T0249896

# Teaching and Learning Computer Programming

## Multiple Research Perspectives

# Teaching and Learning Computer Programming

## Multiple Research Perspectives

Edited by

## Richard E. Mayer
*University of California, Santa Barbara*

Routledge
Taylor & Francis Group
New York   London

First published by Lawrence Erlbaum Associates, Inc., Publishers
10 Industrial Avenue
Mahwah, New Jersey 07430

Reprinted 2008 by Routledge

Routledge

270 Madison Avenue
New York, NY 10016

2 Park Square, Milton Park
Abingdon, Oxon OX14 4RN, UK

Production and interior design: Robin Marks Weisberg
Cover design: Andrea Schettino


**Library of Congress Cataloging in Publication Data**
Teaching and learning computer programming: multiple research
perspectives/edited by Richard E. Mayer.
   p.  cm.
   Based on a Symposium on Research on Teaching and Learning Computer
Programming held Apr. 1, 1987, in Washington, D.C.
   Includes indexes.
   ISBN 0-8058-0073-5
   1. Electronic digital computers—Programming—Research on
Teaching and learning computer programming (1987: Washington, D.C.)
QA76.6.T397 1988
005.1'07—dc19                        88-3831
                                             CIP

10 9 8 7 6 5 4 3 2 1

Dedicated to *Kenny, David, Sarah,*

and all kids who make friends with blinking cursors

# Contents

# 3

# 4

# 5

# 12

# NEW DIRECTIONS IN EDUCATIONAL
# COMPUTING RESEARCH

*Robert H. Seidman*

# Contributors

Juliet Baxter, *Stanford University*

John Bransford, *Vanderbilt University*

Sharon M. Carver, *Carnegie-Mellon University*

Keith N. Clayton, *Vanderbilt University*

Douglas H. Clements, *State University of New York at Buffalo*

Victor Delclos, *Tulane University*

Anne L. Fay, *University of California, Santa Barbara*

Jeffrey J. Franks, *Vanderbilt University*

Thomas Guckenberg, *University of Wisconsin*

Laiani Kuspa, *Stanford University*

Richard Lehrer, *University of Wisconsin*

Sharon Lever, *Vanderbilt University*

Scott Lewis, *University of California, Los Angeles*

Marcia Linn, *University of California, Berkeley*

Joan Littlefield, *University of Wisconsin*

David Littman, *Yale University*

Richard E. Mayer, *University of California, Santa Barbara*

Sheri Merriman, *Kent State University*

D. N. Perkins, *Harvard University*

Ralph Putnam, *Michigan State University*

Leonard Sancilio, *University of Wisconsin*

Steve Schwartz, *Harvard University*

Robert H. Seidman, *New Hampshire College Graduate School*

Rebecca Simmons, *Harvard University*

D. Sleeman, *King's College, University of Aberdeen*

Kathryn Sloane, *University of California, Berkeley*

Elliot Soloway, *Yale University*

James Spohrer, *Yale University*

Noreen Webb, *University of California, Los Angeles*

# Preface

During the decade of the 1980s, computers have become a part of schooling for millions of children, and instruction in programming has increasingly become a part of the curriculum. How can we teach children to use computers productively and what will be the effect on children of learning to program computers? These are the research questions addressed in *Teaching and Learning Computer Programming: Multiple Research Perspectives*.

Ten years ago there was an insufficient research base to answer these questions, but during the past decade researchers have begun to investigate novices' learning of computer programming. This book brings together some of the most productive researchers in the field and asks each to summarize what research says about teaching and learning computer programming. The result is a concise and current account of how instructional techniques affect student learning and how learning of programming affects students' cognitive skills.

In my role as editor, I asked each author to show how research answers two general questions: What kinds of instruction enable students to learn programming productively? What are the cognitive consequences of learning programming languages? In other words, I asked each author to address the two topics in this book's title—*teaching* and *learning*. Similarly, as the subtitle indicates, I asked each author to examine these topics from his or her own research perspective and to provide integrative summaries of relevant research.

As an aid in preparing their chapters, authors exchanged ideas at a "Symposium on Research on Teaching and Learning Computer Programming" held in April of 1987 in Washington, DC. With the exception of one chapter which was reprinted in updated form from refereed sources, each chapter was subjected to peer review and an extensive editorial revision cycle. In the interests of readability, I instructed authors to present chapters in a common format, including chapter outlines and abstracts. An introductory chapter and a summary chapter have been added to provide coherence and context.

I wish to acknowledge those who have made this book possible. I am grateful to the authors who worked in a cooperative and timely fashion in generating excellent chapters on schedule, to the copyright holders who graciously granted permission to reprint material needed for this volume, and to Lawrence Erlbaum and his staff at Lawrence Erlbaum Associates. Finally, I acknowledge that this book would not have been possible without the support given me by my wife, Beverly Mayer, and my children, Kenny, David, and Sarah. I am pleased to dedicate this book to my children, who represent the millions of school children currently learning to use a technology that is also in its childhood.

*Richard E. Mayer*

# 1

# Introduction to Research on Teaching and Learning Computer Programming

Richard E. Mayer
*University of California, Santa Barbara*

## ABSTRACT

Research on teaching and learning computer programming is in its childhood; however, already scholars are reaching some preliminary consensus concerning the respective merits of mediated versus discovery instruction and the conditions for transfer to nonprogramming domains. This chapter begins by briefly summarizing recent developments in educational computing. The next section of the chapter explores two topics that have begun to receive research attention during the past few years: identifying appropriate methods of instruction for computer programming and describing the cognitive consequences of learning computer programming. In the third section, some of the contributions of each chapter in this volume are highlighted. Finally, the chapter closes with an analysis of the implications of current research on teaching and learning computer programming.

## RECENT DEVELOPMENTS

This book is concerned with what research can tell us about teaching and learning computer programming. Computers are rapidly becoming a part of schooling and computer programming is finding its place in the curriculum. Until recently, however, not much was known about *how* students learn or *what* students learn from programming experiences.

The history of research on teaching and learning computer programming can be analyzed into three phases: an initial phase in which many strong claims were made concerning the expected outcomes and best methods of instruction for computer programming, an observation phase in which mounting data pointed to problems in students' learning, and a research phase in which theory-based studies were carried out to systematically understand the processes underlying learning and teaching computer programming.

### Phase 1: Powerful Claims

Imagine an educational revolution in which children, working on their own in a highly responsive environment, could teach themselves to be more systematic and organized problem solvers. This is the vision that underlaid much of the early interest in educational computing and that stimulated claims for discovery teaching and highly transferable learning.

In his influential book, *Mindstorms: Children, Computers and Powerful Ideas*, Papert (1980, p. 19) offered an alternative to using the computer to "put children through their paces." Instead of letting the computer program the child, Papert envisioned a reversal in which the child would program the computer. "My vision of a new kind of learning environment demands free contact between children and computers," Papert (1980, p. 60) proclaimed. Furthermore, "in teaching the computer how to think, children embark on an exploration about how they themselves think" (p. 19). The result is that "powerful intellectual skills are developed in the process" (p. 60).

Papert's (1980) advocacy for computer programming as a worthwhile educational domain seemed to have implications for both the instructional methods and expected outcomes of school programs in computing. First, early advocates for computer programming argued for a discovery approach that allowed for plenty of hands-on programming experience in an unstructured environment. Second, early advocates argued that students who learned how to program computers would also show increases in general cognitive development; that is, in learning to program, children would also learn how to think (Mayer, Dyck, & Vilberg, 1986).

Thus, as the 1980s began, there were many strong claims made for the power of computer programming as a vehicle for learning problem-solving skills and for discovery as the instructional method of choice, but there was no powerful research support for the claims.

## Phase 2: Disappointing Realities

As computer programming projects began to appear with more frequency in schools, observations of student learning did not always match the powerful claims. The ideal vision of students' becoming better problem solvers due to hands-on LOGO learning collided with the documented reality of students' difficulties in learning even the fundamentals of LOGO (Dalbey & Linn, 1985; Fay & Mayer, 1987; Gregg, 1978; Kurland & Pea, 1985; Linn, 1985; Pea & Kurland, 1984; Perkins, 1985; Webb, 1984).

For example, Nickerson, Perkins, and Smith (1985) summarized the unpublished results of a small scale LOGO project involving 16 students conducted by Papert and his colleagues in Brookline, Massachusetts. The instructional method included up to 35 hours of hands-on, nondirective programming experience as advocated by Papert (1980). Case studies of individual children indicated that "students developed a number of skills specific to programming, but we are less certain that they developed powerful general skills" (Nickerson et al., 1985, p. 277).

Nickerson et al. (1985) also summarized some early evaluations of LOGO instruction carried out by Pea and Kurland at the Bank Street College of Education. Approximately 50 children received about 25 hours of hands-on, nondirective instruction. Nickerson et al. (1985, p. 277) summarize the findings as "disappointing" because students performed poorly on predicting what would happen for various LOGO commands, locating bugs in procedures, and writing programs that involved variables or conditional tests. Intensive studies of seven children who received more in depth LOGO programming experience revealed that "students often produced programs without really comprehending how the programs worked" (Nickerson et al., 1985, p. 277).

Learning even the rudiments of LOGO appeared to be difficult for children and transfer to other domains seemed minimal. In a comparison of students who received extensive LOGO programming experience with students who received no programming experience, Pea and Kurland (1984) found no major differences on tests of general planning skill and, hence, no support for the idea that learning to program improves thinking in domains beyond programming. Based on a survey of early studies, Perkins (1985, p. 12) was forced to conclude that research had disclosed "no transfer of skill and poor learning within LOGO itself." Similarly, Dalbey and Linn's (1985, p. 267) review of research in the mid-1980s indicated that "students who learn LOGO fail to generalize this learning to other tasks."

Thus, by the mid-1980s, it was clear that learning how to use a programming language did not seem to result in powerful learning outcomes. The occasional hint of positive transfer (Clements & Gullo, 1984; Gorman & Bourne, 1983) occurred under more guided methods of instruction and was not yet replicated. As Dalbey and Linn (1985, p. 267) observed, in those few documented cases of students learning transferable skills from LOGO, the degree of transfer was restricted to the "specific applications of particular language features" and resulted from "instruction which emphasizes transfer."

## Phase 3:
## Multidisciplinary Research and Theory

As the 1980s draw to a close, we have survived the first two phases—strong claims and disappointing realities—and are entering into a new phase of multi-disciplinary theory-based research. The initial vision of teaching and learning computer programming has been altered in two important ways: First, instead of advocating discovery methods of instruction, current research suggests that more guidance is needed to insure learning. The focus of current research is on understanding how the conditions of instruction affect what is learned. Second, instead of predicting major changes in children's cognitive development, current research suggests that transfer is most likely to occur for skills most similar to those learned in programming. The focus of current research is on understanding the conditions under which transfer can be expected to occur.

Research during this third phase has begun to find evidence for transfer but only under certain conditions. For example, Mayer and Fay (1987) found evidence of positive transfer of spatial cognition skills for students who meaning-fully learned to use several LOGO turtle graphics commands, and Mayer, Dyck, and Vilberg (1986) found evidence of positive transfer of procedure comprehension skills for students who successfully mastered elementary BASIC computer programming. In both cases, an apparent prerequisite for transfer of problem-solving skills beyond programming was that the skill had been successfully understood within the programming domain. Similarly, in both cases transfer occurred for skills in nonprogramming domains that were clearly analogous to skills within the programming domain.

Research since the mid-1980s has become increasingly more theory driven. Instead of asking, "Does learning a programming language affect a child's thinking skills?" a more productive set of questions is, "What is learned from instruction in computer programming?" or "How does the method of instruction affect the student's cognitive processing?" Instead of evaluating the effectiveness of an instructional program, current research begins with a cognitive analysis of programming knowledge into parts that can be specified, evaluated, and taught. Furthermore, current research draws on theories of transfer in order to better understand the cognitive conditions under which transfer occurs.

This book represents a picture of the current state of research on teaching and learning computer programming. Although the vision of the first phase has become more modest, moderated partly by the realities of the second phase, the current phase of research retains the idea that computer programming may ultimately become an exciting and revolutionary part of the curriculum. The challenge for researchers and educators is to understand the relationship between learning to program and learning to think.

The goals for teaching computer programming remain a central issue today as they did for Papert in 1980 but the research goals and theories have begun to mature. Computer programming can be viewed as a subject to be learned for its own sake or as a vehicle for teaching students about their own thinking processes. This latter view still entices and challenges us, and the emerging cognitive theory of computer programming enables us to more fruitfully accept the challenge.

## CURRENT RESEARCH ISSUES

The chapters in this book address the current state of research on two issues: teaching computer programming and learning computer programming.

### Teaching Computer Programming

The teaching issue is concerned with determining instructional factors that contribute to students' productive learning of computer programming. Here, we may begin with the hypothesis, stimulated by Papert (1980), that hands-on computer programming experience in a discovery environment is best. Many of the chapters in this volume report empirical studies of the merits of discovery as a method for teaching computer programming.

The overwhelming consensus among the authors in this volume is that, for most children, a hands-on discovery environment should be complemented with direct instruction and mediation by a teacher. For example, in chapter 2 Clements and Merriman conclude that "it is clear that LOGO programming—especially divorced from mediated instruction—does not represent an educational panacea, as Papert is often misunderstood to have claimed." In chapter 3, Fay and Mayer's study of school children in LOGO classrooms found that many children enter the classrooms with "inaccurate models . . . of the LOGO graphics environment" and may "require more direct instruction or pretraining in the prerequisite skills in order to benefit from LOGO experience." Lehrer et al. (chap. 4) summarize their studies by noting that "mediated instruction in LOGO is a prerequisite for the transfer of LOGO to other domains." Littlefield et al. (chap. 5) report that "mastery of the programming language has not been achieved when LOGO has been taught in a discovery-oriented environment" and "if mastery is not achieved, the discovery and transfer of general thinking skills as a result of learning LOGO cannot occur." In chapter 6, Soloway et al. argue that transfer of programming skills requires that students be given guided learning emphasizing that "there is more than one right answer" to programming problems. Perkins et al. (chap. 9) present research showing that productive learning of programming is enhanced by guiding students' "development of mental models through which they understand what the computer does" and helping students acquire "strategies . . . to organize their problem-solving efforts." In chapter 8, Webb and Lewis's research indicates that learning of computer programming is enhanced when students engage in the following activities: "giving explanations, giving . . . suggestions, receiving responses to questions, receiving . . . suggestions, verbalizing planning and debugging strategies to peers, and to some extent, receiving explanations." In an analysis of high school programming classrooms, Sloane and Linn (chap. 9) found that learning was releated to "the quality of explicit instruction" and "the proportion of time teachers work with individuals in small groups." Sleeman et al. (chap. 10) describe the conceptual errors of students who have learned Pascal and discuss "how easy it would be to remediate the different types of errors." Finally, in chapter 11, Carver's results showed that "students rarely developed effective debugging skills on their own after extensive experience with LOGO."

In summary, in study after study, students appear to need guided or mediated instruction to insure they acquire the concepts and strategies underlying computer programming. In spite of earlier interpretations of Papert's (1980) view of programming, the research summarized in this book clearly points to the limits of pure discovery as a method of instruction for programming. When researchers study real children in real classrooms, the results indicate a need for more guided and mediated instructional methods.

## Learning Computer Programming

The learning issue is concerned with the consequences of learning computer programming. Some of the questions raised by including programming in school curricula are: What do students learn when they are taught computer programming? Will students transfer what they have learned about solving programming problems to solving problems in new domains? Does learning to program affect the way children think in general?

The chapters in this book provide some preliminary answers to these questions. Several authors report studies in which students show evidence of transferring what they have learned about programming to new domains. For example, Clements and Merriman found that students who learned LOGO increased their performance on nonprogramming tests of creativity and metacognitive skills. Fay and Mayer found that students who learned and understood LOGO also excelled on tests of spatial cognition. Lehrer et al. found that appropriate learning of LOGO was related to increases on some tests of metacognition and mathematical problem solving but not on general problem solving tests. Littlefield et al. found some kinds of LOGO learning to be related to tests of spatial cognition but less connected to tests of planning. Perkins et al. found modest evidence of transfer for students learning BASIC. Finally, Carver found that students were able to transfer LOGO debugging strategies to debugging within nonprogramming domains.

In summary, the growing list of successful transfer studies indicates that learning a programming language can have effects on thinking in nonprogramming domains. However, in most cases the greatest amount of transfer is found for tests that are most similar to the original programming tasks. More importantly, these authors have begun to pinpoint the conditions under which learning to program appears to be related to learning to think. These conditions include initial mastery of the syntax of the language, the development of appropriate mental models of the system, and the acquisition of strategies for how to solve procedural problems.

## OVERVIEW OF CHAPTERS

This book contains chapters by researchers who have been asked to describe what their work says about teaching and learning computer programming. The programming languages investigated in these chapters represent the languages most often part of the K–12 school curricula: LOGO, BASIC, and Pascal.

The chapter by Clements and Merriman analyzes LOGO programming skill into metacomponents such as solution monitoring, deciding on the nature of the problem, selecting a mental representation, selecting and combining performance components, and allocating resources. In an extensive series of studies, students who were given instruction in LOGO improved more on several metacognitive and creativity tasks designed to measure these components as compared to control groups that engaged in computer-assisted instruction or some other nonprogramming activity. The authors provide consistent evidence that long-term, mediated instruction for LOGO programming affects students' ability to transfer certain problem-solving skills to nonprogramming domains.

In chapter 3, Fay and Mayer propose that effective LOGO programming requires that the user possess syntactic knowledge, semantic knowledge, and strategies for mapping knowledge to new domains. In one study, Fay and Mayer found that beginning programmers often enter the programming environment with conceptions of navigational commands that conflict with the requirements of LOGO. For example, many students, especially in the primary grade levels, had the idea that directional commands (such as RIGHT or LEFT) refer to the users' orientation rather than the turtle's orientation or the idea that directional commands mean to turn and continue moving. In another study, students showed changes in syntactic knowledge, semantic knowledge, and mapping strategies over the course of several LOGO learning sessions. In particular, over the course of learning, students generated fewer syntactically incorrect commands and displayed fewer misconceptions; in addition, students who showed improvements in semantic knowledge, as indicated by losing their misconceptions, also improved on transfer tests of spatial ability. Fay and Mayer's chapter provides an example of how learning of LOGO can be understood as the acquisition of specific kinds of knowledge.

In chapter 4, Lehrer, Guckenberg, and Sancilio explore the cognitive consequences of learning to program in LOGO, and, in particular, they identify several "transferable aspects of LOGO programming." In a series of studies, students given intensive exposure to LOGO (including 60 computer sessions) displayed better transfer performance than students given less intensive exposure to programming in LOGO. For example, the more intensive group benefited more from being reminded about the relation between a math problem and LOGO and was more likely to effectively deal with ambiguous instructions. Students who were successful in learning LOGO also showed a higher level of understanding of geometry. In a related study, students given LOGO-based instruction in geometry were better able to transfer knowledge between programming and geometry. The authors conclude by noting that mediated instruction in the learning of LOGO is a prerequisite for transfer of LOGO knowledge to planning and execution of a novel task.

In chapter 5, Littlefield, Delclos, Lever, Clayton, Bransford, and Franks examine the effects of various methods of instruction on students' learning of LOGO and transfer to other problem-solving domains. The unstructured method emphasized free, hands-on exploration of LOGO; the structured method emphasized teacher-guided, hands-on activities; and the mediational method was similar to the structured method but added direct instruction in how LOGO skills could be applied to other domains. In a series of studies, Littlefield et al. found that students mastered LOGO commands as well or better in the structured or mediational groups as compared to the unstructured group; however, the mediational method was most successful in producing transfer to new domains. Littlefield et al. conclude by noting that mastery of the LOGO language is a prerequisite for transfer and that mediational methods of instruction promote both mastery and some kinds of transfer.

In chapter 6, Soloway, Spohrer, and Littman argue for changing the way that programming is taught. In particular, Soloway et al. show how instruction in Pascal programming should focus on the *process* of problem solving—such as the idea that there are alternative ways to solve the same programming problem—rather than on the *product* of problem solving—such as rapidly generating a program. For example, the authors show how students can learn to generate alternative ways of specifying a problem, decomposing a problem into parts, and composing plans to solve each part. These suggestions mesh well with research on human problem solving (Mayer, 1983).

In chapter 7, Perkins, Schwartz, and Simmons describe a programming *metacourse* for novices learning BASIC programming. Some of the obstacles facing novices include a lack of specific knowledge about computers, a lack of problem-solving strategic knowledge relevant for programming, and a lack of positive affect for and self-confidence about computing. The metacourse designed by Perkins et al. helps students overcome each of these obstacles by helping students acquire useful mental models of the computer, understand the meaning of the elements of program code, and learn to use appropriate program production strategies. The positive results of the metacourse encourage further research on the nature of prerequisite knowledge that supports effective learning of programming.

In chapter 8, Webb and Lewis examine the social characteristics of effective learning of BASIC and LOGO. In particular, they analyze the verbal interactions among students who worked on programming problems in small groups. Interestingly, programming performance is positively related to peer interactions that generate opportunities for giving explanations and input suggestions, describing problem-solving plans and debugging, and receiving responses to questions and suggestions. In contrast, interactions with teachers do not follow the pattern found for peer interactions. This research suggests that detailed analysis of the social context of learning programming can yield important insights into the nature of effective classroom learning environments.

In chapter 9, Sloane and Linn examine the characteristics of effective programming classrooms, that is, of classrooms in which the students excel in learning Pascal programming. For example, their research shows that student programming performance is influenced by the amount of time that computers are available, the degree of explicitness and individualization in instruction, and the number of opportunities for appropriate feedback. The most effective teachers are able to maintain a balance among the instructional strategies of providing direct instruction, allowing time for students to work independently on computers, individualizing instruction, and providing useful feedback. This research suggests that a careful analysis of classroom conditions can provide useful information about the nature of effective instruction for programming.

In chapter 10, Sleeman, Putnam, Baxter, and Kuspa describe the programming errors made by Pascal students at the end of a semester course. Clinical interviews of students revealed that over 90% had some difficulties and over 50% had major difficulties. Sleeman et al. note two major causes of errors: lack of attention or knowledge and preexisting common-sense knowledge that conflicts with the requirements of Pascal. This latter kind of error is similar to Fay and Mayer's analysis of students' misconceptions of LOGO.

In chapter 11, Carver presents a cognitive task analysis of the processes and knowledge, or *skill components,* required for debugging LOGO programs. Carver presents evidence that students normally do not acquire appropriate debugging skills in LOGO courses that use a discovery method of instruction; however, students do acquire appropriate debugging skills, including the ability to transfer to nonprogramming problems, in LOGO courses that provide explicit instruction in the underlying skill components. Carver concludes by noting that effective programming instruction should be based on conducting a detailed analysis of the cognitive processes and knowledge required, designing instruction that explicitly teaches these required skill components, and evaluating students' learning by measuring the extent to which students have acquired the required skill components.


## IMPLICATIONS

The research presented in this book has implications for future research, theory, and practice.

First, the work presented in this book shows that there is a place for the scientific study of how people learn and use a programming language. The growing body of research on programming shows the advantages of developing *psychologies of subject matter areas:* Instead of studying learning and thinking in general we can study how people learn and think within subject matter domains such as programming, mathematics, science, reading, and writing (see Mayer, 1987). This volume demonstrates that the research literature on the psychology of computer programming can begin to take its place among the older and larger literatures on other subject matter domains.

Second, the work presented in this book contributes to theories of human learning and problem solving. In particular, the common theoretical thread running through the chapters of this volume is the analysis of programming skill or processing into meaningful parts. For example, programming skill can be analyzed into components of knowledge, including specific problem-solving strategies, plans, and mental models of the computer system.

This approach suggests that theories of problem solving and learning must be intimately connected to theories of knowledge for the domain under study. Understanding problem solving in the domain of programming seems to depend on understanding the specific knowledge required. Similarly, theories of learning to program depend on an understanding of the kinds of knowledge a student brings to the classroom and in understanding the changes in knowledge that occur during the course of learning.

Third, the research presented in this book, although still requiring additional research verification, yields many preliminary implications for practice. The initial failures of LOGO programs to create powerful changes in children's thinking may persuade some educators to delete programming from the menu of curriculum options. However, the promising transfer results presented in this volume suggest that it is premature to give up on computer programming as a potentially useful part of school curricula.

It is clear that educators must give more careful consideration to their instructional goals and instructional methods. Educators must decide whether the goal of instruction is proficiency in programming per se or whether the goal is to also help students understand something about their own thinking processes. Different kinds of instructional methods are required to support the different kinds of goals. In particular, when the goal is transfer, instructional methods must provide guidance to students concerning the planning and conceptual knowledge that is required. Pure discovery has a place in the educator's box of instructional tools, but it is clear that nondirective techniques by themselves do not generally produce the desired results. As many authors point out in this book, students need practice and guidance in describing alternative processes for solving various programming problems.

Research presented in this book also suggests that students often bring unproductive preconceptions about programming to the classroom. Learning to program involves not just adding new knowledge to one's memory; in addition, it involves replacing initial misconceptions with more productive mental models and concepts.

Finally, this book suggests some implications for assessment. Instead of focusing only on gross measures of learning, such as whether or not a student can write a program to solve a problem, more attention needs to be paid to specific changes in the students' knowledge. For example, educators should assess their students' mental models of the system, metacognitive skills, understanding of specific programming concepts, and strategic planning skills.

If this book stimulates further research that contributes to theory or practice in computer programming, it should be considered a success.

## REFERENCES

Clements, D. H., & Gullo, D. F. (1984). Effects of computer programming on young children's cognition. *Journal of Educational Psychology, 76,* 1051–1058.

Dalbey, J., & Linn, M. C. (1985). The demands and requirements of computer programming: A literature review. *Journal of Educational Computing Research, 1,* 253–274.

Fay, A. L., & Mayer, R. E. (1987). Children's naive conceptions and confusions about LOGO graphics commands. *Journal of Educational Psychology, 79,* 254–268.

Gorman, H., & Bourne, L. E. (1983). Learning to think by learning LOGO: Rule learning in third grade computer programmers. *Bulletin of the Psychonomic Society, 21,* 165–167.

Gregg, L. W. (1978). Spatial concepts, spatial names, and the development of exocentric representations. In R. Siegler (Ed.), *Children's thinking: What develops?* (pp. 275–290). Hillsdale, NJ: Lawrence Erlbaum Associates.

Kurland, D. M., & Pea, R. D. (1985). Children's mental models of recursive LOGO programs. *Journal of Educational Computing Research, 1,* 235–244.

Linn, M. C. (1985). The cognitive consequences of programming instruction in classrooms. *Educational Researcher, 14,* 14–16, 25–29.

Mayer, R. E. (1983). *Thinking, problem solving, cognition.* New York: Freeman.

Mayer, R. E. (1987). *Educational psychology: A cognitive approach.* Boston: Little, Brown & Co.

Mayer, R. E., Dyck, J. L., & Vilberg, W. (1986). Learning to program and learning to think: What's the connection? *Communications of the ACM, 29,* 605–610.

Mayer, R. E., & Fay, A. L. (1987). A chain of cognitive changes with learning to program in LOGO. *Journal of Educational Psychology, 79,* 269–269.

Nickerson, R. S., Perkins, D. N., & Smith, E. E. (1985). *The teaching of thinking.* Hillsdale, NJ: Lawrence Erlbaum Associates.

Papert, S. (1980). *Mindstorms: Children, computers and powerful ideas.* New York: Basic Books.

Pea, R. D., & Kurland, D. M. (1984). On the cognitive effects of learning computer programming. *New Ideas in Psychology, 2,* 137–168.

Perkins, D. N. (1985). The fingertip effect: How information-processing technology shapes thinking. *Educational Researcher, 14,* 11–17.

Webb, N. M. (1984). Microcomputer learning in small groups: Cognitive requirements and group processes. *Journal of Educational Psychology, 6,* 1076–1088.

# 2

# Componential Developments in LOGO Programming Environments

Douglas H. Clements
*State University of New York at Buffalo*

Sheri Merriman
*Akron City Schools*

13

E. Solution Monitoring
F. Knowledge-Acquisition Components
G. All Meta- and Knowledge-Acquisition Components

## ABSTRACT

First, this chapter presents a theoretical foundation for the implementation of educational LOGO environments and for the investigation of cognitive benefits within those environments. Second, research conducted by the authors, as well as pertinent studies conducted by other researchers relevant to componential development, are analyzed to answer two main questions: What componential abilities do children learn in different LOGO environments? What are the characteristics of LOGO environments most likely to facilitate the development of metacomponents and knowledge-acquisition components? An in-depth look at several recently completed studies, including the Sternbergian-based LOGO environments that they used, proffers concrete examples.

Teaching computer programming to young children is often justified on the basis of its promotion of "computer literacy." Such a goal, however, is both vague and vacuous. A more substantive goal is the development of *problem-solving abilities*. Unfortunately, this term is equally nebulous. This chapter presents a theoretical model for LOGO-based development of specific cognitive skills employed in problem solving. Research conducted based on that model and implications for teaching drawn from this and other related research are discussed.

## INFORMATION PROCESSING:
## A THEORETICAL BASE

### Componential Analysis of Problem Solving

One of the strengths of information-processing theories has been their detailed identification of cognitive processes people use in solving problems. One such theory hypothesizes that different types of problem-solving processes are carried out by separate components of people's information-processing systems (Sternberg, 1985). Components are elementary processes that operate upon internal representations of objects. There are three categories of components.

*Performance Components.*   Performance components are involved in the actual execution of a task. They perform such tasks as encoding, inferring, mapping relationships, comparing one piece of information to another, combining information, and responding.

*Knowledge-Acquisition Components.* Knowledge-acquisition components are processes used in gaining new knowledge and in creative thought. They *selectively* encode, combine, and compare information to determine what is relevant, to integrate separate pieces of knowledge, and to relate newly acquired information to information acquired in the past. Knowledge-acquisition components are fundamental sources of learning, insight, and creativity.

*Metacomponents.* Metacomponents are executive processes that control the operation of the system (person) as a whole and plan and evaluate all information processing. They include: deciding on the nature of the problem, choosing performance components relevant to the solution of the problem, choosing a strategy for combining these performance components, selecting a mental representation, allocating resources for problem solution, and monitoring solution processes.

Sternberg (1985) posited that cognitive development results to a large extent from the ability of the components to learn from their own mistakes. They acquire knowledge about where, how, why, and especially when the various components might be best applied. The solution monitoring metacomponent not only keeps track of what has been done, what is currently being done, and what needs to be done, it also controls intercommunication and interactivation among the components, and thus has been called (with some trepidation) a "metameta-component" (Sternberg, 1985). Only metacomponents activate and receive information from other components. Due to these characteristics, metacomponents are fundamental sources of cognitive development. Metacomponents and knowledge-acquisition components are the focus of this chapter.

## Use of Components in LOGO Environments

As an example of componential employment in a LOGO environment, consider the following recorded episode. Ken and Nick scrutinized a large circle on a computer monitor—a circle that they had named "BASEBALL." Nick, attempting to quickly finish the picture, tried to placate Ken: "It does look like a ball!" Ken, not to be deterred until perfection was attained, protested, "But it doesn't look like a baseball. What's missing?" With sudden insight, Nick asked urgently, "Do you think we could make the stitching?" (selective encoding and comparing, and deciding on the nature of the problem). Ken concurred that the laces were the missing element and said, "Yeah! It would be like parts of a circle with little lines" (selecting a representation). The pair began applying performance components, directed by metacomponential components (selecting and combining performance components), in the creation of arcs apportioned by line segments depicting a baseball's stitches. After several minutes, Ken cautioned Nick: "Before we put all these stitches in we'd better try to put the curve *in* the ball" (monitoring the solution and allocating resources). With several moves, the boys positioned the arc in the appropriate place. "Look," said Nick, "it curves too much. When we put in the other curve, they'll overlap" (solution monitoring). In solving this new problem, the boys then used the information acquired when creating the original circle (the baseball) to determine the size of the needed arc (knowledge-acquisition components). Additional examples of children's use of several metacomponents in a LOGO context are provided in Table 2.1 (recorded during a research project described later in the chapter).

Such examples suggest that children's employment of meta- and knowledge-acquisition components may be frequent within certain LOGO environments. This parallels claims that LOGO programming promotes "thinking about thinking" and "learning about learning" (e.g., Papert, 1980). What characteristics of LOGO programming might serve as catalysts of (unconscious) componential employment? In addition, might certain LOGO environments encourage children's conscious reflection on their own problem-solving processes? The following sections examine these two questions.

## Componential Employment in LOGO Programming

This section describes characteristics of LOGO that may lead children to construct and infer the consequences of causal sequences, thus engaging in the construction and modification of cognitive models, which in turn facilitates the development of metacomponential and knowledge-acquisition processes.

*Solution Monitoring.*   The pedagogical theory upon which LOGO is based attributes central importance to learning from errors. This type of learning requires facilitation of solution monitoring. Markman (1977) stated that the more actively people engage in inferential and constructive processing of information, the more likely they are to recognize information-processing failures. Later, she suggested that children be provided with practice inferring consequences of causal sequences, finding problems, and enacting instructions (Markman, 1981). LOGO programming involves operations of transforming incoming information in the context of constructing, coding, and modifying such causal sequences (e.g., one procedure may invoke a subprocedure, which in turn invokes other subprocedures). Errors (bugs) in turtle graphics projects are highly visible. The nature of the actual "bug," and the steps that must be taken to eliminate it, of course, are not as easily seen. LOGO, however, does provide aids for this activity in its graphic depiction of errors, explicit error messages, and easy-to-use editors. In addition, because the problems are of the child's own creation, and bugs occur in the context of real problems, children are motivated to follow through on relatively difficult debugging ventures. Thus, the act of "debugging" LOGO programs provides children with valuable experience in utilizing their monitoring skills.

TABLE 2.1
Categorization Scheme for Information-Processing Components

| Component | Definition | Examples |
|---|---|---|
| **Metacomponents** | | |
| Deciding on the nature of the problem | Determining what the task is and what it requires | "What do we make here?" "We gotta go over here, then put lines around it like our drawing." |
| Selecting performance components | Determining how to solve the problem; choosing lower-order components | "Read the list [of directions] again, but change all the LEFTs to RIGHTs for this side." |
| | | "How are we gonna make this thing go over this way? We did RIGHT 20. What's 90–70 . . . 20, right? We need, not RIGHT 90, but 70!" |
| | | "We got to add these three numbers." |
| Combining performance components | Sequencing the components selected | "First you have to get it over that way a little . . . LEFT 45 then FORWARD 30." |
| | | "We'll make the turtle go up this way about 10, then RIGHT 90 and 10 down, then FORWARD half way—5—and we're done." |
| Monitoring solution processes | Keeping track of progress and recognizing need to change strategy | "We got it!" "Let's think and make sure." "Put 70." "70? We already did 50 . . . type FORWARD 20." "You're gonna go off the screen, I'm telling you." |
| Selecting a mental representation | Choosing an effective form or organization for representing relevant information | No verbalizations recorded. |
| Allocating resources | Deciding how much time to spend on various components | "That's enough time talking. We should draw it." |
| **Performance Components** | Executing the task; includes encoding and responding | "5 times 7 is 35." "Type R-I-G-H-T-4-5." "It says, 'What is 305–78?' " |
| **Other** | Miscellaneous; includes off-task and uninterpretable verbalizations | "They're recording us, you know." "I'm tired of this, can we do another game?" |

*Deciding on the Nature of the Problem.*   The emphasis on turtle graphics allows children to pose numerous significant problems of varying levels of complexity for themselves. They can generate ideas for their own projects, represent these as goals, and identify the specific problems involved in reaching these goals. Thus, they determine the nature of each problem and subproblem.

*Selecting a Mental Representation.*   The turtle allows a representation of the problem goal, as well as partial solutions (and errors) in a form that is meaningful to young students as it has analogs in their noncomputer experiences, such as moving their bodies or drawing (Papert, 1980). Programming in turtle graphics also promotes representation of the solution process internally as an initial state and a goal state often expressed in pictures, as an intended semantic solution whose organization is frequently verbalized for others (e.g., if working in pairs), and as machine-executable code. Therefore, LOGO programming may offer unique opportunities for the development of the metacomponent of selecting a mental representation.

*Selecting and Combining Performance Components.*   Programming requires the explicit selection and ordering of instructions in solving problems. LOGO's modular nature allows students to combine procedures that they develop in various ways to solve graphic problems. Therefore, given an appropriate context, LOGO programming can support higher level planning of strategies.

*Knowledge-Acquisition Components.*   Children who begin a LOGO project may start by making a drawing (their problem goal; see Clements, 1983/ 1984; Clements & Gullo, 1984). They might selectively encode parts of that drawing to determine basic shapes that can be disembedded and constructed as procedures. In addition, they might encode the salient properties of shapes and relationships among shapes. They then might selectively compare their present problems with past procedures to determine if these old procedures and the methods used to construct them might assist in solving the problems at hand. Children also might selectively combine procedures to create numerous figures from a limited number of components and, more importantly, combining parts of a problem solution into a unified whole.

*Thinking About Thinking*
*(Or, Componential Cognizance)*

*Consciousness of Components.*   Children may receive substantial opportunities to engage in componential processing while programming in LOGO. However, although children may become explicitly aware of their errors and may develop stronger meta- and knowledge-acquisition components, they do not have to be (and normally are not) conscious of the existence of the components themselves or of their own componential functioning. A unique claim is that LOGO fosters explicit awareness of cognition (this represents a popular use of the term *metacognitive*, as compared to the previously-described *executive-level*). Papert (1980) maintained that while programming children reflect on how they might do the task themselves, and therefore, on how they themselves think. Thus, encouraging children to become explicitly aware of their own thinking processes is another way in which using LOGO may help children develop componential abilities.

> The child, even at preschool ages, is in control: The child programs the computer. And in teaching the computer how to think, children embark on an exploration about how they themselves think. The experience can be heady: Thinking about thinking turns the child into an epistemologist, an experience not even shared by most adults. (Papert, 1980, p. 19)

It may be possible for children to learn simple notions about the components, then use that knowledge in solving problems, and finally begin to use the knowledge automatically, without conscious direction. Their use of these processes—initially unconscious and ineffective—may become first conscious and more effective (albeit slow), and ultimately, unconscious and expert (automatic and fast). That is, metacognitive experiences would provide declarative knowledge, which is originally interpreted by general procedures. Through practice, knowledge compilation leads to automatization of the skills, particularly to task-specific automatic procedures. There is both theoretical and empirical support for the existence of such knowledge compilation processes (Anderson, 1983; Sternberg, 1985).

*Metacognitive Experiences.* Can LOGO provide the "metacognitive experiences" necessary for such "thinking about thinking"? Flavell (1981) stated that a metacognitive activity involves analyzing information for what it does and does not afford. This is akin to the Piagetian notion that advanced thinking is marked by the ability to view one's own behavior and thinking abstractly, as something that can be analyzed; that is, to reflect on one's own thinking (e.g., Inhelder & Piaget, 1969). Metacognitive experiences are more likely to occur in situations in which:

1. People engage in and communicate about conscious cognition, particularly when they behave in new and unaccustomed ways.
2. The outcome of what people think and do is important to them.
3. People believe that their cognitions contain errors.

Metacognitive experiences are often a serendipitous benefit of cognitive actions undertaken to achieve other cognitive goals (Flavell, 1981). Parallels in LOGO programming are noteworthy.

1.  Children consciously solve problems using strategies unfamiliar to them. They "communicate" their organization of the task and solution processes to each other (if working in pairs), to the teacher, and to a machine.
2.  Problems are often self-selected; children feel that they "own" LOGO problems (e.g., see Carmichael, Burnett, Higginson, Moore, & Pollard, 1985). Along with their graphic nature, these characteristics make the solution to LOGO problems personally significant to children.
3.  Errors are salient and frequent, but correctable. Solution processes are explicated in greater detail than normal.

Thus, the occurrence of metacognitive experiences during LOGO programming indeed appears likely. Furthermore, LOGO's modularity is critical in allowing computer programs to serve learners as metaphors for the psychological procedurality basic to Sternberg's componential theory. First, children's solutions in LOGO have been externalized; they are now the turtle's solutions. Each LOGO procedure serves as a metaphor for a mental schema representing a solution to one problem. They are therefore "more obtrusive and more accessible to reflection" (Papert, 1980, p. 145) and more likely to encourage "thinking about thinking," or, in Piagetian terms, reflective abstraction. This externalization is aided by LOGO's intermediary position between the concrete (e.g., movement, physical paths) and the abstract (e.g, mathematics). Second, this process-oriented procedurality itself serves as a metaphor for componential functioning. For example, the frequent "debugging" situations in LOGO programming, especially those involving explicit awareness of the nature of the error and its place in a sequence, may facilitate children's ability to become explicitly aware of, and to discuss, their errors and their monitoring processes. Debugging also provides children with a metaphor for understanding the process of solution monitoring. Similarly, children may become more aware and more capable of choosing mental representations, selecting and ordering performance components, selectively encoding and comparing information, and so on, as they reflect on their use of these components in the LOGO context as described in the previous section.

*Difficulties in Teaching Metacognitive Skills.*   In a review of information-processing research, Wagner and Sternberg (1984) agreed that metacognitive as well as cognitive skills should be taught. However, they also provided reasons for being wary of wide scale implementation of this training.

1.  Young children often have a limited idea of what they are doing in performing tasks, and therefore may have insufficient internal referents to take advantage of metacognitive instructions.

2. Externally imposed metacognitive activities may have less effect than those spontaneously generated.

3. Teaching students to be aware of generalized strategies is not enough to result in students using them.

Certain characteristics of LOGO programming, however, may ameliorate most of these potential problems.

1. The LOGO programming task is concrete and understandable to the children (at least as a "drawing task"; ideas from computational science, of course, may not be as easily accommodated). Furthermore, children can become explicitly aware of what they wish to achieve (the representation of the goal) and what they are doing as they perform the task (each LOGO procedure must be explicitly analyzed).

2. The metacognitive activities can be included as an integral part of a motivating task, rather than being externally imposed. Although the task demands that metacognitive strategies be employed, specific strategies are not dictated but must be constructed by the children.

3. Similarly, in programming, students apply the strategies in the execution of actual projects, as well as reflect upon their use of these strategies (if guided to do so).

It becomes apparent that the LOGO environment *could* serve as a vehicle for the delivery of opportunities and situations that facilitate the development of componential skills. What actually happens when LOGO is so employed with such a goal? The following section presents a brief history of a series empirical studies addressing this question conducted by Clements and his colleagues.

## RESEARCH

### Study 1: Original Hypotheses and Pleasant Surprises

Our first study was exploratory in nature and not grounded in any precise theory. We attempted to operationalize some of the claims made (along with our own intuitions) concerning the benefits of LOGO programming. Two resultant hypotheses are pertinent here. First, because LOGO was designed to encourage children to reflect on how they think, programming should lead them to develop metacognitive abilities, especially the ability to realize when they do and do not understand instructions. Second, in LOGO programming, children invent, construct, and modify their own projects; therefore, it might facilitate creative thinking (Clements & Gullo, 1984).

## LOGO Environment

To gather information regarding these hypotheses, we worked with 18 first-grade children, half in a LOGO and half in a computer-assisted instruction (CAI) comparison group. We based the LOGO environment on two tenets: (a) that these young children would need considerable interaction with adults (as well as with each other), and (b) consonant with accepted principles of early childhood education, that they would benefit from considerable opportunities for exploration under their own control. The following environment was constructed. Children worked in groups of two or three with one of the researchers for two 30–40 minute sessions per week for 12 weeks. They spent several sessions in exploratory activity. After gaining familiarity with basic commands, they were guided to plan what they would program the turtle to draw. They drew a picture, then traced each part of it (i.e., each basic shape) with tracing paper. Each part was then defined as a LOGO procedure using support programs that allowed children to define a procedure and simultaneously watch it being executed, editing at any time that was necessary (see Clements, 1983/1984). Finally, children assembled the procedures in a superprocedure.

Children typed messages to the turtle at two levels, each of which involved the use of support programs. For the first 5 weeks children used a program that allowed them to direct the turtle by pressing single keys; for example, pressing F instructed the turtle to move forward 10 units; pressing L instructed the turtle to turn 30° to the left. Also, procedures were defined and executed with single keystrokes. For the last 7 weeks children typed in full LOGO commands; for example, FORWARD 10 to move forward 10 units and LEFT 45 to turn 45° to the left. However, they still used a support program, TEACH, which allowed them to to define a procedure while seeing each command executed immediately. This use of the full LOGO language represented a step away from the intuitive and manipulative and toward the abstract and cognitive. It is more difficult but allows more flexibility and control.

Children learned to: move the turtle and draw lines using the single keystroke procedure (two sessions); write procedures to draw shapes with single keystrokes (four sessions); combine these procedures into superprocedures that draw more complex pictures (four sessions); write and combine procedures in the full language using the special support program just described (eight sessions); and plan the superprocedure first, then subdivide this into subprocedures ("top-down" planning; six sessions). At all times, if a procedure was not doing what the children had anticipated, teachers encouraged them to think it through: "What did you tell the turtle to do? What did it do? What did you want it to do? How could you change your procedure . . ." and so on. Thus, although no theory of metacognitive processing was utilized, metacognitive-oriented questioning techniques were employed. In addition, intense child–child and child–adult interaction was encouraged. There was no attempt, however, to relate LOGO programming to other problem situations.

### Metacomponential Measure: Realizing You Don't Understand

To assess children's metacognitive abilities, we used tasks (from Markman, 1977) whose purpose it was to measure children's ability to monitor and evaluate their own cognitive processes. Children are presented instructions on how to perform two activities, but crucial information for executing them is not included. The question is whether children realize they do not (could not possibly) understand. In the first task, eight alphabet cards are divided equally between the experimenter and the child. Directions provided the child include each player laying out one card at a time, looking for the "special card." There is, however, no mention of what the "special card" might be. Ten prompts or questions are given in an attempt to ascertain whether the child realizes his or her lack of complete comprehension. Once the child verbalizes a relevant question or statement the procedure is terminated. Some of these prompts are quite specific. For example, prompt 1 is "That's it. Those are my instructions"; prompt 2 is "What do you think?"; and prompt 9 is "Did I forget to tell you anything?" The second activity involves a similarly incomplete description of a magic trick. Children are first shown the trick, which involves "pressing" a nickel through a napkin and a saucer into a cup. Then they are taught "how to do" the trick themselves. The explanation offered, however, describes the coin's extrication from the napkin, but not its surprising appearance in the cup.

### Metacomponential Results

The LOGO programming group significantly outperformed the CAI group on both the game and trick tasks (Table 2.2 provides means rounded to the nearest integer; complete data can be found in Clements & Gullo, 1984. Remember that the *more* prompts children needed the *worse* they performed; therefore, for the monitoring tasks in this study, lower scores are better scores.) We hypothesized that the ability to monitor one's own thinking and to realize when one does not understand was positively affected by computer-programming environments in which problems and solution processes were brought to an explicit level of awareness and in which consequent modification of problem solutions was emphasized. Through consistent feedback in the form of a visual representation of the procedures and sequences of one's own thinking processes, children may have learned how to monitor those processes.

TABLE 2.2
Study 1: Pre- and Posttest Means for Treatment Groups

| Measure | LOGO | | Comparison | |
|---|---|---|---|---|
| | Pre | Post | Pre | Post |
| Monitoring | | | | |
| Game task* | | 4 | | 9 |
| Magic task** | | 2 | | 6 |
| TTCT-F | | | | |
| Fluency[a] | 46 | 59 | 39 | 41 |
| Flexibility | 48 | 53 | 42 | 42 |
| Originality[b] | 52 | 67 | 48 | 50 |
| Elaboration | 40 | 50 | 33 | 37 |

*$p < .01$.
**$p < .05$.
[a]Pre–post difference significant for the LOGO group only, $p < .01$.
[b]Pre–post difference significant for the LOGO group only, $p < .05$.

### Knowledge-Acquisition Measure: Creativity

We also administered the Torrance Test of Creative Thinking—Figural Test (Torrance, 1972). The Torrance test measures the ability of the child to think divergently in a nonverbal mode. For example, children are presented with 36 identical circles and are asked how many different objects or figures they can make, using the circles as the main part. Creative thinking ability is then assessed in four ways: fluency—how many original ideas the child had; flexibility—how varied these ideas were one from the other; originality—how original the ideas were when compared to a normative group; and elaboration—how many details were added to the main idea.

### Knowledge-Acquisition Results

Only the LOGO group made significant gains on this instrument, specifically on the fluency, originality, and total scores (see Table 2.2). Thus, the children in the LOGO group increased in their ability to produce a greater number of ideas overall, as well as a greater number of original ideas, presumably because LOGO programming facilitated divergent thinking within a figural context.

Thus, the results of this exploratory study were promising, but served not so much to support hypotheses as to suggest hypotheses for future research and to suggest that a theory of metacognitive processes was requisite to such study.

## Study 2: Using Theory as a Basis for Assessment

To this end, Sternberg's (1985) componential theory was used as a theoretical basis for delineating and assessing metacognitive processing in the second study (Clements, 1986a) and for explicating the rationale for using LOGO environments for the development of metacomponential abilities (Clements, 1986b). This rationale is briefly discussed in the first section of this chapter; changes in the LOGO environment and the new assessment techniques, however, are described in some detail in the following sections.

### LOGO Environment

A total of 72 first- and third-graders were randomly assigned to one of three conditions: LOGO computer programming, CAI comparison, and control. The LOGO environment was similar in most ways to that previously described. The major differences were (a) the use of pictorial flow-charting to plan the superprocedure first, then subdivide this into subprocedures and (b) the provision of 20 additional sessions (for a total of 44) in which children were led to write increasingly complex programs in developing their own major projects. Basic ideas such as procedurality and debugging were explicitly taught. Adult guidance was frequent (at each session, three pairs of children worked with one or two teachers). As before, this guidance took the form of metacognitive prompts and questions whenever possible and appropriate. Two approaches, one observational and one psychometric, were used to assess componential employment in this environment and transfer to other situations, respectively.

### Observational Assessment

A naturalistic observational procedure was employed to investigate children's metacognitive interactions while programming (Clements & Nastasi, 1988). Children in the LOGO group and those in a CAI comparison group were observed while working in pairs. Interval recording was used with occurrence/nonoccurrence of the target behaviors recorded at 10-second intervals. Table 2.1 presents the definitions and examples of these behaviors.

Children in the LOGO group exhibited a higher frequency of behaviors indicative of metacomponential processing (a principal-components factor score, which included the first four metacomponents in Table 2.1, was significantly greater for the LOGO group, $p < .001$). Conversely, children working with CAI spent more time responding to the computer program's feedback and performing the task, as well as more time engaging in off-task behaviors (although these differences were not significant).

## Psychometric Assessment

*Metacomponential Measure.*    As mentioned, tests were also administered as measures of transfer from programming in the LOGO environment to problem solving in other situations. Consider the following four metacomponents: deciding on the nature of the problem, choosing performance components relevant to the solution of the problem, choosing a strategy for combining these performance components, and selecting a mental representation. These four involve decisions related to the nature of the problem and to the processes that are used in solving the problem. An eight-item test designed to measure these metacomponents was constructed (Clements, 1986a). First, children are shown a 3 (shape) × 3 (color) array of geometric pieces with two pieces missing. They are asked, "This is unfinished. What do you need to know to figure out how to find the right piece?" A point for *deciding-nature* (deciding on the nature of the problem) is given if children indicate the need to determine both the shape and the color of the missing piece. Children are then asked, "How exactly would you figure that out (what would you do . . . think, say to yourself)?" "What next?" A point for *selecting-performance* (selecting performance components) is given if children identify the relationship between the spatial orientations (columns and rows) and the attributes. A point for *combining-performance* (deciding how to combine performance components) is given if children indicate that a specific shape and a specific color have to be synthesized into a dual attribution description of the correct piece. The original array is reconstructed for the item assessing *selecting-representation* (selecting a mental representation). Children are told, "Here's how three other children figured it out. Mary said she would say, 'These are all blue and these are all triangles. So it must be a blue triangle.' Bill said he would look here (pointing) and think it would look like these, and it would also have to look like these (pointing). He would see in his head what the piece would look like. Dan said he would pick a piece and see if it fit. Who do you think found the piece the best, Mary, Bill, or Dan? Why?" A point is given if the child selects either of the first two methods and justifies the choice by indicating the efficacy of verbal representation or visual imagery, respectively.

Further items assessing the first two metacomponents are posed as detective stories to be solved. The solution of the first depends on the use of transitive inference; the second, analogy. Children are told, "I'm trying to write a detective story, but I got stuck. Can you help me think of the clues the detective should use to prove who committed the crime?" In the first story, "The detective had to find out which sneaky kid hid the cookie jar. The cookie jar was taken from the high cupboard that only the biggest kid could ever reach. Missy liked cookies. Her bigger brother was Billy. Billy's bigger brother was Timmy. They loved cookies. How could the detective prove who took the cookie jar for sure?" In the second story, "The thief who always wore disguises stole some money from a bank. The detective saw a man dressed like a mailman run out of the bank with the money and drive away in a mail truck, but he couldn't catch him. Another day, money was stolen from another bank. The detective saw a tow truck drive away. He found three suspects dressed like: a garbage man, a gas station man, and a fireman. The fireman had a wallet with some money in it. The garbage man looked mean. How could the detective prove who was the thief?"

For each story, a point is given for *deciding-nature* if the children identifies the relevant clue for problem solution, characters' heights and clothing/occupation, respectively. For *selecting-performance*, a point is given if children identify the reasoning process required, either by answering correctly ("Timmy" or "gas station man") or by describing the process itself ("It had to be the biggest; one was the biggest in the line" or "If the mailman drove a mail truck, it must be the guy dressed to drive a tow truck").

Scores were computed for each of these four metacomponents by summing across tasks and standardizing these raw scores. The four standardized scores were summed to yield a total metacomponent score for the domain of deciding on the problem and on solution processes.

To assess the metacomponent of *allocating-resources*, a measure of impulsivity (typically termed a *cognitive style*) was used. Justification for this can be found in Baron's (1982) interpretation of cognitive styles as differences in peoples' propensities to deviate in setting parameters for separate phases of thinking. Each parameter has an optimal setting determined by a rule; for example, that one should stop thinking when the expected benefit from additional thinking becomes less than the cost of that thinking (this being equivalent to the style of impulsivity–reflectivity). The Matching Familiar Figures (MFF) test (Kagan, Rossman, Day, Albert, & Phillips, 1964) represents a situation in which the optimal match between the setting of the parameter and environmental demands requires reflective behavior. In the MFF test, the child is presented with a picture of a familiar object above an array of highly similar variants. Only one of the pictures in the array is an exact duplicate of the target picture. The child's task is to select the variant that is identical to the standard. Two measures are reported: the time in seconds the child took to choose the first picture (latency time) and the number of errors the child makes before choosing the correct standard. These measures were standardized and combined to provide one continuous variable, the reflectivity index (standardized latency score minus standardized error score; cf. Kagan, Lapidus, & Moore, 1978).

Markman (1977) tasks were used to measure the sixth metacomponent, solution monitoring (these scores were also standardized after being recoded so that higher scores now indicated superior performance). To further validate the measure of the first four metacomponents, correlations were computed. The correlation of this score with the comprehension monitoring score was significant; in comparison, with reading and mathematics achievement as measured by the Wide Range Achievement Test (WRAT), the correlations were near zero and nonsignificant. Note that WRAT tasks include naming letters, recognizing sight words, counting, reading number symbols, and performing computations. Therefore, the metacomponent measures were related more highly to another metacognitive measure than to rote achievement.

Finally, metacognitive tasks from other domains (memory and communication) were administered as a check that the treatment effects were specific. That is, if performance differences occurred on metacomponential tasks but not on metamemorial or metacommunicative tasks, then benefits of working with LOGO could not be attributable to generalized treatment effects (e.g., time spent interacting with the experimenter or with small groups of peers) or to global differences in metacognitive knowledge among the groups despite randomization.

*Metacomponential Results.*   The LOGO group significantly outperformed both the CAI and control groups on the assessment of the first four metacomponents of problem solving, the domain of deciding on the problem and on solution processes. (Table 2.3 provides means; complete data can be found in Clements, 1986a.) However, a nearly significant interaction intimated the possibility that treatment effects were stronger for certain metacomponents. Examination of the means indicated that the LOGO environment may have been relatively more efficacious in developing the metacomponents of deciding on the nature of the problem and selecting a mental representation. It was hypothesized that in working with CAI and regular classroom tasks, children may encounter the need to select and combine performance components. However, because in computer programming children must generate ideas for their own projects, represent this as a goal, and identify the specific problems involved in reaching that goal, LOGO may constitute a more effective environment for developing the ability to decide on the nature of the problem. Similarly, because programming necessitates representation of the solution process internally as an initial and a goal state, as an intended semantic solution, and as machine-executable code, this environment may offer unique opportunities for the development of the metacomponent of selecting a mental representation.

No significant differences were found among treatments on the measure of reflectivity/impulsivity, providing no evidence that the treatments were effective in altering the metacomponent of allocation of time resources. The LOGO group significantly outperformed both other groups on the test of comprehension monitoring. As hypothesized, metacognitive experiences may be frequent in debugging situations, which involve explicit awareness and verbalization of errors, that is, in which people see and discuss their comprehension failure.

No treatment differences were found on the test of metacognitive abilities from other domains. This substantiated the hypothesis that treatment effects on metacognitive skills are limited to those predicted by the proposed theory and could not be attributed to other causes, such as generalized treatment effects.

TABLE 2.3
Study 2: Means for Treatment Groups:
Standardized Metacognitive Posttest Scores

| | LOGO Programming | | CAI Comparison | | Control | |
|---|---|---|---|---|---|---|
| | Grade | | Grade | | Grade | |
| | 1 | 3 | 1 | 3 | 1 | 3 |
| Metacomponents | | | | | | |
| Deciding on problem and solution processes | | | | | | |
| Nature of problem | .22 | .64 | -.63 | .43 | -.51 | -.20 |
| Performance components | .18 | .28 | -.31 | .07 | -.08 | -.15 |
| Combining components | -.28 | .68 | -.76 | .54 | -.41 | .20 |
| Representation | .92 | .55 | -.43 | -.21 | -.43 | -.43 |
| Total[a] | 1.04 | 2.14 | -2.14 | .84 | -1.43 | -.56 |
| Monitoring[a] | .35 | .73 | -.48 | .20 | -.74 | -.05 |
| Resource allocation | -.58 | .82 | -.71 | 1.00 | -.77 | .25 |
| Metacognitive—other | | | | | | |
| Metacommunication | -.23 | .57 | -.84 | .41 | -.72 | .73 |
| Metamemory | -.10 | .26 | .07 | -.04 | -.49 | .28 |
| Metasocial—cognitive | -.28 | .28 | -.38 | .23 | -.75 | .74 |
| Total | -.61 | 1.11 | -1.06 | .60 | -1.92 | 1.75 |

[a]LOGO group significantly outperformed the other two groups.

29

*Knowledge-Acquisition Components (Creativity) Results.* The LOGO group outscored both other groups on the Torrance of creativity (Table 2.4). Interactions revealed that this effect was most pronounced on the originality and elaboration subtests ($p < .01$). These differential results for the subtests may have resulted at least partially from the tendency of the children in the LOGO group to combine an entire page of shapes into one drawing, instead of making several separate drawings. This decreased their flexibility and fluency scores, but increased their originality scores. This tendency may have been a reflection of procedural thinking developed during the LOGO treatment.

Increased creativity in a figural domain may have resulted from an increase in the insightful use of knowledge-acquisition components and in overall organizational adaptability. Alternatively, it may have resulted from experience verbalizing visual information or representations that are held in an encoding that is not isomorphic with language. Because such verbalization implies considerable processing, children in the LOGO treatment may have encoded visual representations (e.g., of simple shapes) in long-term memory with a relatively extensive array of verbal, as well as visual, associations or symbols that could later be accessed. These might then serve as links in associative chains that lead to new reorganizations of memory, and thus to numerous "original" figural formulations. This latter hypothesis, of course, implies the caveat that the creativity engendered may be limited to a graphic domain.

### Limitations

Although these results generally support the study's hypotheses, several limitations remain. As mentioned, there was some indication of a weak effect on some of the metacomponents. The componential instrument used lacked a sufficient number of items to allow accurate statistical delineation of the metacomponents. Certain tests, such as the Markman measure, assessed a constrained application (comprehension monitoring) of a particular metacomponent (solution monitoring). Similarly, the creativity instrument represented only one type of situation in which knowledge-acquisition components might be applied. In addition, parallels between the LOGO treatment and these tasks indicate another possible limitation in the generalizability of the results: both the LOGO and the Markman tasks involve sequences of directions, and both the LOGO and the Torrance tasks involve the construction of graphic figures. Our most recent study was designed to overcome these limitations.

## Study 3: Using the Theory
## as a Basis for Teaching

Although ameliorating limitations in previous studies was a major goal, there was one other. That was the restructuring of the LOGO environment so that it, too, embodied the theoretical foundation on which the study was based.

TABLE 2.4
Study 2: Means for Treatment Groups:
Pre- and Posttest Scores on Creativity Measures

| | LOGO Programming | | | | CAI Comparison | | | | Control | | | |
|---|---|---|---|---|---|---|---|---|---|---|---|---|
| | Grade | | | | Grade | | | | Grade | | | |
| | 1 | | 3 | | 1 | | 3 | | 1 | | 3 | |
| | pre | post | pre | post | pre | post | pre | post | pre | post | pre | post |
| Fluency | 40 | 42 | 49 | 56 | 37 | 36 | 44 | 48 | 38 | 39 | 49 | 50 |
| Flexibility | 44 | 45 | 56 | 56 | 40 | 35 | 52 | 47 | 43 | 40 | 55 | 50 |
| Originality[a] | 37 | 57 | 52 | 77 | 36 | 39 | 46 | 50 | 41 | 40 | 55 | 56 |
| Elaboration[a] | 39 | 60 | 42 | 71 | 38 | 48 | 42 | 59 | 38 | 50 | 45 | 61 |

[a]LOGO posttest scores significantly higher than all other scores.

## LOGO Environment

We worked with third-graders for 26 full weeks, three 45–55 minute sessions per week. This necessitated doubling the size of the group involved during a session, from 6 to 12. For the LOGO group, we formulated a general pedagogical approach and sequence of activities. It was planned that most sessions would consist of four phases. (a) An introduction, including a review and discussion of the previous day's work, questions, and, about once per week, a "programmers' chair" (a pair of students present a completed program, followed by group discussion). (b) A teacher-centered, whole-group lesson, which presented new information (e.g., a new LOGO command) or a structured problem. (c) Independent student work on either teacher-assigned problems (about 25%) or self-selected projects (this included projects for which the teachers introduced "themes" but students were responsible for selecting the specific problem). During this time, the teachers encouraged children to solve problems by themselves, to predict (e.g., Where will the turtle be then? What would happen if you changed . . . ?), and to reflect on their use of strategies (e.g., What are you trying to get the turtle to do? What did you tell it to do? What did it do? Can you find the bug?). (d) The fourth phase, summary and sharing with the whole group, was seldom realized, as students left for their classrooms or for home at different times. Therefore, only the first three phases were consistently implemented.

Turtle graphics was introduced as in Study 2; the following description emphasizes characteristics of the treatment that were unique to Study 3. Procedural thinking was introduced, first through discussions of children's experiences of learning/teaching new routines (gymnastics, classroom) and new ideas and words, then through the notion of teaching LOGO new procedures. Using the support program TEACH, children created a "stairway" via dramatizations, then paper-and-pencil, and finally with LOGO. They were led to construct a STAIR procedure as a subprocedure for STAIRWAY. Thus, problem decomposition and procedurality were introduced from the beginning. Different solutions were compared, and children were encouraged to write a different stairway (e.g., that was taller, had more steps, or had smaller steps). Discussions centered around these different procedures (e.g., What was altered in the procedure to create what effect?) Given an altered procedure (or graphic), students were asked to predict the corresponding graphic produced (or procedure that produced the graphic). In this way, there was an attempt to help children construct mappings between components of procedures and their effects. Finally, students were asked to plan "what they could make with STAIRWAY" (i.e., how STAIRWAY itself could be used as a subprocedure). These programs were in turn analyzed.

At this point, children were introduced to the "homunculi." This set of cartoon characters represented an anthropomorphism of the metacomponential processes. The homunculi were pictured as:

*The Problem Decider*. A person thinking about what a problem means (via a "think cloud"). The Problem Decider often asked questions such as, "What am I trying to do?" "Have I done a similar problem before?" "How do the parts of the problem fit together?" and "What information do I have or need?"

*The Representer*. An artist, thumb raised, looking off into the distance. She was surrounded by an assortment of items: a piece a paper with a graph or chart, another piece of paper with writing, a drawing, and a three-dimensional model. These served as metaphors for various ways to represent a problematic situation. Specific representations were introduced when appropriate (e.g., using a diagram or making a table).

*The Strategy Planner*. A intelligent-looking man with pencils and pens in his pocket, holding a notebook. Spaced over the remaining sessions, useful strategies in the Strategy Planner's repertoire were introduced, such as acting the problem out, looking for patterns, decomposing a problem, and guessing and testing (systematically).

*The Debugger*. An exterminator; a metaphor for solution monitoring (which is actually more omnipresent in problem solving than is "debugging" proper). To develop this more general solution monitoring, students were frequently asked: "'What exactly are you doing?' (Can you describe it?) "Why are you doing it?" (How does it fit into the solution?) "How does it help you?" (What will you do with it when you're done?) "Does this make sense?" For debugging computer programs, the following specific steps were modeled for children (simplified from Carver & Klahr, 1986): Run the program or procedures to see if there are bugs. Describe the discrepancy between your goal picture and the turtle's drawing. Based on this, propose a specific type of bug that might be responsible. For example, if the orientation is off ("This is going over here instead of down"), an angle/rotation is probably buggy. Locate the specific bug by representing the structure of the program. For example, is it in a certain subprocedure? In the worst case, hand trace the entire program. Replace the buggy instruction with the correct one.

*Detective Selective*. A detective, scrutinizing objects through a large magnifying glass as they fall through a sifter (selective encoding). A large "thinking cloud" above his head shows that he is thinking of his last case (successfully solved according to the headlines in the newspaper displayed in the cloud; selective comparing). Concurrently, he is meticulously building an intricate shape by combining several of the objects that have dropped through the sifter (selective combining).

These homunculi were introduced as a part of the LOGO-programming/problem-solving process. They aided four teaching methods: *explication, modeling, scaffolding,* and *reflection*. The goal of *explication* was bringing problem-solving processes to an explicit level of awareness for the children. Teachers used the homunculi to describe processes in which one had to engage to solve many types of problems. When the whole class solved problems, the teachers would use the homunculi metaphor to describe problem-solving processes and make them salient. For example, one might remark, "That drawing seems like a good way to view this problem. Your representer made an excellent choice." Teachers would also *model* the use of the homunculi in solving actual problems. In *scaffolding* students' independent work with LOGO, teachers would try to ascertain the process with which the student was having difficulty (e.g., in selecting a useful representation or strategy) and would offer prompts and hints focusing on this particular process (e.g., "Might there be a pattern you could find that would help? What could you write down to try to find it?"). The characters themselves were often utilized as a "nudge" to cue the students that they will need to exercise their metacomponential and/or knowledge-acquisition skills. The characters were also used as a nudge when it was not apparent to them that certain thinking processes might be useful. For example, when a problem arose in the programming process, the teacher might prompt, "What would Detective Selective do?" Thus the child was reminded subtly that they have available skills to discover the nonpalpable solutions to these problems. If necessary, the teacher would model use of the process directly. (Interestingly, students began talking to each other in these terms; e.g., one said to another, "Your Debugger is working overtime, 'cause your Problem Decider missed the point.") Finally, *reflection* was employed especially in the first phase of the lesson (the programmers' chair), as teachers elicited group discussion about a pair of students' use of homunculi in solving programming problems, and in the third phase, as students were asked to reflect on their use of strategies in terms of the homunculi (as described previously).

A general programming strategy for "The Planner's" repertoire was introduced 3 weeks later. This planning procedure was designed to encourage translation between different embodiments or representations, problem decomposition, and reflection (the steps were introduced briefly to the group, then elaborated as teachers worked with pairs; this sequence was repeated periodically for over 3 months).

1. Make a "creative drawing," a free-hand picture of your project. Remember to keep it simple and label its parts.
2. Then make a Planning Drawing.
   • Use the planning form (basically, paper turned to side with the turtle at HOME).
   • Draw the turtle where it starts the procedure
   • Have turtle end in the same location and same heading at which it started ("state transparent").
   • Label each line, turn, or PROCEDURE.
   • Use a ruler and protractor (a 360° instrument duplicated on transparencies and used on both paper and screen) to measure line segments and angles.

- Show the "moves" between parts of the figure (i.e., those made with the pen up) as dotted lines.
- For each new procedure that needs to be written, make a new planning form (i.e., start at the beginning of step 2 for each new procedure).
3. Have one partner read the instructions in order as the other records them at the right-hand side of the planning form.
4. Type them into the computer.
5. Debug each procedure separately, then the program as a whole.

Children applied these skills and concepts in the completion of various projects throughout the year. Some projects were challenges, often oriented toward seasonal interests, such as writing valentine heart procedures (and thus arcs). Others were contests, such as writing the "shortest" (most elegant) program for a "stacked rectangle pyramid" or the like, or duplicating given shapes (none of which were regular polygons) and utilizing them as many different ways as possible in the creation of a picture. Several weeks were spent on explorations of regular polygons (including the "turtle total turn theorem" or "the rule of 360°"). A final project involved collaborative work on a large mural, for an end-of-the-year party for parents.

The control children also received computer experience under the same conditions as the experimental group (i.e., six pairs of children working with the same teachers), with two important differences. First, the content, designed to develop creative problem solving and literacy, included composition using Milliken's Writing Workshop (an integrated package of prewriting programs, a word processor, and postwriting, or editing, programs), as well as drawing programs. A composition process model, including the processes of prewriting (e.g., brainstorming, nutshelling, and branching), writing, revision (conferencing), and editing (e.g., spelling, style, and grammar checking), served as a framework for instruction. Thus, several characteristics of the LOGO treatment were paralleled with the control group, including self-selection of topics, nonregimented pace, introduction of challenging problems, openness to new ideas and methods, and intense interpersonal interaction. Of course, programming and related homunculi experiences were unique to the LOGO group. Second, they met only once per week for a total of 26 sessions. In addition, a no-treatment control group was administered the group (Torrance) measures; time constraints did not allow the administration of the individual (componential) instrument.

It should be clear from this description that it was not expected that LOGO programming alone would produce changes in children's use of metacomponential processes. LOGO was viewed as an environment in which such processes are particularly useful to children in achieving their aims and as a tool that facilitates the mediation of the teacher. Several features of the treatment were designed to promote elaboration and transfer. Problems were solved in several settings, and translations between settings was required. Explicit awareness of the effectiveness of transferring metacomponential skills from one setting (and one problem) to another was encouraged. Although explicit, anthropomorphic instruction in metacomponential functioning was offered, the emphasis was on the implicit application of metacomponential processes. For example, the "debugger" was discussed, but children spent more time engaged in activities designed to educe their own use of solution monitoring, such as making and testing predictions and plans. This, along with the relatively long duration of the treatment, encouraged mastery.

Active engagement of the children was promoted by allowing them to select their own projects (within the constraints of the goals of the instruction) and to engage in intense interaction with teachers and peers (as well as with LOGO). Finally, it is important to note that one potentially powerful mechanism for promoting transfer was incorporated minimally due to the constraints of the design; that is, relating LOGO programming to other classroom work.

## Assessment

*Pretests.*    Two pretests were administered to check initial equivalence of the groups. There was no significant difference between the groups on achievement (California Achievement Test). However, on the Test of Cognitive Skills, a measure of academic aptitude, the comparison group scored significantly higher.

*Metacomponential Measure.*    An instrument was designed to measure metacomponential functioning in problem-solving situations, obtaining a (delineated) subscore for each metacomponent. The basic strategy was to use problems whose successful solution depends on relatively intensive use of a single metacomponent. Students were first allowed to solve each problem with no help. If they were unsuccessful, they were provided a series of five successively more specific prompts. Their raw score was the number of prompts required. Items measuring each metacomponent were presented in random order.

The basic assumption concerning the prompts was the following: If children are successful, or if they are successful given one or more prompts, then they are utilizing that metacomponent. The number of prompts needed is inversely related to the degree of automaticity of that metacomponent. Two different measures were taken: (a) Utilization, the number of prompts necessary before the children exhibited use of the metacomponent (i.e., they "got the idea"); (b) Correctness, the number of prompts necessary before the children responded correctly.

Scoring for Correctness was straightforward: the prompt number at which the child got the correct answer. For Utilization, the criteria were as follows. Deciding-nature: The child shows a sign that he or she is asking the right questions to solve the problem; he or she understands the structure of the specific problem (or type of problem). He or she may subdivide the problem; redefine goals more in line with the problem; relate the problem to another, similar problem; or start a correct solution process. Selecting performance: The child starts to select and combine set of processes that may lead to correct solution (two or more steps); he or she must indicate a systematic strategy for combining selected components (not trial-and-error generation unless this is systematic). Selecting representation: The child must show evidence of using a mental model related to the problem; for example, mental imagery or a drawn figure, a semantic or arithmetic structure, or the like. Cognitive monitoring: The child must show evidence indicating their belief that "something is wrong."

Criteria for selecting items to measure each component were twofold. First, a logical criterion was established for each metacomponent. Second, empirical data had to demonstrate that children presented with each item benefited most from prompts directed at the metacomponent to be measured (this was established during a pilot study). The logical criteria, along with example items, follow.

Deciding nature: The criterion was that these items were "difficult because people tend to misdefine their nature" (Sternberg, 1985, p. 44). For example, young children often used associative instead of mapping relations in analogy tasks; that is, they misdefined the problem (cf. Clements, 1987; Sternberg, 1985). One analogy problem was:

boy pulling wagon:girl pushing child on swing

is analogous to

car pulling trailer: *(ski lift; bulldozer pushing dirt;*
                     *horse pulling cart; dogs pulling sled)*

(Note these were presented to children in pictorial, matrix-like format.) The prompts were: (a) What do you think I want you to do? (b) What kind of problem is this? (c) Look! These pictures are related (go together) in a certain way. (d) We give you these two pictures. You need to find what goes here so they these two (indicate bottom two, globally) go together in the same way as these two (indicate top two). (e) The boy pulling the wagon and the girl pushing the swing are related to each other; they are doing the opposite. The car pulling the trailer goes together in the same way with one of these (indicate answers).

*Selecting/combining performance:* The criterion was that it should not be sufficient to select performance components; one also must combine these in workable strategy. For example, several mathematics problems were included that required children to both select which operations to use and what order in which to execute them. One problem asked, "John wanted to know how much his cat weighed. But the cat wouldn't stay on the scale unless he was holding it. How could he figure out the cat's weight?" The prompts were: (a) What could you do to solve the problem. (b) What plan would you use? (c) Could John get on the scale with the cat and get on again alone? (d) How would John find out how much the cat weighed alone? (e) Think of the difference between his weight with the cat and his weight alone.

*Selecting representation:* The criterion was that solution of these problems should depend on the way information is represented mentally. That is, solution depends on constructing a mental and/or external representation helpful for solving the problems. For example, syllogisms frequently are solved easily if there are but three elements. But an internal, or most probably external, representation is necessary to solve those with more than three elements. A spatial representation of information can help; children may simply construct a vertical/ linear array and place individuals in the array. The syllogism used was: "Bill is faster than Tom. Pete is slower than Tom. Jack is faster than Bill. Jack is slower than Fred. Who is fastest?" The prompts were (a) What could you picture in your head or on paper to help solve the problem? Think of pictures or words that tell or show you which is the fastest. (b) What picture or diagram could you make on the paper? How would you tell which one was the fastest? (c) Could you make a picture or a line for Bill? Could you put his name next to it to remember which child is which? (d) Could you make a line or picture for Tom? When someone is faster than someone else, would the picture or line be shorter or longer? (e) Make a picture of all the children. Each line will be a child with a name next to it. Longer lines are faster children.

*Solution monitoring:* The criterion was that these be problems for which there is a high probability of making an incorrect decision as to its nature, selection of performance-level processes, or the like. In addition, chidren are purposely misled in some way by extraneous or irrelevant information. Also included are problems in which children typically make incorrect decisions. For example, "When Albert was 6 years old, his sister was 3 times as old as he. Now he is 10 years old and he figures that his sister is 30 years old. How old do you think his sister will be when Albert is 12 years old?" The prompts were: (a) Do you have to watch out for mistakes when you do this problem? (b) Is there something in the problem that could trick you if you weren't careful? (c) Is Albert right when he figures that when he is 10 years old his sister is 30 years old? (d) Will his sister always be 3 times as old as Albert? Is that a mistake? Should you multiply or add years? (e) Don't make a mistake. When Albert was 6, his sister was 18. 12 years older. What would his sister be 1 year later, when Albert was 7 (19, right?)? 12 years older. One year later? (Continue if child does not understand, until you solve Albert's 10/22 problem.)

*Metacomponential Results.*   For each measure, correctness and utilization, the four scores of the metacomponents assessed, deciding nature, selecting/ combining performance, selecting representation, and solution monitoring, were standardized and submitted to a MANOVA (Table 2.5). Results for correctness revealed a significant over all difference favoring the LOGO over the comparison group. Stepwise discriminant analyses, however, showed that only two of the metacomponents, solution monitoring and representation, were significantly

TABLE 2.5
Study 3: Means for Treatment Groups:
Standardized Metacomponential Posttest Scores

|  | LOGO | Comparison |
|---|---|---|
| Correctness | | |
| Deciding nature | .15 | −.15 |
| Selecting/combining-performance | −.06 | .06 |
| Selecting representation | .22 | −.22 |
| Solution monitoring | .27 | −.27 |
| Utilization | | |
| Deciding nature | .37 | −.37 |
| Selecting/combining-performance | .11 | −.11 |
| Selecting representation | .34 | −.34 |
| Solution monitoring | .28 | −.28 |

higher (i.e., had meaningful structural coefficients). Results for utilization also showed a significant overall difference favoring the LOGO group. For the discriminant analyses, only one, selecting/combining performance, was *not* higher for the LOGO group to a meaningful degree.

These results suggest that the theoretically based LOGO environment did indeed positively affect metacomponential functioning. Larger effects for utilization than correctness may indicate that children are instantiating and applying the metacomponents, but have not consolidated their skills to the point of consistently constructing a completely correct response. It may even be that helping children bring formerly intuitive processes into consciousness increased the cognitive load, thereby attenuating other processes; it is reasonable to assume that there was insufficient time for the new processes to become compiled and automatic. Interestingly, support was also given to the hypothesis advanced previously, that the LOGO environment may have been relatively less efficacious in developing the metacomponent of selecting/combining performance. There was not a meaningful difference for either the correctness or utilization metacomponent. Although it was addressed in the LOGO sessions, along with the other metacomponents, it may be that regular classroom tasks and tests already provide substantial experience selecting and combining performance components. On the other hand, skills such as deciding on the nature of the problem, selecting a mental representation, and solution monitoring are emphasized far less frequently. (As one example, the TCS aptitude test used in this study *ensures* that children are *given* the nature of the problems before working each section. In addition, as with most classroom assignments, finishing the task is paramount; furthermore, the student's work is often corrected by the instructor rather than having the student monitor his or her own solution attempts.)

Another possibility is that the skills children developed differed in generalizability. When children were taught to choose and combine performance components in the LOGO environment, specific strategies (rather than general planning skills) consistently were emphasized, such as making a "planning drawing" and writing procedures based on this drawing. In contrast, the teaching of the other metacomponential processes tended to be expressed in general terms as well as being anchored in domain-specific applications; therefore, they may have been more applicable to the assessment tasks. Consider, for example, the self-questioning strategies taught for Nature (e.g., "What am I trying to do?") and Monitoring (e.g., questions such as "Why are you doing what you're doing?", and "Does this make sense?" always preceded questions focused on specific debugging actions). A similar argument may explain results for the Representation items. Those five problems on which the LOGO children performed substantially better were spatially-oriented problems amenable to solution through a relatively straightforward translation of the verbal problem into a picture or diagram (e.g., "A dog walks around a rectangle-shaped fence that is 12 yards around in all. If the rectangle is two times as long as it is wide, how long is each side?"). Such direct, but nevertheless generally applicable, translations between verbal and pictorial/spatial representations were emphasized in the LOGO treatment. The two Representation problems on which the difference between the groups was small required a less manifest translation to a more abstract representation. An observational study of videotapes of these children working in the LOGO environment is presently being conducted to provide additional information regarding these possibilities.

*Knowledge-Acquisition Measure.*   To expand the measure of knowledge-acquisition functioning, two assessments were used in addition to the Torrance Test of Creative Thinking-Figural (TTCT-F). First, the TTCT-V (Verbal) test was administered, to ascertain whether—as suggested in the previous section—creativity engendered by the LOGO environment is limited to the graphic domain.

Second, to measure the children's *convergent* creative thinking ability, an instrument was devised from tasks described by Sternberg as tapping the ability to deal with novel problems. Changes were made to make the items appropriate for third-graders. Subtests were delineated to measure selective encoding skills, selective comparing skills, and selective combining skills.

Problems created to measure the process of selective encoding emphasized the separation of relevant and irrelevant information. An example from the test is: "Gumballs cost 1 penny. In the gumball machine there are 20 blue gumballs and 20 red gumballs. Twin sisters, Mandy and Candy, both want a gumball, and because they are twins, they really want to have gumballs of the same color. What is the least number of pennies their mother will have to put in the gumball machine to be *sure* of getting two gumballs of the same color?" Sternberg (1986) found that people who answered a similar problem incorrectly tended to focus on information in the problem that is irrelevant—the number of red and blue gumballs in the machine.

Selective combination is instrumental in solving problems which require putting pieces of information together in new ways. One such selective combination item from the instrument is: "How many pets do I have if all of them are birds except 2, all of them are dogs except 2, and all of them are cats except 2?" (Sternberg, 1986)." In this problem, selective encoding is not difficult—the relevant information is quite obvious and no irrelevant information is offered as a distractor. The subject must determine how the pieces of information should be combined to provide an answer.

The final subset of the instrument, that of selective comparison, requires the subjects to relate new information to old. Although analogies are good examples of such problems, requiring a draw on prior knowledge and an inference of a relationship, they are generally not particularly novel. Sternberg (1986) created novel analogies by selectively altering the state of the world. In solving the novel analogies, the subject must assume that the statement immediately preceding the analogy is true, then solve the analogy with that assumption taken into account. Of the 10 items included in the instrument, the assumption was true in the real world on 2 items; on 8 items the assumption was false. On 5 items, the assumption should affect the solution the subject will reach; on 5 items, it would not. In the following item, the assumption is false, and it will affect the solution: "Goats are robots. CHICKEN is to HATCHED as GOAT is to [BORN FARM BUILT FACTORY]." Sternberg (1986) found that the pivotal point is the assumption of the truth of the preliminary statement regardless of its truth or falsity in the subject's previous experience, and then the use of that assumption, when necessary, to solve the analogy.

Limitations in both measures of componential functioning should be taken into consideration. They are newly developed research instruments. Because few other measures of metacomponential functioning exist, relevant psychometric data such as that regarding concurrent validity is not available. For reasons such as these, several related theoretical and psychometric questions cannot be answered, including: Are components independent processes? Do items designed to measure a specific component measure the same process (or even isomorphic processes)? Positive answers to such questions were assumed for this study; thus, a caveat concerning the interpretation of the results is warranted.

*Knowledge-Acquisition Results.* The LOGO group scored significantly higher on both the figural and verbal tests of creativity (Table 2.6). Therefore, effects were not limited to the figural/graphic domain. The three knowledge-acquisition scores also were standardized and submitted to a MANOVA (Table 2.7). There was a significant overall difference favoring the LOGO group. In addition, two of these components, selective encoding and selective combining were significantly higher. Given that this instrument was experimental, it may be

## TABLE 2.6
### Study 3: Means for Treatment Groups:
### Standardized Divergent Measure Posttest Scores

| Measure | LOGO | | Comparison | | Control | |
|---|---|---|---|---|---|---|
| | Pre | Post | Pre | Post | Pre | Post |
| TTCT-F | | | | | | |
| Fluency | .15 | .26 | -.23 | .07 | .07 | -.31 |
| Flexibility | -.05 | .36 | -.11 | .12 | .15 | -.46 |
| Originality | -.15 | .83 | -.10 | -.21 | .24 | -.59 |
| Elaboration | -.06 | .35 | .05 | .08 | .01 | -.42 |
| TTCT-V | | | | | | |
| Fluency | .00 | .02 | .20 | .14 | -.19 | -.15 |
| Flexibility | .09 | .16 | .12 | .03 | -.20 | -.19 |
| Originality | .05 | .44 | -.01 | .11 | -.03 | -.54 |

*Note:* TTCT = Torrance Test of Creative Thinking. F = Figural. V = Verbal.

TABLE 2.7
Study 3: Means for Treatment Groups:
Standardized Knowledge-acquisition Posttest Measures

|  | LOGO | Comparison |
|---|---|---|
| Encoding | .68 | −.68 |
| Combining | .56 | −.56 |
| Comparing | .34 | −.34 |

that the selective comparing items were less sensitive or less valid measures. Alternately, the LOGO environment may have been less effective in developing this component. Overall, however, these results suggest that the LOGO environment facilitated the employment and development of knowledge-acquisition components across multiple domains.

## Other Pertinent Research

To end the research section, work by other researchers relevant to componential employment in LOGO environments is reviewed, for two reasons. First, these results frequently temper or extend results of our own work. Second, identification of both consonant and disparate results allow us, in the final section of this chapter, to search for patterns in the treatments used by these studies in an attempt to identify characteristics of those LOGO environments that are efficacious in developing componential abilities. Only "snapshots" of these studies' results is provided in this section.

### Deciding on the Problem and on Solution Processes

Several studies have assessed the effects of LOGO on planning skills, which basically relate to two metacomponents, selecting and combining performance components. For example, early work by researchers at Bank Street (e.g., Pea & Kurland, 1984) found that after considerable experience in programming in LOGO (e.g., a year's work), students did not display greater planning skills on a noncomputer task than a matched group. Conversely, several researchers have observed some development of planning skills within LOGO environments. Primary grade children just learning to program in LOGO tend to use opportunistic planning ("planning-in-action"), except when working with a guiding teacher (e.g., Dytman, Peverly, & Wang, 1985). However, those who became more proficient at programming were more likely to use plans at a high level of abstraction, to plan in modular units and to provide a reasonable top-down plan for structured tasks. Kull (1986) reported that even first-graders engage in preplanning, although it develops slowly and often consists of planning only a few moves ahead. Nevertheless, the combined results of these and our own studies suggest, at best, a weak effect on planning ability.

The results of two additional studies can be interpreted as assessing all four metacomponents in the domain of deciding on the nature of the problem and on solution processes. Bamberger (1985) measured transfer of problem-solving strategies from LOGO programming to a paper-and-pencil mathematics test. After training, fourth-grade students used the strategies of planning and drawing more frequently to solve two topology problems. In the second study, sixth-graders at the concrete level of development significantly improved their ability to analyze problems; that is, to understand the questions being asked, pick out important facts, identify ideas related to solving the problem, and recognize the number sentences and/or standard operational formats needed to solve the problem (Dvarskas, 1984). In one final study in this domain, Lehrer and Randle (1986) did not replicate Clements' (1986a) findings with regard to the metacomponent of selecting a representation (although two other metacognitive tests did show beneficial affects).

### Resource Allocation

Young (1982) reported that impulsive second-grade children shifted in the direction of reflective thinking more when in a LOGO treatment group than when in a control group; however, no statistically significant relationship existed between the treatment and reflectivity posttest scores. Miller and Emihovich (1986), in agreement with Clements (1986a), failed to replicate the rather weak findings of Young (1982) and Clements and Gullo (1984).

### Solution Monitoring

Qualitative reports have suggested that children working with LOGO do indeed "think about their thinking." Kull (1986) observed children spending considerable time discussing "What will we do next" and "Why is this plan better than this other plan?" In a longitudinal study, Lawler (1985) immersed his son and daughter in a LOGO computer culture and observed their learning. This experience allowed them to be sensitive to instruction couched in the language of procedural programming. For example, Mariam used procedural terms learned in computer programming to help her father to jump rope. Speaking of the rope, she told him: "You hold it up when you're jumping . . . You [have] that pull-up bug." Mariam naturally used the language of debugging, specifying three specific bugs during the "lesson."

Miller and Emihovich (1986) employed Flavell's comprehension monitoring tasks with preschoolers and found positive effects of LOGO on one task. Using another of Flavell's tasks, Lehrer and Smith (1986) substantiated these findings with third-graders, and Lehrer and Randle (1986) reported similar results with first-graders on the Markman tasks. Students in Bamberger's (1985) study used the strategies of checking and looking back significantly more frequently than did students in a control group. It is clear that an increase in solution monitoring following LOGO experience is one of the more consistent results of LOGO research.

## Knowledge-Acquisition Components

Dytman et al. (1985) found that novice LOGO programmers tended to seek information through questions that were related to incremental problem solution and were often directed toward obtaining information needed to formulate the next step in a task or to obtaining a specific visual outcome. In contrast, the questions of high-knowledge students were aimed toward (a) understanding teacher and peer explanations of LOGO concepts and procedures, (b) confirming the accuracy of already-formulated steps, or (c) requesting explanations of sets of procedures. This may indicate more highly developed knowledge-acquisition processes in students who have gained LOGO knowledge. Although Gaffney (1985), found no differences between LOGO, BASIC, and control groups on a "learning-to-learn" measure, Lehrer and Randle (1986) found significant differences favoring a LOGO group on their "learning-to-learn" task. In addition, LOGO children performed significantly better on another task, assessing the ability to monitor and integrate old and new information. In another of Lehrer's studies, those students who had experienced a relatively more extensive, teacher-mediated LOGO treatment significantly outperformed a group who received less extensive LOGO instruction on an assessment on integrating new information with old information. The former students were able to use their knowledge of LOGO to solve mathematics problems (i.e., selectively comparing new information to information acquired in the past); the latter were not (Lehrer & Smith, 1986).

Certain measures of higher level cognitive processes serve as indications of children's knowledge-acquisition processing. For example, synthesis requires selective combination, and evaluation involves the selective comparison of newly encoded information to information acquired previously. Odom (1985) reported that 8 weeks of LOGO programming increased fifth- and sixth-graders' analysis and evaluation skills (on the Ross Test of Higher Cognitive Processes; Ross & Ross, 1976), but not their synthesis skills. Similarly, Mohamed (1985) concluded that the LOGO program enhanced the analytic skills in the majority of his LOGO students. Curiously, using the same test, Ramondetta (1985) found an increase in synthesis, but not the other skills, in sixth-graders provided with 7 weeks of LOGO programming. Finally, Rodefer (1985) reported no difference on any subtest of the Ross, whereas Studyvin and Moninger (1986) reported that students significantly improved on all subtests.

The results of two studies assessing children's rule learning following LOGO programming experience agree that LOGO positively affects this ability (Degelman, Free, Scarlato, Blackburn, & Golden, 1986; Gorman & Bourne, 1983). In a similar vein, Findlayson (1984) found that LOGO experience increased students abilities to solve novel mathematical problems, involving either the generalization of patterns and formulations of rules or the identification of relevant information.

There have been observational reports of children demonstrating creative strength in the LOGO environment, although few specific examples were included (e.g., Vaidya & McKeeby, 1984). Reimer (1985) reported gains in elaboration and originality; however, these gains lacked statistical significance. Hlawati (1985) found similar, but significant, pre–post gains in a gifted population exposed to LOGO. Horton and Ryba (1986) also reported significant gains in creativity. They noted that LOGO students' graphic compositions were more fully developed in terms of completeness, originality, and drawing style. It appears that at least some components of creativity are amenable to development within LOGO environments. As before, a tentative conclusion can be made: Certain LOGO environments have the potential to affect knowledge-acquisition processing, but variables related to the implementation of a LOGO learning environment affect outcomes.

## IMPLICATIONS FOR TEACHING

Despite some encouraging results, it is clear that LOGO programming—especially divorced from mediated instruction—does not represent an educational panacea, as Papert is often misunderstood to have claimed. Ideally, the children's educational environment writ large should be structured to facilitate componential development (cf. Papert, 1987); minimally, characteristics of the immediate LOGO environment must be considered.

Although all the studies described in this chapter offer suggestions for constructing LOGO environments facilitative of meta- and knowledge-acquisition components, it is not possible to make prescriptions. Few studies have compared one LOGO environment to another in an attempt to analyze necessary or sufficient conditions for this construction. The environments of both those studies reporting effects and those showing no such effects consist, of course, of a complex constellation of factors that prohibit simple comparison. Exacerbating this situation, the norm is to describe little detail of the LOGO environment used (with the authors apparently making the implicit—and false—assumption that a "LOGO treatment" is already well defined). This tendency is especially prevalent in studies reporting nonsignificant effects, making the elimination of unnecessary environmental characteristics particularly difficult (e.g., Gaffney, 1985, devoted only about 1% of her report to a description of the treatment). Finally, not one of the studies approached ideal conditions, especially because they constituted, at most, an infinitesimal fraction of the children's total educational experience.

Nevertheless, we examined the descriptions from each study reviewed, searching for patterns of characteristics requisite to students' development of componential skills. We offer our inductions as suggestions for constructing efficacious environments, with the palpable caveat that they constitute only a springboard for practitioners and researchers.

## Selecting and Combining Performance Components

The metacomponents of *selecting and combining performance components* (i.e., planning) were, in general, not strongly affected by LOGO experience. Therefore, strong intervention may be especially important. The following teaching methods may have potential.

- Teach specific planning strategies, encouraging children to become explicitly aware of their planning procedures.
- Help children see patterns in the application of different strategies, so that they increase their repertoire of programming templates and approaches to solving problems.
- Discuss alternative approaches to solving LOGO and non-LOGO problems and consider why and when particular approaches might be useful.
- Promote the use of procedurality as a tool (rather than "a way to save pictures") from the beginning of instruction.
- Use such questions as:
  What could you do to get started?
  Can you solve part of the problem?
  What do you want the turtle to do next?
  How will you make the turtle go there?
  Have you used procedures before that could help you solve this problem?

Children should ask themselves:

What plan or strategy worked best for me?
Why was it the best in this situation?

Thus, to develop planning skills, it may be necessary to structure children's work with LOGO so that they predict and plan before programming. It should be remembered, however, that certain children may resist planning their LOGO programs, enjoying instead the opportunity to work with mathematics in an intuitive style that is more natural to them (Papert, 1987).

## Deciding on the Nature of the Problem

Although few studies have addressed the ability to *decide on the nature of the problem*, it is likely that certain environments are more conducive to the growth of this metacomponent. For example, teachers may:

- Challenge students to analyze and compare a wide variety of problem types.
- Help students approach problems confidently, in varied, appropriate ways. For example, sometimes an exploratory approach is useful to "get a feel" for the problem. At other times, students need to develop a clearer picture of what their goal is (at these times especially, "deplanning"—changing one's goal and thus the nature of the problem—should be discouraged).
- Use such questions as:
  In your own words, what is the problem?
  Do you need more information to solve the problem?
  Is this problem similar to any other problems you have solved?
  Remember your ___ project? How did you decide what the problem was then?
  What clues led you to think that?
  What made you think to look for a pattern?

### Selecting a Mental Representation

Catalytic environments for the development of the ability to *select an appropriate representation* are probably those that encourage and support the use of a multiplicity of representations, including diagrams, English descriptions (oral and written in journals), computer code, patterns, tables, and so on. Teachers might explicitly discuss the use of such representations, abstracting the relationships between the types, and recognizing the ways in which the representations facilitated problem solution. Constructing a physical representation of the problem and solution could be encouraged.

### Resource Allocation

Recall that effects on impulsivity, or *resource allocation,* were highly dependent on the characteristics of the LOGO environment. It may be that impulsivity can be attenuated, but only if teachers so structure their students' approaches to the computer tasks, either by insisting on planning and predicting (as mentioned previously) or by closely interacting with the students, modeling and encouraging a reflective approach to problems (including "stop and think" self-statements). Students may also justify their choices to a peer.

### Solution Monitoring

As mentioned, the greatest potential of LOGO to facilitate the development of metacomponents may lie in the realm of solution monitoring. Frequent debugging situations, especially those necessitating explicit awareness of the nature of the error and its place in a chain of causal sequences, may lead to an increased ability to monitor one's comprehension. The following teaching processes have been used successfully in research projects.

- Highlight the need for solution monitoring, point it out when children evidence it, and specifically suggest it when it is needed. Promote a "learning from debugging" atmosphere, expanding this notion beyond a limited "fix a computer program" perspective to the use of debugging as an allegory for cognitive monitoring in myriad situations.
- Help students recognize and clear up misconceptions, especially common ones such as using a natural language meaning for a word instead of the programming meaning, or attributing humanlike interpretive powers to the computer.
- Encourage children to use LOGO's aids in finding and correcting errors rather than to quit or start anew.
- Model specific debugging processes (e.g., see Carver & Klahr, 1986; Clements, 1986a) and arrange for supportive, frequent adult–child interaction that encourages children to apply these processes.
- Use such questions as:
  What have we done already?
  What still needs to be done?
  Why are we doing what we are doing?
  How will it help us?
  What's going to happen when you type that?
  Do you know why that's there?
  Are we solving the problem we set out to solve?
  Something is wrong; what exactly didn't work out?
  Does our solution really solve the problem?
  Does it make sense?

## Knowledge-Acquisition Components

LOGO appears to have the potential to facilitate the development of *knowledge-acquisition components,* although relevant characteristics of efficacious environments are less clear. The following suggestions may have merit.

- Tender LOGO and non-LOGO problems containing irrelevant information. Discuss ways to determine what information is necessary.
- Tolerate unexpected and divergent solution approaches. Encourage children to combine that which they know in novel ways.
- Have children refer to previous problems and projects as an aid to solving new problems.
- Ask such questions as:
  What's important here?
  Do you remember what those were for?

Can you think of a problem just like this one that you have solved before?
Can you create and solve a similar problem?
Can you solve the problem in a different way?
Can you solve a more general problem?

In general, to encourage children's retrieval of declarative knowledge of all componential functioning, all componential processes should be discussed frequently (even if briefly), especially in the context of the children's own work (this serves to increase the level of activation of that knowledge; cf. Anderson, 1983).

Perhaps most importantly, children must learn these processes by applying them. This encourages both initial strengthening of declarative memory (especially concerning when and how the processes are used) and eventual knowledge compilation. Thus, the components should be used in a variety of problems, in and out of the LOGO context. Teachers might frequently ask, "What kind of representation would help you solve this [mathematics, language arts, every-day life, etc.] problem?" or, "You started saying one thing, then you stopped and switched. What did your debugger tell you right then?"

## All Meta- and Knowledge-Acquisition Components

Although the preceding suggestions do have some empirical backing, the most consistent patterns we observed were not tied to any single component. Certain characteristics were shared by most successful LOGO interventions. The teachers in these studies usually would:

- Discuss and provide examples of how the skills used in LOGO could be applied in other contexts, thus facilitating transfer.
- Ensure that students are explicitly aware of the strategies and processes that they are to learn, and guide them to decontextualize these processes by applying them to new situations. In this way, the processes should become conscious, should be abstracted and generalized, and finally, should be used to solve problems in settings different from the original.
- Encourage transfer explicitly; for example, "How is that procedure similar to the process we used yesterday to solve the mathematics problem?"
- Generally, forge links with other knowledge, so that what is learned in a programming context becomes integrated with this knowledge.
- Provide sufficient time for programming.
- Discuss errors and common misunderstandings.
- Provide individualized feedback regarding students' problem-solving efforts.
- Ensure that a sufficient proportion of instruction occurs in small groups or one-on-one situations.
- Promote both child–teacher and child–child interaction.

Interestingly, two characteristics of the studies that we examined did *not* show a consistent pattern. Despite many claims to the contrary, mastery of programming itself was not a consistently significant factor; apparently, it is not the programming skills per se that are being transferred, but the mental processes and strategies. *These* are what must be well learned.

The second characteristic was the degree of structure in the learning environment. On a continuum from unguided discovery to complete didacticism, neither extreme appeared prevalent in successful interventions. Thus, environments that are too loosely or tightly structured may not be effective. However, there was no discernable pattern in the middle of the continuum, preventing any indication of an optimal degree of structure. Perhaps researchers are not being clear about *what* it is that is being structured. Successful interventions did structure children's experiences. Structure in this sense is not equivalent to the use of lockstep teaching methods, however. It involves facilitating children's employment of, and often awareness of, componential processes. This kind of structure is also not equivalent to "control" of students. Several interventions tightly structured, or controlled, the students' minute-by-minute LOGO activities to no avail; what they neglected to do was to structure the environment so as to encourage componential employment. Often children were directed page-by-page through LOGO programming worksheets, but were never encouraged to reflect on their activity.

Although the recommended teaching methods are almost certainly facilitative, almost just as certainly, they alone do not constitute necessary or sufficient conditions of componential development. We are left with that ubiquitous, but nonetheless true, phrase, "more research is needed." As a reminder that some research has indeed shown the potential of a relatively more ideal LOGO environment to facilitate children's metacognitive development, we conclude with two vignettes. A posttest interview of a boy from our third study was winding down. As an afterthought, the interviewer asked, "do you think of the homunculi when you're solving problems?" The boy replied, "No" (the interviewer inwardly groaned) . . . "but you always do use them. Like when a problem pops up. But there should be another homunculi. He would get a problem from the problem decider, drop it off to the representer and to the planner. You could even be writing the answer down and this guy could start the problem decider working on a new problem." This boy had independently constructed a function of the solution monitoring component—the metametacomponent—that we had never discussed: directing the actions of the metacomponents themselves! The second vignette is taken from Lawler's (1985) study of his son and daughter's almost total immersion in a metacognitive-oriented LOGO environment. The two children were discussing the structure of the mind. Mariam proposed an "eraser mind," explaining that thoughts were ideas written on a table that could be erased. Between them, they also postulated "remembering minds" and "talking minds" with "voice boxes" (a reference to a computer's speech synthesizer), and concluded that "You must also have a learning mind, or all your other minds would be empty."

## REFERENCES

Anderson, J. R. (1983). *The architecture of cognition.* Cambridge, MA: Harvard University Press.

Bamberger, H. J. (1985). The effect of LOGO (turtle graphics) on the problem solving strategies used by fourth grade children. *Dissertation Abstracts International, 46,* 918A. (University Microfilms No. DA8512171)

Baron, J. (1982). Personality and intelligence. In R. J. Sternberg (Ed.), *Handbook of human intelligence* (pp. 308–351). Cambridge, MA: Cambridge University Press.

Carmichael, H. W., Burnett, J. D., Higginson, W. C., Moore, B. G., & Pollard, P. J. (1985). *Computers, children and classrooms: A multisite evaluation of the creative use of microcomputers by elementary school children.* Toronto, Ontario, Canada: Ministry of Education.

Carver, S. M., & Klahr, D. (1986). Assessing children's LOGO debugging skills with a formal model. *The Journal of Educational Computing Research, 2,* 487–525.

Clements, D. H. (1983/1984). Supporting young children's LOGO programming. *The Computing Teacher, 11*(5), 24–30.

Clements, D. H. (1986a). Effects of LOGO and CAI environments on cognition and creativity. *Journal of Educational Psychology, 78,* 309–318.

Clements, D. H. (1986b). LOGO and cognition: A theoretical foundation. *Computers in Human Behavior, 2,* 95–110.

Clements, D. H. (1987). Longitudinal study of the effects of LOGO programming on cognitive abilities and achievement. *Journal of Educational Computing Research, 3,* 73–94.

Clements, D. H., & Gullo, D. F. (1984). Effects of computer programming on young children's cognition. *Journal of Educational Psychology, 76,* 1051–1058.

Clements, D. H., & Nastasi, B. K. (1988). Social and cognitive interactions in educational computer environments. *American Educational Research Journal, 25,* 87–106.

Degelman, D., Free, J. V., Scarlato, M., Blackburn, J. M., & Golden, T. (1986). Concept learning in preschool children: Effects of a short-term LOGO experience. *Journal of Educational Computing Research, 2*(2), 199–205.

Dvarskas, D. P. (1984). The effects of introductory computer programming lessons on the learners' ability to analyze mathematical word problems. *Dissertation Abstracts International, 44,* 2665A. (University Microfilms No. DA8400949)

Dytman, J. A., Peverly, S., & Wang, M. C. (1985, April). *An investigation of the role of the learner in LOGO learning environments.* Paper presented at the annual meeting of the American Educational Research Association, Chicago, IL.

Findlayson, H. M. (1984). *The transfer of mathematical problem solving skills from LOGO experience.* D.A.I. Research Paper No. 238. University of Edinburgh, Edinburgh, Scotland.

Flavell, J. H. (1981). Cognitive monitoring. In W. P. Dickson (Ed.), *Children's oral communication skills* (pp. 35–60). New York: Academic Press.

Gaffney, C. R. (1985). Computer languages: Tools for problem-solving? *Dissertation Abstracts International, 45,* 3097B. (University Microfilms No. DA8426831)

Gorman, H., Jr., & Bourne, L. E., Jr. (1983). Learning to think by learning LOGO: Rule learning in third-grade computer programmers. *Bulletin of the Psychonomic Society, 21,* 165–167.

Hlawati, B. (1985). *Effects of LOGO and problem-solving CAI on the cognitive processes of gifted children.* Unpublished doctoral dissertation, Kent State University, Kent, OH.

Horton, J., & Ryba, K. (1986). Assessing learning with LOGO: A pilot study. *The Computing Teacher, 14*(1), 24–28.

Inhelder, B., & Piaget, J. (1969). *The early growth of logic in the child: Classification and seriation* (E. A. Lunzer & D. Papert, Trans.). New York: Norton.

Kagan, J., Lapidus, D. R., & Moore, M. (1978). Infant antecedents of cognitive functioning: A longitudinal study. *Child Development, 49,* 1005–1023.

Kagan, J., Rossman, B. L., Day, D., Albert, J., & Phillips, W. (1964). Information processing in the child. Significance of analytic and reflective attitudes. *Psychological Monographs, 78* (1, Serial No. 578).

Kull, J. A. (1986). Learning and LOGO. In P. F. Campbell & G. G. Fein (Eds.), *Young children and microcomputers* (pp. 103–130). Englewood Cliffs, NJ: Prentice-Hall.

Lawler, R. (1985). *Computer experience and cognitive development: A children's learning in a computer culture.* New York: Wiley.

Lehrer, R., & Randle, L. (1986). *Problem solving, metacognition and composition: The effects of interactive software for first-grade children.* Unpublished manuscript, University of Wisconsin–Madison.

Lehrer, R., & Smith, P. (1986, April). *LOGO learning: Is more better?* Paper presented at the annual meeting of the American Educational Research Association, San Francisco.

Markman, E. M. (1977). Realizing that you don't understand: A preliminary investigation. *Child Development, 48,* 986–992.

Markman, E. M. (1981). Comprehension monitoring. In W. P. Dickson (Ed.), *Children's oral communication skills* (pp. 61–84). New York: Academic Press.

Miller, G. E., & Emihovich, C. (1986). The effects of mediated programming instruction on preschool children's self-monitoring. *Journal of Educational Computing Research, 2*(3), 283–297.

Mohamed, M. A. (1985). *The effects of learning LOGO computer language upon the higher cognitive processes and the analytic/global cognitive styles of elementary school students.* Unpublished doctoral dissertation, University of Pittsburgh, Pittsburgh, PA.

Odom, M. L. N. (1985). The effects of learning the computer programming language LOGO on fifth and sixth grade students' skills of analysis, synthesis, and evaluation. *Dissertation Abstracts International, 45,* 2390-A. (University Microfilms No. DA8426197).

Papert, S. (1980). *Mindstorms: Children, computers and powerful ideas.* New York: Basic Books.

Papert, S. (1987). Computer criticism vs. technocentric thinking. *Educational Researcher, 16,* 22–30.

Pea, R. D., & Kurland, D. M. (1984). *LOGO programming and the development of planning skills* (Tech. Rep. No. 16). New York: Bank Street College of Education, Center for Children and Technology.

Ramondetta, J. (1985). *The effect of learning computer programming using LOGO on the higher cognitive processes of sixth grade students.* Paper presented at the LOGO 85 conference, MIT, Cambridge, MA.

Reimer, G. (1985). The effects of a LOGO computer programming experience on readiness for first grade, creativity, and self concept. "A pilot study in kindergarten." *AEDS Monitor, 23,* 8–12.

Rodefer, J. C. (1985). *Teaching higher-level thinking skills through LOGO.* Unpublished dissertation, West Virginia University, Morgantown, WV.

Ross, D., & Ross, C. (1976). *Ross Test of Higher Cognitive Processes.* Novato, CA: Academic Therapy Pub.

Sternberg, R. J. (1985). *Beyond IQ: A triarchic theory of human intelligence.* Cambridge, MA: Cambridge University Press.

Sternberg, R. J. (1986). *Intelligence applied.* Orlando, FL: Harcourt Brace Jovanovich.

Studyvin, D., & Moninger, M. (1986). *LOGO as an enhancement to critical thinking.* Paper presented at the LOGO 86 Conference, Cambridge, MA.

Torrance, E. P. (1972). *Torrance tests of creative thinking.* Lexington, MA: Personnel Press.

Vaidya, S., & McKeeby, J. (1984, September). Computer turtle graphics: Do they affect children's thought processes? *Educational Technology,* pp. 46–47.

Wagner, R. K., & Sternberg, R. J. (1984). Alternative conceptions of intelligence and their implications for education. *Review of Educational Research, 54,* 179–223.

Young, L. (1982). *An analysis of the effect of the LOGO computer programming environment upon the reflective and impulsive cognitive styles of second-grade students.* Unpublished doctoral dissertation, University of Pittsburgh, Pittsburgh, PA.

# 3

# Learning LOGO: A Cognitive Analysis

Anne L. Fay
Richard E. Mayer
*University of California, Santa Barbara*

## ABSTRACT

What is learned when a child is taught to issue navigational commands in a LOGO turtle graphics environment? First, the child acquires syntactic knowledge, including knowing the legal command elements (such as RT or LT), rules for combining the elements into commands (such as knowing that RT must be followed by a number), and rules for combining commands into programs. Second, the child acquires semantic knowledge specific to LOGO, such as a mental model of the locations, objects, and actions carried out in the computer. Third, the child acquires semantic knowledge that can be mapped onto domains beyond programming, such as comprehending and issuing commands for spatial navigation using maps. This chapter examines the chain of cognitive changes—including changes in syntactic, semantic, and mapping knowledge—that occur as children learn to use LOGO turtle graphics commands.

## WHAT IS LEARNED BY LOGO USERS?

Imagine that you are sitting in front of a computer terminal. There is a triangular cursor (called the "turtle") in the middle of the terminal screen as shown in Fig. 3.1.

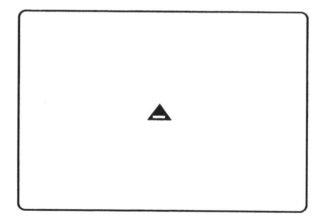

FIG. 3.1. Computer screen with turtle at 0° heading. Copyright 1987 by the American Psychological Association. Reprinted by permission of the publisher.

Further, imagine that you can type in commands at the keyboard that will move the turtle around the screen, based on the following instructions.

In the LOGO graphics environment, the turtle creates designs by leaving a visible trace of its path as it moves around on the screen. There are four elementary commands that control the actions of the turtle: RIGHT, LEFT, FORWARD, and BACK (abbreviated as RT, LT, FD, and BK, respectively). Each of these commands must be followed by a space and then a number, which determines the magnitude of the action. For example, the command "RT" followed by the argument "90" rotates the turtle 90° clockwise, "LT 45" rotates it 45° counterclockwise, "FD 50" moves it forward 50 turtle steps, and "BK 20" moves it backward 20 turtle steps.

Next, you are given the following tasks to complete.[1]

1. Circle the commands that are incorrect and rewrite them so that they are correct.
   (a) FD 75     (b) 50 BK     (c) R30

2. Draw what would appear on the screen after the commands "FD 50 RT 90 FD 50" were entered (See Fig. 3.2.)

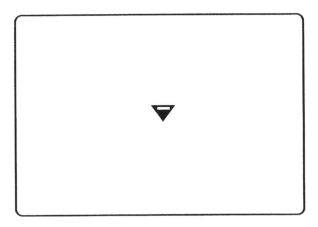

FIG. 3.2. The position and heading of the turtle before the commands are entered. Copyright 1987 by the American Psychological Association. Reprinted by permission of the publisher.

3. Using the map provided, write the directions that will get a person from point A to point B.

---

[1]Answers: (1) FD 75 is correct, 50 BK should be changed to BK 50, and R30 should be changed to RT 30. (2) The screen would look like this:

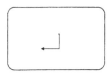

(3) The directions are: Move forward, turn right, move forward, turn left, move forward, turn right, move forward, turn left, move forward, turn left, move forward.

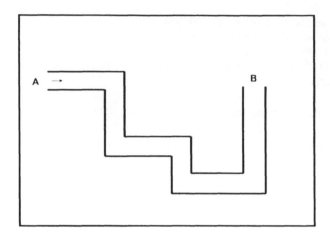

FIG. 3.3.    Map for question 3.

The first two tasks are designed to evaluate knowledge of two basic skills for computer programming: writing programming code and comprehending programming code. Although you may have found these tasks easy to solve, previous research has shown that many novice programmers have considerable difficulty in solving similar tasks (Anderson, Farrel, & Sauers, 1984; Bayman & Mayer, 1983; Bonar & Soloway, 1985; Fay & Mayer, 1987). To understand why these tasks are difficult, it is necessary to analyze the tasks in terms of the knowledge required to accomplish them successfully.

The first task is a code recognition/production task, in which the learner has to recognize and generate legal programming code. This task requires knowledge of the programming language *syntax*, that is, the lexicon and grammar used for programming the movement of the turtle.

The second task is a comprehension task, in which the learner has to predict the output that would be produced by a set of commands. This task provides the command syntax, but requires knowledge of the meaning of the commands, that is, the *semantics* of the programming language.

These two types of knowledge, the syntax and the semantics of the programming language, are major knowledge components of a computer programming language. Once a learner has acquired this knowledge (along with related strategic knowledge not discussed in this chapter), he or she will be able to write programming code to produce desired output.

The third task is not designed to evaluate programming knowledge. This task is used to evaluate the learner's ability to transfer knowledge acquired in the programming environment to a new problem-solving domain. This task presents a problem from a non-LOGO domain that can be solved by applying knowledge components from the LOGO programming environment. Learner performance on this type of task is of interest to many educators and researchers because it evaluates the role that computer programming can play in enhancing general problem-solving skills.

In this chapter we examine the knowledge that is required to successfully accomplish each of these tasks, and propose the sequence in which this knowledge is acquired. We describe three kinds of knowledge that can be acquired through experience with LOGO graphics programming: syntactic knowledge of LOGO, semantic knowledge of LOGO, and semantic knowledge of spatial navigation. For each type of knowledge we provide a definition and report research that shows the initial difficulties that children have in acquiring these knowledge components and the changes in their knowledge as a result of experience.

We close with a discussion of the chain of cognitive changes model, which proposes a sequence in which the three types of knowledge are acquired. In particular, the model proposes that acquisition of language syntax is a prerequisite for success in learning the semantics of programming, and semantic knowledge is a prerequisite for success in learning to transfer skills to domains outside of programming. Finally, we discuss the implications of our model, for both educational practice and future research.

## SYNTACTIC KNOWLEDGE

### What is Syntactic Knowledge?

In this section we analyze the syntactic structure of the LOGO graphics environment. The syntactic structure of all programming languages consists of three components: the elements, the rules for combining elements into commands, and the rules for combining commands into programs or program segments. Although all programming languages have the same syntactical components, the contents of the components are uniquely (and somewhat arbitrarily) determined for each language. Throughout this section, we describe two of the syntactical components (the elements and the rules for combining elements into commands) and the specific syntactic knowledge required to program in the LOGO graphics environment and in the Pascal turtle graphics environment. The purpose of this comparison is to highlight the difference between the syntactic structure, which is language-independent, and the syntactic content, which is language-dependent.

*Elements.* The elements of a programming language include keywords, punctuation marks, and arguments (e.g., numeric or string). In LOGO graphics, for example, the four elementary keywords are FORWARD, BACK, LEFT, and RIGHT; the punctuation marks are blank spaces; and the arguments are integers or variables that store integers. In comparison, in Pascal turtle graphics the primary keywords are TURN and MOVE; the punctuation marks are blank spaces, parentheses, and semi-colons; and the arguments are integers or variables that store integers. As you can see, the two languages have the same element subcomponents, but they differ in terms of their specific contents.

*Rules.* The second syntactic component consists of the rules for combining the elements into commands or programming statements. Each command has its own format, or way that it must be written in order to be accepted by the system. In LOGO, the graphic elements must be combined according to the following rule:

KEYWORD space ARGUMENT

For example, "FD 50" consists of the correct LOGO elements and is written in the legal form. However, "50 FD", although containing the correct elements, would be unacceptable because it fails to follow the combination rule. In contrast, Pascal's rule for combining elements in its turtle graphics environment is:

KEYWORD space (numerical argument);

For example, "MOVE (50);" is syntactically correct for Pascal's turtle graphics, whereas "(50) MOVE;" is incorrect because it fails to follow the rule for combining elements. Again, you can see that the two languages are similar in that they each contain rules for combining elements, but they are different in terms of the specific rules they use. A syntactically correct command in LOGO, such as "RT 90", would be incorrect in Pascal; first, because "RT" is not one of the Pascal elements; and second, because the rule for placing delimiters in Pascal has been violated.

Knowledge of the programming language syntax is necessary for successful computer programming. In order for the computer to execute some action, the learner must input syntactially correct commands. For example, in LOGO, until a learner knows that FD, BK, LT, and RT, followed by a space and a numerical argument are the commands to make the turtle move and turn, he or she will be unable to program the computer to produce output. Once syntactic languages features are known however, the learner can program the turtle to produce various graphic designs.

## Research on Acquiring Syntactic Knowledge

There have been only a few studies that have examined children's acquisition of LOGO syntax. Heller (1986) examined fourth-grade students' knowledge of LOGO graphics syntax after 3 and 12 weeks of LOGO experience. After 3 weeks of LOGO experience, the mean percentage correct on a LOGO syntax test was approximately 48%, and after 12 weeks, performance rose to 65% correct. In our research the acquisition of syntax was measured informally. Fourth-grade students were given simple graphic projects to complete in each of two LOGO sessions. All the students successfully completed the projects, which indicates that they had acquired the syntactic features of LOGO. However, informal observation revealed that they made several syntactic errors before accomplishing their goals. For example, students often entered keywords without arguments, omitted the space between the keyword and the argument, and entered multiple arguments after a keyword. Although these errors can be due to mistyping, the students often required an explanation as to why they were incorrect, which points to a lack of knowledge rather than to mere typing slips. These studies demonstrate that the acquisition of the LOGO syntax can be difficult for some children and it may require extensive practice and experience before mastery will occur.

## SEMANTIC KNOWLEDGE

### What Is Semantic Knowledge?

The second type of knowledge that can be acquired through programming experience is semantic knowledge. Unlike the syntactic structure, the semantic structure of a programming environment is not arbitrary; it has a logical structure that is dependent on the functional components of the programming domain. There are three functional components that can be used to describe the semantics of commands in all programming languages: operations, which are the actions that can be performed; objects, which are the entities that are operated upon; and locations, which refer to where in the computer the operation occurs. Every aspect of a programming command can be described as an operation that is applied to an object at some location. Although all programming languages can be analyzed in terms of these three components, each may differ in the actual operations, objects, and locations that are available to them (see Mayer, 1979, 1985).

In the first part of this section we describe the semantic structure of the LOGO graphics environment in terms of the operations, objects, and locations that are available to it. We also provide a similar description of Pascal's turtle graphics environment to further clarify the distinction between the components (which are language-independent) and the specific elements of the components (which are language-dependent). In the second part of this section we discuss the common misconceptions that student's often develop of the LOGO graphics commands. We also discuss how these misconceptions change as a result of continued experience with LOGO.

*Operations.* In LOGO turtle graphics, an operation is comprised of two subcomponents: an action and an action modifier. Knowledge of the action component involves the ability to discriminate among the actions available in the programming environment and the ability to map each of these actions onto its appropriate keyword. In the LOGO graphics environment, there are four elementary actions: clockwise rotation, counterclockwise rotation, forward movement, and backward movement. A complete understanding of the actions would consist of knowing that the keyword "RT" invokes the action of clockwise rotation, the keyword "LT" invokes the action of counterclockwise rotation, the keyword "FD" invokes the action of forward movement, and the keyword "BK" invokes the action of backward movement. In contrast, there are only two elementary actions in Pascal's turtle graphics: counterclockwise rotation, which is invoked by the keyword "TURN"; and forward movement, which is invoked by the keyword "MOVE".

The action modifier is the numerical argument that accompanies the action. The function of the action modifier is to determine the magnitude of the action. When used to modify a rotation, the argument refers to the number of degrees. For example, RT 90 and RT 45 invoke the same action (i.e., clockwise rotation) but the former refers to a 90° rotation and the latter refers to a 45° rotation. When used to modify a movement, the argument refers to the distance travelled as measured in turtle steps. For example, BK 50 and BK 100 invoke the same action (i.e., backward movement) but the former refers to a distance of 50 steps and the latter refers to a distance of 100 steps. In Pascal, the same relationship exists; the action modifier is the numerical argument and it refers to the number of degrees of rotation when paired with the keyword "TURN" and the number of steps when paired with the keyword "MOVE".

*Objects.*    Although a child may understand the operations invoked by different programming commands, his or her semantic knowledge may still be incomplete or inaccurate. The child must also have knowledge of the objects upon which the operations apply. In LOGO graphics, as well as in Pascal turtle graphics, the turtle is the object of the operations. The turtle has spatial features (i.e., front, back, left side, and right side) and a current state (i.e., orientation and position). When operations are applied to the turtle, they are interpreted in reference to the turtle's spatial labels or to its current orientation and position. For example, the command "RT 90" can be interpreted as "rotate the turtle 90° to its right" or as "rotate the turtle 90° clockwise from it current orientation."

*Locations.*    The third component is the location, which refers to where the operation on the object is to take place. In the LOGO graphics environment the most common location is the CRT screen, but it can also be the floor, as in the case where a robotic Turtle is used. In Pascal, the location is usually the CRT screen, once again very similar to LOGO's environment.

Once the components are known, each command can be understood in terms of its underlying actions, objects, and locations. For example, "rotate the turtle on the screen 60° counterclockwise" is the underlying meaning of the command

"LT 60." This is also the meaning underlying the Pascal command "TURN (60);". As you can see, different languages will have similar semantic structures to the degree that they have the same semantic component elements, regardless of any differences between their syntactical structures.

Knowledge of the semantic structure of the programming environment must be acquired in order for the learner to be able to program effectively. Although output can be generated from knowledge of only the language syntax, the learner would be unable to predict the output generated by the entered commands. It is only when the learner has also acquired semantic knowledge that he or she will be able to accurately predict the output of a command and so be able to systematically and efficiently write programs. Note that we use semantic knowledge to refer to the underlying conception of "actions on objects at locations" as well as to the mapping of these concepts onto appropriate syntactic labels.

## Research on Acquiring
## Semantic Knowledge

*Users' Preconceptions.*  Recent research has demonstrated that many students have difficulty acquiring the semantic structure of the programming environment (Bayman & Mayer, 1983; Mayer & Fay, 1987; Sleeman, Putnam, Baxter, & Kuspa, 1986; Soloway, Ehrlich, Bonar & Greenspan, 1982). One source of difficulty can stem from the preconceptions (or intuitive knowledge) that the learner brings with him or her to the programming environment (Bonar & Soloway, 1985; Mayer & Fay, 1987). When these preconceptions conflict with the semantic structure of the programming environment, it can result in the construction of faulty or inaccurate mental models of the programming statements. For example, in everyday English when someone says "turn right" it usually means to turn right and keep moving forward, but this conflicts with the meaning of the LOGO command "RIGHT", which means to rotate clockwise. If a child enters the LOGO environment and applies the everyday meaning of "turn right" to the command "RIGHT", that child will have an inaccurate mental model of the command.

The term *mental model* refers to the user's conception of the transformations that occur between the time a command is entered and until it is finally executed (Young, 1981). The semantic analysis of the commands described previously provides a framework for analyzing the mental models that students possess of the LOGO graphics environment. The misconceptions that they have, as inferred from the errors in their programming performance, can be attributed to incomplete or inaccurate knowledge of the actions, objects, and locations underlying the commands.

We conducted a study to find out what kinds of misconceptions students had after initial exposure to LOGO and to see if there were any developmental trends in the frequency and type of misconceptions that students held. Fourth, fifth,

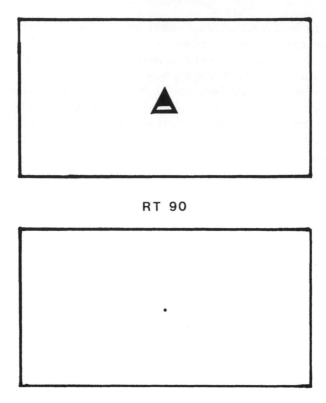

FIG. 3.4.   Example item from the LOGO prediction problem test. (Copyright 1987 by the American Psychological Association. Reprinted by permission of the publisher)

sixth, and eighth-grade students were given a hands-on introduction to LOGO turtle graphics followed by a LOGO prediction test. On the test, each child was presented with a set of 24 problems, like that shown in Fig. 3.4, and was asked to draw the output of the command in the lower frame.

An analysis of the responses revealed two misconceptions, which accounted for most of the errors that students made: interpretation bugs, in which a student maps the wrong action onto a keyword (e.g., interpreting a turn command to mean move or turn and move), and egocentric bugs, in which a student interprets the object of the action incorrectly, (e.g., LT 90 means to face the left side of the screen or to the student's left rather than to the turtle's left). These misconceptions, occurring alone or together, resulted in four major response categories:

*No Bugs (CC)*, in which the turtle is rotated relative to its current orientation for turn commands or moved relative to its position for move commands, *Interpretation Bugs (XC)*, in which the turtle is moved or turned and moved relative to its orientation for turn commands or turned and moved relative to its orientation for move commands,

*Egocentric Bugs (CX)*, in which the turtle is faced in the direction of the command for turn commands and moved in the direction of the command for move commands,
*Interpretation and Egocentric Bugs (XX)*, in which some combination of both the Interpretation Bug and the Egocentric Bug occurs.

Table 3.1 provides a description of each response category for the command RT 90, when the turtle's heading is 180°.

There were also several cases where the child had misconceptions regarding the action-modifier. Many students interpreted the argument as determining

TABLE 3.1
Response Categories for LOGO Prediction Problems

| Type of Bug | Description | RT 90 means: | Drawing for RT 90 (heading = 180°) |
|---|---|---|---|
| No Bugs (CC) | TURN the Turtle relative to its orientation. | Rotate the Turtle 90° clockwise. | |
| Interpretation Bug (XC) | MOVE the Turtle relative to its orientation. | MOVE the Turtle to its right. | |
| | TURN and MOVE the Turtle relative to its orientation. | Rotate the Turtle 90° clockwise and MOVE it forward. | |
| Egocentric Bug (CX) | FACE the Turtle in the direction of the command. | Make the Turtle FACE the right side of the screen. | |
| Interpretation and Egocentric Bug (XX) | Slide the Turtle in the direction of the command. | MOVE the Turtle to the right side of the screen. | |
| | FACE and MOVE the Turtle in the direction of the command. | Make the Turtle FACE and MOVE to the right side of the screen. | |

distance and not as determining rotation. For example, students would predict that RT 90 would rotate the turtle clockwise 90° and move it forward 90 steps and that RT 45 would also rotate the turtle clockwise 90° but move it forward only 45 steps.

These results show that many children initially hold inaccurate models of the semantic components of the LOGO graphics environment. These misconceptions may be due to the knowledge that the child brings with him or her to the programming environment. For example, children who possess an egocentric conception of space (Piaget & Inhelder, 1956) would fail to recognize that when the turtle is at a 180° orientation, its right corresponds to the child's left. Alternatively, the egocentric child may focus on end states and interpret a command as referring to a static location or orientation, rather than as a transformation from one state to another state (Piaget & Inhelder, 1958.)

The development of spatial knowledge involves a change from an egocentric perspective to a relative perspective. Thus we would expect that younger children would display egocentric bugs more frequently than older children. In our study, 35% of the younger students (fourth and fifth grade) displayed egocentric errors on turn commands compared to only 7% of the older students (sixth and eighth grade). For move commands (FORWARD and BACK) the same trend was found: 22% of the younger students had egocentric errors compared to 2% of the older students. These results show that the tendency to commit egocentric errors declines with age.

Children may also apply their previous knowledge of English words to the LOGO environment. In the LOGO graphics environment, interpreting the commands in the same way as in ordinary English would be indicated by interpreting turn commands (e.g., LT 90) to mean turn and move. Although "turn and move" is the usual interpretation in English when we instruct someone to turn left, in LOGO "LT 90" means to rotate the turtle 90° counterclockwise, without changing its location. In our study, 26% of the younger students and 7% of the older students interpreted turn commands to mean turn and move, which suggests that they have the tendency to apply their prior knowledge of words to the LOGO environment.

The results of this study support the notion that acquiring the semantics of LOGO can be difficult for two reasons: The learner lacks the necessary conceptual skills, (e.g., when a child is unable to take the perspective of the turtle) or the learner inappropriately maps the meanings that the keywords have in everyday language onto the commands in the LOGO environment. In both cases, the learner is entering the LOGO environment with misconceptions that conflict with the semantic structure of LOGO. Therefore, acquiring the semantic structure involves replacing these misconceptions with conceptions that are appropriate for the LOGO domain.

*Changes in Semantic Knowledge.*   In order to examine the process of acquiring semantic knowledge, we continued to provide LOGO experience and evaluation to our fourth-grade students from the study described previously. After each of three LOGO sessions, the students completed the 24 LOGO prediction problems. We then compared the response category that each student was best fitted to for each command type across the three LOGO tests. Table 3.2 summarizes, for each type of command, the number of students who showed no change in their misconceptions, reduced misconceptions, and increased misconceptions from LOGO session 1 to LOGO session 3.

The table shows two patterns: The students showed no change in their semantic knowledge (i.e., they had the same number of misconceptions from day 1 to day 3) or they showed an improvement in their semantic knowledge (i.e., they reduced the number of misconceptions from day 1 to day 3). As shown in Fig. 3.5, the proportion of students possessing the correct conception tends to increase across the three sessions, the proportion of students with one misconception (either egocentric or interpretation bugs) tends to remain constant, and the proportion of students possessing both misconceptions (egocentric and interpretation bugs) tends to decrease across sessions.

In summary, repeated experience in LOGO can result in an improvement in the ability to think within the domain of LOGO, that is, in the acquisition of the semantics of LOGO. A significant number of children showed a decrease in the number of misconceptions they held concerning the semantics of LOGO with continued experience. However, the fact that many children failed to show improvement provides us with information concerning the difficulty of acquiring the semantics of LOGO. These results suggest that at certain ages or stages of development, certain misconceptions in the LOGO environment are to be expected and may be difficult to eliminate, even when the students are given hands-on experience.


## MAPPING SEMANTIC KNOWLEDGE
## ONTO ANOTHER DOMAIN


### What Is Mapping?

Much of the impetus for teaching LOGO to children is based on the claim that experience with LOGO can enhance general and high-level thinking skills (Papert, 1980). This phenomenon is often referred to as transfer: The knowledge acquired in one domain is applied, without the benefit of learning or experience, to a novel domain. Unfortunately, research results often have failed to provide support for this claim (Pea & Kurland, 1984; Pea, Kurland, & Hawkins, 1985). However, some studies have reported gains in certain areas of problem solving (e.g., Clements & Gullo, 1984; Gorman & Bourne, 1983). These conflicting findings lead to the question of when LOGO will lead to the enhancement of general problem-solving skills and what kinds of problem-solving skills should

TABLE 3.2
Number of Students showing Reduced, Increased, or Unchanged Misconceptions
from Day 1 to Day 3 for Three Types of Commands

| Type of Command | No Change | Reduced Misconceptions | Increased Misconception |
|---|---|---|---|
| RT and LT | 13 | 11* | 1 |
| FD | 7 | 6* | 0 |
| BK | 12 | 10* | 0 |

Note: Only those students who displayed misconceptions on Day 1 are included.
*The proportion of students who changed by reducing misconceptions is significantly greater than chance, $p < .01$

be affected. In this section we focus on these two questions and propose that there are two conditions that must be met in order for transfer to occur. First, the relevant syntactic and semantic knowledge components must be acquired (to some degree) in the original learning environment, and second, the knowledge acquired in the original domain must be recognized as relevant for the new domain.

The first condition that must be met in order for transfer to occur is the acquisition of the target skill in the original domain. If a skill is to be transferred from one domain to another, it must first exist in one of the domains. Most of the studies conducted to examine the transfer of problem-solving skills from programming to a new domain failed to evaluate the subjects' mastery of syntactic and semantic knowledge in the programming domain or to evaluate which programming constructs were used, which may explain the mixed results.

In the LOGO graphics environment, one of the knowledge components involves recognizing the turtle as the object of the operations. If a child learns that the commands are interpreted in reference to the turtle's perspective and acquires the ability to interpret the commands accordingly, he or she may be able to transfer that skill to situations requiring giving directions from some other object's or person's perspective.

Although the child may have the necessary knowledge to solve the new task, this is not a guarantee that he or she will apply that knowledge in the new situation. The child must also recognize the relevance of the acquired knowledge to the new domain. For example, Pea, Hawkins, and Sheingold (1983) found that students who could successfully use a programming construct in one LOGO context often failed to use it in another LOGO context where it was applicable. Such evidence suggests that the acquisition of the concept is not sufficient to ensure its transfer to another applicable domain. We suggest that the child must also recognize the new domain as having components that are analogous to the components in the original learning environment.

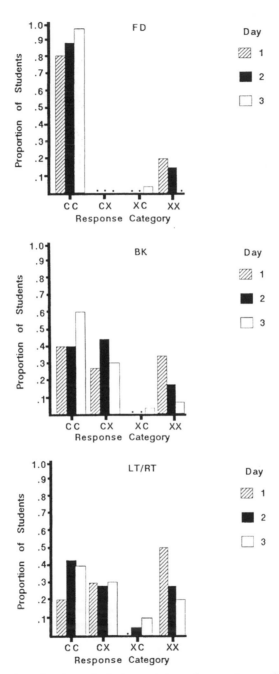

FIG. 3.5.   Proportion of students displaying each type of conception on three instructional days by type of command. (Copyright 1987 by the American Psychological Association. Reprinted by permission of the publisher)

### Research on Transfer of Knowledge

In order to assess the effects of learning LOGO on spatial skills, we gave our fourth-grade students a Map test prior to their exposure to LOGO and again after three sessions of hands-on LOGO learning. The task was to write the directions that would lead a person from the start position to home, as shown in Fig. 3.6. Based on their responses on the LOGO test booklets, we divided the students into three groups: (a) No Change/Egocentric, which refers to students who had egocentric bugs on their first LOGO test and on their final LOGO test (b) Change/Egocentric-to-Turtle-Centric, which refers to students who had egocentric bugs on their first LOGO test but who eliminated this bug by the final LOGO test and (c) No Change/Turtle-Centric, which refers to students who never displayed egocentric bugs. The results show that only the Change and No Change/Turtle-Centric groups made significant gains in their pretest to posttest Map scores. The children who had egocentric bugs on LOGO Test 1 and who still had egocentric bugs on LOGO Test 3 failed to show any gains in their Map posttest. Table 3.3 shows the proportion correct for the Map pretest and the Map posttest and the proportion of students who showed gains in their scores for each of the three types of LOGO learners. As you can see, not all of the students in the

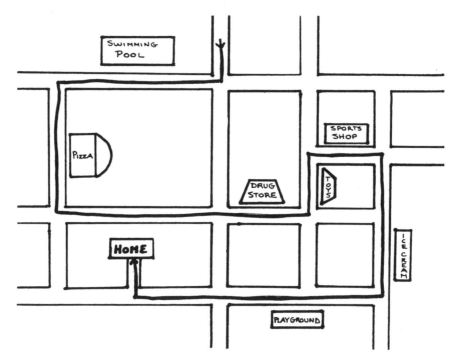

FIG. 3.6.    Example item from the Map test. (Copyright 1987 by the American Psychological Association. Reprinted by permission of the publisher)

TABLE 3.3
Pretest to Posttest Changes in Map Test for Three Groups of LOGO Learners

| Group | Pretest Score (Proportion Correct) | Posttest Score (Proportion Correct) | Proportion of Gainers |
|-------|------------------------------------|-------------------------------------|-----------------------|
| Change: Egocentric to turtle-centric ($N=10$) | .51 | .66* | .90* |
| No change: turtle-centric ($N=11$) | .53 | .74* | 1.00* |
| No change: Egocentric ($N=6$) | .50 | .44 | .00 |

*The increase in proportion correct and/or the proportion of gainers is significantly greater than chance, $p < .05$

Change group showed pretest to posttest gains. Although these students acquired and displayed the target skill in the LOGO environment, they were unable to apply this knowledge to the Map posttest. Together, these findings support the idea that acquisition of the target skill in the original environment (i.e., LOGO) is a necessary but not a sufficient condition for the transfer of the skill to a new domain (i.e., giving directions). As mentioned previously, we suggest that recognition of the analogous components between the original and new domain is also necessary, and that the acquisition of these two knowledge components may be sufficient for skill transfer.

The results indicate that those children who acquired one aspect of the semantics of LOGO (i.e., that the turtle is the spatial referent for the commands) were able to transfer this knowledge to another domain (i.e., giving directions of spatial navigation from a map). Those children who failed to acquire this knowledge did not demonstrate transfer. The results of this study provide evidence that learning of the target skill in the original domain (e.g., LOGO) and recognition of the relevance of the skill to the new domain are prerequisites for the transfer of that skill to the new domain (e.g., giving directions from a map).

## CONCLUSION

### The Chain of Cognitive Changes

In the first section of this chapter we examined three kinds of knowledge that could be acquired when a child learns to program a computer. The first type of knowledge is syntactic, or what Linn (1985) called learning the language features. The second type of knowledge is semantic knowledge of LOGO, or learning to think within the programming domain. Finally, the third type of knowledge is semantic knowledge of spatial navigation, or learning to think beyond the programming domain. These three cognitive changes are the knowledge components of the cognitive changes model. Similar to a model proposed by Linn (1985), the model stipulates that learning the language features is a prerequisite for learning the programming semantics and that acquisition of programming semantics is a prerequisite for learning to think in domains beyond programming.

The first component of the chain is the acquisition of syntactic knowledge. As discussed previously, until a child can write syntactically correct commands, he or she will be unable to produce program output. The command output serves as the major source of feedback of the semantic structure of the command (i.e., the change in the state of the turtle after command execution provides information regarding how the command is interpreted), and as a result the ability to produce command output is a prerequisite for semantic knowledge acquisition. The results from our research (Mayer & Fay, 1987) and Heller's (1986) demonstrate that children do have difficulty acquiring the syntax of LOGO graphics commands. If acquiring the syntax is too cognitively demanding, a child may not have enough cognitive resources available to attend to the semantics of programming. Research in other domains, such as writing (Scardamalia, 1981; Scardamalia, Bereiter, & Goelman, 1982) suggests that when the cognitive demands of the basic skills (i.e., writing syntactically correct sentences) are great, the higher level skills (i.e., story composition) are executed poorly. If we assume that programming skills follow a similar process, then some degree of mastery or automaticity in writing programming code would be necessary before acquisition of the language semantics could occur. An alternative to syntactic mastery is to remove or reduce the syntactic constraints, making it less cognitively demanding and thereby increasing the cognitive resources available for the acquisition of the semantics of the programming language. For example, computer systems could be used that accept pseudocode or natural language, thereby eliminating the need to learn and write commands according to the strict syntactic structure of the programming language.

Once the syntax is acquired (or the syntactic constraints have been removed), the child can concentrate on acquiring the semantic structure of the commands. Some of the semantic components of the programming environment will be transferable to nonprogramming problem-solving domains. However, as our results suggest, the acquisition of the semantic component within the LOGO environment is a prerequisite for the transfer of that skill to a new domain. Carver (this volume) also found that the transfer of higher level programming skills to another domain is related to the degree of mastery of the skill in the programming environment. These results suggest that the acquisition of problem-solving skills does not automatically occur as a result of learning to program. Rather it is dependent upon the skill learning that takes place within the programming environment. Our results indicate that programming can serve as a vehicle for learning general thinking skills but only if those skills are learned and practiced in the programming environment and their applicability to other domains is recognized.

## Implications

The chain of cognitive changes model has implications for the teaching of LOGO to children. The first link in the chain requires the mastery of the language syntax. The model implies that the acquisition of the semantics of LOGO can be accelerated by simplifying the syntax or by reducing the syntactic constraints of LOGO so that the child will be able to devote more attention to the semantic structure of LOGO (such as the turtle as the spatial referent of the commands). Although some studies have introduced subjects to LOGO using simplified syntactic constructions (e.g., Campbell, Fein, Scholnick, Schwartz, & Frank, 1986; Clements & Gullo, 1984), as yet there is no empirical evidence to suggest that this affects the acquisition of semantic knowledge of LOGO. However, promising research by Dyck (1987) indicates that novices can acquire some semantic knowledge of BASIC before they learn BASIC syntax if they are first given experience solving procedural problems written in English. Further research in this area is necessary to determine if reducing the syntactic constraints of LOGO facilitates the acquisition of LOGO semantics and if so, which syntactic manipulations are the most effective.

The second link in the chain concerns the transfer of skills acquired in the programming environment to other domains. As the results suggest, transfer can occur provided that the target skill is acquired in the programming environment and that the learner recognizes the applicability of the skill to the new domain. This implies that effort should be made to ensure that the target skill is being taught and practiced in the programming environment. Even if the target skill is explicitly taught, however, some students may not be as cognitively "ready" to acquire the skill as others. As noted by Littlefield et al. (this volume) these students might require more direct instruction or pretraining in the prerequisite skills in order to benefit from LOGO experience.

## ACKNOWLEDGMENT

This research was supported by Grant MDR-8470248 from the National Science Foundation.

## REFERENCES

Anderson, J. R., Farrell, R., & Sauers, R. (1984). Learning to program in LISP. *Cognitive Science*, *8*, 87–129.
Bayman, P., & Mayer, R. E. (1983). Diagnosis of beginning programmers' misconceptions of BASIC programming statements. *Communications of the ACM, 26*, 519–521.

Bonar, J., & Soloway, E. (1985). Preprogramming knowledge: A major source of misconceptions in novice programmers. *Human–Computer Interaction, 1,* 133–161.

Campbell, P. F., Fein, G. G., Scholnick, E. K., Schwartz, S. S., & Frank, R. E. (1986). Initial mastery of the syntax and semantics of LOGO positioning commands. *Journal of Educational Computing Research, 2,* 357–378.

Clements, D. H., & Gullo, D. F. (1984). Effects of computer programming on young children's cognition. *Journal of Educational Psychology, 76,* 1051–1058.

Dyck, J. L. (1987). *Learning and Comprehension of BASIC and Natural Language Computer Programming by Novices.* Unpublished doctoral dissertation. University of California, Santa Barbara.

Fay, A. L., & Mayer, R. E. (1987). Children's naive conceptions and confusions about LOGO graphics commands. *Journal of Educational Psychology, 79,* 254–268.

Gorman, H., & Bourne, L. E. (1983). Learning to think by learning LOGO: Rule learning in third grade computer programmers. *Bulletin of the Psychonomic Society, 21,* 165–167.

Heller, R. S. (1986). Different LOGO teaching styles: Do they really matter. In E. Soloway & S. Iyenger (Eds.), *Empirical studies of programmers.* Norwood, NJ: Ablex.

Linn, M. C. (1985). The cognitive consequences of programming instruction in classrooms. *Educational Psychologist, 14,* 14–16, 25–29.

Mayer, R. E. (1979). A psychology of learning BASIC. *Computing Surveys, 13,* 121–141.

Mayer, R. E. (1985). Learning in complex domains: A cognitive analysis of computer programming. In G. Bower (Ed.), *Psychology of learning and motivation* (Vol. 19, pp. 89–130). New York: Academic Press.

Mayer, R. E., & Fay, A. L. (1987). A chain of cognitive changes with learning to program in LOGO. *Journal of Educational Psychology, 79,* 269–279.

Papert, S. (1980). *Mindstorms: Children, computers and powerful ideas.* New York: Basic Books.

Pea, R. D., Hawkins, J., & Sheingold, K. (1983, April). *Developmental studies on learning LOGO computer programming.* Paper presented at the Annual Meeting of the Society for Research in Child Development, Detroit, MI.

Pea, R. D., & Kurland, D. M. (1984). On the cognitive effects of learning computer programming. *New Ideas in Psychology, 2,* 137–168.

Pea, R. D., Kurland, D. M., & Hawkins, J. (1985). LOGO and the development of thinking skills. In M. Chen & W. Paisley (Eds.), *Children and microcomputers: Formative studies* (pp. 193–212). Beverly Hills, CA: Sage.

Piaget, J., & Inhelder, B. (1956). *The child's conception of space.* London: Routledge & Kegan Paul.

Scardamalia, M. (1981). How children cope with the cognitive demands of writing. In C. H. Frederikson & J. F. Dominic (Eds.), *Writing, Volume 2* (pp. 81–103). Hillsdale, NJ: Lawrence Erlbaum Associates.

Scardamalia, M., Bereiter, C., & Goelman, H. (1982). The role of production factors in writing ability. In M. Nystrand (Ed.), *What writers know: The language, process and structure of written discourse.* New York: Academic Press.

Sleeman, D., Putnam, R. T., Baxter, J., & Kuspa, L. (1986). Pascal and high school students: A study of errors. *Journal of Educational Computing Research, 2,* 5–23.

Soloway, E., Ehrlich, J., Bonar, J., & Greenspan, J. (1982). What do novices know about programming? In B. Shneiderman & A. Badre (Eds.), *Directions in Human–Computer Interactions* (pp. 27–54). Norwood, NJ: Ablex.

Young, R. M. (1981). The machine inside the machine: User's models of pocket calculators. *International Journal of Man-Machine Studies, 15,* 51–85.

# 4

# Influences of LOGO on Children's Intellectual Development

Richard Lehrer
Thomas Guckenberg
Leonard Sancilio
*University of Wisconsin-Madison*

## ABSTRACT

Expectations concerning the influence of learning to program on children's intellectual development originate in the plurality of conceptions endorsed by various models of mind. Proceeding from a general systems perspective, we formulated and tested several questions concerning the cognitive consequences of learning to program in LOGO. Research questions focused on transferable aspects of programming skills and also on the degree to which use of LOGO's turtle geometry results in the restructuring of children's understanding of Euclidean geometry. Measures employed in the research studies differentiated between knowledge acquisition and knowledge application. Results suggest that transferable aspects of learning LOGO hinge on the method of instruction. When mediated inquiry-based instruction was employed, children demonstrated increases in the cognitive skills associated with comprehension monitoring and with defining the nature of problem constraints. Prolonged instruction in programming apparently resulted in the development of a component of academic self-concept oriented toward computer-based learning. In all studies, turtle geometry helped students restructure their understanding of geometry according to the van Hiele framework. The chapter concludes with a discussion of how instruction in LOGO can mediate a transition between narratively and paradigmatically based reasoning.

Does learning to program contribute to intellectual development? To what extent should young children be taught programming? How should instruction proceed? To what end? Questions such as these provided the context for the empirical research summarized in this chapter and motivated the theoretical framework developed to guide our inquiry.

On the one hand, proponents of teaching programming skills to children suggest that learning to program facilitates the development of thought. On the other hand, critics suggest that learning to program is, at best, no more useful than learning other complex cognitive skills, such as Latin, and at worst, may promote an epidemic of "instrumental thinking"—thinking that advocates reason as a tool rather than as an end (Broughton, 1985; Dreyfus & Dreyfus, 1986). To explore the implications of this dialectic, in the first section of this chapter we outline a control-theory perspective and consider its potential as a framework for understanding the pedagogical implications of instruction in programming for young children. In the second section, we consider a range of possible cognitive consequences that may ensue as a child learns to program. The third section contains a summary of three successive studies of the influence of mediated instruction in the LOGO programming language on the intellectual development of third- and fourth-grade children. In these studies, four general categories of children's intellectual development are examined: (a) planning and problem solving, (b) the influence of LOGO's "turtle geometry" on the acquisition and application of geometric concepts such as angle, (c) metacognition, and (d) programming-related components of self-concept. In the concluding section, we discuss the implications of our findings for a theory of instructional practice.

## MODELS OF MIND AND LEARNING TO PROGRAM

Diversity in expectations concerning the influence of learning to program on children's intellectual development originates in the plurality of conceptions endorsed by various models of "mind" and of "intellect." For example, Sternberg (1985) distinguished six root metaphors governing the construction of various theories of intelligence. Research in programming then takes place in the penumbra of the metaphor for intellect that guides the conduct of inquiry (Lehrer, 1986). Our research program adopts a contextualist metaphor for mind in which students construct knowledge by their actions and in which cognitive development is interpenetrated with social structure (Mead, 1934; Pepper, 1942). By the latter, we refer to the type and extent of mediation provided to students as they learn to program, and the extent to which computers and programming are part of the culture of the classroom (Papert, 1987).

Because learning to program may influence intellectual development in a variety of ways, we distinguish among three types of programming effects on learning: cognitive, metacognitive, and epistemic (Lehrer, 1986). *Cognitive* effects refer to the influences of programming on the search processes and the knowledge structures involved in thinking. For instance, learning to program in LOGO may influence children's ability to formulate a plan, or it may affect how children represent some geometric concepts. *Metacognitive* effects refer to the influences of programming on processes that serve to monitor the progress and products of cognition. For instance, a child may reflect on the programming statements used to solve a programming problem, perhaps comparing her solution to that suggested by a teacher. This reflection-on-action may then lead to a reorganization of the program or the amplification of a programming template that could then be applied to similar problems. Proponents of LOGO suggest that metacognitive activities such as these will make a child more likely to apply similar metacognitive strategies in other contexts.

Finally, the *epistemic* effects of programming perhaps have been most widely discussed (Papert, 1980). Epistemology here refers to the interpretative framework the learner applies to the instructional context, regulating thought according to the learner's criteria for what constitutes knowledge, the relative certainty of that knowledge, and its potential range of application. For example, proponents of programming often suggest that it may instill a new attitude toward learning in that failures encountered during programming exercises will cease to be perceived as serious obstacles and will instead be considered as opportunities to learn. Children presumably will then apply this interpretation of mistakes to other activities both in and outside the school. Also in this view, the absence of transfer of programming skills to nonprogramming contexts may simply reflect a learner's failure to recognize commonality in culture between a programming context and a second context.

## APPLICATIONS OF CONTROL THEORY TO PROGRAMMING

Having identified several ways in which programming may influence intellectual development, we now consider how these influences are related. To this end, we adopt a systems, or control-theory, perspective toward learning how to program (Carver & Scheier, 1981, 1982; Powers, 1973). Briefly stated, control theory proposes a model of learning in which learning goals are organized hierarchically into levels according to the complexity of their structure. For example, goals concerning what constitutes "the good program," or other similar epistemic principles, regulate those governing the actions undertaken to identify "good-ness." The system is maintained by satisfying goals; it undergoes reorganization when goals cannot be satisfied. It is also assumed that the system attempts to understand input at the highest possible level. To illustrate, understanding of a simple action such as pressing a key to make the turtle move is biased toward identifying the action more abstractly, perhaps as a subgoal in the larger matter of "drawing a house" or "playing with LOGO." To connect this systems perspective with our proposals concerning LOGO's influence on thought, we later associate different potential influences with different levels of control.

### Control by Matching to Standards

The basic unit of control in the systems perspective is the negative feedback loop. A feedback loop consists of a goal, or standard, against which perceptions are matched, and the discrepancy between the standard and the perceptions is then evaluated (Miller, Galanter, & Pribram, 1960). The system is maintained by minimizing (negating) discrepancies. For instance, a novice programmer's efforts usually are guided by the goal of creating a program that runs, with little attention to qualities such as visibility to other potential readers of the code (Joni & Soloway, 1986). Accordingly, for novices any program that runs minimizes discrepancy with respect to the standard of "write a good program."

When discrepancies persist, two forms of systemic reorganization can occur. First, lower order standards can be reorganized so that their output better matches the higher order standard. Considering our previous example, an instructor could introduce the notion that good programs not only run, but they are also visible to other programmers. A novice can resolve the discrepancy between the instructor's standard of good programming and her program by reorganizing her lower order standards to include heuristics for making programs more visible, such as "initialize variables," "create program blocks," and the like.

Second, selection of a new higher order standard can, as in the previous example, initiate a series of lower level changes, or it can provide a bridge between previously diverse elements of experience. For example, children often disagree about how to implement a particular LOGO program. At first, these disagreements are often sources of discomfort, but over time, they appear to be subsumed by the higher level standard of "discussing with my partner," and thus become a more acceptable, and a more readily anticipated, component of learning LOGO.

## Hierarchical Control

Hierarchical control among various goals or standards is maintained by the time-order course of feedback (Mancuso & Lehrer, 1986). Components of the system that integrate feedback over longer durations regulate those that act more quickly. This occurs because higher order standards take as inputs the outputs from lower order standards. Hence, each step up the control hierarchy integrates the information from the preceding level. To illustrate, the goal of writing a good program requires evidence about many of its constituents. Accordingly, matching to this standard involves integrating (possibly conflicting) information from multiple sources—a time-intensive process. In contrast, testing for adherence to a single discourse rule such as "explicit initialization of all variables" involves a shorter feedback loop. Generally speaking, more abstract or complex standards in principle require longer feedback loops for adequate comparisons between standards and perceptions.

## Levels of Standards

In this regard, Powers (1973) distinguished among several levels of abstractness for standards that we illustrate in Fig. 4.1 with reference to the goal of repairing a program error. At the highest level, the activity of repairing a program error is

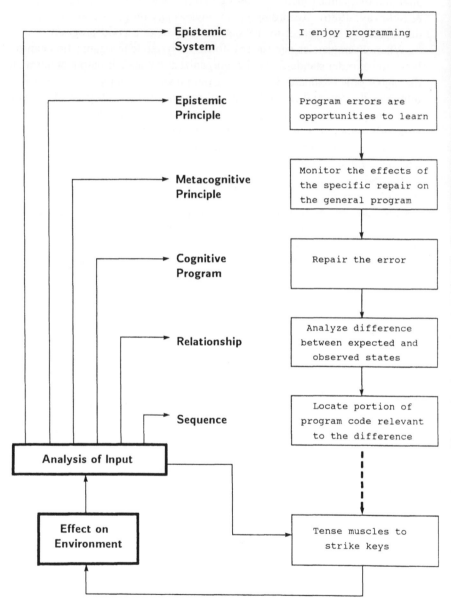

FIG. 4.1.  Application of a control system hierarchy to fixing a programming error

identified with respect to how computer programming fits in with one's definition of self. Powers (1973) regarded such overarching conceptions as indicative
of a systems level; these standards have broad implications for self-regulation.
Output from this systems level guides the selection of principles at succeeding
levels of the hierarchy. We have differentiated two types of principles in Fig. 4.1
to reflect our previous distinction between epistemic and metacognitive qualities
of thought. Epistemically, we can view an error as evidence of an opportunity to
learn. This principle can be expressed in a variety of programming contexts and
may involve many different types of errors. Similarly, the metacognitive principle presented in Fig. 4.1 also applies to many programming situations. Hence,
the principled level may be likened to a theme that guides the selection of other
standards for its realization.

Principles are enacted by recourse to program standards that specify general
scripts (Schank, 1980), such as "repairing program errors." Here the output from
the principled level selects and sets an appropriate standard at the program level.
The program level in turn specifies other standards; these standards regulate
increasingly precise actions as one descends the hierarchy, as depicted in the
relationship and sequence levels in Fig. 4.1. Other lower order standards necessary to complete the cycle have been omitted, such as those regulating some
aspects of editing code. However, two axioms are evident in Fig. 4.1. First,
processing proceeds primarily in a top-down fashion. Second, more abstract
standards integrate information received from less abstract standards. What is not
evident in Fig. 4.1 is that the system can behave recursively. That is, partial
repairs can be undertaken, evaluated, and the results can initiate a new cycle of
repair.

## Pedagogical Implications

The control-theory perspective invites us to consider the educator as a moderator
of novelty. This role is twofold. On the one hand, an instructor introduces
discrepancy to instigate systemic reorganization. For example, a child draws a
square with LOGO and an instructor responds by eliciting a prediction: "How
many different ones could you possibly make?" Here the instructor is indirectly
introducing a higher level standard: square as a generalization rather than as an
instance. On the other hand, an instructor also buffers discrepancy, perhaps by
providing children with strategies to implement such high level standards as
"break the problem down". Much of instruction then consists of a balancing act
between systemic maintenance and emergence.

A second pedagogical implication of the control-theory framework is that
evidence concerning high-level standards accumulates more slowly than that for
low-level standards. Consequently, high-level standards are most stable, but they
are also most resistant to change. As a result, the time course of feedback

necessary for developing relations between epistemic or metacognitive principles and programming practices likely involves prolonged periods of programming instruction. In short, powerful ideas develop slowly.

Third, the child's focus of attention determines which of the various levels available will serve as the pragmatic superordinate standard at a particular moment of instruction. Attention has the effect of making a particular level accessible; control is exerted from that level downward. For example, a student instructed in how to initialize variables could focus on the program level, without recognizing the role of variable initialization in regard to the higher level principle of increasing program visibility. Hence, the student may use the rule in class and forget about it elsewhere. Conversely, simply urging students to adopt higher order standards such as that governing error in Fig. 4.1 does not guarantee its use in self-regulation. For instance, if a student is told that an error is an opportunity to learn, but is not informed of the program-level actions necessary to debug the written code, then it is not likely that he or she will continue to view errors as opportunities for very long. Hence, instructional efforts must be made to develop integration among the various standards regulating a programming activity.

Last, the systems perspective invokes a culturally determined view of transfer in which the perception of similarity between contexts is regulated by the systems and principle levels (Powers, 1973). These levels typically describe aspects of self-regulation associated with the definition of a cultural context, such as self-perception. In contrast to more traditional perspectives, such as "identical elements" (Thorndike, 1903), transfer between domains does not principally depend on the program-level elements typically attended to by such theories, but rather on the capacity of the learner to subsume programming in his identification of "what am I doing now." In short, the learner must be able to invoke a superordinate standard that links programming actions to other actions. This perspective then indicates the importance of instruction that *mediates* and *bridges* the learner's identification of actions taken in the programming context with those taken in other contexts.

## TRANSFERABLE ASPECTS OF LOGO PROGRAMMING

Exploring more fully transferable aspects of LOGO programming, in the sections that follow we distinguish between two fundamental types of transfer, and trace the implications of this difference with respect to the systems theory just described. In defining transferable components, we draw on Gentner's theory of analogy (Gentner, 1983; Gentner & Toupin, 1986). Gentner proposed that an *analogy* succeeds when a system of relations in one domain corresponds validly to a system of relations in a second domain. For example, "an atom is like a solar system" involves mapping relations concerning attractive force from the solar system to the atom. Similarly, "he's another Alice" invites the reader to apply the personality traits (and their relations) of Alice to the target person. In contrast, a perception of *similarity* between objects in different domains involves a comparable mapping process but with the exception that what is mapped includes literal attributes. Hence, "she's like Alice" could refer to the brown eyes and gender each possess. In this view, similarity and analogy define ends of a continuum; they differ more in degree than in kind.

## Two Types of Transfer

Applying this theoretical perspective to the problem of the transfer of programming skills to other domains, we distinguish two types of transfer. On the one hand, literal components of the programming environment may map directly to components of a second domain. For example, a programming template developed to sort numbers may be applied to sort party invitations. This *similarity-dominated* form of transfer will most likely occur spontaneously when programming templates have been repeatedly practiced to the point of automaticity. Salomon and Perkins (1987) characterize this type of transfer as "low-road"; it invokes the *program-level standard* without any necessary recourse or connection to the higher order principle or systems levels.

On the other hand, *analogically dominated* transfer occurs when relationships (but not literal features) developed in programming contexts are transferred to other contexts. This type of transfer typically involves the principle and systems level. For example, one could make the attribution of "successful student" in the programming domain and then attempt to apply this attribution to another school subject area. Analogically dominated transfer is akin to the "high road" transfer discussed by Salomon and Perkins and as such, often requires reflective efforts to map from the programming domain to a target domain. The degree of transfer is limited by the "systematicity" (Gentner, 1983), or depth of nesting of the relations, to be encoded and mapped from the programming to the target domains. Assuming that more systematic relations place higher demands on working memory, it is likely that individual differences in working memory constrain what may be transferred. In what follows, we distinguish among transferable components by referring to various levels of a control hierarchy, applying the similarity analogy bifurcation to each level.

## Transfer at the Program Level

At the program level of control, strategies used to solve problems presented in LOGO may apply to other problems as well. Candidates include weak methods such as means–ends analysis and hill-climbing, presumably as a result of increased practice and corresponding "strengthening" (Anderson, 1983) of these strategies as children solve problems in LOGO. This is a form of analogically based transfer at the program level insofar as these methods are comparatively domain independent. Alternatively, children could develop systematic programming approaches or programming "templates" to problems in LOGO and then apply these to problems in other formal domains (Linn, 1985). The specificity of these templates suggest that this is a form of similarity-based transfer. However, we believe both possibilities unlikely. In the case of weak methods, demonstrations of their use by very young children indicate that they constitute a rudimentary ferature of the cognitive architecture (Anderson, 1986; Klahr, 1985). Hence, the problem for the child is to figure out how to apply these weak methods to new domains such as programming (Anderson, Farrell, & Sauers, 1984). On the other hand, it seems unlikely that children who have relatively little experience in programming develop well-organized and automatically accessed templates for particular programming problems that they then apply spontaneously to new problems in other domains. Stated another way, the possibilities for similarity-dominated transfer of problem-solving strategies appear remote.

## Transfer at the Principled Level

Programming in LOGO affords children an opportunity to develop a series of principles. Although a plethora of possibilities exist, that of making problem constraints explicit constitutes a principle that appears to apply to nearly every programming problem. That is, constraints known declaratively in the task environment must be translated into programming goals (and so made explicit) in the problem space, and these programming goals must be interrelated. For example, to draw a house in LOGO, the declarative knowledge of the constraint, roof on-top-of main structure, must be translated into a series of programming goals, such as those concerning the orientation of the turtle on the screen. In summary, constraints must be translated into actions and goals that guide their satisfaction. In this way, every programming problem involves deciding on the nature of constraints (see Clements & Merriman, chap. 2, regarding "deciding on the nature of the problem") and testing these decisions in the crucible of the program. Making constraints explicit is not sufficient to solve a particular programming problem, but it is necessary. And it entails a principle that can be mapped to related formal domains in which this type of constraint explication is important (Katovsky, Hayes, & Simon, 1983). Because making constraints explicit transcends the specific instances of it application, we consider this a form of analogically dominated transfer.

*Metacognitive Transfer.* In a related vein, ideal programming practices demand continued monitoring to assess the effects of current programming composition on previously written sections of code, much in the way in which authors monitor the relationship between their current choice of words and the text composed previously. For instance, if a LOGO procedure is changed, the change may have ramifications for other procedures that interface with the revised procedure. In short, the child ideally should evolve a principled understanding of the importance of monitoring the relationship between new (current programming statements) and previous states of knowledge (previously written code). Previous research, however, suggests that this type of principle is difficult for young children to apply in a novel context (Flavell, Green, & Flavell, 1985). And the discussion of control theory indicates that it is unlikely to develop in classroom settings without specific pedagogical interventions designed to focus processing at this level.

## Transfer at the Systems Level

Although Papert (1980) spoke of an epistemological revolution as a possible benefit for instruction in programming, our earlier presentation of control theory suggests that this question is not testable in the limited time frame of most research studies. That is, such a revolution would involve massive change at the systems level. A less ambitious change at this level might involve some (small) component of self-concept. Hence, we have focused on the ways in which programming may restructure academic self-concept (Shavelson & Bolus, 1982). Because the self constitutes a high-level reference standard in most schema-based accounts of identity (Greenwald & Pratkanis, 1984), potentially it can amplify self-congruent inputs and inhibit those that are incongruent with self-definition (Bandura, 1978). Bereiter (1985) referred to this property of self-related control as a means of "bootstrapping" more complex conceptual structures from less-complex ones. According to the control-theory axiom of regulation from the highest order standard that applies, retention of programming-related concepts will be regulated according to the degree to which students' academic self-concepts are defined by their programming experiences.

## KNOWLEDGE RESTRUCTURING WITH LOGO:
## THE CASE OF TURTLE GEOMETRY

Although transfer of knowledge inevitably entails its reorganization, use of LOGO with children also has the potential to fundamentally influence the way some types of knowledge are encoded and organized. Briefly stated, LOGO may be used as a teaching tool—a means to restructure knowledge. In this regard, LOGO's graphical interface and associated turtle geometry provides a tool for teaching geometry (Abelson & diSessa, 1980).

## Intrinsic Geometry

Turtle geometry only depends on the internal (intrinsic) state of the turtle, not on the relationship between the turtle and an external frame of reference. Change of state operators in LOGO permit a figure such as a circle to be represented by repetitive turtle movements rather than as an equation anchored to a Cartesian (or other) coordinate system. Stated another way, a figure may be represented as a path as well as by the more traditional concepts of intersecting line segments and the like. In addition, features of the LOGO language, such as procedures, are aids to representing paths more abstractly. For instance, a child usually constructs a procedure by re-representing some subset of actions taken in immediate mode to draw a figure. Building a procedure also requires that a child distinguish between necessary and sufficient operators to change the turtle's state when constructing a figure. For example, FORWARD may be a necessary operator to define a square, but it is not sufficient for it's definition. Of course, some sequences of operators may be neither necessary nor suffcient.

## Linking Representations

Instruction in LOGO then creates a context for linking observed properties of figures and of space with procedural transformations of a screen object (the turtle) that produce these observed properties. This alternative language provides a means to link two systems of representation: knowledge of the properties of figures and knowledge of the corresponding state of change operators required to construct the equivalent turtle path. Integrated linkages are constructed when the learner is able to reversibly transform one symbolic system (e.g., Euclidean geometry) into a second symbolic system (e.g., turtle geometry). From the perspective of a spreading activation model of retrieval from long-term memory (Anderson, 1983; Collins & Loftus, 1975), these integrated knowledge structures are more easily retrieved because they offer multiple encodings of a concept with corresponding multiple paths of access to that concept. These integrated knowledge structures are then more likely to be activated when needed (Bransford, Sherwood, Vye, & Reisser, 1986).

## van Hiele Theory

Our measurement of children's development of knowledge in geometry hinges upon the developmental progression first outlined by the van Hieles (Burger & Shaughnessy, 1986; Fuys, 1985; Hoffer, 1983; van Hiele, 1986). By means of clinical interviews and structured tasks, researchers in this tradition propose an orthogenetic sequence (Werner & Kaplan, 1963) in which knowledge of geometry is first organized about surface features such as "slanty lines" or the simple contour of the figure (the visual level). With instruction, children's knowledge of space becomes more differentiated; understanding is now organized about properties of figures (the descriptive level). Properties are then hierarchically organized so that, for example, the child can make a judgment about ordered relations among polygons and the like (the theoretical level). (Subsequent levels of this framework describe proof and are not relevant here.)

Instruction in LOGO offers many avenues for increased understanding of geometry according to the van Hiele framework. To begin with, at the visual level, contour-based recognition of figures may be supplanted by the dynamic concept of a turtle path. Second, building a procedure compels the child to reflect upon operators that produce a given path. Hence, LOGO may provide an impetus to the descriptive level with its focus on the analysis of properties of figures. Finally, at the theoretical level, variables in procedures serve as instruments to develop relationships among the properties of figures. For example, to draw an n-sided regular polygon with LOGO, a simple computational relationship exists between the number of sides and the amount the turtle must be turned (the exterior angle of the figure) before drawing each side. As a result, one could expect instruction with LOGO to enhance children's understanding of relationships between the properties of sideness and angle for regular polygons.

## OVERVIEW OF RESEARCH STUDIES

The control-theory perspective suggests that instruction in programming should proceed in mediated learning contexts; programming languages are means not ends. Consideration of the types of transfer possible with instruction in programming further suggests that the influences of programming on intellectual development are apt to be multiple and most pervasive when bridges are established between programming activities and other types of learning. In a related vein, the use of LOGO in the classroom may provide a means to restructure knowledge of geometry. Accordingly, the research studies reported here ask multiple questions and employ multiple measures to discern the influences of learning to program on children's intellectual development. The research questions generally reflect the tripartite division of cognition (cognitive, metacognitive, epistemic) described previously. And the measures of programming influences may be broadly described as indicators of knowledge acquisition (What does a child learn?) and knowledge application (Is the learning transferable?). In each investigation, the research context was intended to simulate aspects of a computer "culture" in the classroom. As a result, children had continual access to computers throughout the duration of the research studies.

The first study contrasted the cognitive consequences of more intensive, mediated instruction in LOGO versus less intensive, discovery oriented instruction for two intact classes of third-grade children. Here we examined the effects of the form of instruction on the acquisition and application of LOGO skills. In the second study, the goals of the mediated instruction in LOGO were varied, and we assessed the effects of this variation, again with respect to the tripartite division of cognition proposed previously. Lastly, the third study contrasted LOGO-aided instruction in geometry to instruction using more traditional tools. Results of these instructional variations were assessed with regard to the acquisition and the application of knowledge about geometry.

## STUDY 1

### Research Context

The first study (Lehrer & Smith, 1986a, 1986b) contrasted the effects of mediated, more intensive instruction in LOGO with less-intensive, discovery-oriented instruction in two intact third-grade classes. The less-intensive, discovery-oriented group was intended as a control for the simple presence of instructors and LOGO. Students in the mediated (experimental) class received instruction in pairs for 12 weeks in 31 sessions of 20–25 minutes. Four microcomputers were located in the class; the classroom teacher supervised an additional 2–3 practice sessions each week. Hence, each child in this class participated on the average in 60 computer sessions. All instruction was embedded in the context of student projects that represented a blend of student initiative and instructors' suggestions in a guided-discovery approach. Projects were extended over time as indicated by inspection of Fig. 4.2a where a student composition, Box 130, is the successor of a series of progenitors. Figure 4.2b displays the results of two children playing with lists, variables, and self-reference during one session. Programming topics included an introduction to programming with the Big-Trak robot (Lehrer & DeBernard, 1987), estimation of length using the Big-Trak as a standard unit of measure, LOGO graphics and the Turtle Tot robot, estimation of angle and distance, use of variables, work-space management, procedures to create regular polygons, and applying a problem decomposition heuristic to solve problems in LOGO (Identify parts, Make procedures for each parts, Decide on how the procedures relate, Compose the whole-IMDC model).

In contrast, students in the control class received formal instruction in LOGO once a week for 9 weeks, 45 minutes each week, and had access to only one computer for practice for 12 weeks. We suspect that such practices are typical of computer-based instruction in many elementary schools and in this regard, this study may be considered a test of such practices. We summarize the consequences of this instructional disparity with respect to the research questions.

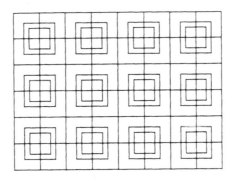

(a) **Box 130**

```
TO M :YOU :ME
  PR [I LIKE COMPUTERS, GIRL SCOUTS, FRIENDS
  AND MY LITTLE PONYS. WHO AM I?}]
  PR ( SE [YOU ARE] :YOU )]
  PR [I LIKE GO-BOTS, SOCCER, MATH, BASEBALL,
  COMPUTERS AND MYSELF. WHO AM I?]
  PR ( SE [YOU ARE] :ME )]
END
```

(b) **Me**

FIG. 4.2.    Representative programming projects for the first study

## Research Questions and Results

1. *Does instruction in LOGO transfer to other contexts that involve application of general problem-solving skills?*

The Tower of Hanoi puzzle provided an exemplar of a problem that could be solved by application of the general strategy (weak method) of means-ends analysis (Klahr, 1985). Children in each class completed a computer-assisted version of this puzzle before the beginning and after the completion of instruction. Several measures of problem-solving efficiency were collected including the moves to solution, time to solution, and the percent of time spent backtracking (repeating an earlier move). Analysis of covariance (ANCOVA) with the pretest score serving as a covariate for each dependent measure indicated no reliable differences between groups. Hence, we found little evidence of transfer of a general problem-solving skill according to the degree of instruction with LOGO.

2. *Can instruction in LOGO serve as an analogical bridge to bootstrap performance in a related domain?*

Studies in cognitive science suggest that well-organized knowledge may be used more flexibly than poorly organized or deficient knowledge (Bransford et al., 1986). In this instance, we examined children's ability to use their knowledge of LOGO as an analogical bridge to help them solve word problems in the familiar domain of mathematics. The methodology consisted of explicitly reminding (Ross, 1984) some of the children in each class (Mediated and Discovery) of correspondences between components of LOGO procedures and components of the mathematical problems. Failure to find any transfer effects under such ameliorating circumstances in either instructional group would be very discouraging to theories of the transferability of programming experience to other contexts. On the other hand, differential transfer between instructional conditions could be taken as evidence for the importance of specification of the duration and type of instruction for future reasonable discussion of transfer effects. It would also highlight the importance of knowledge organization for creating transferable elements of instruction.

*Subjects and Methods.* To this end, children within each class were randomly assigned by ranks (Maxwell, Delaney, & Dill, 1984) on the mathematics subtest of the Iowa Test of Basic Skills (ITBS) to either a reminding or a no-reminding mathematics problem-solving condition. Five mathematics word problems were solved by children in both conditions. For example, children solved: "In a party, there are 360 pieces of candy and six children. If everyone gets the same number of pieces, how many will each child get?" Children in the *reminding* condition were reminded to "think about LOGO to help you solve this one" and were provided specific analogical bridges such as "360 pieces of candy is like 360 turtle turns." Children in the no-reminding condition received no analogical cues.

*Results of Question 2.* Means and standard deviations by condition and class are displayed in Table 4.1. Inspection of this table suggests that remindings were effective for class M (mediated instruction) but not for class D. Separate ANCOVA for classes M ($n = 24$) and D ($n = 22$) indicated a statistically significant relationship between problem-solving and mathematical ability; $F(1, 21) = 31.88$, $p < .01$ and $F(1, 19) = 29.21$, $p < .01$, for classes M and D, respectively. However, only children in class M found the reminding useful; $F(1, 21) = 9.31$, $p < .01$ whereas in class D it was not, $F(1, 18) < 1.00$, $p > .95$. These results suggest then that transfer of LOGO-based knowledge to other contexts requires a well-organized body of LOGO-related knowledge.

TABLE 4.1
Remindings Results: Means and (Standard Deviations) for
Word Problems

|  |  | Reminding Provided | |
|---|---|---|---|
|  |  | No | Yes |
| Group | Mediated | 2.58 (2.78) | 4.58 (2.19) |
|  | Discovery | 2.82 (2.64) | 3.00 (2.86) |

### 3. Can instruction in LOGO transfer spontaneously to a metacognitive task?

Although a variety of metacognitive tasks could be used to assess this type of transfer, we measured children's ability to establish and monitor the relationship between new and old information, in part because this skill is implicated in most discussion of ideal programming practices such as those concerning program debugging. We employed a map-reading and direction-following task developed by Flavell et al. (1985). Task administration and format closely paralleled those described in Flavell et al. (1985). The task is divided into two types of situations: those in which an initial ambiguity (e.g., "take a road") in a two-part set of directions is resolved by the second part of the directions ("then take the orange road," and it's the only orange road on the map) and those in which it is not, although the directions make sense in a local context. For instance, the uncertainty of "take the road to a house" when there are two such landmarks on the map will not be ameliorated by a second direction, "then turn on the nearest road," even if that direction makes sense in the local context defined by a particular portion of the map. In this second instance, the child must realize that although the second set of directions is not locally ambiguous (i.e., there is an identifiable landmark), it does not resolve the initial ambiguity (there is a similar landmark elsewhere on the map that could be intended by the directions). Hence the directions remain globally ambiguous.

In summary, despite initial ambiguity about the intended location on the map, to resolve directions that are globally unambiguous, the child need only monitor the last set of directions. However, to detect directions that are globally ambiguous, the child must monitor the relationship between the two sets of directions and must understand their contradictory nature.

If LOGO-based instruction aids in the development of this type of metacognition, then one would expect differences between classes only in the case of the globally ambiguous directions. Inspection of Table 4.2 tends to corroborate this expectation, which is confirmed by ANCOVA; $F(1, 44) < 1.00$, $p > .36$ for the

TABLE 4.2
Comprehension Monitoring: Means and Standard Deviations

|       |           | Globally Unambiguous | | Globally Ambiguous | |
|-------|-----------|------|--------|------|--------|
| Group | Mediated  | 9.29 | (1.97) | 5.46 | (2.81) |
|       | Discovery | 8.78 | (1.91) | 2.87 | (2.00) |

globally unambiguous directions and $F(1, 44) = 13.22, p < .01$ for the globally ambiguous directions. In summary, instruction in LOGO had no effect on the ability to decipher an unambiguous set of directions. However, mediated instruction in LOGO apparently aided children's detection of ambiguity, indicating an increased ability to monitor the relationship among different states of information. Considered in conjunction with results pertaining to the previous research question, these results suggest that the quality and duration of instruction in LOGO significantly influences its transferability. This is not surprising, but it does tend to put a damper on the aspirations of those who see LOGO as an educational panacea.

4. *Does computer-based instruction influence academic self-concept? If so, what are the effects on the long-term retention of information acquired in this computer context?*

Investigation of this issue entailed development of measures of (a) computing self-concept, and (b) mastery of LOGO, followed by an assessment of the role of this facet of self-concept in children's retention of LOGO. We begin by briefly describing each measure and then present the results obtained.

*Assessing Computing Self-Concept.* A modification of the self-concept inventory developed by Marsh, Parker, and Smith (1983), the Self-Description Questionnaire (SDQ), was administered to all children. The SDQ is based on Shavelson's model (Shavelson & Bolus, 1982) of a hierarchical self-concept that distinguishes between academic and nonacademic components. We added eight items concerning computer-based experience (e.g., "I look forward to using computers") to the SDQ scales of parent, peer, reading, mathematics and overall school subjects and deleted items relating to physical abilities and appearance and also those that were negatively worded (see Marsh, Barnes, Cairns, & Tidman, 1984). A confirmatory principal components analysis (six "factors" were extracted followed by varimax rotation) of children's responses to this modified SDQ indicated the existence of a separate component describing children's responses to the computer-oriented questions. All eight items correlated highly ($r > .6$) with this computer-based component of academic self-concept, which accounted for over 10% of the total variation among subjects. Responses to each of the six components of self-concept were summarized by subscale scores. As expected, correlations within the two nonacademic subscales and the four academic subscales exceeded those between the nonacademic and academic subscales. Internal consistency (reliability) for the computing component of the academic self-concept was .79. Internal consistency for all other subscales of the SDQ was comparable to that reported by Marsh et al.

*Assessing Knowledge of LOGO.*    We developed an instrument, the Test of LOGO Knowledge (TOLK), to measure children's mastery at LOGO. The TOLK consisted of 86 (items) measuring knowledge of five major facets of LOGO: (a) commands that control the turtle's position and direction (36), (b) the flow of control and debugging (11), (c) variables (15), (d) list processing (9), and (e) workspace management and miscellaneous commands (15).

Each item was administered individually by a single examiner. To test concepts relating to position and direction, a green felt turtle was placed on a felt board. The heading of the turtle was varied systematically, and students enacted with the felt turtle their understanding of the effects of the command. The time to complete the entire test was approximately 15–20 minutes. Each item was scored as right or wrong. Item sums defined subtest scores and the total score. Test-retest reliability at a 7–10 day interval was .97. The median KR20 reliability coefficient for the five subtests was .84. Prior performance on the mathematics subtest of the ITBS predicted the total TOLK score well, $r = .66$. As expected, statistically reliable differences were observed between classes on the means of every subtest. Hence, the TOLK was a valid measure for its intended purposes.

*Procedure.*    The TOLK was administered at the completion of instruction in each class and again 5 months later. At this later time, the modified version of the SDQ was also administered.

*Results of Question 4.*    The development of the computing component of the academic self-concept varied with the degree of instruction. The mean computing-related subscale score for children in class M was 32.5. In contrast, that for children in class D was 28.1. The difference was statistically significant; $t(38) = 2.09$, $p < .05$. Because children in the control class learned less about LOGO, we confined analysis of long-term retention to children in the ex-perimental class. The results of a multiple regression analysis indicated that both the computer-oriented academic self-concept subscale score and the first TOLK score predicted long-term retention well, but no other facet of the self-concept was similarly predictive. When prior academic achievement was added to the model, it also contributed little to the prediction. Hence, instruction in computing influenced the development of this facet of self-concept, and the degree to which the self was construed as involved with computer-based instruction was associated highly with the retention of information learned in this context.

5. *Does instruction in LOGO help students restructure their knowledge of geometry?*

Data concerning this question and the next were gathered only in class M, because each presumes comparatively well-organized knowledge of LOGO. For this research question, we applied the van Hiele model to analyze children's responses to clinical interviews. The structured interview technique employed in this portion of the research allowed for follow-up questioning to elicit children's understanding and reasoning about geometry concepts. For example, children were asked: "How are a square and a triangle alike? different?" and "How are a circle and a square alike? different?" Responses to these questions were categorized in terms of van Hiele levels. That is, responses such as "They're both pointy or slanty" were judged to indicate reasoning at the first, visual level. Similarly, "One has three angles (or the turtle turns 3 times) and the other has four (or the turtle turns four times)" and like responses usually indicated reasoning at the second, descriptive level. Finally, responses such as "they're alike cause even though they have different sides (number of) the total amount of the turtle turns is 360 for both" was scored as indicating relational reasoning of the type suggested by the third, theoretical level.

Other interview questions probed children's understanding of linkages between knowledge of LOGO and knowledge of geometry. For example, questions about a square included "How do you make a square using LOGO?" (knowledge of the LOGO procedure), "Are the sides of a square all of the same length?" (knowledge of properties), "What part of the procedure tells you that?" (knowledge of the relation between the procedure and the property), and "Why do you turn 90? Why not 120?" (expression of knowledge of the relationship among properties in the LOGO language).

*Results of Question 5.* Categorization of children's responses to questions concerning linkages between LOGO procedures and geometric properties yielded three major categories of understanding (interrater agreement = 96%). Sixty percent of the children linked properties of figures with components of associated LOGO procedures. Of the remaining students, 33% appeared to establish two systems of representation—one for LOGO and one for Euclidean figures that were linked only at the most global level. For instance, a child might know that a LOGO procedure could produce a square and could describe properties of the square, but could not specify (or misconceived) how components of procedures related to observed properties of figures. The remaining children appeared to understand properties of figures exclusively in terms of

LOGO procedures. For these children, figures were not described at a descriptive level unless the language of LOGO was employed.

Analysis of children's responses to the questions concerning similarities and differences among figures were usually framed in terms of computational adjustments that would transform one LOGO procedure into another, so as to transform one figure (e.g., a triangle) into a second figure (e.g., a square). Categorization of these responses indicated that most children appeared to reason at the descriptive level, analyzing figures with respect to the components of LOGO procedures used to construct them. This finding was in sharp contrast to the visual-level responses usually offered by children of this age.

Analysis of relations between knowledge of LOGO and responses to the similarity/difference questions proceeded by transforming children's modal responses into a 4-point scale. Contour-dominated responses defined the lowest end point of the scale (1) whereas reasoning about relationships among properties defined the highest end point (4). Partial correlations were then calculated between this scale score and each of the subtests of the TOLK with the influence of mathematics ability (ITBS) statistically controlled. The highest partial correlation was .49 ($p < .02$), obtained with the debugging subtest, perhaps because successful debugging of graphics procedures often required knowledge of relations among the properties of figures.

6. *How does the instructional context influence children's problem-solving processes?*

Although most theories of planning and problem-solving model individual processes, collective processes dominate many instances of problem solving in schools, especially when microcomputers are in use. Vygotsky (1978) suggested that collaborative enterprises lead to the development of higher mental functions such as reflection. He proposed that schooling entailed a "zone of proximal development" in which socializing agents, such as teachers or peers, "scaffold" (Wood, Bruner, & Ross, 1976) instructional activities so that students' reach may exceed their grasp insofar as their knowledge acquisition in an appropriately structured context may exceed the rate characteristic of solitary learning environments.

Extending this rationale, we contrasted the problem-solving processes of children confronted with a novel problem (drawing a tower in LOGO) either with a partner or alone. To this end, children in class M were assigned randomly to either a collective ($n = 12$, 6 dyads) or soliloquy context ($n = 12$). All problem-solving activities were videotaped. Children in the soliloquy context thought aloud; we simply recorded the conversation of partners. Tapes were scored for (a) *problem-solving efficiency* measured by moves and time to solution, (b) *global* planning, measured by statements indicative of problem decomposition and assessment of interactions among components of the problem,

(c) *local* planning, measured by statements predicting the immediate consequences of a proposed move for a portion of the problem, and (d) the use of
procedures, a measure of *problem decomposition.*

We expected children in the collective context to plan more abstractly, in part
because the working memory limitations of abstract planning (see Anderson,
1983) would be ameliorated by collaborative efforts to "divide and conquer" the
problem. We also expected more abstract planning to lead to more efficient
solutions.

*Results of Question 6.*   We observed no differences between conditions in
problem solving efficiency, as measured by moves or time to solution. Nevertheless, those in the collective context elaborated their representations of the
problem space in several ways. They were more likely to decompose the problem
into subproblems, shown by their propensity to use procedures (83% for dyads
vs. 42% for individuals) and to plan globally ($M = 4.2$ planning statements for
dyads vs. 2.0 for individuals). In addition, they were less likely to use a simple
means-ends strategy, shown by fewer local planning statements ($M = 1.6$ for
dyads vs. 2.4 for individuals). Our analysis also suggested that procedures
served as visible and stable topics guiding communication between pairs.

In summary, children working together elaborated their representation of the
problem whereas those working alone typically said: "All I'm trying to do is get
this done." The latter emphasis is reminiscent of the focus on "answers" prevalent in much of schooling, a focus that leads to efficient problem solution at the
expense of the more valued pedagogical goal of developing a schema for a
subject (Gick, 1986; Owen & Sweller, 1985).

## Summary

Results of this first study indicate that mediated instruction in LOGO is a
prerequisite for the transfer of LOGO knowledge to other domains, perhaps
because such instruction results in the construction of comparatively well-
organized networks of knowledge (see Mayer, chap. 1, this volume; Mayer,
Bayman, & Dyck, 1987). There was little evidence of transfer of general
problem-solving skills, such as those embodied by the weak method of means-
ends analysis that children employed to solve the Tower-of-Hanoi puzzle.
However, experience with LOGO contributed to the development of the metacognitive skill of monitoring the relationship between new and old states of
knowledge. More intensive, mediated instruction in LOGO also contributed to
the development of a distinct facet of self-concept oriented toward classroom
computing. With respect to knowledge restructuring, responses to clinical interviews concerning children's understanding of common plane figures suggested a role for turtle geometry in altering children's conceptions of space.
Finally,   student   problem-solving   processes   appeared   more   schematically

oriented in a dyad as compared to a solitary context. Hence, there may be good reason (other than financial) to foster a group context when teaching LOGO to young children.

## STUDY 2

### Research Context

In the second study, the mediated (guided discovery) approach to LOGO instruction of the first study was extended for another group of third-grade students to encompass two distinct instructional goals. Children in one condition ($n = 15$) used LOGO as a problem solving tool in that they received mediated instruction in how to apply the problem decomposition heuristic presented previously (IMDC) to solve a variety of problems in LOGO. Children in the other condition ($n = 15$) used LOGO as a vehicle for understanding geometry concepts. In both conditions, instructional goals were embedded within problem constraints that encouraged children to elaborate their representation of the problem. For instance, children in the geometry condition completed a face where the perimeter of the "eyes" was the same as that of the "mouth," but where the eyes and mouth comprised different shapes, as displayed in Figure 4.3a. Figure 4.3b displays a student project in the problem-solving condition that satisfied a variety of constraints such as "place the flower on the table." Both forms of LOGO instruction were contrasted to a third condition ($n = 15$) where children used problem-solving software such as "The Pond" or "Rocky's Boots" (Lehrer, Guckenberg, & Lee, in press).

The overall design of the study included blocking (by alternate ranks, see Maxwell, Delaney, & Dill, 1984) on the mathematics subtest of the ITBS and random assignment to instructional conditions. Four instructors rotated among pairs of children twice each week for 7 months and a total of 47 sessions. Three computers were placed in each classroom for student practice under the supervision of their classroom teachers. Students practiced for 2–3 times each week for 20 minutes each time. Hence, each student interacted with the computer approximately 118 times during the course of the study. This estimate is conservative as it does not take into account practice before and after school, during recess hours, and so on.

*Overview of Findings.*    As in the first study, we investigated the cognitive consequences of these instructional variations. We assessed children's (a) general problem solving, (b) planning, (c) mastery of LOGO, (d) knowledge of geometry, (e) metacognition, and (f) attitudes toward mathematics and computers. As in the first study, no transfer of general problem solving strategies was evident. However, children instructed in LOGO solved a planning task more efficiently than their counterparts in the problem-solving software condition. In

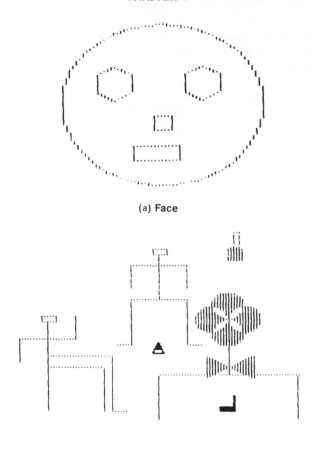

(a) **Face**

(b) **Kitchen**

FIG. 4.3.   Programming projects satisfying instructional constraints

addition, children in either LOGO condition demonstrated more sophisticated understanding, in terms of van Hiele-based scoring, of a variety of geometric concepts than did the other students, although these differences were most pronounced for children who used LOGO as a vehicle to understand geometric concepts. Geometric understanding was related systematically to children's knowledge of LOGO. The metacognitive results obtained in the first study were again observed for children instructed with "bridges" between geometry and LOGO. Lastly, children's attitude toward computer-based learning did not vary by instructional condition, but differences in attitude were observed with respect to mathematics. In the following, we elaborate briefly on some of these results, posing the research questions that motivated this second study.

## Research Questions and Results

1. *Does instruction in LOGO transfer to other contexts that involve application of general problem-solving skills?*

As in the first study, children responded to problems whose solution relied upon employment of weak methods (general strategies). Two types of general strategies were assessed. The first, means-ends analysis, was measured as in the first study by performance on a computer-assisted version of the Tower-of-Hanoi problem. The second weak method, "hill-climbing," proceeds by generating candidate solutions to a problem, picking the one that seems best according to some evaluation function, and then repeating the process until the problem is solved. It is analogous to climbing a hill in a series of small steps where one can not see the peak (the solution) but where one can know the direction of the climb (up or down). Use of this strategy was measured by children's performance on an eights puzzle (see Klahr, 1985). An eights puzzle consists of nine tiles of which eight are occupied. The task is to achieve a goal pattern among the eight tiles by rearranging them using the minimum number of moves.

Strategic efficiency for both problems was defined as the number of moves to solution and the time to solution. Each problem was administered twice to assess the possbility of a "learning to learn" phenomenon.

*Results of Question 1.* As in the first study, no differences among conditions were apparent between conditions with respect to any measure of problem-solving efficiency on the Tower-of-Hanoi task. This finding also applied to the eights puzzle. These results corroborate those of the first study.

2. *Does instruction in LOGO influence problem representation in a novel context?*

We designed a variation of the errand task presented by Hayes-Roth and Hayes-Roth (1979) to elucidate opportunistic planning. The task was chosen because it was not easily susceptible to the problem decomposition heuristic taught in the problem-solving condition. Instead, we expected that children would plan opportunistically, a type of "planning on the go." Hence, task performance would measure provide a fair transfer for children in both LOGO conditions.

The task was presented to students as a chore-planning task in which the object was to complete a set of chores (e.g., feed the dog) distributed throughout a "house" with a minimum number of moves so as to avoid a "tired" turtle. A turtle was used as the main character to cue the same interpretative context that children might apply to a LOGO problem. However, the moves were not defined in the same metric as used by LOGO. As in studies by Pea, Kurland, and Hawkins (1985), children's plans had to take into account problem constraints such as "dust before vacuum" and "pickup (the toys) before dust." In this way, we could assess any differences among instructional conditions with regard to how constraints affected planning. Children were directed to think aloud (Ericsson & Simon, 1984), and their planning statements were coded by raters into two levels. Lower level statements referred to actions contemplated to satisfy a single constraint. In contrast, planning statements referring to the relations between constraints were considered more abstract.

*Results of Question 2.* Results of ANCOVA with the ITBS as a covariate indicated that the total distance to solution was associated with the within-group regression on the ITBS; $F(1, 41) = 5.06, p < .03$. Children in either LOGO condition solved the problem more efficiently (less distance) than their counterparts in the control condition; $F(1, 41) = 4.41, p < .05$. Analysis of the planning statements (verbal protocols) and solution paths for each child indicated that children in the control condition were likely to follow the structure of the problem constraints in a serial manner, an instance of less-abstract planning, whereas children in either LOGO condition were more likely to establish relationships among sets of problem constraints, an instance of higher order planning. As a result, the incidence of higher level planning statements was higher in the protocols of children in either LOGO condition than that of the control condition. In summary, children in the LOGO conditions appeared to represent and translate problem constraints more abstractly when contrasted to their counterparts in the control condition.

### 3. Can instruction in LOGO transfer spontaneously to a metacognitive task?

The map-direction task was again employed to assess children's ability to monitor the relationship between new and old states of information. Although children in the mediated geometry LOGO condition performed at a higher level than their counterparts in the control condition, children in the other LOGO condition did not. Hence, there is some indication that the use of LOGO per se is less important than the instructional goals one adopts to promote such transfer (also see Lehrer & Randle, 1987).

### 4. Does instruction in LOGO help students restructure their knowledge of geometry?

Each child responded to a revision of the clinical interview used in the first study to measure knowledge of (a) relations among polygons, (b) variables, (c) angles, (d) parallel lines and (e) perimeter. Scoring guidelines were arranged to code responses numerically from low to high levels of van Hiele based understanding. Two raters independently scored transcripts of every interview with adequate interrater agreement (96%). Each child's knowledge of these five components of geometric understanding was represented by a subtest score derived from the coding of responses.

*Results of Question 4.*    Children instructed in LOGO generally developed more sophisticated conceptions of geometry, according to our van Hiele-based scoring of their responses, when contrasted to their counterparts in the control condition. For instance, children in the control condition typically responded to questions concerning relationships among (regular) polygons almost exclusively in terms of visual perception, "This one looks more pointy." In contrast, children instructed in LOGO described such relations by appeal to a general polygon procedure that allowed them to see each polygon as an instance of the more general concept of a regular polygon. Here manipulation of the variables of a LOGO procedure enabled children to reason about geometric relationships. Similarly, children in the control condition often associated angles with the static conception of "slanty lines," reasoning then that triangles had three angles and squares, none. In contrast, children in both LOGO conditions tended to associate angles with the more dynamic concept of rotation, and children in the geometry condition typically could also indicate how combinations of turtle turns (e.g., RT) and turtle movements (e.g., FD) could produce "slanty lines." The geometry orientation of one form of LOGO instruction appeared to facilitate an integration between the Euclidean orientation of children's classroom instruction and LOGO's turtle-path metaphor.

Responses obtained during the clinical interviews corresponded highly with TOLK (LOGO mastery) subtest scores even when the (linearly related) influence of mathematics ability was removed. For example, the partial correlation of the TOLK subtest of variable knowledge with the interview-based measure of knowledge of variables was .58. Similarly, the partial correlation of the TOLK-based measure of knowledge of turtle position and direction commands with the interview-based measure of knowledge about angles (e.g., estimation and definition of angles) was .64. Hence, learning of LOGO increased closely allied mathematical skills.

5. *Is the acquisition of LOGO related to mathematics ability, short-term memory, or working memory?*

Recent research suggests that limitations in processing efficiency rather than simply processing capacity constrains performance in complex domains (Case, 1985). Because LOGO constitutes a comparatively complex domain, we expected that children's working memory (processing efficiency) would be predictive of their ability to acquire and comprehend LOGO. Moreover, an index of general ability to acquire school subjects should also be predictive of the acquisition of LOGO, as we found in the first study. Hence, the question was whether or not working memory would make a further predictive contribution over and above that provided by knowledge of children's general academic ability. At the same time, we expected that short-term memory would not be predictive of the acquisition of LOGO when the first two predictors were taken into account.

Children's mathematics subtest ITBS scores served as the measure of general (mathematical) ability. The digit span subtest of the WISC-R (Wechsler, 1974) indicated children's short-term memory. We adapted a sentence-span measure developed by Daneman and Carpenter (1980, 1983) for use with young children as a measure of working memory. Our adaptation followed the procedures outlined by Daneman and Carpenter with sentences appropriate for third grade children. Responses to the TOLK in the form of a total score indicated children's mastery of LOGO.

*Results of Question 5.* A step-wise regression indicated that working memory and prior achievement (ITBS mathematics score) were sufficient predictors of the child's mastery of LOGO.

6. *Do differences among conditions result in corresponding differences in children's attitude either toward computing or toward mathematics?*

Instruction in LOGO has been promoted as an ideal vehicle for instruction in mathematics and as a means for introducing computers in the classroom (Papert, 1980). Hence, one might expect more positive regard for mathematics from children instructed in LOGO when contrasted to their counterparts in the control condition. On the other hand, all instructional conditions featured bridging or mediated instruction. In this regard, differences among conditions due to media would not necessarily lead to more positive regard, perhaps because attitude is most closely aligned with instructional style, not medium.

At the end of instruction, children responded to paper-and-pencil measures of attitude toward mathematics (15 Likert scale items with a reliability of .91) and attitude toward computers (15 Likert scale items with a reliability of .89). A sum score indexed children's attitude on each scale.

*Results of Question 6.* Children's attitudes toward their computer experiences were highly positive, but there were no reliable differences among conditions. On the other hand, children instructed with software such as Number

Stumper and Bumble Plot (control condition) developed a more positive attitude toward mathematics when contrasted to the LOGO conditions. This difference was statistically reliable. Follow-up interviews with the children suggested that they equated computation with mathematics. Hence, their higher positive regard when instructed with software of the type used in the control condition. On the other hand, several children went so far as to suggest that "LOGO does not have any math."

## Summary

As in the first study, LOGO-based learning was not transferable to general problem-solving skills. However, children instructed in LOGO appeared to represent problem constraints more adequately when contrasted to their peers in the control condition. As a result, they solved a planning task in fewer moves. With respect to metacognition, results were mixed, with children participating in one type of mediated instruction demonstrating enhanced monitoring skills. But similar benefits did not accrue to children participating in the second mediated condition. The strongest results concerned the use of LOGO as a tool to restructure children's understanding of geometry. Here, linkages between LOGO and plane geometry resulted in higher levels of understanding, according to the van Hiele model. Acquisition of LOGO was predicted by children's general mathematical ability and also by a measure of their working memory. Lastly, children's attitudes toward computer-based instruction did not vary with the medium, indicating the potential role of instructional variables in the development of children's attitudes toward computer-assisted learning (see Littlefield et al., chap. 5, this volume).

## STUDY 3

### Research Context

In this study (Lehrer, Randle, & Sancilio, 1988), we investigated more closely the relationship between the development of geometric concepts and instruction in LOGO. To use LOGO as a tool, one must know LOGO. Consequently, we blocked by mathematics ability and randomly assigned 32 of the fourth-grade students who had participated in the second study the previous year to one of two instructional conditions. Children learned about the same geometric facts in each instructional condition with matching instructional goals and techniques. For example, all children learned that a square was a type of rectangle. However, in one condition children used LOGO to develop procedural representations of this factual knowledge (Anderson, 1983; Reif, 1987). That is, they used LOGO to transform properties of figures into turtle states and changes thereof. But in the other condition, they used conventional tools such as protractors and rulers to develop procedural representations.

## Hypotheses and Rationale

We expected no instructionally related differences for knowledge of geometric facts because both groups received identical instruction in this component of knowledge. On the other hand, we expected that children in the LOGO condition would learn more by doing, because the LOGO learning environment offered many opportunities to develop linked representations (factual, procedural) of geometric concepts. For example, the concept of parallel lines can be reexpressed in turtle geometry as two noncoincident turtle paths with identical headings (or a simple reflection in headings). Consider further the following abbreviated task analysis. Children learned the fact that every square is also a rectangle. In the LOGO condition, such knowledge was interpreted procedurally by adjusting a "rectangle" program to create a square. Hence, the fact (a class inclusion relationship) was embodied in the form of a program, and the additional constraints necessary to transform a rectangle into a square were represented as variables of the program. As a result, the LOGO program was a tool to think with; the rectangle program could serve as an avenue for reasoning about relations between figures. Recalling our previous discussion of control theory, the use of a modifiable program focused attention on the higher order relationship between two programs, rather than on each program in turn.

In the other condition, however, to represent this class inclusion at the level of action, children constructed separate figures for a rectangle and for a square. They then had to conserve a trace of the relationship between their respective constructions. This conservation appears more demanding of working memory and imagination than simply adjusting a procedure.

At the conclusion of 17 instructional sessions, eight tasks ranging along an application of knowledge continuum were individually administered to each subject. Order of task administration was counterbalanced across subjects. The first three tasks measured facts only, such as "Which of these is a right angle?" or "How many sides does a triangle have?" These low-level tasks were augmented by two intermediate tasks that required some use of knowledge. For example, "What is the smallest number of sides that a polygon can have? Why?" Collectively, we refer to these first five measures as knowledge-acquisition tasks due to their emphasis on facts. The final three, high-level tasks measured knowledge application. For example, students were presented with an intersection task that required coordination of knowledge about two sets of geometric objects (e.g., parallelograms and right trapezoids) in order to choose an object appropriate for both sets (e.g., a rectangle) and to justify their choice. Other high-level tasks required children to distinguish between necessary and sufficient properties of figures or to reason about ordered relations among quadrilaterals (Burger & Shaughnessy, 1986; Shaughnessy & Burger, 1985).

## Results

For purposes of analysis, a single composite variable was created to represent children's performance on the five knowledge acquisition tasks. Similarly, a second composite variable represented student performance on the three knowledge acquisition tasks. As expected, no differences were observed between instructional conditions with respect to knowledge acquisition; $F(1, 28) = 1.39$, $p > .24$. However, large differences were observed between instructional conditions with respect to knowledge application; $F(1, 28) = 30.96$, $p < .001$. These results were confirmed again after delayed retention intervals of 10 and 16 weeks. Hence, LOGO-based instruction in geometry robustly influenced children's application of geometric knowledge but not its initial acquisition.

## GENERAL DISCUSSION

The results of our studies suggest that although LOGO is not something that we can recommend as an all-purpose educational panacea, it does fulfill much of its original promise in carefully crafted instructional contexts (Papert, 1987). In the studies reported, students had easy and longitudinal access to computers, and they received instruction in LOGO that emphasized the role of the student as a codeveloper of knowledge. None of our instructional contexts exemplified pure discovery learning. We suspect that if this was the case, most children would have used LOGO as an electronic etch-a-sketch. On the contrary, we provided problem-solving themes in the forms of problem constraints and helped students elaborate upon these themes. In these contexts, students working collaboratively amplified the scaffolding potential of their instructors.

Considering the control model of LOGO learning initially presented, it is evident that the teaching and learning of LOGO can influence the development of intellect at a variety of levels. In this regard, although the feedback loops necessary to develop more elaborate principles and systems concepts are necessarily long, there is some evidence from this research that systematic instruction in programming may influence children's development of such higher order standards. For example, more intensive and mediated instruction in LOGO was associated with the development of a separable facet of academic self-concept oriented toward computer-based learning. This development was associated with the long-term retention of programming-related concepts. More research is needed, however, to elucidate the ontogenesis of self-concept in computational environments.

In a similar vein, there is some evidence that experience in programming fosters the development of monitoring the relationship between new and old information. However, we replicated this result in one form of LOGO instruction but not another. Hence, fostering these types of higher-order processes may be more highly associated with the instructional method than with the medium. In this regard, the flexibility of the LOGO environment provides a context easily extended to suit a variety of instructional goals (Lehrer & Randle, 1987). Moreover, because working memory capacity predicted the acquisition of LOGO, instructional methods should be analyzed with respect to the working memory demands they place on students. Hence, the important role for instruction that mediates between contexts; cross-contextual comparisons may simply exceed the working memory capacity of young children.

Contrary to some previous studies (Pea et al., 1985), mediated experience with LOGO programming facilitated children's planning and execution of a novel task. We attribute differences in performance between programmers and nonprogrammers to the many opportunities children had in the programming environments to make problem constraints explicit and to translate these constraints from facts into acts. For young children, this is a type of learning by doing that may transfer to other formal domains, even though specific programming templates or more general skills (e.g., weak methods) may not. Stated another way, results obtained from this research locate the source of improved problem-solving performance for these young children in problem representation, not in the development of general problem-solving skills.

Discrepancies between the finding just noted and those obtained by Pea et al. (1985) may be attributed to a number of sources including potential differences in the method of instruction, sensitivity of the experimental design, and children's prior knowledge of relationships among problem constraints. For instance, the Pea et al. task involved classroom chores with constraints that were perhaps familiar to children. If so, the planning task would assess general problem solving skills, and no differences between groups then would be expected. On the other hand, Pea et al. replicated their findings, and we have not (but see Lehrer & Randle, 1987). Further research efforts are required to differentiate among these and other alternatives.

Looking at all three studies, LOGO can be used as a tool to restructure children's understanding of geometry. LOGO-based instruction can help children establish links between the observed properties of figures and the actions needed to construct them (Abelson & diSessa, 1980). For the child, viewing geometry as a set of transformations provides a new window to a world dominated by more static conceptions of contour and property lists. Moreover, in our studies these new understandings were manifested in van Heile-based measures that provided a metric for assessing change. Individual differences in knowledge of various components of LOGO corresponded to individual differences in knowledge of geometric concepts even when the influence of general mathematics ability was accounted for statistically. This correspondence in conjunction with results obtained in the third study buttresses our belief that increased understanding of geometry was, at least in part, due to the unique qualities of the LOGO environment (Papert, 1980).

Along these lines, we suggest further that LOGO and other dynamic software contexts bridge the gap between what Bruner (1986) described as two distinct modes of thought: the narrative and the paradigmatic. The former mode of thought invokes the metaphor of a person as a dramatist. In this instance, a child may personify the action of the turtle, and instruction in LOGO may profitably be embedded within a narrative context (Lehrer & DeBernard, 1987). Hence, LOGO becomes a vehicle for story-telling rather than "programming." On the other hand, many of the features of LOGO tend to provide a concrete medium for developing paradigmatic thought—thought that relies on formal argument rather than personal appeal. Here, the building block of LOGO, the procedure, involves a primitive form of formal generalization. For instance, a child constructing a square may come to recognize that particular values of an operator (e.g., FD) merely generate instances; the more general definition of a square is determined by the structure of its defining procedure.

Finally, we reiterate the important role for self-structure in the maintenance and future development of computer-based learning. In short, like other school subjects, instruction in programming creates a context that most likely will elaborated in proportion to a student's perception of its congruence with personal goals.

## ACKNOWLEDGMENTS

Parts of this research were funded by a grant from the Spencer Foundation to the School of Education, University of Wisconsin-Madison, and by grant no. NIE-84-0008 to the Wisconsin Center for Education Research from the National Institute of Education. The usual disclaimers apply. We thank Dean John Palmer for making available the microcomputers used to conduct this research. We appreciate the cooperation provided by the children, parents, and teachers of the Verona Elementary School. Special thanks to Linda Christensen, Director of Curriculum for the Verona School District. The assistance of Okhwa Lee, Miheon Lee, and Paul C. Smith in the conduct of some of the research reported here was invaluable. David N. Perkins, James C. Mancuso, Marty Rosenheck, and an anonymous reviewer contributed constructive criticisms of an earlier version of this chapter.

## REFERENCES

Abelson, R. P., & diSessa, A. (1980). *Turtle geometry: The computer as a medium for exploring mathematics*. Cambridge, MA: MIT Press.

Anderson, J. R. (1986). *A theory of human knowledge*. Unpublished manuscript.

Anderson, J. R. (1983). *The architecture of cognition*. Cambridge, MA: Harvard University Press.

Anderson, J. R., Farrell, R., & Sauers, R. (1984). Learning to program in LISP. *Cognitive Science, 8*, 87–129.

Bandura, A. (1978). The self system in reciprocal determinism. *American Psychologist, 33*, 344–358.

Bereiter, C. (1985). Toward a solution of the learning paradox. *Review of Educational Research, 55*, 201–226.

Bransford, J., Sherwood, R., Vye, N., & Reisser, J. (1986). Teaching thinking and problem solving: Research foundations. *American Psychologist, 41*, 1078–1089.

Broughton, J. M. (1985). The surrender of control: Computer literacy as political socialization of the child. In D. Sloan (Ed.), *The computer in education* (pp. 102–122). New York: Teachers College Press.

Bruner, J. (1986). *Actual minds, possible worlds*. Cambridge, MA: Harvard University Press.

Burger, W. F., & Shaughnessy, J. M. (1986). Characterizing the van Hiele levels of development in geometry. *Journal of Research in Mathematics Education, 17*, 31–48.

Case, R. (1985). *Intellectual development*. New York: Academic Press.

Carver, C. S., & Scheier, M. F. (1981). *Attention and self-regulation: A control-theory approach to human behavior*. New York: Springer-Verlag.

Carver, C. S., & Scheier, M. F. (1982). Control theory: A useful concept of framework for personality-social, clinical, and health psychology. *Psychological Bulletin, 92*, 111–135.

Clements, D. H. (1986). Effects of LOGO and CAI environments on cognition and creativity. *Journal of Educational Psychology, 78*, 309–318.

Collins, A. M., & Loftus, E. F. (1975). A spreading activation theory of semantic processing. *Psychological Review, 82*, 407–428.

Daneman, M., & Carpenter, P. A. (1980). Individual differences in working memory and reading. *Journal of Verbal Learning and Verbal Behavior, 19*, 450–466.

Daneman, M., & Carpenter, P. A. (1983). Individual differences in integrating information between and within sentences. *Journal of Experimental Psychology: Learning, Memory, and Cognition, 9*, 561–582.

Dreyfus, H. L., & Dreyfus, S. E. (1986). *Mind over machine*. New York: Free Press.

Ericsson, K. A., & Simon, H. A. (1984). *Protocol analysis: Verbal reports as data*. Cambridge, MA: MIT Press.

Flavell, J. H., Green, F. L., & Flavell, E. R. (1985). The road not taken: Understanding the implications of initial uncertainty in evaluating spatial directions. *Developmental Psychology, 21*, 207–216.

Fuys, D. (1985). van Hiele levels of thinking in geometry. *Education and Urban Society, 17*, 447–462.

Gentner, D. (1983). Structure-mapping: A theoretical framework for analogy. *Cognitive Science, 7*, 155–170.

Gentner, D., & Toupin, C. (1986). Systematicity and surface similarity in the development of analogy. *Cognitive Science, 10*, 277–300.

Gick, M. L. (1986). Problem-solving strategies. *Educational Psychologist, 21*, 99–120.

Greenwald, A. G., & Pratkanis, A. R. (1984). The self. In R. S. Wyer & T. K. Srull (Eds.), *Handbook of social cognition* (pp. 129–178). Hillsdale, NJ: Lawrence Erlbaum Associates.

Hayes-Roth, B., & Hayes-Roth, F. (1979). A cognitive model of planning. *Cognitive Science, 3*, 275–310.

Hoffer, A. (1983). van Hiele-based research. In R. Lesh & M. Landau (Eds.), *Acquisition of mathematics concepts and processes* (pp. 205–227). New York: Academic Press.

Joni, S. A., & Soloway, E. (1986). But my program runs! Discourse rules for novice programmers. *Journal of Educational Computing Research, 2,* 95–125.

Katovsky, K., Hayes, J. R., & Simon, H. A. (1983). Why are some problems hard? Evidence from Tower of Hanoi. *Cognitive Psychology, 17,* 248–294.

Klahr, D. (1985). Solving problems with ambiguous subgoal ordering: Preschooler's performance. *Child Development, 56,* 940–952.

Lehrer, R. (1986). LOGO as a strategy for developing thinking? *Educational Psychologist, 21,* 121–137.

Lehrer, R., & DeBernard, A. (1987). The language of learning and the language of computing: The perceptual-language model. *Journal of Educational Psychology, 79,* 41–48.

Lehrer, R., Guckenberg, T., & Lee, O. (in press). A comparative study of the cognitive consequences of inquiry-based instruction with LOGO. *Journal of Educational Psychology.*

Lehrer, R., & Randle, L. (1987). Problem solving, metacognition, and composition: The effects of interactive software for first-grade children. *Journal of Educational Computing Research, 3,* 409–427

Lehrer, R., Randle, L., & Sancilio, L. (1988). *Learning pre-proof geometry with LOGO.* Manuscript submitted for publication.

Lehrer, R., & Smith, P. C. (1986a). *LOGO learning. Is more better?* Paper presented at the annual meeting of the American Educational Research Association, San Francisco.

Lehrer, R., & Smith, P. C. (1986b). *LOGO learning: Are two heads better than one?* Paper presented a the annual meeting of the American Research Association, San Francisco.

Linn, M. C. (1985). The cognitive consequences of programming instruction in classrooms. *Educational Researcher, 14*(5), 14–29.

Mancuso, J. C., & Lehrer, R. (1986). Cognitive processes during reactions to rule violation. In R. D. Ashmore & D. M. Brodzinsky (Eds.), *Thinking about the family: Views of parents and children* (pp. 67–93). Hillsdale, NJ: Lawrence Erlbaum Associates.

Marsh, H. W., Barnes, J., Cairns, L., & Tidman, M. (1984). Self-description questionnaire: Age and sex effects in the structure and level of self-concept for preadolescent children. *Journal of Educational Psychology, 76,* 940–956.

Marsh, H. W., Parker, J. W., & Smith, I. D. (1983). Preadolescent self-concept: Its relation to self-concept as inferred by teachers and to academic ability. *British Journal of Educational Psychology, 53,* 60–78.

Maxwell, S. E., Delaney, H. D., & Dill, C. A. (1984). Another look at ANCOVA versus blocking. *Psychological Bulletin, 93,* 136–147.

Mayer, R. E. (1983). *Thinking, problem solving, cognition.* New York: W. H. Freeman.

Mayer, R. E., Bayman, P., & Dyck, J. L. (1987). Learning programming languages: Research and applications. In P. E. Berger, K. Pezdek, & W. P. Banks (Eds.), *Applications of cognitive psychology: Problem solving, education, and computing* (pp. 33–45). Hillsdale, NJ: Lawrence Erlbaum Associates.

Mead, G. H. (1934). *Mind, self, and society.* Chicago: University of Chicago Press.

Miller, G. A., Galanter, E., & Pribram, K. H. (1960). *Plans and the structure of behavior.* New York: Holt, Rinehart & Winston.

Owen, E., & Sweller, J. (1985). What do students learn while solving mathematics problems? *Journal of Educational Psychology, 77,* 272–284.

Papert, S. (1980). *Mindstorms: Children, computers and powerful ideas.* New York: Basic Books.

Papert, S. (1987). Computer criticism vs. technocentric thinking. *Educational Researcher, 16,* 22–30.

Pea, R. D., Kurland, D. M., & Hawkins, J. (1985). LOGO and the development of thinking skills. In M. Chen & W. Paisley (Eds.), *Children and microcomputers: Research on the newest medium* (pp. 193–212). Beverly Hills: Sage Publications.

Pepper, S. C. (1942). *World hypotheses*. Berkeley: University of California Press.

Powers, W. T. (1973). *Behavior: The control of perception*. Chicago: Aldine.

Reif, F. (1987). Interpretation of scientific or mathematical concepts: Cognitive issues and instructional implications. *cognitive Science, 11,* 595–416.

Ross, B. H. (1984). Remindings and their effects in learning a cognitive skill. *Cognitive Psychology, 16,* 371–416.

Rumelhart, D. E., & Norman, D. A. (1981). Analogical processes in learning. In J. R. Anderson (Ed.), *Cognitive skills and their acquisition* (pp. 335–359). Hillsdale, NJ: Lawrence Erlbaum Associates.

Salomon, G., & Perkins, D. N. (1987). Transfer of cognitive skills from programming: When and how? *Journal of Educational Computing Research, 3,* 149–169.

Schank, R. C. (1980). Language and memory. *Cognitive Science, 4,* 243–284.

Shaughnessy, J. M., & Burger, W. F. (1985). Spadework prior to deduction in geometry. *Mathematics Teacher, 78,* 419–428.

Shavelson, R. J., & Bolus, R. (1982). Analogical processes in learning. In J. R. Anderson (Ed.), *Cognitive skills and their acquisition* (pp. 335–359). Hillsdale, NJ: Lawrence Erlbaum Associates.

Sternberg, R. J. (1985). Human intelligence: The model is the message. *Science, 230,* 1111–1118.

Thorndike, E. L. (1903). *Educational Psychology*. New York: Lemke & Buechner.

van Hiele, P. M. (1986). *Structure and insight: A theory of mathematics education*. New York: Academic Press.

Vygotsky, L. S. (1978). *Mind in society: The development of higher psychological processes*. Cambridge, MA: Harvard University press.

Wechsler, D. (1974). *Manual for the Wechsler intelligence scale for children-Revised*. New York: Psychological Corporation.

Werner, H., & Kaplan, B. (1963). *Symbol formation*. New York: Wiley.

Wood, D., Bruner, J. S., & Ross, G. (1976). The role of tutoring in problem solving. *Journal of Child Psychology and Psychiatry, 17,* 89–100.

# 5

# Learning LOGO:
# Method of Teaching,
# Transfer of General Skills,
# and Attitudes Toward
# School and Computers

Joan Littlefield                    Victor R. Delclos
*University of Wisconsin-Madison*        *Tulane University*
Sharon Lever, Keith N. Clayton, John D. Bransford
Jeffrey J. Franks
*Vanderbilt University*

## ABSTRACT

A summary of a 3-year project investigating the cognitive and attitudinal effects of learning LOGO is presented. Previous studies using a discovery method of teaching LOGO make the assumption that general problem-solving skills will be developed

111

and transferred spontaneously. Our research is based on the theoretical viewpoint that more explicit emphasis is needed in the teaching environment on the skills to be developed and how such skills are useful in other contexts. Experimental comparisons of three teaching methods are presented. A structured teaching method produced higher levels of language mastery than an unstructured, although neither group showed consistent evidence of transfer. Comparisons of structured and mediational methods showed no differences in language mastery, but the mediational method was more effective in producing transfer to a near-transfer test. A Computer/School Questionnaire was administered to LOGO-trained and control students. LOGO-trained students showed positive changes in attitudes relative to controls. The implications of the studies for the teaching and learning of computer programming are discussed.

In recent years a great deal of attention has been focused on the issue of helping people improve their abilities to think, learn, and solve problems. The goal of improving thinking and learning skills is by no means only a recent concern, however. Programs for teaching thinking have been discussed for centuries and have taken a number of forms, ranging from training in mathematics to learning Latin (see Mann, 1979, for a history of cognitive process training). Twentieth century educators now offer programs that include a wide variety of exercises, teaching methods, and recommended time spans (Feuerstein, Rand, Hoffman, & Miller, 1980; Lipman, 1985; Whimbey & Lochhead, 1980). A number of these programs are described and analyzed in Chipman, Segal, and Glaser (1985), Glaser (1984), and Segal, Chipman, and Glaser (1985).

Recent advances in technology have led to the hope that computers can play an important role in developing people's abilities to solve problems. Some investigators argue that the experience of learning to *program* computers—as opposed to using them as a tool or for drill and practice—is especially important for improving problem-solving abilities (e.g., Papert, 1980; Taylor, 1980). The proponents of this view argue that when learning to program a computer, one is in essence teaching the computer how to think. According to Seymour Papert, one of the strongest supporters of this view, "in teaching the computer how to think, children embark on an exploration of how they themselves think" (1980, p. 19). Taylor (1980) added that "learners gain new insights into their own thinking through learning to program" (p. 4).

## THE BENEFITS OF LEARNING LOGO

### Cognitive Benefits

Programming computers in the language LOGO has been highlighted as being particularly conducive to the development of problem-solving skills. LOGO is a computer language created for use in educational settings. It was designed by

Papert and his colleagues at the Massachusetts Institute of Technology to be easy enough so that even very young children could be introduced to programming. This language is usually introduced through the use of computer graphics, which serves to attract and maintain children's interest and lets them see how the basic commands they are learning can be put together in different ways to yield very complex designs. (See Delclos, 1987, and Papert, 1980, for full discussions of the LOGO language.)

There are a number of reasons for assuming that LOGO programming might be especially suited for facilitating problem-solving abilities. First, LOGO provides a problem-rich environment that encourages a great deal of practice at solving programming problems. Because it is rarely the case that a program will do exactly what the programmer intended the first time, meaningful problems of various kinds occur spontaneously and very frequently during the normal course of programming. Second, the structure of the LOGO language facilitates activities such as breaking problems into subproblems and devising systematic plans for finding errors (i.e., debugging). Third, the turtle graphics component of LOGO, which involves instructing a "turtle" to draw intricate patterns, makes LOGO programming simple enough so that even kindergarten children are able to successfully learn something about programming. The turtle graphics component also makes LOGO a highly motivating environment, contributing to the sense of excitement and anticipation that many students feel when programming in LOGO.

## Positive Effects on Attitudes

It has been hypothesized that learning LOGO not only has cognitive benefits, but that it can also have positive effects on children's general attitudes toward learning. Papert presents several examples of students who have entered "the LOGO lab hating numbers as alien objects and have left loving them" (1980, p. 68). Similarly, he discussed how children who hold very negative attitudes toward learning in general can come to view learning as an enjoyable task. This change in attitudes is partially attributed to students' realization of the usefulness of certain concepts they have been forced to "learn" (i.e., memorize) in classrooms. In the case of mathematics, Papert argued that the LOGO environment can provide essential links between the fundamentals of mathematics and children's everyday life, and thus help children understand why the things they are being asked to learn are meaningful. This comprehension of the usefulness of concepts presumably leads to more complete understanding as well as increased motivation to learn.

A second reason that LOGO may facilitate positive attitudes toward learning concerns the attitude generally taken toward errors when programming. Errors are commonplace in LOGO and are to be learned from, rather than simply marked as incorrect. The emphasis is on improving programs by finding and correcting errors, rather than throwing the program away and starting anew each time an error is encountered. This attitude toward errors is in sharp contrast to what most children typically encounter in school. It may contribute to an understanding that answers are not necessarily "incorrect" and, therefore, bad; rather they are "not completely correct" and can even be useful. Thus, LOGO may promote the more positive attitude that learning does not have to mean getting the right answer on the first try. Instead, learning involves starting with an initial try and then improving upon it.

Finally, LOGO may enhance positive attitudes toward learning in general due to increases in self-esteem as a result of children's successful experiences in LOGO. As noted before, LOGO was developed so that even complex designs can be produced by using fairly simple commands. Thus, children can begin producing interesting and unique designs quickly without having to first spend a great deal of time learning a lot of commands. For students who have a history of being less successful in school, this experience of beginning to master a computer language and produce complex pictures may foster the idea that they are capable of learning. Indeed, observations of students in LOGO classes seem to indicate that both academically successful and less successful children are very interested in and excited about learning LOGO, and that off-task behaviors are very low in frequency (Kinzer, Littlefield, Delclos, & Bransford, 1985). Perhaps the excitement and interest generated in the LOGO classroom can result in a more positive attitude toward learning in general, even in children who have had little success in the traditional school curriculum.

Although there is little research investigating the effects of learning LOGO on students' attitudes toward school in general, D. H. Clements and Nastasi (1985) reported that students receiving LOGO training expressed "more pleasure at discovery of new information or solving a problem" (p. 25) than did students receiving training using computer-assisted instruction. Although no differences were found in self-esteem between the LOGO-trained and computer-assisted instruction groups, students in the latter group showed a higher incidence of dependency behaviors, perhaps indicating lower self-confidence. Thus, there is some evidence that students trained in LOGO show positive changes in affective variables, although attitudes toward computers in particular and toward school in general have not been directly assessed.

Part of the research to be discussed in this chapter concerns changes in student attitudes as a result of learning LOGO. Interest in attitudes associated with learning LOGO was motivated by our observation that students in LOGO classes were very interested and excited about learning LOGO, and by our belief that these effects are potentially important. If students who previously had neutral or negative attitudes toward school in general can become excited about being in school and about learning in general, this may prove to be one of the greatest contributions that LOGO has to offer. This would constitute not merely a change in what students learn in school, but in their desire to learn—surely a remarkable feat. Although not the major focus of our LOGO project, a portion of the project was designed to determine whether the excitement seemingly generated in the course of learning LOGO resulted in measurable differences in attitudes toward school and computers.

## Research Investigating LOGO's Cognitive Effects

Despite the enthusiastic claims about the cognitive benefits of LOGO programming, studies of the effects of LOGO programming have found mixed results concerning transfer of problem-solving abilities to non-LOGO problems. For example, a project conducted at Bank Street College included three studies of 8- to 12-year-old children receiving 1 year of LOGO training (Pea & Kurland, 1983). The studies were designed to assess the degree of programming expertise developed, the depth of understanding of certain programming concepts (e.g., recursion), and the development and spontaneous transfer of planning skills to other problems and situations. In all three studies LOGO was taught in a discovery-oriented environment where children were allowed to work on programs of their own choosing. Although the children enjoyed the experience, the results suggested they did not seem to progress very far in programming expertise, depth of understanding of programming concepts, or planning and problem-solving skills. The researchers also found that even some of the best programmers in the class did not understand a number of concepts (e.g., recursion and use of variables) even though they had used them in their own programs. Finally, 1 year of LOGO training seemed to have no effects on children's ability to solve a problem that required them to develop a schedule of classroom chores—a problem that seems to involve some of the same planning strategies as those used in LOGO programming.

The Bank Street researchers have found similar results in subsequent studies, even in those using a near-transfer measure of planning skills that involved a robot testing environment very similar to that of LOGO. Data provided clear evidence of improvements in the efficiency of plans across time and in reorganization of initial plans into more efficient ones, but the changes occurred regardless of whether students were trained in LOGO (see Pea, Kurland, & Hawkins, 1985).

The Bank Street researchers are not the only ones who have failed to find evidence that LOGO programming increases the problem-solving skills of students. Other researchers have reported similar results (e.g., see Maddux, 1985). However, there is some support for LOGO's effect on cognitive skills. D. H. Clements and Gullo (1984) taught LOGO to first-grade children for a total of 16 hours over 12 weeks. Although no differences were found between the LOGO-trained children and children receiving computer-assisted instruction on several general cognitive measures from the McCarthy Screening Test or on several Piagetian tasks of operational competence, positive changes for the LOGO-trained children were seen on measures of divergent thinking, awareness of comprehension failure, and describing directions. Children in the computer-assisted instruction group did not show such differences. Significant positive changes in measures of reflectivity–impulsivity were also found, but have failed to be replicated in subsequent studies.

Subsequent work by Clements has also indicated positive effects of LOGO training, relative to a group of students receiving computer-assisted instruction, on students' abilities to decide on the nature of a problem and on the processes used in solving the problem, as well as on their abilities to monitor their own understanding (D. H. Clements, 1986). It is interesting to note that the LOGO instruction in these studies seems to differ from that in many other studies in that there was more structure in the way LOGO was taught. For example, students in these classes were asked to sketch their drawings on pieces of paper prior to programming them in LOGO. With the instructor's assistance, sketches were broken into subparts. Each subpart was programmed and then the subparts assembled. Through the instructor's questions and prompts, students were actively encouraged to think through problems encountered while programming. Thus, it seems that the LOGO instruction in the studies that have yielded evidence of LOGO's effects on problem-solving skills differs in important ways from the instruction in other studies.

## Importance of Teaching Method

We note in the preceding section that evidence concerning LOGO's effect on the development and transfer of general skills is mixed, and that one possible reason might involve methods of instruction. The method that has been used to teach LOGO is typically reported to be a "discovery" method. Although details in most reports are sketchy, we assume that this method involves the presentation of basic commands followed by a free time period during which children are able to work on whatever they choose. Teachers intervene when children need help.

In order for the discovery method to show evidence of transfer from LOGO to more general problem-solving tasks, children must (a) achieve some minimal level of mastery of the programming language, (b) develop the general skills, and then (c) transfer these skills spontaneously without anyone making any special efforts to ensure that mastery has been achieved or that general problem-solving skills have been developed. From previous reports, the indication is that even the first of these three requirements has not been achieved when LOGO has been taught in a discovery-oriented environment (Pea, 1983; Pea & Kurland, 1983). If mastery is not achieved, the discovery and transfer of general problem-solving skills as a result of learning LOGO cannot occur.

An assumption underlying the "discovery" method is that problem-solving skills will be spontaneously developed and transferred in the free interaction of the learner and LOGO environment. We have a different perspective. We believe that even if the programming environment has potential for encouraging the development of general problem-solving skills, simply placing children in this environment and teaching them the basics of programming need not necessarily result in improved problem-solving skills. We strongly suspect that more is needed. Recent evaluations of several thinking skills programs have emphasized the importance of the presentation method. A recurring theme in this literature is that no content, standing alone, can spontaneously produce generalizable learning (Bransford, Stein, Arbitman-Smith, & Vye, 1985; Delclos, Bransford, & Haywood, 1984; Nelson, 1983). Instead, some structure in the method of teaching or learning must exist to facilitate mastery of the material, development of general problem-solving skills, and transfer of skills to other domains.

One of the major goals of our reseach was to investigate the effects of different methods of teaching LOGO on (a) mastery of the language and (b) transfer of general problem-solving skills to non-LOGO problems. Our discussion of this research has the following organization. The next section summarizes the characteristics of the students participating in the project and provides an overview of the general procedure followed throughout the project. Following this general orientation is a description of the teaching methods we have investigated and results of experiments comparing the effects of these methods. Next is a discussion of our work investigating the effects of learning LOGO on students' attitudes toward school in general and toward computers in particular. Finally, we discuss the significance of our findings for the general topics of teaching and learning computer programming.

## RESEARCH SETTING

Academically successful and less successful fifth-grade children from Nashville, Tennessee middle schools have participated in all the studies we have conducted. Success level was determined on the basis of students' Math and Reading scores on the Comprehensive Test of Basic Skills and on the basis of teacher ratings. Equal numbers of successful and less successful students in each study served as experimental students who received LOGO training and as control students who did not receive any computer instruction. Both experimental and control students were given tests of general problem-solving skills before and after the LOGO instruction. Several near-transfer tests that shared more obvious similarities with the LOGO environment were also administered to the students who participated in the last year of our research.

Students receiving LOGO instruction reported to "the computer room" every afternoon for a full 6-week period. Because of the time required to administer tests, these students actually learned and worked with LOGO for 1 hour a day, 5 days a week, for 5 weeks. Students were taught in groups of five to six with one teacher per group. Each group was homogeneous with respect to the success level of the students. Each student worked individually on his or her own computer, although students were allowed to freely interact.

## UNSTRUCTURED AND STRUCTURED TEACHING METHODS

### Teaching Methods

The first study we conducted compared the effects of an unstructured teaching method with a more structured one. The unstructured method was based on the open, discovery-oriented environment used in previous studies. Each day, the teacher presented a group of new commands or concepts. One or two concrete examples of the use of this material were completed by the teacher and related to the previous day's work. The rest of the lesson was given to free exploration time, with the students allowed to do whatever they chose as long as they were using LOGO. The teacher observed all work and answered questions. When students could not think of anything to do, the teacher suggested they try to practice the material learned that day.

As noted before, some previous reports indicated that children in unstructured LOGO classes had failed to achieve mastery of the LOGO language as well as failed to show evidence of the development and transfer of general skills. Lack of LOGO mastery could be due in part to a phenomenon we have noticed while observing children in unstructured LOGO classes. Many children in the unstructured environment tend to engage in impulsive, random play with the turtle and its capabilities. For example, some students quickly discover that they can generate interesting patterns by turning the turtle just a little to the right or left and instructing it to move forward thousands of steps. Many children continue random variations on this theme for several classes. These children generally do not try to predict what will be created or analyze why the commands produced the particular drawing that resulted. Although these children are actively engaged in using LOGO and are producing interesting designs (see Kinzer et al., 1985), they do not seem to reach an understanding of why the patterns look as they do, nor do they develop an ability to predict what will be drawn when they give the turtle a specific set of commands.

Not all children follow the pattern just described; in fact, some children have done well in the unstructured learning environment. We have noticed that those who did learn from this approach were those who set specific structured goals and limits for themselves, even in the absence of such structure from the instructors. These students set out to produce a specific figure and worked until they succeeded—a sharp contrast to the random exploration just described. This suggests that some degree of structure in the LOGO learning experience is necessary to ensure mastery of basic commands and proficiency in planning and writing programs. If this basic material is not mastered, transfer is a moot point: A process not learned cannot, by definition, be generalized.

Our second teaching method was more structured. We believed this structuring would help students avoid the random play just described and achieve a better mastery of the language. In the structured method the material covered and examples used were the same as those in the unstructured method. The structured method differed from the unstructured method in that, rather than having free exploration time, each student was given a sheet with a variety of pictures that could be made using the material that had been presented previously. Some examples are shown in Fig. 5.1.

Students were instructed to select one of the pictures and write a program to draw it. The teacher answered questions and continually checked to assure that

FIG. 5.1. Examples of practice figures used for the structured and mediated teaching methods

children worked on this assigned task. After completing the pictures as shown, students usually added their own personal touches to them (e.g., special doors, windows, or chimneys to the house; different kinds of eyes, hats, noses to the robot face, etc.) or used parts of these pictures in other pictures of their own creation. This enabled students to not only practice the particular commands the instructors wished to emphasize, but also to create their own personalized pictures.

## Tests of General Problem-Solving Skills

Three tests were used as pretest and posttest measures of general problem-solving skills. The tests that we used were chosen because they measured skills that seemed to be intrinsic to LOGO mastery and because they did not presuppose content knowledge that the students were lacking (e.g., see Bransford et al., 1985). The Organization of Dots test and the Instructions test were adapted from Feuerstein's Instrumental Enrichment Program (Feuerstein, Rand, & Hoffman, 1979). A third test, Set Variations I, was taken directly from the Learning Potential Assessment Device (Feuerstein et al., 1980). In addition to standard administrations of all three tests, the Organization of Dots and Set Variations I tests were also administered using adaptations of the dynamic assessment procedures for group testing outlined by Feuerstein et al. (1980). Dynamic procedures assess transfer by measuring learning or adaptation in new situations. It has been argued that dynamic assessments are especially appropriate as measures of general problem-solving skills, because such skills are presumably the basis for adaptation and learning (Bransford et al., 1985; Campione, Brown, & Ferrara, 1982; Feuerstein et al., 1979). If general problem-solving skills are enhanced through experience with LOGO, the students may show evidence of such skills on a dynamically administered test even if no evidence is seen in evaluations of students' independent performance.

## A Test of LOGO Mastery

A LOGO mastery test was developed that assessed three aspects of LOGO mastery: command mastery, prediction mastery, and production mastery. Examples of the mastery test items are included in Fig. 5.2. Command mastery refers to knowledge of basic LOGO commands and was assessed by fill-in-the-blank items. Prediction mastery refers to the ability to predict the drawing that would result from a set of LOGO commands and was assessed by having children choose which of four alternative figures a given set of commands would produce. Production mastery refers to the ability to write a LOGO program that would produce a given figure. This third aspect was assessed by having children write LOGO programs on paper and pencil that would produce the figures shown on the test page.

Command mastery items:
To make the turtle go forward 20 steps you type_____.
To make the turtle go back 20 steps you type_____.

If the turtle is pointing straight up like this △ , how much do you

have to turn it to make it point straight out to the side like this

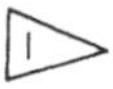

▷ ? _____.
Prediction mastery items:

?ED "SQ50
Repeat 4 [FD 50 RT 90]
END
?Repeat 3 [SQ50 Rt 90]

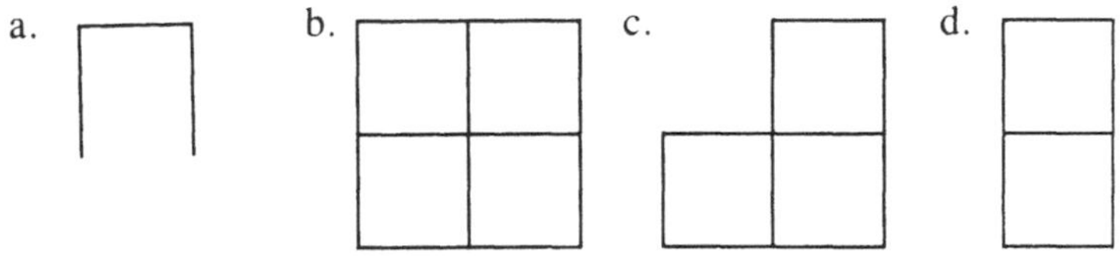

Production mastery items:
  Teach the turtle a new word that will make a picture like this one.

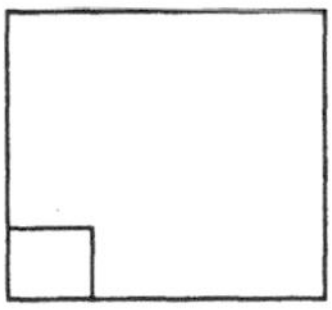

Call the picture BOXES. Write the definition for BOXES on the line
below. Remember, you have to teach the turtle *everything* it needs to know
to draw BOXES.

FIG. 5.2.  Examples of mastery test items

Our concern with different types of mastery developed as a result of informal
observations of pilot students learning LOGO in the unstructured environment
described earlier. It seemed that a number of students were very good at some
aspects of LOGO (e.g., what specific commands stand for and when a number is
required to use them) but not other aspects (e.g., they were unable to predict the
drawing a given set of commands would produce or to write a program to
produce a given figure). Thus, the mastery test was developed to see which
particular aspects of LOGO are mastered under different training conditions.

Following 3 weeks of instruction using the two different teaching methods, all
experimental students were given the LOGO mastery test. These mastery results
indicated low levels of mastery by students in the unstructured condition; there-

fore, during the last 2 weeks of instruction both instructional groups were taught using the structured method. Our goal was to get both groups to a level where some possibility for transfer would be plausible.

## Mastery of LOGO

Analyses were conducted separately for each of the three types of mastery as well as for the total mastery test score. The results showed that the unstructured and structured methods of teaching resulted in comparable levels of command mastery. However, the structured group scored significantly higher than the unstructured group for both prediction and production mastery and for the total Mastery test score. This was true for both successful and less successful students. Thus, both successful and less successful students performed significantly better when taught LOGO using the structured teaching method than with the unstructured method on the parts of the mastery test that required more than basic knowledge of LOGO commands (i.e., on the prediction and production mastery test items). This indicates that the structured method was more effective for teaching the language.

## Transfer to Non-LOGO Problems

To assess any enhancement in problem-solving skills from pretest to posttest, the difference between pre- and posttest administrations of the tests of problem-solving skills was calculated (i.e., posttest score minus pretest score). Difference scores for the experimental group (including all students taught LOGO, regardless of teaching method) and for the control group were analyzed for each of the three tests of general problem-solving skills. No differences between the experimental and control groups were found for any of the tests.

The effect of the particular method used to teach LOGO was assessed by comparing the difference scores of the two experimental conditions only, omitting the scores of the control group. There were no significant differences between the unstructured and structured groups for any of the three tests.

The analyses of the difference scores seem to indicate that learning LOGO does not result in the transfer of the general problem-solving skills assessed. In addition, the particular method used to teach LOGO does not seem to have any effect on the general problem-solving skills assessed, although teaching method did have differential effects on comprehension and production mastery. Note that these difference scores were the results of measures that were administered using a static testing format. That is, they are measures of performance by students who worked independently, that is, without prompts.

If learning LOGO affects general problem-solving skills, it is possible that this effect may be more readily seen in students' abilities to profit from help given in the testing situation, that is, in a more dynamic testing situation. In order to evaluate this possibility, analyses were conducted in which the dependent measure was the difference between the dynamic and static administrations of two of the posttests: the Organization of Dots and Set Variations I tests. These analyses showed that, for the Organization of Dots test, the students taught LOGO had higher scores than the control students. This difference was not seen on the Set Variations I test. Analyses conducted to examine the effects of teaching method compared the dynamic posttest scores of students in the structured versus those in the unstructured teaching groups. No differences were found.

In summary, the major finding of this study was that discovery training methods may often lead to degrees of LOGO learning that are inadequate to support any general transfer. Without adequate mastery, one would hardly expect such transfer. Our structured teaching method provided systematic practice on a variety of figures and designs with each command learned. Compared with the discovery learning condition, this procedure appears to increase children's understanding of LOGO basics and enhance their ability to predict what a given set of commands will produce. However, even our structured teaching method did not result in clear evidence of transfer of general skills. Although the dynamic administration of two of the tests did show a difference between the experimental and control students, this difference was found on only one test.

Our second study extended the first in two directions: (a) we further modified our methods used to teach LOGO in ways designed to promote better transfer and (b) we developed additional transfer tests to assess the possibility that our previous measures were not sufficiently sensitive to reflect the skills learned in LOGO. This second study is discussed in the following section.

## STRUCTURED AND MEDIATIONAL TEACHING METHODS

### Teaching Methods

Based on theories that emphasize the role of mediation in the promotion of effective learning (Bransford et al., 1985; Feuerstein et al., 1980), we developed a mediational teaching method designed to explicitly focus students' attention on the general problem-solving skills used in LOGO and on how these skills could be useful in other contexts. The mediational teaching method was similar to the structured and unstructured methods described earlier in the chapter in terms of the material covered and the examples used to demonstrate the commands and concepts. This method was also like the structured method in that students were given exercises like those shown in Fig. 5.1. The critical difference between the mediational method and the other two is that the teacher explicitly talked about and provided numerous examples of how the skills used in LOGO could be applied in other contexts. Breaking problems into parts, identifying errors, and planning ahead were particularly emphasized. This bridging of general skills to other contexts was accomplished by familiarizing students with two specific contexts other than LOGO in order to help children understand that the skills discussed during LOGO programming were useful across a variety of situations. These contexts were developed in detail during the first few sessions of computer instruction, and the students and teachers referred back to them frequently during the course of learning LOGO.

The first context was introduced by having students view a 10-minute segment of Indiana Jones in the film *Raiders of the Lost Ark*. The segment portrays Indiana Jones searching for a golden idol in the South American jungle. After the children viewed the film segment, the teacher led a discussion of how Indiana (a) broke large problems (e.g., finding the idol) into smaller, more manageable ones (e.g., hiring an airplane to get to the jungle, finding a guide to the cave where the idol was kept); (b) planned ahead (e.g., determining the supplies needed for the trip and purchasing them, planning an escape route); and (c) identified and corrected errors in his plans. Children generated examples of how Indiana used these skills and what the consequences might have been had he failed to apply these general skills (e.g., what if he hadn't planned how much food he would need, or if he hadn't thought about the possibility of needing to leave the jungle in a hurry after locating the idol).

Following the discussion of general problem-solving skills in the Indiana Jones context, the teacher elicited examples of other contexts in which these general ideas could be useful. The second specific context used in our mediated LOGO instruction was developed as an example of another, more familiar context in which the general problem-solving skills being discussed might be useful. This context involved planning a party. Students discussed (a) breaking the large problem of planning a party into smaller problems (e.g., developing a guest list, deciding on the kind and amount of refreshments, buying and mailing invitations, etc.); (b) planning ahead (e.g., what are the advantages of planning the different aspects of the party and assigning different people to be responsible for the different parts); and (c) identifying and correcting errors in plans for a party (e.g., identifying that an error existed if one person had been assigned to pick up the guest of honor for the party at the same time that she was supposed to decorate the room).

While learning LOGO, the children in the mediated group were encouraged to plan their designs ahead of time and break the designs down into smaller, meaningful subparts. In addition, when students encountered problems, references to the other two contexts were made to encourage students to think about the way in which problems had been solved in other contexts and to consider whether the present problem could be approached in a similar manner. For example, if a student wished to write a program to draw an alien spaceship but said that she didn't know where to start, the teacher might prompt her to think about what the first step had been in planning a party. This was intended to remind the student that sometimes large, complex problems can be more easily solved by breaking them into smaller, more manageable subparts. Thus, a useful approach might be to break the alien spaceship picture into smaller components which could be programmed separately and later put together. Conversely, when students succeeded in solving a problem in LOGO, the teacher prompted the students to think about how the process used to solve the LOGO problem was an example of using one of the general problem-solving skills discussed in class, how the process could be successfully applied to other LOGO problems, and how the process could be successfully used in the Indiana Jones or the party-planning contexts. Thus, the teacher in the mediational teaching method, in essence, focused on facilitating transfer by pointing out the general problem-solving skills involved in completing the LOGO tasks and providing numerous, explicit examples of the usefulness of these skills in non-LOGO contexts.

The structured teaching method used in this study was identical to the structured method described previously in this chapter except that, as in the mediational method, the teacher explicitly emphasized breaking problems into parts, identifying errors, and planning ahead. However, these skills were discussed *only* in terms of their use in LOGO—examples of their usefulness in other contexts were not discussed. Thus, if a student in the structured group wanted to write a program to produce an alien spaceship but didn't know where to start, the teacher would encourage him to break the larger problem into subcomponents by prompting him to think about how he had proceeded in programming other complex LOGO projects. Similarly, when a LOGO programming problem was solved in the structured group, the teacher would prompt students to think about how they had used the same problem-solving skill (e.g., breaking big problems into smaller ones) to successfully solve prior LOGO problems. The teacher did *not*, however, provide or elicit examples of how the general skills might be useful in other non-LOGO problems or contexts.

## Near-Transfer Tests

Thus far, we have focused on the possibility that the method of teaching LOGO is the reason that previous studies have not found clear evidence of transfer of general skills. A second possible explanation is that the tests used to examine general skills were very dissimilar to LOGO programming. To evaluate this possibility, we created two additional transfer tests, each designed to share obvious similarities to the LOGO environment. A map test was designed to be administered using a static testing format while a classroom cleaning task was designed for dynamic assessment.

A map test was developed that contained more obvious similarities to the LOGO environment than the tests of general skills used in the first study. The map test was developed to test the ability to be precise in following and giving directions, to identify and correct errors in given sets of directions, and to make use of subprocedures in writing and correcting sets of directions. The task was to instruct a robot how to get to various places in the hypothetical town illustrated in Fig. 5.3. There were three parts to the test. In the first part, the robot knew only a few basic commands (e.g., go straight ahead $X$ blocks, turn right, etc.). In the second, the robot knew the basic commands and two complete sets of directions (e.g., a set of directions concerning how to go from the Home to the Town Circle, and a set concerning how to go from the Town Circle to Home). In the third, the robot knew only the basic commands, but could be taught different sets of directions. It could remember these sets and use them in other problems. The robot in the map test is analogous to the turtle in LOGO in that it must receive directions from a limited set of commands and the goal of the task is to manipulate its spatial orientation. In addition, the robots in Parts 2 and 3 of the map test could make use of "subprocedures" just as the turtle in LOGO could. These similarities should make transfer of skills more likely to occur.

It is also possible that even if students' independent performance on near- and far-transfer tests did not show evidence of the general problem-solving skills discussed in LOGO, differences would emerge when students were given hints on a near transfer task, that is, a dynamically administered test. To assess this possibility, students were individually tested using a modification of the class-

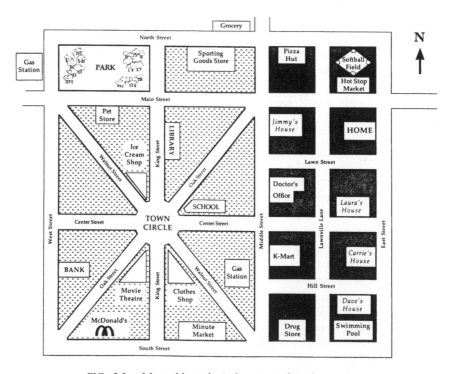

FIG. 5.3.   Map of hypothetical town used in the map test

room cleaning task developed by Pea and Kurland (1983). The modified class-room cleaning task involved planning the most efficient way for a group of five children to clean a classroom using a limited number of tools and equipment. Specifically, it tested students' abilities to be precise in the assignment of people and tools to tasks, to appropriately sequence tasks, and to debug a given problem solution.

The task was to develop a plan for cleaning classrooms in school using a limited number of people and tools. Each student was interviewed individually and the task situation presented verbally. The student was given approximately 2 minutes for an initial response. After this protocol was obtained, the experimenter asked a series of five questions designed to prompt the student to think about the skills discussed in the LOGO programming class. The interview was audiotaped and the tapes later transcribed and rated for quality of the assignment of people and tools to tasks and quality of sequencing of the tasks. Each student received assignment and sequencing scores on the initial protocol and after the prompts. In addition, each student received a score ranging from 0 to 2 on a question concerning the usefulness of taking notes to help solve this problem and on a question concerning the identification and correction of an error in a plan developed by the experimenter.

Overall, students in this study comparing the effects of structured and mediated teaching methods received two near-transfer tests at posttest: the map test and the dynamically administered classroom cleaning task. These students also completed four far-transfer tests of general skills at pre- and posttest (i.e., the Organization of Dots, Instructions, and Set Variations I tests used in the first study, as well as a modified version of the Analytic Perception test from Feuerstein et al.'s Instrumental Enrichment Program). Organization of Dots was administered both statically to obtain a measure of students' independent performance and dynamically to obtain a measure of prompted performance. In addition, the experimental students completed the LOGO mastery test after the 5-week instructional period to assess the three aspects of LOGO mastery previously discussed.

## Mastery of LOGO

Overall, the different methods of instruction did not lead to differences in mastery. The mastery test data indicate that both the structured and mediational teaching methods result in comparable levels of LOGO mastery.

## Transfer to Problems Similar to LOGO

The means and standard deviations of the number correct for each of the three parts of the map test are illustrated in Fig. 5.4. For all three parts of the map test, the mediated group scored significantly higher than the structured group, and the structured group scored significantly higher than the control group. There were

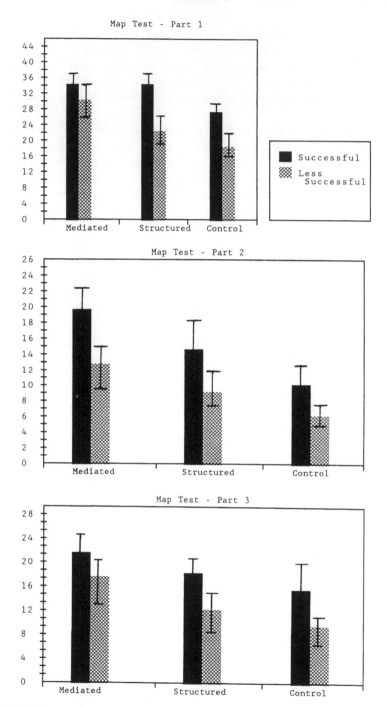

FIG. 5.4.   Mean performance on map test of mediated, structured, and control groups (bars indicate standard deviations)

no interactions of students' success level and teaching method for any part of the map test, indicating that the mediational teaching method was more effective in producing evidence of transfer on this task for both successful and less successful students.

For the dynamically assessed classroom cleaning task, separate analyses were conducted using students' unprompted assignment and sequencing scores, prompted assignment and sequencing scores, total assignment and sequencing scores (i.e., prompted plus unprompted), and scores on the questions concerning taking notes and debugging. The results showed that for both unprompted assignment scores and the total assignment scores, students in the mediated group performed significantly better than control students. The level of performance of students in the structured group was between, and did not differ from, those in the mediated or control groups. On the question concerning the usefulness of taking notes, successful students scored significantly higher than less successful students.

Performance on the new transfer tasks indicated that LOGO learning does seem to develop skills that are transferable, at least to situations that are fairly similar to the LOGO environment. Furthermore, mediational instructional methods seem to be especially effective in promoting this transfer.

## Far-Transfer Performance

For all students, the posttest minus pretest difference scores were calculated for each of the four far-transfer measures of general problem-solving skills; these formed the static assessment measures. For the Organization of Dots test, the dynamic posttest minus the static posttest scores were also calculated. Essentially, there was no difference in performance among conditions. The mediated and structured learning conditions showed comparable performance on these far-transfer measures and, perhaps more importantly, they performed no better than the control condition. Thus, we found no evidence that learning LOGO can aid in transfer to situations that differ substantially from the LOGO environment.

In summary, the results of this experiment indicate that, although the structured and mediated teaching methods produced comparable mastery levels, the mediational method was most effective in producing transfer, at least as measured by a test which closely resembled the LOGO environment. Neither instructional method showed consistent evidence of transfer on the four pretest and posttest measures of general skills. The classroom-cleaning test showed some evidence of transfer, but only for students in the mediated instructional group and only for questions involving precise assignment of people and tools to tasks. This test does not share as many similarities with the LOGO programming environment as the map test (e.g., the task does not require giving directions in order to manipulate spatial orientation), but is more similar to the LOGO environment than the four general tests (e.g., it does require precision in assignment and logical sequential ordering of tasks).

Of course it is still possible that LOGO training might promote far transfer. On one hand, it may be that our far-transfer measures just did not involve the type of skills developed in LOGO (even though we tried to choose ones that did). Alternatively, it may be that our students just did not receive sufficient LOGO training for the development of such general cognitive skills. Perhaps the length of the LOGO training was not sufficient to show transfer to tests that are very dissimilar from the original training conditions. With an increase in the length of instruction, it might be that the patterns of differences seen on the map test would appear on other transfer tests, with evidence of transfer perhaps first becoming apparent on the classroom-cleaning test and only later on the four far-transfer tests.

## LOGO'S EFFECTS ON STUDENTS' ATTITUDES

Informal records during the first 2 years of our LOGO project indicated that most students enjoyed learning LOGO and wished they could work on the computers every day in school. Such records of students' reactions raised the question of how universal these attitudes might be and whether they might alter the students' attitudes toward school in general. As noted before, little work has been done on this specific question, although there is evidence that LOGO-trained students show more positive attitudes toward solving problems and show less evidence of dependency behaviors than children trained in computer-assisted instruction. Other studies not focused on LOGO have investigated the general advantages of computer classes over other, more traditional classrooms (F. J. Clements, 1981; Lawton & Gerschner, 1982). Features such as the type of interaction allowed (or encouraged) between students, the pacing of instruction, the type of feedback students receive, and the nature of the tasks undertaken by students may serve to make computer classrooms quite different from other classes and potentially more motivating for students.

In light of these considerations, a study was designed to assess whether students' attitudes toward computers and toward school in general are improved through experience in a LOGO class. A Computer/School Attitude Questionnaire was developed and the students' attitudes assessed before and after learning LOGO (Lever, Sherrod, & Bransford, in press). Students who took the LOGO class were expected to show improved attitudes toward school upon completion of the class.

### The Computer/School Questionnaire

The Computer/School questionnaire is a 50-item survey (see Table 5.1 for examples of questionnaire items). Half the items pertain to school in general and half to computers in particular. A three point rating scale was used for each

TABLE 5.1
Examples of Items on the Computer/School Attitude Questionnaire

---

38. It is hard to do well at computers.
    Yes     Maybe     No
39. Some days I hate school.
    Yes     Maybe     No
40. It is important to me that I learn how to use computers.
    Yes     Maybe     No
41. Making plans helps people solve problems at school.
    Yes     Maybe     No
42. Learning about computers would make me feel important.
    Yes     Maybe     No
43. I admire people who work in schools.
    Yes     Maybe     No
44. Whoever invented computers must have liked kids.
    Yes     Maybe     No
45. Most of the time I hate school.
    Yes     Maybe     No
46. I don't work as hard as I ought on computers.
    Yes     Maybe     No
47. You can learn a lot by going to school.
    Yes     Maybe     No
48. I would be happy if I never saw another computer.
    Yes     Maybe     No

---

question, with positive, neutral, and negative response options. Half the questions were based on positive statements about school and computers and half were negative.

The Computer/School Questionnaire is similar to surveys developed by others in terms of the questions regarding school (Barker & Lunn, 1969; Fitt, 1956; Tennenbaum, 1944), but differs from those previously published in its inclusion of computer questions. Alpha internal consistency for the scale is .804.

## Changes in Attitude

Analyses of the pre- and posttest scores on the total survey show that, after taking the computer class, experimental students' attitudes became more positive toward school and computers, whereas the students who were not in computer class did not alter their attitudes. There was also a significant interaction of gender across time, which shows that female students became more positive toward school and computers by posttest than did males. There was no significant interaction of success level with time of administration, indicating that successful and less successful students did not differ in the degree to which their attitude improved.

Analyses of only those questions pertaining to attitudes toward school show that those students who learned LOGO showed improved attitudes toward school, whereas control students did not change their attitudes toward school.

For the questions pertaining to attitudes toward computers in particular, the results indicate that those students who had taken the computer class showed improved attitudes toward computers, whereas control students did not. The interaction of gender with time of administration was also significant, and it indicated that females who had been part of the computer class showed more improvement in their attitudes toward computers than males who had taken the class. In addition, male control students viewed computers less positively at posttest than at pretest, whereas control females did not change their attitudes.

## Relationship of Attitudes and LOGO Mastery

Pearson Product Moment correlations were computed between the LOGO mastery scores of the experimental students and these students' scores on the total Computer/School Attitude Questionnaire, their Computer subscale score, and their School subscale score. No significant correlations were found.

These results indicate that the LOGO programming course resulted in positive changes in attitude scores for both successful and less successful students toward both school and computers. The computer class in this study offered students a novel kind of activity (i.e., computer programming) in a way that was different from their regular classrooms. For example, students were encouraged to interact and work together to solve problems that arose. Such interaction is often not allowed in other kinds of classrooms and may have served to increase interest, motivation, and positive attitudes. In addition, the computer class allowed each student to work on their own computer, at their own pace, with constant feedback regarding their performance. These differences may have fostered an excitement and a motivation to learn about computers, thus contributing to the more positive attitudes seen at posttest. Further research is needed to determine whether the positive attitudes of the experimental students are maintained over extended periods of time and if they are maintained in the absence of participation in the programming class.

No relationship between attitudes and LOGO mastery was found. Perhaps all students, successful and less sucessful, felt they had accomplished a great deal in the class. The pictures designed and the programs written were a source of pride for the students, and students felt they had mastered the computer after completing their LOGO projects. In addition, students never saw the results of the paper-and-pencil mastery test; therefore, they did not have any evidence to suggest that they had not done as well as they believed they had.

Finally, this experiment showed interesting gender effects, with the experimental females showing greater increases in measured attitude toward school and computers than the experimental males. It is possible that this effect may be due in part to modeling. Both the computer teachers in the LOGO project were female. It was obvious to the students that these females were comfortable around the computers and knew what they were doing. If the teachers could feel this way about computers then perhaps the female students began to feel that they could also be competent in computer class, and thus developed more positive attitudes.

## GENERAL DISCUSSION

Unlike other computer programming languages, LOGO is generally taught in elementary schools with the idea that children will learn more than just the LOGO language. It has been viewed by many as a quick, effective fix for the difficulties encountered in teaching general problem-solving skills to children. Whether or not this perception is an accurate reflection of the developer's conception of LOGO, it unfortunately has become a widespread view. As a result, LOGO has generated a great deal of excitement and enthusiasm among educators. As early negative reports and later more mixed results have appeared concerning LOGO's effects on thinking skills, the enthusiasm and excitement have begun to give way to a disappointment in LOGO that could ultimately lead to the unfortunate consequence of throwing LOGO out with the rest of the educational programs that "didn't work." We think this is not only unfortunate, but unfair. Our work, as well as that of D. H. Clements, seems to suggest that LOGO does have merit and can potentially be useful in facilitating the development of general problem-solving skills. It cannot, however, be expected to work miracles.

We think that perhaps the best way to view LOGO is as one context that can be useful for facilitating the development of general problem-solving skills. It is a very good context for this purpose for reasons outlined previously (i.e., it is a problem-rich environment, a procedural language, and is accessible to young children), but it is one of an array of tools that can be utilized to foster the development of problem-solving ability. To accomplish this end, LOGO requires that someone (e.g., the instructor, a parent, or the child) provide structure in the learning environment and explicit emphasis on problem-solving skills, as well as explicit bridging to decontextualize the skills developed and encourage transfer to other contexts.

Thus, the implications of our work for teaching and learning LOGO are clear: Serious attention to the method used to teach LOGO is critical if the goal is to develop general problem-solving skills. Structure and emphasis on the general skills are needed to ensure that the general skills will develop, and mediation is needed to decontextualize the skills and facilitate their transfer to other contexts.

Finally, the results of our attitude survey indicate that students have more positive views of school in general after having learned LOGO. Clearly, more work is needed to clarify which particular aspects of the LOGO environment are responsible for these changes, whether the changes are maintained over time, and to identify the source of the observed gender differences in attitude change. However, these results are encouraging. For many students it seems that the greatest barriers to learning are the lack of motivation to learn and the belief that one cannot learn effectively. If experience with LOGO can help students overcome these barriers by fostering the belief that school is a positive place to be, it would clearly be a powerful tool for learning.

## ACKNOWLEDGMENTS

The present research was supported by National Institute of Mental Health Grant MH38235 to John D. Bransford, Jeffrey J. Franks, and Keith N. Clayton.

We gratefully acknowledge the cooperation of Dr. George Kersey, principal, and the fifth-grade students and teachers at Carter-Lawrence Middle School in Nashville, TN for their generous and continued support in this research project.

## REFERENCES

Barker, C., & Lunn, J. C. (1969). The development of scales to measure junior school children's attitudes. *British Journal of Education, 39*, 64–71.

Bransford, J. D., Stein, B. S., Arbitman-Smith, R., & Vye, N. J. (1985). Three approaches to improving thinking and learning skills. In J. Segal, S. Chipman, & R. Glaser (Eds.) *Thinking and learning skills: Relating instruction to basic research (Vol. 1*, pp. 133–206). Hillsdale, NJ: Lawrence Erlbaum Associates.

Camione, J. C., Brown, A. L., & Ferrara, R. A. (1982). Mental retardation and intelligence. In R. J. Sternberg (Ed.), *Handbook of human intelligence* (pp. 392–490). Cambridge: Cambridge University Press.

Chipman, S. F., Segal, J. W., & Glaser, R. (1985). *Thinking and learning skills: Research and open questions (Vol. 2)*. Hillsdale, NJ: Lawrence Erlbaum Associates.

Clements, D. H. (1986). Effects of LOGO and CAI environments on cognition and creativity. *Journal of Educational Psychology, 78*(4), 309–318.

Clements, D. H., & Gullo, D. F. (1984). Effects of computer programming on young children's cognition. *Journal of Educational Psychology, 76*(6), 1051–1058.

Clements, D. H., & Nastasi, B. K. (1985). Effects of computer environments of social-emotional development: LOGO and computer-assisted instruction. *Computers in the Schools, 2*(2/3), 11–32.

Clements, F. J. (1981). Affective considerations in computer based education. *Educational Technology, 10*, 28–32.

Delclos, V. R. (1987). An introduction to programming in LOGO. In C. K. Kinzer, R. D. Sherwood, & J. D. Bransford (Eds.), *Computer strategies for education: Foundation and content-area applications*. Columbus, OH: Merrill Publishing.

Delclos, V. R., Bransford, J. D., & Haywood, H. C. (1984). Instrumental enrichment: A program for teaching thinking. *Childhood Education, 60*, 256–259.

Feuerstein, R., Rand, Y., & Hoffman, M. (1979). *Dynamic assessment of retarded performers.* Baltimore, MD: University Park Press.

Feuerstein, R., Rand, Y., Hoffman, M., & Miller, R. (1980). *Instrumental enrichment: An intervention program for cognitive modifiability*. Baltimore, MD: University Park Press.

Fitt, A. B. (1956). An experimental study of children's attitudes toward school in Auckland, N.Z. *British Journal of Educational Psychology, 26,* 26–30.

Glaser, R. (1984). Education and thinking: The role of knowledge. *American Psychologist, 39,* 93–104.

Kinzer, C. K., Littlefield, J., Delclos, V. R., & Bransford, J. D. (1985). Different LOGO learning environments and mastery: Relationships between engagement and learning. *Computers in the Schools, 2*(2/3), 33–44.

Lawton, J., & Gerschner, J. (1982). A review of literature on attitudes toward computers and computerized instruction. *Journal of Research and Development of Education, 16,* 51–55.

Lever, S., Sherrod, K., & Bransford, J. D. (in press). Computers and student attitudes toward school. *Computers in the Schools.*

Lipman, M. (1985). Thinking skills fostered by philosophy for children. In J. Segal, S. Chipman, & R. Glaser (Eds.), *Thinking and learning skills: Relating instruction to basic research (Vol. 1*, pp. 83–108). Hillsdale, NJ: Lawrence Erlbaum Associates

Maddux, C. D. (Ed.). (1985). *LOGO in the schools.* New York: Hawthorne Press.

Mann, L. (1979). *On the trail of process: A historical perspective on cognitive processes and their training.* New York: Grune & Stratton.

Nelson, W. L. (1983). Literature as a process: An approach for the gifted. *Roeper Review, 5,* 14–17.

Papert, S. (1980). *Mindstorms: Children, computers and powerful ideas.* New York: Basic Books.

Pea, R. D. (1983). *LOGO programming and problem solving.* (Tech. Rep. No. 12). New York: Bank Street College of Education, Center for Children and Technology.

Pea, R. D., & Kurland, D. M. (1983). *On the cognitive effects of learning computer programming* (Tech. Rep. No. 9). New York: Bank Street College of Education, Center for Children and Technology.

Pea, R. D., Kurland, D. M., & Hawkins, J. (1985). LOGO and the development of thinking skills. In M. Chen & W. Paisley (Eds.), *Children and microcomputers: Research on the newest medium* (pp. 193–212). Newbury Park, CA: Sage.

Segal, J. W., Chipman, S. F., & Glaser, R. (1985). *Thinking and learning skills: Relating instruction to basic research (Vol. 1).* Hillsdale, NJ: Lawrence Erlbaum Associates.

Taylor, R. (Ed.). (1980). *The computer and the school.* New York: Teachers College Press.

Tennenbaum, S. (1944). Attitudes of elementary school children to school, teachers, and classmates. *Journal of Education, 28,* 134–141.

Whimbey, A., & Lochhead, J. (1980). *Problem solving and comprehension: A short course in analytical reasoning.* Philadelphia: The Franklin Institute Press.

# 6

# *E Unum Pluribus:* Generating Alternative Designs

Elliot Soloway
James Spohrer
David Littman
*Yale University*

## ABSTRACT

This chapter identifies one critical aspect of teaching problem solving skills—teaching students to explore alternative ways of solving the same problem. In the context of designing computer programs, we show how current attempts to teach students to consider alternatives is too tied to the *product* that is the result of a problem solving episode rather than to the *process* that leads to the product. Focusing on the process, rather than the product, we illustrate how students can be encouraged to explore variability in early phases of the program design process. We suggest several heuristics that can be taught to students so that they can productively control their problem solving processes and avoid becoming locked into a single approach.

137

## INTRODUCTION: MOTIVATION AND GOALS

As it is now taught, computer programming appears to have little impact on facilitating enhanced problem solving. We believe that the failure to find transfer from programming to others kinds of problem solving is due to looking for it in the wrong place. Our position is that if one views programming as really designing artifacts that serve some needs, then programming can be seen to have significant educational value. In particular, programming *qua* design fills a gap in the current curriculum: Although there is major emphasis on analysis skills, there is precious little explicit instruction in synthesis skills—design skills. This is an unfortunate weakness: In their everyday lives, people are constantly constructing artifacts that help them achieve their goals, for example, constructing travel plans, constructing financial plans, constructing a sandbox or a backyard swingset.

Given that we want to teach students good design principles, and given that programming is an excellent medium in which to carry out this instruction—views for which we argue at length (see Soloway, in press)—in this chapter, we focus on one design principle that is particularly important: It is important that students learn that there are multiple ways to construct an artifact, that is to say, there is more than one right answer. A good artifact is not one which simply "works." Rather, there are better and worse artifacts. For example, one evaluates an artifact in terms of numerous criteria (e.g., how effective is it?). How easy it is to change? How easy is it to build? Typically, one artifact won't meet all the desiderata, and thus one *must* have alternatives from which to choose. Besides its effect on the current artifact, generating alternatives has a long-term effect: It helps one to better understand the particular problem under consideration as well as the class of similar problems, and in turn, it helps one to better understand the space of solutions to that problem class. Because people tend to be faced with similar problems, this long-term effect can be quite beneficial.

If teaching students to develop alternative solutions is a good idea, how does that square with what is being taught in programming classes? First, students are dismayed when they do not get full credit for a program that "runs," that is, computes the specified values. They do not view a program as they would an essay—as an entity for which there is no one right answer. Second, this view is fostered by the textbooks themselves: They either emphasize efficiency as a criteria for a good program (which is silly given the speed of today's computers and the tinyness of students' programs) or they provide excellent examples of nonprincipled, inappropriate variation, for example, the use one construct to mimic another. Thus, it is no wonder that students stop when they come up with one solution: they have no good model for doing otherwise.

In this chapter then, we describe how we attempt to encourage students to generate alternative solutions—in a principled manner—to their assignments. First, however, we describe in more detail how the vast majority of current introductory programming textbooks deal with variability. Next, we introduce our five-phase strategy for developing artifacts, and then show how principled variability can be encouraged during each of the first three phases.

## HOW VARIABILITY IS CURRENTLY TAUGHT

Authors of programming textbooks want to teach "structured programming." Although this term has an elusive quality, the basic point is that no one wants to teach students to write programs with spaghetti-style control structures (e.g., indiscriminate use of GO TOs). As we argued (Soloway, Spohrer, & Littman, 1987), by focusing on structured programming, one has already missed the real point: the program is the last product of the design process; the important and creative work is done before the program is produced. Be that as it may, in trying to rid the world of idiosyncratic code, the textbooks have essentially thrown the baby out with the bath water: They invariably focus on nice, clean, straightforward "step-wise" refinements of problems into programs. Students nod their heads at every step in the transformation but don't see—because they are not shown—the myriad of design decisions that have been left out.[1] Thus, because the textbook shows that only one decomposition is needed to derive a program, students believe that they too should only need to do one decomposition.

There are instances, however, when textbooks do show *program* variability. (Again, notice the ill-advised focus on program variability.) For example, there are two classic instances when Pascal textbooks show more than one way to solve a problem. First, textbooks typically show how the WHILE construct can be used to emulate the FOR loop construct. (See Fig. 6.1.) Showing students this example results in two unfortunate outcomes: (a) Students tend to see the WHILE construct as all they need to learn and so become proficient only in the use of it, and (b) in so doing, miss the point that each looping construct corresponds to a different type of problem.

- FOR PROBLEM: When one knows the specific number of times to loop.
- WHILE PROBLEM: When one does not know the specific number of times to loop, but only knows a stopping condition, such as reading in a sentinel or stopping value, which may cause the loop to stop without being executed even once.

The point is that different looping constructs were designed for different kinds of problems. Unfortunately, by showing variability at the construct level, most

---

[1] Anderson (Pirolli & Anderson, 1984) made this same point well in discussing how proofs in geometry are taught.

```
FOR count := 1 to 10 do                count := 1;
  begin                                WHILE (count <= 10) do
    writeln('Input a number');           begin
    readln(input);                         writeln('Input a number');
    sum := sum + input;                    readln(input);
  end;                                     sum := sum + input;
                                           count := count + 1;
                                         end;
```

FIG. 6.1.   Variability at construct level: FOR versus WHILE.

```
STACKED IF-THEN:                       NESTED IF-THEN-ELSE:
if winning_player=0                    if winning_player=0
  then writeln('Draw game.');            then writeln('Draw game.')
if winning_player=1                      else if winning_player=1
  then writeln('Player 1 Wins!');          then writeln('Player 1 Wins!')
if winning_player=2                        else writeln('Player 2 Wins!');
  then writeln('Player 2 Wins!');
```

FIG. 6.2.   Variability at construct level: IF-THEN versus IF-THEN-ELSE.

standard instruction encourages students to ignore the problem-dependent aspects of the looping constructs.

Second, textbooks illustrate variability by showing the equivalence of various combinations of IF-THEN-ELSE. For example, in Fig. 6.2, we show how a nested IF-THEN-ELSE structure is equivalent to a stacked set of IF-THEN statements. What is the student supposed to learn from this variability? When is one more appropriate than the other? For example, there is little discussion of which type of structure is more readable, easier to change, and so on. Thus, students are not even given criteria to choose between the two structures. Why then do textbooks show both? What sense can students make of the two structures? All the student can ask is: Why should I learn both structures, when one is equivalent to the other? (Note this is the same argument that can be voiced about not learning the FOR and REPEAT structures, because the WHILE loop is equivalent.)[2] Note that later we argue that there is a big difference between the two formulations in Fig. 6.2. However, we introduce the differences—the variability—not at the code level, but in one of the levels in the design process.

In sum, then, the little variability that is explicitly shown in the majority of textbooks actually gives students the wrong idea of why variability is important: Textbooks focus on twiddles at the construct level. It is intriguing to note that similar observations of low-level variation have been seen in essay writing: Bereiter and Scardamalia (1982) observed that students rewriting essays tend to make only local changes to their original drafts, focusing on word changes or

---

[2]This sort of argument can degenerate into saying: Well, Bohm-Jacopini showed that we need only three primitive control structures to emulate all the others, so why not simply learn those three.

sentence rewrites, but rarely modifying the global structure of the essay. In what follows, we try to show how to introduce the notion of variability at an earlier—more productive—point in the design process.

## VARIABILITY IN NOVICE PROGRAMMER PROBLEM SOLVING

The problem with construct-based variability is that it does not require the students to think about the problem in "radically" different ways. A student who generates an initially "poor" solution will be able only to produce minor perturbations of the solution using different constructs. Assuming that students would be able to recognize a "better" solution if they were presented with it, the problem becomes one of helping students break out of a local search to perform a more global search (a view not uncommon in some popular guides to better problem-solving, e.g., Adams, 1979; Gardner, 1978; Polya, 1973).

What can be done to help novices break out of the local searches and generate more global types of variability so that they may, in fact, be able to generate "better" solutions? The answer lies in two main skills:

- *Solution Evaluation Skills*. Novices need better evaluation skills so that they can better characterize and differentiate "poor" solutions from "better" solutions.
- *Variability Exploration Skills*. Novices need to understand the sources of variability that precede simply twiddling with language constructs, for the ability to generate "radically" different solutions resides lies in the skill of exploring alternatives in those earlier problem-solving phases where

Due to space limitations, we focus on this latter point in the remainder of this chapter and only touch on the former. In the next section we describe some of the earlier problem-solving phases and what kinds of variability novices should be encouraged to explore.

### Phases in the Novice Program Generation Process

When we teach introductory "programming," which we have done now for 5 years, we tell the students that there are five phases in developing a design artifact–or program:

- *Phase 1: Understand problem specification.* The goal here is simply to understand what the problem is asking for. Two heuristics that are helpful for understanding the problem are: (a) try concrete cases, and (b) simplify the problem.

- *Phase 2: Decompose problem into programmable goals and objects.* During this phase, the objective is to "lay the components of the solution on the table," that is, *decompose* the problem and *identify* the solution components. By components we mean three types of entities:

  *Goals.* These are the objectives specified in the problem specification.

  *Plans.* These are the methods by which the goals are achieved. One of the objectives of the course is to have the students build a library of stored routines, or plans, that they can use when solving new problems (Rich, 1981; Soloway, 1986; Soloway & Ehrlich, 1984).

  *Objects.* These are the pieces of data that will go into the solution. For example, there are simple data objects (e.g., a counter) and there are more complex data objects, for example, a series of games composed of individual games, which are in turn composed of individual player moves.
- *Phase 3: Select and compose plans to solve problems.* During this phase the pieces of the solution are woven together, that is, the components are composed to form a working whole (see Fig. 6.3).
- *Phase 4: Implement plans in language constructs.* During this phase, one actually instantiates the plans in some programming language.
- *Phase 5: Reflect—Evaluate final artifact and overall design process.* When all is said and done, a good strategy is to look back over what has been done and learn from both the successes and failures.

Initially, we suggest that these five phases occur one after the other. However, as the problems the students tackle become more complex, we point out that in fact these phases are really "activities" and that there may be (will be!) some jumping around—back and forth. We recognize that (a) these stages do not accord with the standard step-wise refinement paradigm (Soloway et al., 1987 laid out the differences in detail) and (b) that jumping around is not supposed to be done (Adelson & Soloway, 1985). However, in our studies with expert software

## ROCK-PAPER-SCISSORS PROBLEM

Rock-Paper-Scissors is a two player game. Each player simultaneously makes one of three possible gestures, signifying either rock, paper, or scissors. The winner is determined by the following rules:

1. paper covers rock → paper wins
2. scissors cut paper → scissors win
3. rock breaks scissors → rock wins
4. same gesture → draw

Write a program that takes as input the two players' gestures and determines who the winning player is, player 1, player 2, or neither. The input should be encoded as follows: 1=rock, 2=paper, 3=scissors. Your program should also ask for how many games to play and then play that many games, keeping track of the number of player 1 wins, player 2 wins, and draws. Print out the over-all results after all games have been played.

FIG. 6.3.   The Rock-Paper-Scissors (RPS) Problem.

designers, for example, they did carry out these five activities and they did jump around. Nonetheless, we recognize that our prescriptions for design are a fiction; however, we feel they are much less a fiction than those promulgated continually in introductory textbooks on programming.

In the following section we describe how variability can be introduced during the first three phases of the design process.

## Introducing Variation During Phase I: Understand Problem Specification

The first step in understanding the problem specification is to develop an initial characterization. An initial characterization of a problem is the knowledge that results from an initial reading of a problem specification. An initial characterization might determine what the general type of problem is, what major goals must be solved, possible "danger issues" to take into account, what looks easy/familiar, what looks hard/novel, and so on. Note that the skills that are called upon to build the initial characterization can be totally decoupled from programming, and therefore should be useful for all sorts of other design problems.

Variability can enter the design process during the initial characterization phase. For example, consider the problem specification for the Rock–Paper–Scissors (RPS) Problem shown in Fig. 6.3, and the following two possible characterizations, depicted graphically in Fig. 6.4.

- The "Rules" Characterization: The first approach characterizes the game in terms of four *rules* and appears to be a simple restatement of the rules provided in the problem specification. The rules identify relationships between pairs of gestures made by players and the winning gesture.
- The "Payoff Matrix" Characterization: The second approach characterizes the game in terms of a *payoff matrix*. A payoff matrix is a specific form of a more general representation—a *table* that captures the relationship between different objects' values in a systematic set of rows and columns. Thus, the payoff matrix for Rock–Paper–Scissors captures the relationship between the two players' gestures and who the winning player is.

Verbal rules (Chaiklin, 1984) and payoff matrices are just two of the many *representational devices* novices can use in characterizing a problem. Another representational device would be a *graph* showing the three possible gestures arranged in a circle and connected by arrows indicating the cyclic dominance of successive gestures. Thus, one source of variation in characterizing the problem is in the choice of representational device, such as rules, payoff matrices, tables, or graphs.

```
-------------------------------------------------------------------------
THE ''RULES'' CHARACTERIZATION

1. IF the two gestures are paper and rock, THEN the winning gesture is paper.
2. IF the two gestures are scissors and paper, THEN the winning gesture is scissors.
3. IF the two gestures are rock and scissors, THEN the winning gesture is rock.
4. IF the two gestures are the same, THEN neither gesture wins.

ENCODED RULES
1. IF the two gestures are 2 and 1, THEN 2 wins.
2. IF the two gestures are 3 and 2, THEN 3 wins.
3. IF the two gestures are 1 and 3, THEN 1 wins.
4. IF the two gestures are the same, THEN neither gestures wins.

   OBJECT:GESTURE                    OBJECT:WINNING-GESTURE
 1 = rock is the gesture          0 = neither gesture wins
 2 = paper is the gesture         1 = rock is winning gesture
 3 = scissors is the gesture      2 = paper is winning gesture
                                  3 = scissors is winning gesture
-------------------------------------------------------------------------
THE ''PAYOFF MATRIX'' CHARACTERIZATION


                                                  ENCODED PAYOFF MATRIX
                      PLAYER2                      PLAYER2'S GESTURE
              rock      paper    scissors           1        2        3
            +---------+---------+---------+    P  +---------+---------+---------+
  P   rock  | Draw    | Player2 | Player1 |    L G 1 |   0   |    2    |    1    |
  L         |         | Wins    | Wins    |    A E   |       |         |         |
  A         +---------+---------+---------+    Y S +---------+---------+---------+
  Y   paper | Player1 | Draw    | Player2 |    E T 2 |   1   |    0    |    2    |
  E         | Wins    |         | Wins    |    R U   |       |         |         |
  R         +---------+---------+---------+    1 R +---------+---------+---------+
  1 scissors| Player2 | Player1 | Draw    |    ' E 3 |   2   |    1    |    0    |
            | Wins    | Wins    |         |    S     |       |         |         |
            +---------+---------+---------+      +---------+---------+---------+


     OBJECT:GESTURE                OBJECT:WINNING-PLAYER
 1 = rock is gesture          0 = draw, no player wins
 2 = paper is gesture         1 = player1 is the winning player
 3 = scissors is gesture      2 = player2 is the winning player
-------------------------------------------------------------------------
```

Figure 4: Two alternative characterizations of the Rock-Paper-Scissors Problem.

FIG. 6.4.   Two alternative characterizations of the Rock-Paper-Scissors Problem.

The important point about these alternative characterizations is that each may lead to "radically" different solutions to the problem of determining the winner. For instance, the first characterization uses rules that lend themselves naturally to implementation via a sequence of IF-THEN constructs. However, in the second characterization, after encoding both the players' gestures and the three possible outcomes in a payoff matrix, one might try to devise a mathematical formula to implement the particular numeric relationship (e.g., winning-player := (gesture1 = gesture2 + 3) mod 3;). In our terminology, the problem of determining the winner is a *goal* of the RPS problem, and the two alternative solutions are called *plans:* A sequence of IF-THEN constructs is a *selection plan*, and a mathematical formula is a *formula plan*. Goals correspond to what must be done, and plans correspond to how it will be done. These observations give rise to our first heuristic for helping novices generate globally different solutions to design problems:

- *Variability heuristic 1.* Instruct students to explore alternative characterizations by using different representational devices, such as rules, tables, payoff matrices, and graphs.

Each representational device, along with the way in which it encodes values, may lend itself to a different type of plan—we have just seen rules leading to a selection plan and a payoff matrix leading to a mathematical formula plan.

Even a novice who knows how to generate alternative characterizations might stop after generating the first. Unless they are explicitly instructed in the value of, and simple methods for, generating alternative characterizations, novices will typically use the first characterization that comes to mind. Usually, the problem specification biases most novices toward a particular characterization (i.e., rules in the case of RPS), even though an alternative characterization that might lead to a "better" solution is just lurking around the corner. Of course, the alternative characterization might lead to a "worse" solution, but even then it would be an opportunity for the novices to improve their plan evaluation and differentiation skills. For instance, in the case of rules versus payoff matrix for RPS, students might be encouraged to generate observations like:

- The payoff matrix characterization leads to a formula plan that is very concise, but may be hard to understand because it is so concise.
- The rules characterization leads to a less concise selection plan, but it may be easier to understand because it is similar to our common-sense intuitions about how people actually play the game.

Thus, this example illustrates that, well before they begin to generate programs, students should be confronted with the necessity and desirability of generating alternative characterizations. In addition, the example shows that generating alternative characterizations puts the student in a position to make informed judgments in identifying the advantages and disadvantages of alternative plans. As we see in the next section, variability does not stop with the initial characterization.

## Introducing Variation During Phase II:
## Decompose Problem into Programmable Goals and Objects

Once a student has decided on an initial characterization of the problem, the initial characterization must be reformulated into a set of goals and subgoals whose form is appropriate for writing computer programs. Although students solving the RPS problem can initially characterize some goals in ways that can be programmed directly (e.g., a goal to get information from the user is specified as Readln(UserInput), other goals must be carefully analyzed before appropriate programming plans can be associated with them. We call this process of analyzing goals "specifying" them, and it is at the heart of the problem decomposition phase. This further specification that occurs during decomposition entails such activities as inferring implicit goals and identifying intermediate results that may have to be computed on the way to a final answer. These decomposition activities must be carried out before a student has the right kind of information to begin designing a program.

Like the initial problem characterization phase, problem decomposition also leads to variation. To continue our example of the RPS game, there are two distinct ways to solve the problem given an initial understanding in terms of rules, rather than in terms of a payoff matrix:

- The "INDIRECT" Decomposition: In the indirect decomposition, the student reasons about how he or she would keep score in a game played by two friends. Thus, the student reasons introspectively about common-sense knowledge to determine that he or she would (a) see each player make a gesture, (b) identify one of the two gestures as the winning gesture (or note that there was a tie), and (c) then finally, "connect up" the winning gesture with the winning player. Connecting up the winning gesture with the winning player is easy in real life: You just look up to see to whom the hand with the winning gesture is attached. The big problem in programming RPS using the rules provided in the specification is, however, just this—connecting up the winning gesture with the player. To do so the student creates an intermediate result, the "winning gesture." With the winning gesture in hand, the student then needs a way of tracing it back to the player who made it. As Fig. 6.5 shows, the student has constructed a selection plan that uses the fact that gesture1 was made by player1 and gesture2 was made by player2 to decide who made the winning gesture.
- The "DIRECT" Decomposition: In the direct decomposition, the student is motivated to use rules that directly determine the winning player. Thus, the student does not use the intermediate step of determining the winning gesture. Instead, the student exhaustively enumerates all of the nine possible games using a nine-way selection plan (as shown in Fig. 6.5) and "hard-wires" in which player wins each of the nine games.

Thus, as this example shows, variability enters into the programming process at the stage of problem decomposition; such variability is not at all trivial. As we have seen, the alternative decompositions result in "radically" different solutions to the problem.

Teaching students the methods for seeking alternative decompositions helps students avoid the trap of "going with the first obvious solution." Thus, our second heuristic for helping novices generate different solutions is:

- *Variability heuristic 2*. Instruct students in exploring alternative ways of decomposing problems. Common-sense plans provide one source of knowledge about decomposing problems. Introspecting on the nature of the

```
--------------------------------------------------------------------------
THE ''INDIRECT'' DECOMPOSITION (VIA WINNING_GESTURE)

if gesture1=gesture2 then winning_gesture:=0;
if ((gesture1=1) and (gesture2=3)) or
   ((gesture1=3) and (gesture2=1)) then winning_gesture:=1;
if ((gesture1=1) and (gesture2=2)) or
   ((gesture1=2) and (gesture2=1)) then winning_gesture:=2;
if ((gesture1=2) and (gesture2=3)) or
   ((gesture1=3) and (gesture2=2)) then winning_gesture:=3;

if winning_gesture=0 then winning_player:=0;
if winning_gesture=gesture1 then winning_player:=1;
if winning_gesture=gesture2 then winning_player:=2;
--------------------------------------------------------------------------
THE ''DIRECT'' DECOMPOSITION

if (gesture1=1) and (gesture2=1) then winning_player:=0;
if (gesture1=1) and (gesture2=2) then winning_player:=2;
if (gesture1=1) and (gesture2=3) then winning_player:=1;
if (gesture1=2) and (gesture2=1) then winning_player:=1;
if (gesture1=2) and (gesture2=2) then winning_player:=0;
if (gesture1=2) and (gesture2=3) then winning_player:=2;
if (gesture1=3) and (gesture2=1) then winning_player:=2;
if (gesture1=3) and (gesture2=2) then winning_player:=1;
if (gesture1=3) and (gesture2=3) then winning_player:=0;
--------------------------------------------------------------------------
```

FIG. 6.5.   Two decompositions of the rule-based characterization for Rock-Paper-Scissors.

subgoals in common-sense plans, which can help identify intermediate steps that may or may not be part of the final solution, highlights differences among direct and indirect decompositions.[3]

In addition, we would like students to actively evaluate the relative merits of their alternative decompositions. They should be taught skills so that they can generate observations like:

- The "indirect" decomposition has the advantage of being a straightforward implementation of the rules mentioned in the specification and may also be easier to understand, because it is similar to the common-sense notion of how the winning player is determined in real-life play.
- The "direct" decomposition has the advantage of being a single plan made up of nine very similar subgoals. The ordering of the nine possible games makes it easier to verify that no possibility has been left out, and no unforeseen interactions will occur between the subcomponents.

---

[3]A more detailed theory of alternative decomposition and why novices generate them can be found in (Spohrer, 1987).

In sum, the phase of problem decomposition leads to variability just as phase of problem understanding does.

### Introducing Variation During Phase III:
### Select and Compose Plans to Solve Problem

After characterizing a problem and settling on a particular decomposition, the student must select plans to achieve the goals and compose the plans. In this section, we can only sketch out (due to space limitations) how variability is introduced via the four methods for composing plans (Soloway 1986; Soloway et al., 1987):

- ABUTTING: One plan after another in a simple linear sequence.
- NESTING: One plan inside (or around) another plan.
- INTERLEAVING: Two plans with multiple subgoals are "shuffled" together so that the ordering of the subgoals is alternated.
- MERGING: Instead of duplicating similar subgoals, a single integrated plan shares whatever is in common between them.

Four plan compositions for RPS are shown in Fig. 6.6 and described below:

- ABUTTED PLANS: Two plans are abutted—the first plan prints out who the winning player is, and the second plan updates the appropriate counter.
- NESTED PLANS: The plan to print out the winning player and the plan to update the counters are still abutted, but the subgoals within these two plans are now nested.
- INTERLEAVED PLANS: This is like the first composition (abutted), except that the plan to print out the winning player and the plan to update the appropriate counter have been interleaved. Interleaving the plans results in three sections of code that correspond to the three possible outcomes of a game.
- MERGED PLANS: Similar to the interleaved, except the common conditionals have been merged.

If students are aware of the space of alternative composition methods, they can explore many more plan compositions. This observation gives rise to our third heuristic for helping novices generate globally different solutions to design problems:

- *Variability heuristic 3.* Instruct students in exploring the use of alternative composition methods, such as abutting, nesting, interleaving, and merging.

In addition, evaluating the four alternative compositions might lead to observations like:

- Abutting the plans that output and count the outcome of each game highlights these two goals but spatially separates the three possible outcomes: draw, player1 wins, or player2 wins.
- Nesting the subgoals eliminates the need for the final condition in each case, but requires that the three possible values of winning-player be mutually exclusive and exhaustive possibilities. Run-time efficiency is not

```
------------------------------------------------------------------------------
THE ''ABUTTED'' COMPOSITION

if winning_player=0 then writeln('Draw game; neither player wins.');
if winning_player=1 then writeln('Player 1 Wins!');
if winning_player=2 then writeln('Player 2 Wins!');

if winning_player=0 then draw_counter:=draw_counter+1;
if winning_player=1 then player1_win_counter:=player1_win_counter+1;
if winning_player=2 then player2_win_counter:=player2_win_counter+1;
------------------------------------------------------------------------------
THE ''NESTED'' COMPOSITION

if winning_player=0
   then writeln('Draw game; neither player wins.')
   else if winning_player=1
           then writeln('Player 1 Wins!')
           else writeln('Player 2 Wins!');

if winning_player=0
   then draw_counter:=draw_counter+1
   else if winning_player=1
           then player1_win_counter:=player1_win_counter+1
           else player2_win_counter:=player2_win_counter+1;
------------------------------------------------------------------------------
THE ''INTERLEAVED'' COMPOSITION

if winning_player=0 then writeln('Draw game; neither player wins.');
if winning_player=0 then draw_counter:=draw_counter+1;

if winning_player=1 then writeln('Player 1 Wins!');
if winning_player=1 then player1_win_counter:=player1_win_counter+1;

if winning_player=2 then writeln('Player 2 Wins!');
if winning_player=2 then player2_win_counter:=player2_win_counter+1;
------------------------------------------------------------------------------
THE ''MERGED'' COMPOSITION

if winning_player=0  then begin
                          writeln('Draw game; neither player wins.');
                          draw_counter:=draw_counter+1;
                          end;
if winning_player=1  then begin
                          writeln('Player 1 Wins!');
                          player1_win_counter:=player1_win_counter+1;
                          end;
if winning_player=2  then begin
                          writeln('Player 2 Wins!');
                          player2_win_counter:=player2_win_counter+1;
                          end;
------------------------------------------------------------------------------
```

FIG. 6.6.  Four compositions of plans for the Rock-Paper-Scissors Problem.

an issue in this short interactive program, but in larger programs nesting would be more run-time efficient than abutting. Nesting seems less readable than abutting in this case.

- Interleaving the plans for output and count for each of the three outcomes highlights the three possible outcomes, but highlights without taking advantage of the possible sharing that can occur.
- Merging the plans that output and count the winner for each of the three possible outcomes is more concise than the other compositions.

In sum, exploring alternative compositions may help novices break out of local search and find globally "better" solutions.

## CONCLUDING REMARKS

We have put forth the argument that we should encourage students to explore variations in the design process because it is a good design principle. To this end we have suggested three heuristics that should be taught explicitly, heuristics which we have collected in Fig. 6.7. For example, the first heuristic is designed to help students explore variability during the phase of problem understanding. This heuristic, which is stated in the WHAT portion of the first column of the figure, is intended to help students explore alternative representational devices— we argued earlier that alternative representational devices were a useful basis for variation in problem understanding. In the HOW portion of the first column we have indicated four steps that might be taught to students to help them explore the use of alternative representational devices during problem understanding. The remaining two heuristics are presented in a similar manner in the table.

Although the principle of exploring variation, and the associated heuristics, can be taught in other design domains (e.g., English composition) programming is a particularly good vehicle for instruction for the following reason: There is a formal target language (the programming language), and there are formalizable intermediate languages (goals, plans, and objects) that can be made explicit. These explicit languages provide a concreteness to the notions of design activities and of variability that are not nearly as evident in more amorphous domains such as English composition.[4]

Realistically, can we teach students to generate alternative solutions? For starters, textbooks would need to double or triple in size in order to explain the alternatives. Moreover, there is no way to cover all the topics (language con-

---

[4]We really need a computer-based design environment that supports all the design activities and that give first-class status to the intermediate languages; see BRIDGE (Bonar, 1987), KBEmacs (Rich, 1981; Waters, 1985) for first steps in that direction.

| PHASE I | PHASE II | PHASE III |
|---|---|---|
| UNDERSTAND | DECOMPOSE | COMPOSE |
| WHAT: | WHAT: | WHAT: |
| To explore alternative Representational Devices (RDs), e.g, Rules, Tables. | To explore both direct and indirect ways to decompose problems. | To explore the four methods of composing plans. |
| HOW: | HOW: | HOW: |
| 1. Recognize RD implicit in specification. | 1. Consider several commonsense plans. | 1. Note composition methods in generated solution. |
| 2. Select alternative from stock of RDs. | 2. Identify intermediate steps in commonsense plans. | 2. Attempt to compose plans with other methods. |
| 3. Rewrite specification to use each RD. | 3. Include intermediate steps in decomposition. | 3. Note changes needed to use other methods. |
| 4. Evaluate advantages and disadvantages of each RD. | 4. Evaluate advantages and disadvantages of including steps. | 4. Evaluate advantages and disadvantages of changes. |

FIG. 6.7.   Summary of three heuristics for generating variability.

structs!) normally covered in an introductory programming course *and* teach variability, all in a single semester. The next question to ask is: How can we assess whether students are learning something and whether that learning transfers? It is extremely problematic to grade exams and homework where the student's task is to show variability in their designs: What are the criteria? And transfer, well that one is even more problematical.

The cognitive science approach to education is a heady enterprise; researchers and practitioners feel that they are truly breaking new ground and they can make a difference in education. Thus, these worries should be treated as new mountains to climb and should not hold back our efforts at exploring what really counts as expertise and what ways there might be for teaching it.

## ACKNOWLEDGMENTS

This work was sponsored by the National Science Foundation under grants MDR-8751361 and IST-8505019.

# REFERENCES

Adams, J. L. (1979). *Conceptual Blockbusting: A guide to better ideas.* Norton: New York.

Adelson, B., & Soloway, E. (1985, November). The role of domain experience in software design. *IEEE Transactions on Software Engineering, SE-11(11)1351–1360.*

Bereiter, C., & Scardamalia, M. (1982). From conversation to composition: The role of instruction in a developmental process. In R. Glaser (Ed.), *Advances in instructional psychology* (Vol. 2). Hillsdale, NJ: Lawrence Erlbaum Associates.

Bonar, J. (1987). *BRIDGE: A programming environment for novice programmers.* Unpublished manuscript.

Chaiklin, S. (1984). On the nature of verbal rules and their role in problem solving. *Cognitive Science, 8,* 131–155.

Gardner, M. (1978). *Aha! Aha! Insight.* New York: Scientific American.

Pirolli, P. L., & Anderson, J. R. (1984). The role of learning from examples in the acquisition of recursive programming skills. *Canadian Journal of Psychology, 39(2),* 240–272.

Polya, G. (1973). *How to solve it: A new aspect of mathematical method.* Princeton, NJ: Princeton University Press.

Rich, C. (1981). *Inspection methods in programming* (Report No. AI-TR-604). Cambridge, MA: MIT AI Lab.

Soloway, E., & Ehrlich, K. (1984, September). Empirical studies of programming knowledge. *IEEE Transactions on Software Engineering, 10(5),* 595–609

Soloway, E. (1986). Learning to program—learning to construct mechanisms and explanations. *Communications of the ACM, 29(9),* September.

Soloway, E. (in press). It's 2020: Do you know what your children are learning in programming class? In R. Nickerson & P. Zodiahtes (Eds.), *Technology in education: Looking toward 2020.* Hillsdale, NJ: Lawrence Erlbaum Associates.

Soloway, E., Spohrer, J. C., & Littman, D. (1987). *There's more to understanding step-wise refinement than what they taught you in school.* Unpublished manuscript.

Spohrer, J. C. (1987). *A generative theory of the bugs and plan variations produced by novice programmers.* Unpublished doctoral dissertation.

Waters, R. (1985). *KBEmacs: A step towards the Programmer's Apprentice* (Report No. AI-TR-753). Cambridge, MA: MIT AI Lab.

# 7

# Instructional Strategies
# for the Problems
# of Novice Programmers

D. N. Perkins
Steve Schwartz
Rebecca Simmons
*Educational Technology Center*
*Harvard Graduate School of Education*

## ABSTRACT

This chapter addresses major pedagogical concerns in computer programming instruction. The authors identify three sources of difficulty common to many novice programmers: (1) a "fragile knowledge" of the domain, (2) a notable shortfall in elementary problem-solving strategies, and (3) attitudinal problems of confidence and control. The authors then discuss a "metacourse" designed to address these programming difficulties. The metacourse intervention consists of a series of lessons that supplements a teacher's BASIC introductory curriculum, introducing a set of problem-solving strategies as well as a visual model of the computer. Results from a recent experiment indicate a substantial positive effect of the metacourse on programming performance of beginning BASIC students. Treatment groups outperformed control groups in all major categories, including simple commands, hand execution, debugging, and program production. A measure of general cognitive skills transfer was administered with less promising results. Implications for future programming instruction are discussed.

## INTRODUCTION

What makes something hard to learn, and what can we do about it? Those two questions arise again and again for particular subject matters and parts of subject matters. For example, precise use of English syntax or the writing of a well-organized essay are chronic trouble spots in the language arts. The understanding of fractions or the solving of algebra word problems are enterprises that confuse generation after generation of students. But it is by no means the case that most children find most of English or mathematics unmanageable. On the contrary, the larger part of the school population muddles through elementary English and math well enough.

Now imagine a subject matter that is almost all "trouble spot." Most students do not muddle through this subject matter "well enough." On the contrary, the larger portion of students soon evince discouragingly limited understanding. We might wonder whether the subject matter really belongs in the curriculum, what students' poor performance says about their intellectual abilities, or what the shortfall indicates about the effectiveness of a system of education that cannot deliver this subject matter effectively. In moments of lesser dismay and greater curiosity, we might even ask again those key questions: What makes this subject matter so hard to learn, and what can we do about it?

There is no reason to play out this scenario in the abstract. Elementary instruction in programming does not fall so very far from the profile sketched here. Considerable research has shown that most students at the elementary and high-school levels do not attain anything like the level of competence one would hope for from a semester or more of instruction in LOGO or BASIC (Kurland,

Pea, Clement, & Mawby, 1986; Linn, 1985; Pea & Kurland, 1984a, 1984b). Students with a semester or more of instruction often display remarkable naivete about the language that they have been studying and often prove unable to manage dismayingly simple programming problems.

One answer is that programming is not so hard to learn, but in general is not well taught. If only teachers gained better mastery of programming themselves and taught it with the same competence they exercise in other subject areas, better results would ensue. We have argued, on the contrary, that programming presents special challenges not found in most school subjects as typically taught (Perkins, Farady et al., 1986; Perkins, Hancock, Hobbs, Martin, & Simmons, 1986; Perkins & Martin, 1986; Perkins, Martin, & Farady, 1986). Moreover, we have urged that other school subjects *should* be taught so as to pose challenges akin to those of programming.

In particular, in contrast to most other subjects, programming is problem-solving intensive. It requires the ability to break a given task down into sub-components that allow programming solutions, as well as the ability to compose the proper code for those subcomponents. This often involves formulating patterns of code for which the programmer has no direct precedent. Moreover, the process of debugging asks the programmer to diagnose and repair often obscure difficulties in the program, a task that plainly requires sophisticated problem-solving skills. To be sure, other school subjects, perhaps most notably mathematics, pose such demands from time to time, but most are not nearly as persistently demanding as programming.

Besides being problem-solving intensive, programming also is precision intensive. More so than most other school subjects, it calls for an extraordinarily high degree of precision in order to obtain a relatively modest degree of success. Contrast a spelling test in which 90% of the words are spelled correctly with a computer program in which 90% of the statements are coded correctly. In the former case, the student will probably receive an A; in the latter, the program is not going to do anything like what it is supposed to do, and an A is out of the question. Furthermore, the 10% shortfall in the program may introduce several interacting errors that will make the debugging process exceedingly demanding and frustrating, so that achieving a workable program becomes a difficult task indeed.

The problem-solving intensive and precision-intensive nature of programming offers a broad first-order understanding of what makes programming hard to learn. In search of a more precise characterization of students' difficulties, the programming group at the Educational Technology Center of the Harvard Graduate School of Education has conducted a series of clinical studies examining the thinking of elementary school and high school novice programmers as they work. A review of these studies follows. As to the second question, "What can we do about it," the greater part of this article describes an instructional approach we are developing based on our analysis of the nature of the difficulties, an approach that may enhance students' learning of programming. Generalized, the approach may also enhance students' learning of other subjects when they are taught in a more substantive problem-solving and precision-intensive way. Some empirical results on the effectiveness of this approach are outlined.

The concluding section turns to a third question, "Why bother?" That is, given the considerable challenges of learning to program, what cognitive impact can we reasonably expect upon students of programming that makes instruction worth the trouble? The discussion examines such potential benefits as practical programming skills, general cognitive skills, and understanding of a society in which information processing plays a major role. An argument is advanced that these somewhat different objectives invite instruction fine-tuned to their special challenges: There is no universal "good programming instruction."

## THREE CATEGORIES OF DIFFICULTY

The programming group chose to investigate students' development of programming skills using clinical methods, because we noted that most prior work in the field had employed pretest–posttest methods and felt that the contrasting clinical approach might complement what had already been done. The details of this clinical approach have been described elsewhere (Perkins, Hancock, et al., 1986; Perkins & Martin, 1986), but a few words about its broad character may be helpful. The subjects were students of LOGO in elementary school and students of BASIC in high school. The inquiries focused on the first and second semesters of instruction in programming, because it is in this period that most students encounter great difficulties and many founder entirely. The investigators worked mostly one-on-one or one-on-two with students seated at microcomputers. How did a typical clinical interview proceed? The investigator posed a programming problem to a student and observed as the student attempted to solve the problem. When the student encountered difficulties, the investigator "scaffolded" the students' efforts, providing as much guidance as proved necessary—but as little as possible—to help the student over the trouble spot (Greenfield, 1984; Rogoff & Gardner, 1984). Records were kept both of what the student did and what help the investigator provided. Both the work the student completed without help and the scaffolding the investigator offered became data for an analysis of the aspects of the programming process that the student managed well and which not so well. Besides these clinical efforts, the research team often collected more conventional posttest data on written tests of programming achievement.

The clinical interviews coupled with the posttest data provided a rich body of information allowing many sorts of analysis. We have found it heuristic to discuss results under three headings: Knowledge base, problem-solving strategies, and affect and attitude.

## Knowledge Base and the Problem of Fragile Knowledge

Mastering a computer language, of course, requires learning the primitives of the language and how to use them. Not surprisingly, the clinical research disclosed that many students of BASIC and LOGO appeared to lack knowledge of the purpose, effect, and syntax of many commands that, in fact, they had studied. However, clinical probes disclosed that one could not simply characterize the students as suffering from "missing knowledge" (Perkins, Farady et al., 1986; Perkins & Martin, 1986; Perkins, Martin, & Farady, 1986). Often the students knew more about the commands in question than they seemed to initially. For instance, sometimes they exhibited "inert knowledge" (cf. Bereiter & Scardamalia, 1985; Bransford, Franks, Vye, & Sherwood, 1986; Perfetto, Bransford, & Franks, 1983), failing to retrieve a command which, upon prompting, they could recall and apply correctly.

For example, one of the students in the study was trying to write a program to print out a square of stars (5 rows by 5 columns of asterisks) (Perkins & Martin, 1986). He had coded two nested FOR loops but his output resulted in a horizontal row of stars. He pondered his output for awhile, without success. When prompted by the experimenter with "What do you need to do," the student was able to define the next step: Make the stars into a block and then go on to solve the difficulty by inserting a blank PRINT line after the first NEXT statement to force a carriage return and make rows of stars. Here the experimenter's general prompt led the student to see through to the nature of the problem and retrieve a command that would solve it.

Students exhibited other types of fragile knowledge as well. Sometimes they mixed two commands or parts of commands up, combining them in odd ways that, nonetheless, disclosed some garbled knowledge. For example, one student attempted to print a row of 5 stars in a horizontal row by writing the statement, PRINT 5 "*". Students were also seen to compose plausible but incorrect commands and failed to hand-execute them with a mental model of the machine in mind, either lacking or neglecting to evoke such a model. Such problems constituted a sizable portion of their knowledge-base difficulties.

With these sorts of problems in mind, one might characterize the students' difficulties as a matter of "fragile knowledge," rather than just missing knowledge (Perkins & Martin, 1986; Perkins, Martin, & Farady, 1986). The notion of fragile knowledge has theoretical interest because it emphasizes that students' behavior cannot be accounted for simply as a matter of missing knowledge: Half-knowing something is not just a state of knowing half of it, but something considerably more complex. The notion of fragile knowledge has instructional importance because it suggests instructional remedies quite different from those that would suit simply missing knowledge. Missing knowledge alone urges more review, perhaps with drill and practice to consolidate the knowledge base. In the case of fragile knowledge, the students have knowledge to work with and build upon. An integrative mental model of the computer should allow students to check better tentative responses founded on a fragile knowledge base about particular commands, as well as to learn commands with more precision. Stronger retrieval strategies should allow students to accomplish much more with a fragile knowledge base even as they extend it. This introduces the next theme.

## Problem-Solving Strategies and Strategic Shortfall

The clinical investigations also suggested that many students of programming suffer from a shortfall in elementary problem-solving strategies. They fail to prompt themselves with such queries as, "What do I want this line of code to do," "Do I know a command that does that sort of thing," or "Exactly what does the line of code I just wrote do, if I hand-execute it?" What suggests that such self-prompts may be helpful? When provided by an experimenter, they often allowed students to resolve difficulties and proceed with the programming task (Perkins & Martin, 1986; Perkins, Martin, & Farady, 1986). Note that such prompts do not reflect any special knowledge the experimenter might have of the particular nature of the subject's difficulty at the moment. All are prompts that students in principle might give themselves.

For example, in the square of stars problem described previously (Perkins & Martin, 1986), after a student indicated a need to repeat a row of stars the desired number of times, but was unable to proceed from there, the prompt, "Do you know a command for repeating?" often helped the student to get back on track (Perkins & Martin, 1986). Although other research suggests that problem solving benefits from a sophisticated heuristic repertoire (e.g., Schoenfeld, 1982; Schoenfeld & Herrmann, 1982), it is interesting in these studies of young programmers to discover what appears to be a need for some quite elementary heuristics of problem management.

## Affect and Attitude:
## Problems of Confidence and Control

The clinical research also disclosed problems of confidence and control in systematically pursuing programming problems. We identified a "stopper-mover" continuum, characterizing some students as "stoppers," because they would disengage from a programming task at the first sign of difficulty, and other students at the opposite extreme as "movers," because no matter what the tangle, they would keep trying to work toward a solution (Perkins, Hancock et al., 1986). Interestingly, stoppers were not necessarily especially inept nor movers especially able. With some encouragement, a student who seemed to be a stopper often could solve the problem.

Consider, for example, a student who tended to leave a current problem and go onto the next, without making an effort to understand what was wrong

(Perkins, Hancock, et. al., 1986). While running a program that used array subscripts, he received the error message, "subscript out of range." He paused for a few seconds and then, without a word, began to look at the next problem. The researcher stopped him and asked him what he thought the error message meant, to which he responded that he didn't know. However, when pressed for an answer, he thought for a moment and then said that maybe the number in the parentheses neeeded to be smaller. Once prompted, he tried this idea out at the computer, and the program ran without error. This student then continued on his own initiative to test various values until he had established the appropriate range.

In contrast, with this "stopper," some students moved along continuously. But these "movers" often proceeded in a haphazard way. For instance, often "movers" would try some simple fix, and when it did not work, leave the changed code in place, adding yet another misconceived repair. The program would soon become a maze of useless modifications. In a sense, these haphazard movers, like stoppers, were not genuinely engaging the problem, but rather proceeding in an extreme trial-and-error fashion that evaded any genuine intellectual confrontation with the difficulties presented by the program. Such patterns of behavior may relate to tacit models of learning and one's efficacy as a learner held by many students (Dweck & Bempechat, 1980; Dweck & Licht, 1980; Zelman, 1985).

## A "METACOURSE" FOR ENHANCING THE LEARNING OF PROGRAMMING

With the difficulties faced by young programmers somewhat clarified, it seemed reasonable to investigate instructional interventions that might help students to cope better with the demands of learning to program. Accordingly, the research team constructed and tested a "metacourse" for students in the first semester of the study of BASIC; a second-generation version of the metacourse is currently under development. The metacourse consists of nine lessons formulated to equip the students with thinking and learning heuristics specialized to learning programming (i.e., heuristics designed to moderate the problem of fragile knowledge), provide some elementary problem-solving strategies, and encourage systematic engagement with programming problems. For example, the metacourse provides students with a better mental model of the computer, a systematic approach to breaking problems down, and a systematic framework for learning new commands.

Teachers receive the lessons in written form. Each lesson contains an introductory page that lists pertinent organizing information for the teacher such as prerequisites for the lesson, new vocabulary, lesson objectives, target performances, and approach of the lesson. The body of the lesson is presented in a scripted format that the teacher is encouraged to follow fairly closely, making adjustments for personal style and student level. The focus is on whole group presentation and discussion, though some of the activities are geared toward individual or small group work. The lessons also include optional prepared overheads for teacher use and worksheets for the students. The lessons are taught periodically, once every week or two, as the students advance through their regular BASIC curriculum. The metacourse can be interpolated into any conventional first-semester program of instruction in BASIC.

The sections that follow detail the design of the metacourse and discuss empirical results. Here, by way of introduction, several fundamental questions about the notion of a metacourse as an investigative and educational endeavor are addressed.

## Why Focus on BASIC?

It is natural to think twice about organizing educational experiments around BASIC, a language much criticized for not fostering structured programming and other inadequacies. However, upon careful consideration, a number of factors emerge that make BASIC an attractive choice. Most practically speaking, investigations such as the present one call for wide-scale testing, and BASIC courses are easily found in local high schools. Regarding the inadequacies of BASIC, a renaissance in BASIC is now occurring, brought on by recognition of the limitations in the classic form of the language and the introduction of several structured BASICs with extended powers; these superior BASICs are finding their way into high-school instruction even now.

This point aside, it is crucial to recognize that the many difficulties students encounter in their first forays into BASIC programming do not even reflect the structural inadequacies of the language but much simpler, indeed seemingly trivial, matters. People occasionally argue, "If only the students were learning a structured language, they would do okay." This runs contrary to the findings of the clinical investigations discussed previously and the literature on elementary programming generally, which show that many students encounter major difficulties well before programming projects become large enough for the advantages of structured programming to become prominent.

Finally, and perhaps most important of all, the choice of BASIC in the line of experimentation discussed here is an incidental convenience rather than an essential feature of the metacourse concept. A metacourse could be constructed in essentially the same spirit, and with most of the same concepts, for LOGO or Pascal, for example. If the metacourse design proves effective in enhancing BASIC instruction, it seems plausible that a similar metacourse would be equally effective with other languages.

## Why a Metacourse Instead of a Full Course?

An obvious alternative to the metacourse just outlined (and described more fully later) is to design an entire semester or even year of instruction in BASIC, incorporating the metacourse ideas. This route certainly has its attractions. The present line of investigation was developed for the metacourse idea instead for two reasons. First of all a practical constraint: Resources have not been available to design a full semester of instruction with proper attention to detail. But second and more interesting, the idea of a metacourse may represent a neglected "ecological niche" in education; the potentials of the metacourse concept consequently invite exploration.

Pursuing this notion, consider how the idea of a metacourse contrasts with other instructional interventions. Some educational development efforts design a whole course, with associated text and materials. Unfortunately, such a course typically sees only limited adoption, because substantial materials costs are entailed as well as total reorientation of the teacher to the new materials. Other educational development efforts consist mostly in in-service teacher training designed to help teachers change their patterns of interaction with students and promote more mindful instruction. This approach is notorious for yielding no real change in teacher behavior.

In contrast to both, the metacourse approach steers a middle course, providing specific materials and lessons that *concisely* address specific metacognitive and other matters that conventional instruction apears to neglect. The hope is that a metacourse would be small enough in size to minimize material costs, modest enough in scope to be readily accepted by teachers, and yet specific enough in content to have a significant impact on students. Indeed, the present development effort can be viewed as an exploration of the metacourse idea that may have significance for entirely different subject matters. For instance, one might design metacourse materials for mathematics, physics, or English at various levels with the same agenda of providing generally neglected metacognitive skills, mental models, and so on.

## In What Sense is the Metacourse a Research Effort?

It is reasonable to ask how the metacourse development relates to the clinical research already outlined and other research on novice programmers. Certainly far more laboratory and clinical research could be done to probe fundamental issues of students' understanding of programming. How do experiments in instructional design like the present one contribute, if at all? Broadly speaking, the design and testing of a metacourse may be seen as a rough test of the present theoretical analysis of students' difficulties. Taking this step, of course, implies that the existing research in our judgment has revealed enough about the character of students' difficulties to inform a thoughtful design effort; although we recognize that much remains to be filled in, we suggest that our and others' research has developed a clear picture of students' difficulties. Taking a step toward implementation also recognizes a risk of pure laboratory research: The construction of theories that explains the phenomenon from a certain perspective but gives little instructional leverage upon it. Our aim is to evolve an analysis that does both.

To be sure, the soundness of the analysis does not, strictly speaking, stand or fall with the success of the metacourse as an instructional intervention; many other factors would figure in the latter. Nonetheless, the research team is conscious of the presence of these other factors and is appraising them as part of the development and testing. Accordingly, research on the metacourse will yield a broad assessment of the merits of the underlying analysis. If the metacourse, and hence the underlying theory, proves promising, it may be appropriate to consider a finer grain of analysis.

We turn now to the details of a metacourse for enhancing the learning of programming.

## DESIGN OF THE METACOURSE

The metacourse seeks to assist students in acquiring a comprehensive model of the task of programming. Such an endeavor calls for (a) assisting students in constructing a clear mental model of the computer, (b) providing students with heuristics that can help them conceptualize and organize the constituent elements of the programming language, and (c) equipping students with tools and problem-solving strategies that will enable them to tackle the complex demands of program planning and production. Table 7.1 displays the titles and content of the metacourse lessons. Some particulars follow.

### Building a Strong Model of the Computer

We attribute students' fragile knowledge of programming in considerable part to a lack of a mental model of the computer that helps learners to encode and consolidate their knowledge of programming. The concept of a mental model is key in the design of the metacourse. The concern with helping students construct a robust mental model of the computer arises from recent work in the field of cognition (cf. Gentner & Stevens, 1983; Johnson-Laird, 1983; Mayer, 1976, 1981). In addition, Mayer has presented empirical evidence that a stronger mental model of the computer can help students gain programming competence (Mayer, 1976, 1981). In the metacourse, students learn a visual model of what happens inside the computer to help them interpret exactly what commands do (cf. DuBoulay, 1986; DuBoulay, O'Shea, & Monk, 1981). The model is func-

TABLE 7.1
Content of Metacourse Lessons

---

*Lesson 1:*  *Actions in the Computer World.* Introduces the computer world (via the paper computer) and its parts. Introduces actions of individual commands in the computer world and tracking the action of a whole program.

*Lesson 2:*  *Learning About Commands.* Introduces the purpose-syntax-action framework for understanding commands using the INPUT command as a sample case.

*Lesson 3:*  *Program Purposes and Interactions.* Introduces the terms *program purpose* and *program interaction* in the context of a user specfication form.

*Lesson 4:*  *Reading What It Really Says.* Alerts students to the dangers of misreading a program by projecting one's intentions onto it.

*Lesson 5:*  *Patterns in Programming.* Introduces the concept of a pattern, using the examples of summing and counting patterns.

*Lesson 6:*  *Managing a Programming Task: Planning a Program.* Introduces steps to follow before actual coding begins, including defining the purpose of the program, describing interactions, grouping tasks into sections, and checking for omissions or organizational problems.

*Lesson 7:*  *Managing a Programming Task: Writing, Debugging, and Revising a Program.* Introduces steps for effective coding, debugging, testing, and revision of programs.

*Lesson 8:*  *Associating Patterns with Specific Commands.* Introduces the utility of associating patterns with their core commands, using branching patterns commonly associated with IF-THEN as an example.

*Lesson 9:*  *Using Patterns to Build Programs.* Introduces the utility of combining patterns to accomplish multiple purposes within a program.

---

tional rather than technical in nature, so that, for example, the student thinks of a variable as the name of a box in memory with a number in it. The key concepts of visibility and simplicity promote optimal understanding.

This visual model is called the "paper computer," because students receive forms displaying the visual model on which they hand execute programs. The paper computer reflects the operation of BASIC, showing variables and their values, characters on the screen, and flow of control between lines of the program. As noted in the introduction, part of the fragile knowledge syndrome is an uncertain grasp of exactly what commands do. The paper computer, then, offers a mental model of the machine in terms of which students can represent to themselves the effects of command execution.

An additional feature of the paper computer is a personified "interpreter." This robotlike persona acts as a mediator between the instructions given by the

## The Computer World

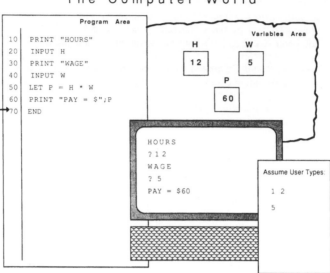

FIG. 7.1.   The paper computer

program and what happens in the computer. For instance, faced with a command such as INPUT 'Cost'; X, students would imagine the robot fetching the string 'Cost' from the instruction itself, carrying the string over to the screen and leaving it there, waiting for a number from the keyboard, and carrying that over to the storage area to store in the box labelled X.

The rationale for representing the interpreter as an agency in the paper computer is twofold. First, it gives the students a ready means of visualizing how program instructions get changed into effects. Second, recent research in programming has shown that many errors made by novice programmers can be attributed to a tendency to understand the computer as a personlike entity that comprehends intentions (Bonar & Soloway, 1985; Pea, 1986; Sleeman, Putnam, Baxter, & Kuspa, 1986). It is as though students expect the computer to "do what I mean." The robot interpreter provides a way of drawing a sharp contrast between what the computer knows and does and what people know and do. For instance, one can discuss with students the ignorance of the robot, emphasizing that it does not know the purpose of programs or the meaning of variable names.

### Building a Model of Program Constituents

To further reduce students' fragile knowledge, the students learn an analytical scheme for comprehending commands and command lines. The metacourse emphasizes the usefulness of attending to the following: (a) the purpose of a command, (b) its legal syntax, and (c) its action in the computer world as shown on the paper computer. Students are encouraged to use this framework as a way to organize their learning of each new command. In addition, the metacourse emphasizes the utility of employing the purpose-syntax-action framework when trying to understand the lines of a program during checking and testing of program parts or whole programs.

The choice of terms in the triad is in part drawn from the contrast between pragmatics, syntax, and semantics and in part from a framework for learning called "knowledge as design" developed by Perkins (1986a, 1986b). Purpose has a major role because of the results of the clinical analyses discussed earlier (Perkins & Martin, 1986; Perkins, Martin, & Farady, 1986). It was found that often students had a knowledge of relevant command structures, but could not retrieve them, apparently failing to make the connection between what needed to happen in the program and the commands that would serve the purpose. This fragile-knowledge problem of knowledge not well-accessed by means-end thinking ("inert knowledge") is commonplace in education, as noted earlier (Bereiter & Scardamalia, 1985; Bransford et al., 1986; Perfetto et al., 1983). The attention to syntax is motivated by observations of how novice BASIC and LOGO programming performance can be affected by difficulties of a purely syntactic nature (Perkins, Farady et al., 1986; Perkins, Martin, & Farady, 1986). Action refers to the precise effect on the computer state by the execution of a command line. The emphasis on action reflects the observation that students cannot reliably hand-execute command lines, one of the manifestations of fragile knowledge and a sign that the students have a partial and misleading mental model of the machine (cf. Pea, 1986; Sleeman et al., 1986).

Concepts like purpose, syntax, and action in effect provide students with elementary self-prompts tuned to the programming context that add to their repertoire of elementary problem-solving strategies and that should help them to navigate through the task of learning to program. The gradual induction of self-guiding and self-monitoring heuristics is an instructional strategy that has seen other successes in efforts to teach problem-solving, so it is reasonable to think that it may serve here as well (Collins, Brown, & Newman (1987); Schoenfeld, 1982; Schoenfeld & Herrmann, 1982; Meichenbaum, 1977; Nickerson, Perkins, & Smith, 1985; Palincsar & Brown, 1984).

In addition to an emphasis on individual command lines, the metacourse also aims to build students' problem-solving abilities by increasing their awareness of lines of code that work together to accomplish a particular job. In the metacourse, such recurrent schema are called "patterns," a term roughly synonymous with the "programming plans" described by Soloway and colleagues (Soloway & Ehrlich, 1984; Joni & Soloway, 1986). Patterns provide an intermediate level of analysis between the whole program and individual command lines and offer a way of helping students to organize and comprehend code used for counter variables, certain compound conditional branches, and the like. The metacourse stresses the importance of patterns for efficient comprehension of programs and program segments as well as their utility and portability in the construction of whole programs.

At a more abstract level of problem solving and program comprehension, the metacourse teaches the concept of metapatterns. Metapatterns are broad features of flow of control such as "repeats" and "decides" that provide the major structural building blocks of programs. For example, a program to read in and accumulate costs until a "0" cost is input can be said to *repeat* the cycle of reading and adding until the program *decides* to quit because it "saw" a 0. Metapatterns are more generalized than patterns (programming plans) and allow a more holistic description of a program. When more precision is called for, as is often the case, metapatterns provide a high-level organizer within which to examine the function of particular patterns and code sequences in general.

A final tool provided by the metacourse to assist students in the comprehension of programming constituents is the "minimanual," a quick easy-access reference of BASIC commands and patterns. Commands are presented in the purpose-syntax-action framework, accompanied by examples. The minimanual is designed to help the student overcome some of the initial information overload associated with learning a programming language.

## Building a Model of Program Production

The metacourse extends the problem-solving strategies and mental models for understanding the computer and its operations with further strategies for program production. A major point of emphasis is that writing programs is a process of refinement, involving multiple rounds of planning, writing, and testing code.

As a first step in top-level planning, students are encouraged to think in terms of interactions with the user. The term *Interactions* refers to the sequence of computer outputs and user inputs that occurs as a user uses a program. This heuristic offers a concrete beginning point for the novice programmer, who frequently experiences difficulties in moving from a given problem statement to the initial stages of task decomposition. For many programs, an outline according to the "rounds" of interaction provides a decomposition into subunits that amount to subproblems in the programming task. An initial focus on interactions as the student begins a programming task can help to avoid the frequent problem of moving from a problem statement directly to a coding phase without sufficient thought and effort devoted to planning.

An additional top-level planning strategy involves looking for metapatterns around which to organize the program. This can help the student to conceptualize the program in terms of major elements of flow of control. Thus, for example, suppose a student were given the assignment of writing a program that added inputs together until receiving a zero and then output the result. The student might reason, "Is there anything that the program needs to *repeat*? Yes, the reading in and adding up gets repeated over and over. What about *decide*? Well, the program has to decide when to stop—when it gets a zero. So now, what commands can I use to get the *repeat?* FOR-NEXT makes repeats, and I can also build up repeats out of a GOTO. Let's see . . ." and so on.

As an aid in refining a broad flow-of-control plan, students are encouraged to conceptualize program sections in terms of the patterns that might serve the section purposes. Patterns provide the student with the tools to manage and create code above the level of the single command line. Students are taught the utility of having a repertoire of patterns that are portable across programs. Thus, for examaple, if a student recognizes the need in a program to implement code that will trap unreasonable inputs from the user, the student can call on a "bulletproofing" pattern to help with that task. This simple pattern includes a conditional branch that rejects inappropriate inputs, prompting the user for another input.

At each level of the planning and coding stages students are encouraged to consider the purpose of chunks of code and the action those chunks actually effect. Students are taught to check their code, mentally simulating the action of the program line by line to catch the "easy" bugs before a program is actually run and tested. The metacourse also emphasizes that bugs and debugging are inevitable and integral parts of program production, not reflections of poor-programming performance.

The foregoing discussion makes plain how the metacourse incorporates a number of elements designed to address the problems of fragile knowledge presented in the introduction and to provide students with some useful problem-solving strategies as they attempt to manage the complexities of writing programs. As to problems of confidence and control, the third category mentioned, no specific steps were taken in the metacourse to deal with this beyond those addressing the fragile knowledge and strategy problems. We conjectured that attention to these would help also with confidence and control. Now the question remains: How does the metacourse play out in practice? We turn now to some empirical results on this question.

## THE IMPACT OF THE METACOURSE

An experiment was carried out to investigate the impact of the metacourse on high school students taking their first term of programming instruction in BASIC. The metacourse employed in the experiment lacked a few features mentioned previously that are being worked into the latest version. In particular, the metacourse used in the experiment included the paper computer but not the robot interpreter, and although patterns figured importantly, the metapatterns aforementioned had no role. However, in general tone and substance, the metacourse used in the experiments was as described.

The study was conducted within the context of another Educational Technology Center Study, the "Laboratory Sites" project. This broader study aimed to involve the teachers using the metacourse (as well as trying out interventions in two other subject matters) in the discussion and evaluation of the educational innovations they were implementing in their classrooms. Thus, instructors teaching the metacourse received more support in their efforts to adapt to the new materials than would normally be the case. The main extra supports were monthly meetings with the research team and a research assistant, who acted in an advisory capacity, to discuss issues pertaining to the implementation of the metacourse, and modest monetary compensation for the extra time required. The same level of support was not present in the control sites, although control teachers did receive a small honorarium. The control-site teachers, however, were not faced with the problem of introducing and infusing new, innovative materials into their well-practiced normal BASIC curriculum.

The experimental group consisted of six teachers of BASIC, who taught 9 classes and 132 students at four high-school laboratory sites. The control group pool consisted of nine teachers who taught 13 classes and 239 students at eight control sites. Students in both groups ranged from Grades 9 through 12.

All teachers were experienced programming instructors, beginning the semester with at least 2 years of previous experience teaching BASIC classes. The classes were straightforward programming courses, meeting on an average five times a week for 40-minute periods throughout one semester. Just prior to the beginning of the semester, the research group met with the experimental group teachers. At this meeting, teachers were presented with the outline of the metacourse materials and introduced to central concepts such as the paper computer mental model and the purpose-syntax-action framework. Teachers were urged to infuse these concepts throughout their course as well as teaching the metacourse lessons per se.

Teachers in the experimental classes taught a typical BASIC curriculum, which varied in minor ways from teacher to teacher. They interspersed the eight metacourse lessons at a pace of 1 per week for the first four lessons, and about one every 2 weeks for the rest. Adjustments in the curriculum were made at the discretion of the teacher to accommodate the infusion of the metacourse concepts. Thus, the students were quickly introduced to the metacourse framework and then had periodic lessons to reinforce these concepts throughout the semester. Each of the teachers in the control classes, of course, followed his or her normal curriculum.

## Tests and Measures

### Cognitive Skills Pretest–Posttest

A cognitive skills test was developed with two purposes in mind. First, such a measure might be expected to correlate with programming performance (most cognitive skills are interrelated) and thus serve as an indicator of level of general student ability in comparing treatment and control students. In addition, it seemed sensible to probe the possibility of transfer of a few cognitive skills. General findings on transfer from programming have been negative (Blume, 1984; Kurland et al., 1987; Kurland et al., 1986; Land & Turner, 1985; Linn, 1985; Mawby, in 1987; Pea & Kurland, 1984a, 1984b; Salomon & Perkins, 1987), nor was the metacourse particularly designed to promote transfer. However, there have been occasional positive findings (Clements, 1985; Clements & Gullo, 1984) and the issue has great currency, warranting an effort to examine the question of transfer in the present study.

The cognitive skills instrument was designed to test skill in complex linear reasoning (e.g., "If the day after tomorrow were Thursday, what would the day before yesterday be?") and field-independence and planning (a task of counting the number of triangles in a complex diagram). In addition, the test incorporated an algebraic version of the well-known students-and-professors problem (Clement, Lochhead, & Monk, 1981), where students typically have great difficulty translating a simple algebra word problem into an algebraic equation. Soloway and his colleagues have suggested that computer programming experience may help students to deal with this sort of problem more effectively (Ehrlich, Soloway, & Abbott, 1982; Soloway, Lochhead, & Clement, 1982). A further item relating to accuracy and precision of observation and description required the student to describe accurately a complex geometric figure in order for another student to be able to recognize it among a set of similar figures. Finally, the cognitive-skills test included a problem of a type quite similar in character to a programming problem involving combining patterns in a programlike way.[1] In prior research, when the rare case of transfer from programming has been found, it has emerged most often on tasks with marked similarity to programming (cf. Kurland et al., 1986; Linn, 1985).

## BASIC Posttest

The BASIC posttest was a fairly conventional paper-and-pencil programming test, comprising 16 items. The problems were formulated to evaluate certain general programming skills, in particular: (a) knowledge of programming commands typically presented in an introductory BASIC course (e.g., PRINT, LET, INPUT, FOR/NEXT, IF-THEN), (b) the ability to hand-execute a problem, (c) debugging skills, and (d) the ability to write whole programs. Certain language-independent bugs identified by Pea (1986), such as personifying the computer and attributing intelligence to it, as well as a programming version of the students-and-professors problem previously already cited were included.

---

[1] The design of this problem was suggested by Ellen Mandinach of the Educational Testing Service.

## Classroom Observations

Researchers conducted classroom observations at all treatment sites, systematically recording a number of features of the classroom dynamics and instructional style. The major purpose was to ascertain if the teachers could present the metacourse material in a reasonably faithful fashion and if students would be responsive. An observation instrument was designed to aid the observers in recording salient features of the classroom activities. The majority of the items on the observation instrument were rated on 7-point Likert scales, where 7 was the most desirable score. These included situational factors such as student–teacher and student–student interaction, student responsiveness and engagement, and teacher presentational style. Items relating specifically to the metacourse included fidelity to the metacourse and infusion of metacourse concepts into the metacourse lessons. Teachers were also rated on factors such as mode of instruction (e.g., presentational, interactive) and on degree of comfort with the material. In addition, observers used the seven-point scale to give an overall rating of effectiveness of instruction.

## Student Questionnaire

At the beginning of the semester students filled out a short questionnaire concerning their previous experience with computers and computer programming. Items were designed to determine the students' general experience with computers in the schools, with computers in the home, and in other outside activities as well as previous experience in BASIC and/or other programming languages.

# Results

How did it all come out? Here, it is appropriate to consider three questions: Did the metacourse prove "teachable," leading to an implementation that smoothly provided the intended concepts and practice in their use? Did the metacourse have the hoped-for impact on students' mastery of programming? Did the metacourse, or the normal programming instruction in the control groups, have a cognitive impact beyond the targeted instruction?

## Teachability of the Metacourse

First, were the metacourse lessons adequately taught? The data indicate that at least for experienced teachers under conditions of support the metacourse was quite teachable and could be integrated into the normal curriculum in BASIC. Although the metacourse lessons produced a variety of differences in teacher style of presentation as well as student behavior compared to the normal lessons, both teachers and students appeared to adapt well to the new material with a number of indicators pointing to effective classes. The lessons were presented more or less as they were written. Teachers were rated as covering over three-quarters of the material in each lesson quite adequately and also as referring appropriately during the metacourse lessons to the major principles stressed in the metacourse, (e.g., the paper computer, purpose, syntax, action, patterns), with the exception of the minimanual which was rarely mentioned.

In comparing differences between metacourse and ordinary lessons, there were few surprises. The teachers seemed somewhat more comfortable when presenting their own lessons, compared to the new metacourse material. Student behavior during both types of classes was rated as quite responsive, attentive, engaged, and interactive with their teachers. However, there was apparently significantly more interaction among students during the nonmetacourse lessons. Some of these differences might be due to the fact that this was the first time the teachers used the materials; such contrasts might diminish as teachers become more familiar with the material.

### Impact on Programming Performance

Now, let us turn to the second question: Did the metacourse have a positive impact on the students' mastery of BASIC? Before considering the students' performance in BASIC we need to examine the matching of the experimental and control groups. The cognitive pretest was assumed to be an indicator of general ability that might relate to later BASIC performance, and in fact significant correlations were obtained between the cognitive pretest and the BASIC posttest in both the experimental group ($r = .69$, $p < .01$) and the control group ($r = .40$, $p < .01$). Overall the control group performed significantly better than the experimental group on the cognitive pretest ($p < .001$), committing on average about 12 errors compared to 16 errors for the experimental group. Thus, the control group appeared to be of somewhat higher ability than the experimental group.

In addition to the cognitive pretest, students also filled out a short questionnaire about previous computing experience. Three-quarters of the experimental group and 84% of the control group had no previous exposure to BASIC. Those few with experience had minimal exposure, typically a week or two. Although 24% of the experimental group had some experience with another programming language compared to only 5% in the control group, this consisted in all but two cases in each group of some exposure to LOGO, often some years back.

Despite the apparent higher general ability of the control group, the data indicate that the experimental group performed significantly better on the BASIC test. The experimental group averaged about 5.5 fewer errors than the control group, nearly half a standard deviation overall. The treatment group produced about 77% correct responses compared to about 66% for the controls (out of a maximum of 61 errors). Experimental groups outperformed control groups in all major categories—simple one-line commands, hand execution, debugging, and production—with the smallest advantage on the simple one-line command problems and production problems (about a third of a standard deviation), and the largest advantage on the hand-execution problems (nearly two-thirds of a standard deviation). In three of the groups (hand execution, debugging, and production) the experimental group had significantly fewer errors on every problem except one requiring the use of an IF-THEN loop. In fact, both groups found it more difficult to write a program using IF-THEN after being asked to create a program that generated identical results but used the more natural FOR loop.

### Impact on General Cognitive Skills

Although the cognitive posttest provided an occasion to examine possible transfer of cognitive skills from programming instruction, it should be recalled that such findings were not necessarily expected from the metacourse treatment. As indicated previously the control group made significantly fewer errors on the pretest overall than the experimental group. Analysis by subtests indicated that this superiority manifested itself on three of the five subtests (conditional reasoning, precise visual description, and repeats and decides), although no initial differences were found on the visual planning or professors/students problems. Surprisingly, the experimental group improved by about three fewer errors on the posttest, compared to virtually no gain for the control group ($p < .001$). Analysis of the data from the component tests indicates that this result was due almost entirely to the considerable improvement of the experimental group on the Repeats and Decides subtest, compared to a modest decline in performance on the part of the control group on that same problem. No improvement on the students-and-professors problem was noted, in contrast to findings of other research (Ehrlich et al., 1982; Sloway et al., 1982). Thus some evidence of transfer was observed, but it occurred only on the problem most closely related in its formal structure to that of producing coherent commands in a programming language.

### TARGETS AND TRADEOFFS
### OF PROGRAMMING INSTRUCTION

Why do we teach programming? The current enthusiasm for teaching computer programming in elementary schools and high schools involves several targets. For students on their way toward science, engineering, accounting, and related fields, a first course in computer programming is their introduction to a technical skill that they may need to develop more fully later. Some may actually become professional programmers, but many more will need to know a bit about programming to judge best how they can call on existing programs or call for the design of new programs to serve their particular needs. For students in general, some knowledge of computer programming can be viewed as a piece of culture, a dipping of one's toe into the stream of information processing that flows so strongly in today's technologically oriented society, for the sake of comprehending better the modern world. Yet another familiar target is the development of cognitive skills. Many scholars have urged that programming may help to foster patterns of thinking that learners could carry over to other contexts (e.g., Feurzeig, Horwitz, & Nickerson, 1981; Linn, 1985; Papert, 1980).

One can argue about the appropriateness of these different goals for programming instruction, but more important, the present findings concern two related questions: *Can* computer programming instruction serve these goals significantly, and *what kind* of computer programming instruction? We focus especially on the targets of computer-programming skill and general cognitive skills.

As to the "can" side of the question, it must be said that the initial picture is not encouraging. As reviewed at the beginning of this chapter, primary and secondary school instruction in computer programming typically lead to very low levels of mastery: Many, perhaps most, students do not learn to program with any reasonable degree of flexibility. According to our clinical work, students are plagued by fragile knowledge, a sparse repertoire of elementary problem-solving strategies, and problems of confidence and systematicity. What about general cognitive skills? As reviewed earlier, most studies seeking transfer from programming experience have not found any effects. In sum, neither the programming competency target nor the general cognitive skills target is easy to hit.

However, the thesis of this chapter and the metacourse development project has been that programming instruction can be improved. One can teach programming in substantially more effective ways by paying more heed to the students' development of mental models through which they understand what the computer does, strategies by which to organize their problem-solving efforts, and so on. Certainly the single experiment reported in these pages falls far from proving that marked improvement on a wide scale is possible, but at least the results are encouraging. So perhaps the targets of programming competency and general cognitive skills are more accessible than recent history suggests.

It is natural to suppose that the very same arrow—good programming instruction—would hit both these targets. Here, however, one needs to confront an important dilemma in educational design: It seems likely that teaching for programming competency is a somewhat different enterprise than teaching for transfer of cognitive skills from programming. The kind of programming instruction one wants will vary with the ultimate objective one selects. To be sure, compromises can be struck to serve both objectives equally, or more time could be secured for programming instruction to pursue both objectives vigorously. But the possibility of such measures should not obscure the reality of certain tradeoffs in designing instruction to hit both targets.

Why might this tradeoff exist? Considerable research on transfer of learning in various contexts argues that transfer comes hard: Without specific provocation, it typically does not come at all (cf. Perkins, 1985; Perkins & Salomon, 1987; Salomon & Perkins, 1987). Yet attention to transfer may have a performance cost for the core task. Mayer (1976), for instance, presented results demonstrating a tradeoff between teaching for a narrow programming performance and for a somewhat broader one still within the province of programming: Students receiving the second treatment showed better performance overall but somewhat *worse* performance on exercises very like those the first treatment focused on entirely. In general, teaching for transfer involves mediating the making of connections between the particular content being learned, its generic significance, and/or applications to other domains (cf. Clements, 1985; Clements & Gullo, 1984; Delclos, Littlefield, & Bransford, 1985). Mediating this connection-making consumes class time that could instead contribute directly to the building of domain-specific skills. Moreover, often content can be formulated in ways that make clearer the domain-specific point, or, by sacrificing a little clarity, facilitate making a more general point.

These remarks can be illustrated through the design of the metacourse discussed here. Early in its evolution, a policy decision was made to focus on the development of programming competency when tradeoffs arose. So what sorts of tradeoffs does the current metacourse reflect? For instance, the metacourse teaches a mental model of the computer—the paper computer. The idea of mental models is a powerful one; students are often well advised to seek out or try to construct mental models of situations. Yet the metacourse does not capitalize on the opportunity to introduce the *general* idea of a mental model, but simply presents the paper computer. Why? Because time is at a premium in the metacourse design and the policy decision alluded to recommends investing that time in matters directly bearing on programming competency.

This kind of tradeoff pervades the metacourse. For example, as remarked earlier, many of the ideas in the metacourse reflect a general pedagogical method called "knowledge as design" (Perkins, 1986a, 1986b). This method uses a crosscutting framework of four concepts—purpose, structure, model cases (roughly, examples), and argument—to organize all instruction. In the metacourse, the term *purpose* is used as such, but *structure* is assimilated into various other terms—*syntax, action,* and *interaction* for instance. Both illustrative examples and the paper computer are models, but are not identified as such. The role of arguments is assimilated into particular activities such as checking a program. These adaptations of the framework contextualize it in ways that make the computer concepts in themselves more accessible, but, at the same time, make the analogical connections to other domains and procedures less salient.

The policy decision to resolve tradeoffs in the direction of programming competency reflected a number of particular factors about the ongoing project, not a general commitment of our research group. Indeed, we have thought about, although have not had the opportunity to develop, what might be called a "bridge course" in programming. A bridge course, like the metacourse, would be an add-on, designed to supplement normal programming instruction by providing appropriate strategies and mental models. The bridge course probably would use many of the broad concepts that appear in the metacourse. However, when tradeoffs between the objectives of fostering programming competency and cognitive skills appeared, the resolution would favor the latter rather than the former.

This does not mean that attention to programming competency would be abandoned, of course. After all, one would still be trying to foster cognitive skills *through* programming, and that could hardly be done without managing better the development of the programming skills themselves. But even within that constraint, many choices can be made. For instance, one would select vocabulary somewhat less contextualized to programming, that still works adequately for programming (albeit not quite as smoothly), but that made salient connections with other domains.

In summary, we urge that a more powerful pedagogy of programming is a possibility that deserves pursuit. Such a pedagogy could serve such targets of development as programming competency, cognitive skills, or an understanding of modern times. The metacourse presented here, the bridge course briefly characterized, and, of course, other innovations, are potential contributors to such a pedagogy. At the same time, however, we urge that differences in the demand characteristics of these different targets need to be recognized. Programming instruction optimized for the development of programming, cognitive skills, or a perspective on contemporary culture would not take just the same form, although it would involve many of the same broad principles—attention to mental models, strategies, and so on. Thus, it is really not reasonable to ask sweepingly how programming can be taught effectively. One needs to ask: Programming instruction to what end?

## ACKNOWLEDGMENTS

The "Metacourse" discussed here is the product of the programming group at the Educational Technology Center, all the members of which are thanked for their many contributions. The research reported here was supported by the Office of Educational Research and Improvement (contract #OERI 400-83-0041). Opinions expressed herein are not necessarily shared by OERI and do not represent Office policy.

## REFERENCES

Bereiter, C., & Scardamalia, M. (1985). Cognitive coping strategies and the problem of inert knowledge. In S. S. Chipman, J. W. Segal, & R. Glaser (Eds.), *Thinking and learning skills, Vol. 2: Current research and open questions* (pp. 65–80). Hillsdale, NJ: Lawrence Erlbaum Associates.

Blume, B. W. (1984, April). *A review of research on the effects of computer programming on mathematical problem solving*. Paper presented at the annual meeting of the American Educational Research Association, New Orleans.

Bonar, J., & Soloway, E. (1985). *Pre-programming knowledge: A major source of misconceptions in novice programmers*. Pittsburgh, PA: Learning Research and Development Center. (ERIC Document Reproduction Service No. ED 258 805.)

Bransford, J. D., Franks, J. J., Vye, N. J., & Sherwood, R. D. (1986, June). *New approaches to instruction: Because wisdom can't be told*. Paper presented at the Conference on Similarity and Analogy, University of Illinois, Urbana.

Clement, J., Lochhead, J., & Monk, G. (1981). Translation difficulties in learning mathematics. *American Mathematical Monthly, 88,* 26–40.

Clements, D. H. (1985, April). *Effects of LOGO programming on cognition, metacognitive skills, and achievement*. Presentation at the American Educational Research Association conference, Chicago, IL.

Clements, D. H., & Gullo, D. F. (1984). Effects of computer programming on young children's cognition. *Journal of Educational Psychology, 76*(6), 1051–1058.

Collins, A., Brown, J. S., Newman, S. E., (1987). *Teaching the craft of reading, writing, and mathematics* (Report No. 403.) Cambridge, MA: Bolt, Beranek and Newman. University of Illinois, Urbana, Center for the Study of Reading (ERIC Document Reproduction Service No. ED 284 181)

Delclos, V. R., Littlefield, J., & Bransford, J. D. (1985). Teaching thinking through LOGO: The importance of method. *Roeper Review, 7*(3), 153–156.

DuBoulay, B. (1986). Some difficulties of learning to program. *Journal of Educational Computing Research, 2*(1), 57–73.

DuBoulay, B., O'Shea, T., & Monk, J. (1981). The black box inside the glass box: Presenting computing concepts to novices. *International Journal of Man–Machine Studies, 14,* 237–249.

Dweck, C. S., & Bempechat, J. (1980). Children's theories of intelligence: Consequences for learning. In S. G. Paris, G. M. Olson, & H. W. Stevenson (Eds.), *Learning and motivation in the classroom* (pp. 239–256). Hillsdale, NJ: Lawrence Erlbaum Associates.

Dweck, C. S., & Licht, B. G. (1980). Learned helplessness and intellectual achievement. In J. Garbar & M. Seligman (Eds.), *Human helplessness* (pp. 197–221). New York: Academic Press.

Ehrlich, K., Soloway, E., & Abbott, V. (1982). *Transfer effects from programming to algebra word problems: A preliminary study* (Rep. No. 257). New Haven: Yale University Department of Computer Science.

Feurzeig, W., Horwitz, P., & Nickerson, R. (1981). *Microcomputers in education* (Rep. No. 4798). Cambridge, Massachusetts: Bolt, Beranek, & Newman.

Gentner, D., & Stevens, A. L. (Eds.). (1983). *Mental models*. Hillsdale, NJ: Lawrence Erlbaum Associates.

Greenfield, P. M. (1984). A theory of the teacher in the learning activities of everyday life. In B. Rogoff & J. Lave (Eds.), *Everyday cognition: Its development in social context* (pp. 117–138). Cambridge, MA: Harvard University Press.

Johnson-Laird, P. N. (1983). *Mental models*. Cambridge, MA: Harvard University Press.

Joni, S. A., & Soloway, E. (1986). But my program Runs! Discourse rules for novice programmers. *Journal of Edcuational Computing Research, 2*(1), 95–125.

Kurland, D. M., Pea, R. D., Clement, C., & Mawby, R. (1986). *A study of the development of programming ability and thinking skills in high school students*. New York: Bank Street College of Education, Center for Children and Technology.

Kurland, M. D., Clement, C., Mawby, R., & Pea, R. D. (1987). Mapping the cognitive demands of learning to program. In D. N. Perkins, J. Lochhead, & J. Bishop (Eds.), *Thinking: The second international conference,* (pp. 333–358). Hillsdale, NJ: Lawrence Erlbaum Associates.

Land, M. L., & Turner, S. V. (1985). *What are the effects of computer programming on cognitive skills?* Paper presented at the annual meeting of the Association for Educational Data Systems, Toronto.

Linn, M. C. (1985). the cognitive consequences of programming instruction in classrooms. *Educational Researcher, 14*, 14–29.

Mawby, R. (1987). Proficiency conditions for the development of thinking skills through programming. In D. N. Perkins, J. Lochhead, & J. Bishop (Eds.), *Thinking: The second international conference* (pp. 359–371). Hillsdale, NJ: Lawrence Erlbaum Associates.

Mayer, R. E. (1976). Some conditions of meaningful learning for computer programming: Advance organizers and subject control of frame order. *Journal of Educational Psychology, 68*, 143–150.

Mayer, R. E. (1981). The psychology of how novices learn computer programming. *Computing Surveys, 13*)11), 121–141.

Meichenbaum, D. (1977). *Cognitive-behavior modification.* New York: Plenum Press.

Nickerson, R., Perkins, D. N., & Smith, E. (1985). *The teaching of thinking.* Hillsdale, NJ: Lawrence Erlbaum Associates.

Palincsar, A. S., & Brown, A. L. (1984). Reciprocal teaching of comprehension-fostering and comprehension-monitoring activities. *Cognition and Instruction, 1*, 117–175.

Papert, S. (1980). *Mindstorms: Children, computers, and powerful ideas.* New York: Basic books.

Pea, R. D. (1986). Language-independent conceptual "bugs" in novice programming. *Journal of Educational Computing Research, 2*(1), 25–36.

Pea, R. D., & Kurland, D. M. (1984a). On the cognitive effects of learning computer programming. *New Ideas in Psychology, 2*(2), 137–168.

Pea, R. D., & Kurland, D. M. (1984b). *LOGO programming and the development of planning skills* (Rep. No. 16). New York: Bank Street College.

Perfetto, G. A., Bransford, J. D., & Franks, J. J. (1983). Constraints on access in a problem solving context. *Memory & Cognition, 11*(1), 24–31.

Perkins, D. N. (1985). The fingertip effect: How information-processing technology changes thinking. *Educational Researcher, 14*(7), 11–17.

Perkins, D. N. (1986a). *Knowledge as design.* Hillsdale, NJ: Lawrence Erlbaum Associates.

Perkins, D. N. (1986b). Knowledge as design: Teaching thinking through content. In J. B. Baron & R. S. Sternberg (Eds.), *Teaching thinking skills: Theory and practice* (pp. 62–85). New York: W. H. Freeman.

Perkins, D. N., Farady, M., Hancock, C., Hobbs, R., Simmons, R., Tuck, T., & Villa, E. (1986). *Nontrivial pursuit: The hidden complexity of elementary LOGO programming* (Tech. Rep.). Harvard Graduate School of Education, Cambridge, MA: Educational Technology Center.

Perkins, D. N., Hancock, C., Hobbs, R., Martin, F., & Simmons, R. (1986). Conditions of learning in novice programmers. *Journal of Educational Computing Research, 2*(1), 37–56.

Perkins, D. N., & Martin, F. (1986). Fragile knowledge and neglected strategies in novice programmers. In E. Soloway & S. Iyengar (Eds.), *Empirical studies of programmers* (pp. 213–229). Norwood, NJ: Ablex.

Perkins, D. N., Martin, F., & Farady, M. (1986). *Loci of difficulty in learning to program* (Educational Technology Center technical report). Cambridge, MA: Educational Technology Center, Harvard Graduate School of Education.

Perkins, D., & Salomon, G. (1987). Transfer and teaching thinking. In D. N. Perkins, J. Lochhead, & J. Bishop (Eds.), *Thinking: The second international conference* (pp. 285–303). Hillsdale, NJ: Lawrence Erlbaum Associates.

Rogoff, B., & Gardner, W. (1984). Adult guidance of cognitive development. In B. Rogoff & J. Lave (Eds.), *Everyday cognition: Its development in social context* (pp. 95–116). Cambridge, MA: Harvard University Press.

Salomon, G., & Perkins, D. N. (1987). Transfer of cognitive skills from programming: When and how? *Journal of Educational Computing Research, 3*, 149–169.

Schoenfeld, A. H. (1982). Measures of problem-solving performance and of problem-solving instruction. *Journal for Research in Mathematics Education, 13*(1), 31–49.

Schoenfeld, A. H., & Herrmann, D. J. (1982). Problem perception and knowledge structure in expert and novice mathematical problem solvers. *Journal of Experimental Psychology: Learning, Memory, and Cognition, 8*, 484–494.

Sleeman, D., Putnam, R. T., Baxter, J. & Kuspa, L. (1986). Pascal and high school students: A study of errors. *Journal of Educational Computing Research, 2*(1), 5–24.

Soloway, E., & Ehrlich, K. (1984). Empirical studies of programming knowledge. *IEEE Transactions on Software engineering, SE-10*(5), 595–609.

Soloway, E., Lochhead, J., & Clement, J. (1982). Does computer programming enhance problem solving ability? Some positive evidence on algebra word problems. In R. Seidel, R. Anderson, & B. Hunter (EDs.), *Computer literacy* (pp. 171–185). New York: Academic Press.

Zelman, S. (1985, April). *Individual differences and the computer learning environment: Motivational constraints to learning LOGO.* Paper presented at the American Educational Research Association Annual Meeting, Chicago, IL.

# 8

# The Social Context
# of Learning Computer
# Programming

Noreen M. Webb
Scott Lewis
*University of California, Los Angeles*

## ABSTRACT

This chapter examines the social context of learning computer programming. It first describes theoretical perspectives that predict how and when peer-directed learning in small groups may be beneficial for learning. It next describes two studies that

179

investigated the relationship between peer interaction and achievement among junior high-school students learning LOGO or BASIC in small groups. Verbal behavior variables related to achievement included giving explanations, giving input suggestions, receiving input suggestions, receiving responses to questions, planning using students' own words, debugging errors (positively related), receiving no help when needed (negatively related), and verbalizing planning and debugging during conversations with the instructor (not related). Student demographic characteristics, aptitudes, and cognitive style did not predict behavior in small groups. The final sections discuss implications for classroom instruction and describe suggestions for future research.

## INTRODUCTION

Much of the use of microcomputers in the classroom is social. Teachers often structure their classrooms so that students share computers. The National Survey of School Uses of Microcomputers (Becker, 1984), for example, found that teachers assigned groups of students to a computer 46% of the time. For another 20% of the time, teachers encouraged students to help each other even if they each had access to a computer.

Not only do teachers often encourage social interaction when using computers, but students frequently exhibit interaction spontaneously. Anecdotal observations of spontaneous interaction abound (Campbell, 1986; Diem, 1986a, 1986b; Jewson & Pea, 1982; Kull, 1986; Shade, Nida, Lipinski, & Watson, 1986; Shrock et al., 1985; Swigger & Swigger, 1984). Systematic quantitative reports of peer work are consistent with the anecdotal observations: Several studies report that most of the interaction in the classroom is between students and not between teacher and student (percentages are as high as 63% of total classroom interaction (Genishi et al., 1985; Littlejohn, Ross, & Gump, 1984; Muller & Perlmutter, 1985).

Whatever the reasons for the abundance of social interaction around computers (e.g., a management tool for teachers who do not have enough computers for every child), theoretical and empirical work on social cognition suggests ways in which peer interaction may be beneficial for learning. Several theoretical perspectives have emerged to suggest that interacting with peers may promote cognitive restructuring in significant ways. Cognitive restructuring may occur when students give and receive help from each other. In formulating explanations to give to another student, students may reorganize or clarify the material in ways they had not previously thought of (Bargh & Schul, 1980). This reorganization and clarification would help the explainer understand the material better than before as well as help him or her to recognize gaps in understanding. Receiving information and explanations may help students to reshape their ideas, correct misunderstandings, and learn new information that they might not discover on their own (Gall & Gall, 1976; Heap, 1986; Riel, 1983; Rubin, 1983; Slavin, 1977).

Furthermore, group settings provide a diversity of skills and knowledge among students that promotes the exchange of information and ideas. This diversity may help individual students learn how to solve problems or complete tasks that they would not be able to complete on their own. In the first step of this process, students may pool their unique skills and knowledge and assume complementary roles to complete a task or solve a problem. Students guide and correct each other and build on each other's ideas until they reach the solution in a process called "scaffolding" (Forman & Cazden, 1985; Palincsar, 1986; Palincsar & Brown, 1984; Wood, Bruner, & Ross, 1976). In the second step, students may internalize aspects of the completed solution and solution process, problem-solving strategies, and the language the group used to solve the problem (Damon, 1984; Forman & Cazden, 1985; Vygotsky, 1981; Wertsch, 1979).

The diversity of ideas in a group may also give rise to conceptual conflict and conflict resolution, which have been hypothesized to promote cognitive restructuring. Peer interaction provides opportunities for interpersonal controversy and conceptual conflict (doubt, perplexity, contradiction, incongruity, confusion, irrelevance, surprise, Berlyne, 1965a, 1965b). In the process of resolving disagreements among group members, students retrieve prior knowledge, seek new information, retrieve prior knowledge, evaluate their own and others' answers, ideas, and opinions, confront their own misunderstandings and lack of knowledge, and as a consequence, restructure their own thinking (Bearison, Magzamen, & Filardo, 1986; Dickinson, 1985; Doise, Mugny, & Perret-Clermont, 1975; Forman & Cazden, 1985; Hatano, 1986; Johnson & Johnson, 1979; Kuhn, 1972; Mugny & Doise, 1978; F. B. Murray, 1972; Perlmutter, Behrend, Kuo, & Muller, 1986; Perret-Clermont, 1980; Piaget, 1970; Weinstein & Bearison, 1985).

Others have theorized that peer interaction provides opportunities for modeling and imitation, particularly of strategies for solving problems or completing tasks (Cohen, 1986; Hythecker et al., 1985). Although researchers have claimed that peer models are effective because of the similarity between viewer and model (e.g., Bandura, 1969; Bronfenbrenner, 1970), in an extensive review of the literature, Schunk (1987) suggested that peers may provide better models than an adult primarily when students doubt their own capabilities. In this case, Schunk (1987, p. 166) suggested that "viewing a peer successfully perform a task may raise children's self-efficacy for performing well more than observing an adult." Schunk also concluded that, for students encountering difficulties or who doubt their own capabilities, observing coping models (those who initially experience difficulty and doubts but gradually develop competence and self-confidence) may be more effective than observing mastery models (those who are successful at the outset). For students who do not have high confidence in their ability, then, observing their peers learning how to complete a task or solve a problem may be more effective than observing the teacher demonstrate the same problem.

An extended view of modeling and imitation from developmental psychology suggests two modifications. First, students will imitate only models whose behavior indicates more advanced understanding than that of the observer, not less. For example, children classified as partial conservers on a Piagetian conservation task may improve their understanding of conservation by observing a model who conserves, but the reverse does not occur (i.e., conservers watching partial conservers do not regress; J. P. Murray, 1974; see also Kuhn, 1972). Second, modeling will be effective only when the observer's understanding is not a great deal less than the model's. In J. P. Murray's (1974) study, although partial conservers watching conserving models improved their understanding of conservation, nonconservers watching conservers did not improve.

Proponents of several of the preceding perspectives have hypothesized that communication among students may be more effective than between teachers and students. This may be related to the fact that students discuss material in ways that they can easily understand: by using familiar language (Buckholdt & Wodarski, 1978; Noddings, 1985), by being direct without hedging words (Damon, 1984), and, because they are working on the same problem simultaneously, by being able to "tune into" each others' thinking and problem-solving processes (Vedder, 1985) or cognitive framework (Cohen, 1986) better than a teacher can. This may allow students to understand what others are thinking when they make errors or ask questions and so enable them to give precise, relevant, and, consequently, effective feedback.

The ability to correctly evaluate what students think and understand is also at the heart of the scaffolding process mentioned earlier. The aim of scaffolding, whether carried out by a teacher or by peer collaborators, is to move students from one level of competence to another (see Palincsar, 1986). Because the potential change in competence that can arise in this situation (called the "zone of proximal development" by Vygotsky, 1978, and "region of sensitivity to instruction" by Wood and Middleton, 1975) may differ from student to student, feedback must be tailored to the needs of the individual student. Students working on a common problem may be in an excellent position to give each other the feedback needed to make the scaffolding effective.

Socioemotional factors have also been hypothesized to suggest positive effects of peer interaction on learning. Peer learning settings, particularly cooperative settings in which a group is rewarded for the learning of all group members, may increase students' motivation to work hard and to help each other (Hammond & Goldman, 1961; Slavin, 1977, 1983), may lower their level of anxiety (Buckholdt & Wodarski, 1978), may increase their willingness to ask for help (Artzt, 1979; Jackson & Reissman, 1977), and may increase their willingness to take feedback seriously (Damon, 1984).

Of course, predictions about the effects of peer interaction on learning are not always positive. The positive effects just described will not take place when members do not actively participate in group work (Noddings, 1985; Okey &

Majer, 1976), when they lack the requisite skills to do the work (Ellis & Rogoff, 1982), or when they fail to receive the help they need (Webb, 1982).

These theoretical predictions make it clear that working with other students may be beneficial or detrimental for learning, depending on the conditions that prevail in the group. And, indeed, the empirical research comparing small group and individual learning settings is inconclusive, both in noncomputer settings (see Webb, 1982) and in computer settings. Of the five studies that have compared learning of computer programming in group and individual settings, for example, two reported greater achievement in the group setting than in the individual setting (Cheney, 1977; Perlmutter et al., 1986, Study 3) and three found no difference between individual and group settings (Perlmutter et al., 1986, Studies 2 and 3; Webb, 1985). The discrepant findings between studies may be due to the kinds of interaction in which students engaged. The important question, then, is not which setting is better for learning computer programming, but is, rather, what kinds of behavior are beneficial for learning in either setting. This chapter explores this question for the group setting.

The foregoing hypotheses about the effects of peer interaction on learning are just beginning to be tested empirically. We know relatively little about the relationship between peer interaction and learning in noncomputer settings (see Webb, 1982) and even less about the relationship in computer settings. Before suggesting behaviors to encourage and discourage in small groups learning computer programming, we first need to investigate the kinds of behavior that seem to influence learning. This chapter, then, examines the links between some aspects of peer interaction discussed previously (particularly helping behavior and the exchange of information and ideas) and learning.

Specifically, this chapter summarizes the results of two studies that have linked specific kinds of behavior in peer-directed small groups to achievement outcomes in computer programming. The next section describes the methodology and results of two studies that were designed to link interaction in social settings to learning of computer programming. The final sections discuss the implications of the findings for classroom instruction and describe the next steps for research.

## THE RELATIONSHIP BETWEEN SOCIAL INTERACTION AND LEARNING IN GROUP LEARNING CONTEXTS

### Methodology of the Studies

The findings directly bearing on the relationship between peer interaction and learning of computer programming come from two studies that explicitly investigated the link between them. The first study examined LOGO (Webb, 1984a) and the second examined BASIC (Webb, Ender, & Lewis, 1986). This section describes the methodology and findings of those studies.

## Students and Instructors

The two studies of peer interaction and computer programming used similar student populations, designs, and procedures. The students in both studies were 11- to 14-year-old volunteers from Los Angeles area schools (Grades 7, 8, and 9). Students in the BASIC study had no previous experience in computer programming. Approximately one third of the students in the LOGO study had some previous experience in computer programming.

The primary instructor was the same in both studies. He had many years of teaching experience, primarily at the university level. He had much expertise in computer programming, having designed instructional materials and having taught classes in several computer programming languages. Several other helpers were present to answer students' questions when the primary instructor was busy with another group. Most of them were university students with some knowledge of the computer programming language (LOGO or BASIC), but only a few had any teaching background. Most of the interaction between students and instructor took place with the primary instructor.

## Design

In the LOGO study, students worked in three-person, peer-directed groups for 5 days (a total of 15–20 hours). Students were assigned to groups so that groups would be homogeneous on previous experience with computers and would have both girls and boys. In the BASIC study, students worked in two-person, peer-directed groups for one day (3–4 hours). Students were assigned to pairs at random.

## Curriculum

In both studies (LOGO and BASIC), the curriculum consisted of a series of lessons that guided students through basic commands, more complex concepts, and interpreting and writing programs. The materials were designed to be self-sufficient and self-pacing, and to require little intervention from the instructor. The topics of the BASIC lessons included the operating system, input and output commands, logical relations, branching, looping, data types, arithmetic operators, and relations. The topics of the LOGO lessons included basic commands, repeating sequences of commands, programming simple geometric shapes, combining shapes to make complex figures, writing recursive programs, incorporating random placement into pictures, changing sizes of figures within a program, and programming with words and sentences to play interactive games with the computer. Embedded within each curriculum were short programs for students to write. Student interaction was tape-recorded while they developed and tested these programs. The transcripts of the audio tapes served as the data on interaction among students.

## Instructional Method

In both studies, the primary instructor gave an introduction to computers and to the computer language prior to group work. Then students were given the worksheets for the different lessons. Students in all groups in both studies were instructed to work with each other, to ask each other for help, and to consult the instructor only if no one in the group knew how to proceed.

Prior to the study, the instructor and assistants were instructed to use a very indirect style of teaching: to refrain from helping students to complete their programs, to encourage students to rely on each other for help, and to give the minimum help needed when students asked the instructor questions. To determine whether the instructors followed these instructions, instructor talk with students was coded to examine the nature of instructor behavior within conversations with students. The frequencies of different instructor behaviors are presented in Table 8.1. Table 8.1 shows that during conversations with students, the instructor played a largely reactive role. Of instructor behavior, 85% was in response to students' questions or suggestions (defined as "reactive behavior" in Table 8.1). Even when students asked questions, the instructor tended not to give information in response. Of the 42.1 instances of reactive behavior per group on the average, only about 28% included specific information or suggestions. The remaining 72% included referring students back to previous lessons, asking students leading questions (asking students questions that encouraged them to generate their own answers, e.g., "What do you have to put in that line so that the computer will print that statement?"), and reflecting students questions back to them (repeating the students' own questions). Only about 11% of instructor talk consisted of unsolicited suggestions.

## Measures

*Pretests.* Prior to instruction, all students completed tests of mathematical computation and reasoning, verbal inference, nonverbal reasoning (a short form of Raven's Progressive Matrices; Raven, 1958), spatial reasoning (Paper Folding, Form Board, and Surface Development; French, Ekstrom, & Price, 1963), field independence (Hidden Figures; French et al., 1963), and holistic processing (Gestalt Completion; French et al., 1963). In the BASIC study a composite ability measure was created from all of the pretests that significantly correlated with one or more achievement outcomes: mathematics, verbal inference, nonverbal reasoning, spatial ability, and age. The ability composite was the sum of these five scores, with each score weighted by the inverse of its standard deviation. This ability composite was used as the control variable in the partial correlations presented in the results section. In the LOGO study, the partial correlations controlled for mathematics ability, spatial reasoning, and field independence, which were the best predictors of achievement outcomes.

TABLE 8.1
Frequency of Instructor Behavior

| Behavior | M[a] | SD |
|---|---|---|
| *Proactive behavior* | | |
| Points out mistakes unnoticed by students | 1.8 | 2.0 |
| Gives specific suggestions | 5.4 | 4.4 |
| *Reactive Behavior* | | |
| Gives information in response to question | 11.9 | 11.6 |
| Refers student to previous lesson | 5.9 | 5.3 |
| Asks leading question | 23.2 | 26.1 |
| Reflects question back to students | 1.1 | 1.4 |

[a]Mean frequency per group transcript.

TABLE 8.2
Example Items for Each Achievement Outcome

Knowledge of Commands
LOGO       Which command clears the screen and returns the turtle to the center, pointing up?
BASIC      Which command will make the word "AMOS" appear on the screen?

Syntax
LOGO       Make the necessary correction in the following command: SETXY 100 PD.
BASIC      Make the necessary correction in the following statement: PRINT WHAT YEAR IS IT?

Interpreting Programs
LOGO       What will be displayed on the screen when the following program is run: REPEAT 4 [RT 90 FD 20]
BASIC      What will be displayed on the screen when this program is run?
```
100    A=15
110    IF A<20 THEN PRINT "FUN";
120    IF A>10 THEN PRINT "RUN";
130    PRINT "GUN"
```

Generating Programs
LOGO       Graphics: Write a program to make the computer draw the initials IBM.
           Logical Relations: Write a program to make the computer count by 5's and print out each number.
BASIC      Write a program that will ask a person their first name, last name, height, and weight. After obtaining this information, the program should display it on the screen. The following display is an example for Mary Evans, who is 62 inches tall and weighs 105 pounds:
```
FIRST NAME:   MARY
LAST NAME:    EVANS
HEIGHT:    62 INCHES
WEIGHT:    105 POUNDS
```

*Posttest.*    At the end of the workshop, all students took an achievement test (individually). For both LOGO and BASIC, the tests measured their mastery of basic commands, principles of syntax, ability to interpret programs, and ability to generate programs. Example items for each type of outcome are presented in Table 8.2.

*Peer Interaction Variables.*    Students' conversations about their work were coded in terms of the interaction directed at each other (peer-directed interaction was coded in both the LOGO and BASIC studies) and in terms of the kinds of planning behavior that students carried out with each other (BASIC study only).

Six categories of peer-directed interaction were coded (see Table 8.3). "Gives explanation" included describing the function or purpose of a command or series of commands to another student. "Receives explanation" was the receipt of the aforementioned information. Students gave other students explanations after they had made an error and in response to requests for explanations (e.g., "Why do you do FD?"). The distinction between receiving explanations after errors and receiving explanations after requests was made only in the LOGO study; in the BASIC study, these categories could not be reliably distinguished and so were combined. "Gives input suggestion" was a suggestion for what to type on the keyboard and included no elaboration. "Receives input suggestion" was the receipt of those suggestions. "Receives response to question" included the response to questions students asked of each other that did not fall into the other categories. "Receives no help" occurred in the LOGO study in three ways. First, sometimes students made errors without other students giving subsequent feedback about why a statement or program was incorrect. Second, students sometimes requested information and did not receive any response. Finally, students sometimes asked for an explanation and did not receive one. None of this behavior occurred in the BASIC study.

*Planning and Debugging Variables.*    Planning and debugging are considered critical activities in computer programming and much empirical work has focused on planning and debugging styles of expert and novice computer programmers (Atwood, Jeffries, & Polson, 1980; Dalbey & Linn, 1984; Galanter, 1983; Nagy & Pennebaker, 1971; Papert, Watt, diSessa, & Weir, 1979; Pea, 1983; Pea & Kurland, 1983). The few studies to examine the link between planning and learning of computer programming used broad variables and found mixed results: Schneiderman, Mayer, McKay, and Heller (1977) found no benefits of flowcharts for achievement, whereas Bradley (1986) found a positive relationship between a top-down approach toward LOGO problem-solving and learning outcomes. Because of the hypothesized importance of planning and debugging for computer programming, and the fact that these variables have never been examined in group contexts for learning, they were included here.

Although planning and debugging is examined here in a small group context, the interpretations may also generalize to individual learning settings.

A variety of planning and debugging categories were coded in the BASIC study (see Table 8.4). First, planning was carried out at different levels of abstraction (the labels were derived from the work of Hayes-Roth & Hayes-Roth, 1979). The most abstract level was design planning, in which the student described the general approach to writing the computer program or part of it using natural English rather than computer terms, for example, "*He* [the computer] has to say what city he [the person at the keyboard] lives in. He has to say it." (Webb et al., 1986, p. 248). This student was trying to determine the relationship between the PRINT statements and the INPUT statements in the first part of the program. An intermediate level of planning (called "procedure planning") explicitly identified a computer command to be used (e.g., INPUT), but did not specify a particular line of code to enter into the computer. The least abstract level of planning was "operation planning." Here, the student specified the exact computer code to enter on the keyboard, for example, "Put hello and then put . . . wait, I'll show you. You gotta put quote, you gotta put quote, quotation" (Webb et al., 1986, p. 249). All debugging was carried out at the operation level.

Second, planning concerned two amounts of the computer program: a single statement or chunks consisting of more than one statement. Chunks typically consisted of two or three lines of code. Students never planned their program in entirety before entering lines of code. Only design planning dealt with chunks as well as single statements. All specification of lines of code (operation planning) was done with single statements, even though several statements had the same, or similar, formats. All debugging was carried out with single statements, even though students often made the same mistake in more than one statement.

Finally, planning and debugging was carried out either without any instructor being present at the time or during conversations with an instructor. For example, when students asked an instructor for help, the instructor sometimes asked them leading questions to prompt them to verbalize how to complete the program. In responding to the instructor's leading question, students often verbalized the answer to their own questions.

## Results

Three sets of findings are presented and discussed here: the relationship between peer-directed interaction and achievement, the relationship between planning and debugging behavior and achievement, and the relationship between student characteristics and behavior. The results of the computer-programming studies are placed in the context of previous research in noncomputer studies investigating the same or similar variables.

Based on previous research in noncomputer settings (described in detail in the following section), several predictions were made here. Concerning the relationship between peer interaction and achievement, it was hypothesized that giving explanations and possibly receiving explanations would be positively related to achievement, and that *not* receiving help when needed would be negatively related to achievement. Giving and receiving information other than explanations were not expected to relate to achievement. Concerning planning and debugging behavior, it was hypothesized that planning at a general level in students' own words would be positively related to achievement. Finally, the students who gave the most help to other students were expected to be high-ability students.

## Peer-Directed Interaction and Programming Achievement

Table 8.3 presents the partial correlations between peer-directed interaction variables and achievement controlling for ability. Because the interest here is in determining the effects of peer interaction on learning, it is necessary to present partial correlations controlling for ability to test the counterhypothesis that interaction is a function of achievement. Significant partial correlations help support the hypothesis that interaction influences achievement and not vice versa. (See the previous section for description of the ability measures used as control variables.)

All of the interaction variables significantly predicted at least one programming outcome measure, although the results were not always consistent across studies. Giving explanations was positively related to command knowledge and the ability to interpret programs in the BASIC study, but did not relate to any programming outcome in the LOGO study. Previous research has consistently found a positive relationship between giving explanations and achievement (typically in mathematics classrooms, e.g., Peterson & Janicki, 1979; Peterson, Janicki, & Swing, 1981; Peterson & Swing, 1984; Swing & Peterson, 1982; Webb 1980a, 1980b, 1982a, 1982b, 1982c, 1984c; Webb & Kenderski, 1984). Giving explanations is hypothesized to help the explainer restructure and clarify material in his or her own mind while preparing to explain it to another (see Bargh & Schul, 1980). The lack of any significant correlation in the LOGO study was, therefore, unexpected.

The explanations given in the two studies were reexamined to determine whether the explanations of LOGO were less accurate or less complete than explanations of BASIC. The results, however, showed comparable levels of accuracy (high) and elaboration among the explanations in the two studies. Another post hoc hypothesis for the different results between studies concerns differences between the computer languages. Nearly all of the aforementioned research showing a positive relationship between giving explanations and achievement involved mathematics topics (e.g., computation, metric system, exponential notation, area and volume). Perhaps BASIC is more similar to these mathematical topics than LOGO (Papert, 1980a, 1980b, pointed out aspects of

TABLE 8.3
Partial Correlations Between
Peer-Directed Interaction and Achievement

| Interaction Measure | Command Knowledge | Syntax | Interpreting Programs | Generating Programs |
|---|---|---|---|---|
| **Gives explanation** | | | | |
| LOGO | .05 | .12 | −.04 | .11 |
| BASIC | .33* | −.30 | .52** | .19 |
| **Gives input suggestion** | | | | |
| LOGO | −.09 | .06 | .09 | −.09 |
| BASIC | .26 | −.13 | .36* | .01 |
| **Receives explanation** | | | | |
| LOGO | | | | |
|   After error | .24 | .30* | .11 | .24 |
|   After request | −.47** | −.08 | −.03 | −.18 |
| BASIC(a) | .45* | −.23 | .29 | −.03 |
| **Receives response to question** | | | | |
| LOGO | .08 | −.13 | −.09 | −.16 |
| BASIC | .44** | .08 | .43** | .12 |
| **Receives input suggestion** | | | | |
| LOGO | .31* | −.29 | .02 | .09 |
| BASIC | .29 | .11 | −.04 | −.20 |
| **Receives no help** | | | | |
| LOGO | | | | |
|   After error | −.19 | −.35* | −.08 | −.23 |
|   After request for information | −.27 | −.31* | −.22 | −.32* |
|   After request for explanation | −.30* | −.17 | .02 | −.29 |
| BASIC | (b) | (b) | (b) | (b) |

*Note.* Partial correlations control for ability; see text.

*Note.* Data for the LOGO study are from "Microcomputer learning in small groups: Cognitive requirements and group processes" by N. M. Webb, 1984, *Journal of Educational Psychology, 76,* p. 1083. Copyright 1984, by the American Psychological Association.

*Note.* Some data for the BASIC study are from "Problem-solving strategies and group processes in small groups learning computer programming" by N. M. Webb, P. Ender, and S. Lewis, 1986, *American Educational Research Journal, 23,* p. 253. Copyright 1986 by the American Educational Research Association. Adapted by permission.

[a]Distinction between errors and requests not possible in BASIC study: see text.
[b]Behavior did not occur in BASIC study.
*$p < .05$.
**$p < .01$

LOGO that differ from conventional "school mathematics"). Another possibility is that there was more important nonverbal behavior occurring in the LOGO study than in the BASIC study. For example, explanations of LOGO may have included statements drawing figures for each other. These kinds of explanations could not be captured by the audiotapes. Clearly, further analysis of the LOGO explanations must be conducted to explain the lack of significant correlations, as well as further research using videotapes to document nonverbal behavior.

Receiving explanations also had mixed results across studies. This is consistent with mixed relationship between receiving explanations and achievement found in previous research: some studies found positive relationships (see Webb, 1983), some found no relationship (Peterson & Janicki, 1979; Peterson, Janicki, & Swing, 1981), and others found negative relationships (Swing & Peterson, 1982). Two out of the three statistically significant relationships were positive; one was negative. The positive relationships are intuitively reasonable. Receiving explanations should help the student learn how to correct an error or complete the program.

The negative relationship between receiving an explanation in response to a request for one and command knowledge in the LOGO study ($r = -.47$, see Table 8.3) was hypothesized in the original study to be the result of students depending on the explanations to complete their programming, rather than learning from the explanations (see Webb, 1984a). If students were relying on others' explanations to complete the program (specifically, to use the correct commands) rather than learning the meaning of commands, the more often they asked others for help, the less they would be expected to learn. Although this explanation could account for a negative relationship, why it would apply only to learning commands and only in the LOGO study is unclear. More work needs to be done to unravel this complex set of results.

Receiving responses to questions was positively related to command knowledge and the ability to interpret programs in the BASIC study, but not in the LOGO study. The difference in results between studies may be related to the kinds of questions that students asked each other. Informal inspection of questions asked showed that in the BASIC study, students asked each other for specific information about commands or lines of code. They debated how to correct errors as well as the sequencing of commands in a line of code. In the LOGO study, in contrast, students often asked each other for confirmation that their programs were correct or asked other students to help them complete their programs or detect errors. Furthermore, the questions in the LOGO study were often phrased very generally ("What do we do now?", "What do I push now?") whereas the questions in the BASIC study often requested specific information ("What does the dollar sign do?", "What [variable] name should we use?").

When previous studies with noncomputer tasks have distinguished between different kinds of questions, they have found that questions requesting specific information and those that were phrased explicitly were more effective for learning than questions phrased generally or ambiguously (Peterson Wilkinson, Spinelli, & Swing, 1984; Webb & Kenderski, 1985; Wilkinson & Calculator, 1982a, 1982b). A comprehensive analysis of the kinds of questions asked may clarify the different results between those two studies, as well as in other studies that have found no relationship between responses to questions and achievement (see Webb, 1982c).

The other interaction variable that has been examined in previous research is receiving no help. Receiving no help, either after making an error, after requesting information, or after requesting an explanation, was negatively related to command knowledge, knowledge of syntax, and the ability to generate programs in the LOGO study. All but one of the nonsignificant partial correlation coefficients were also negative. This set of findings is consistent with the previous research with noncomputer activities. When students make an error or ask for help, they typically do not understand the function of commands or how to complete a program. Receiving no help from others in these circumstances logically would be detrimental to their learning. Without receiving help, they would not be able to correct their misunderstanding or learn how to complete the program correctly (see Webb, 1982c).

A further check was done to make sure that requesting help (rather than the response to requests) was not the key variable. Requesting help did not correlate significantly with ability (correlations ranged from $-.22$, $p < .11$, to $.17$, $p < .18$). Nor did requesting help correlate significantly with achievement (partial correlations controlling for ability ranged from $-.29$, $p < .06$, to $-.01$, $p < .49$). These results help support the interpretation that the responses to requests for help were more important for learning than was the frequency of asking for help.

The interaction category receiving no help never occurred in the BASIC study. Students always corrected each other's errors (when they recognized that one had been made), and they always answered each other's questions. A likely explanation for this result is the group size—two. When there are only two students working at a computer, it is quite clear who is being asked the question. To ignore a question would be obvious and rude. In the LOGO study, in contrast, students in the three-person groups could assume that another student would answer the question and so not take responsibility for answering it.

The remaining two interaction variables presented in Table 8.2, giving and receiving input suggestions, have no counterparts in noncomputer studies. Giving input suggestions was positively related to interpreting programs in the BASIC study, but not in the LOGO study. Conversely, receiving input suggestions was positively related to command knowledge in the LOGO study, but not in the BASIC study. Giving input suggestions would be expected to have a positive effect on learning when the student used that opportunity to think through the outcome of the suggestion, or to test his or her hypotheses about the correct command or program. Giving input suggestions would not have much effect on learning if they were guesses or were not used as opportunities to test hypotheses about how to complete a program correctly. Similar claims can be made about receiving input suggestions. Merely using them to complete the program would not be related to learning, whereas trying to understand the suggestion in the context of the program would be beneficial for learning. It is possible, then, that different processes were occurring in the two studies.

In summary, the kinds of peer-directed interaction that showed positive relationships with achievement appeared mostly in the BASIC study. They included giving explanations (two significant correlations), giving input suggestions (one significant correlation), receiving responses to questions (two significant correlations), and receiving input suggestions (one significant correlation). Receiving no help when needed occurred only in the LOGO study. This behavior was negatively related to achievement (four significant correlations). Receiving explanations had mixed results across studies with two positive correlations and one negative correlation. These results suggest that actively participating in group discussions, by giving explanations and input suggestions and receiving information, may be beneficial for learning at least some aspects of computer programming. Some next steps for research (discussed in more detail in later sections) are to determine how to encourage students to engage in the behaviors that seem to be positively related to achievement and discourage students from engaging in the behaviors found to be negatively related to achievement.

### Planning and Debugging Behavior and Programming Achievement

Table 8.4 presents the partial correlations between planning and debugging behavior and programming achievement in the BASIC study. These variables were not examined in the LOGO study.

*Presence of the Instructor.*    The most striking finding is that much of the planning and debugging carried out without the presence of an instructor was positively related to most achievement outcomes, whereas verbalizing the same kinds of behavior to an instructor was negatively related or not related to achievement. This finding is consistent with those of Durling and Schick (1976), who compared concept attainment across three conditions: verbalizing to a peer also learning the task, verbalizing to a confederate supposedly learning the task, and verbalizing to the experimenter who supposedly had already mastered the task. On most performance criteria, students verbalizing to a peer or confederate performed better than students verbalizing to the experimenter.

Durling and Schick suggested that students verbalizing to another student may have viewed themselves as teachers, whereas those verbalizing to the experimenter may have viewed themselves as students. And, as Bargh and Schul

TABLE 8.4
Partial Correlations Between Planning Behavior
and Achievement in BASIC

| Behavior | Command Knowledge | Syntax | Interpreting Programs | Generating Programs |
|---|---|---|---|---|
| No instructor present | | | | |
| Design planning | | | | |
| Chunk | .41* | .17 | .47** | .49** |
| Statement | −.01 | .08 | .33* | −.13 |
| Procedure planning | −.16 | −.10 | −.14 | −.24 |
| Operation planning | .16 | −.13 | .34* | −.01 |
| Operation debugging | .50** | .02 | .58*** | .44** |
| Instructor present | | | | |
| Design planning | | | | |
| Chunk | −.29 | −.23 | .03 | .18 |
| Statement | −.41* | −.14 | −.15 | .09 |
| Procedure planning | −.36* | −.22 | −.06 | .23 |
| Operation planning | −.37* | −.27 | −.10 | −.01 |
| Operation debugging | −.27 | .02 | −.32* | .11 |

*Note.* From "Problem-solving strategies and group processes in small groups learning computer programming" by N. M. Webb, P. Ender, and S. Lewis, 1986, *American Educational Research Journal, 23,* p. 250. Copyright 1986 by the American Educational Research Association, Washington, D.C. Adapted by permission.

*Note.* Procedure planning, operation planning, and operation debugging occurred for statements only.

$^*p < .05.$   $^{**}p < .01$   $^{***}p < .001$

(1980) suggested, students preparing to teach material to another student may produce a more highly organized cognitive structure as a result of reorganizing and clarifying the material for effective presentation. Perhaps students expended more mental effort and greater mindfulness, to use the concepts of Salomon (1983, 1985) and Langer and Imber (1979), when communicating to another student than when communicating to the instructor. The greater mental effort when communicating with students would be expected to lead to greater learning (see Salomon, 1985).

Before placing too much emphasis on the difference in outcomes between the presence and absence of the instructor, however, it is important to ascertain whether the students who carried out much planning and debugging with the instructor were those who had particular problems with the work. If true, this would explain the lack of positive correlations in Table 8.4. Further analyses were conducted, then, to investigate this possible counterhypothesis.

For simplicity, the further analyses used a summary variable created to represent verbalizing planning and debugging to the instructor: the sum of the relevant variables in Table 8.4. Furthermore, the group mean was used as the unit of analysis because many of the variables (the incidence of errors and instructor talk) could not be reliably coded for individual students.

Groups who frequently verbalized their planning and debugging strategies to the instructor did not have lower ability than other groups (correlation between ability and verbalizing planning and debugging: $r = -.29, p < .15$) nor did they make more errors than other groups (correlation between number of errors and verbalizing planning and debugging: $r = -.30, p < .14$). They did, however, ask more questions of the instructor than other groups did (correlation between asking the instructor questions and verbalizing planning and debugging to the instructor: $r = 0.77, p < .001$). Furthermore, these groups also received more reactive instructor behavior than other groups did: The instructor behaviors that significantly correlated with student verbalizing of planning and debugging to the instructor were giving information in response to a question ($r = .72, p < .001$), referring students to previous lessons ($r = .64, p < .01$), and asking leading questions ($r = .92, p < .001$).

These results help clarify the sequence of student and instructor behavior within these student–instructor conversations. Students who frequently asked the instructor questions received the kinds of responses from the instructor that would encourage them to generate their own answers. Students then verbalized to the instructor what they thought their next action should be. The evidence presented here suggests that this sequence was a characteristic of these groups' working style rather than an indication that they were having difficulty.

It is important to note that we cannot draw any conclusions from these results about the recommended instructor behavior. The indirect and reactive style of the instructor in this study had few effects on students' learning. Although some of the correlations were negative, suggesting that students who often verbalized to the instructor learned less of some aspects of BASIC than students who exhibited this behavior less frequently, it is not appropriate to conclude that students should refrain from interacting with the instructor. First, the results come from basically only one instructor and so are based on a limited sample of observations. Second, some other style of instructor behavior may have promoted student–instructor interaction that was positively related to achievement. In fact, the results of the study by Sloane and Linn (chap. 9, this volume) show that explicit teaching ("the extent to which teachers provide explicit instruction in strategies for solving problems, explain difficult concepts, lead student discussion about the assignments, and encourage students to discuss how topics relate or how previously learned procedures can be applied to new problems") and extensive feedback may be effective for learning. If the instructor in this study had used a more direct style of interaction, the effects of verbalizing to the instructor may have been different.

*Levels of Planning and Debugging.*    Of the three levels of planning verbalized without an instructor being present, design planning was most consistently related to programming outcomes. When students discussed in their own words how to construct part of a computer program (design planning of chunks), it was effective for learning. Putting their ideas about planning portions of a program into their own words probably helped them form the structure of the program and remember it (see also Bower, 1973; Gagné & Smith, 1962; Mayer, 1979, 1981; O'Neill, 1978; Paivio, 1969). Why the positive effect was much weaker for design planning of single statements is not clear.

Procedure planning without an instructor showed no relationship with learning outcomes, and operation planning was positively related only to the ability to interpret programs. In the process of planning lines of code, they may have formed hypotheses about the possible outcomes of that code. This activity would help them interpret outcomes.

Operation debugging was positively related to three of the four achievement outcomes. The more discussion students had about how to correct their errors, the more they learned. Because a high frequency of debugging behavior could be explained by a large number of errors, or extensive discussion of each error, or both, it is important to separate out these two potential interpretations. To do this, the total number of errors that students made was calculated and used as a control variable in partial correlations. Although there was a marginally significant simple correlation between the frequency of debugging and number of errors ($r = .30, p < .06$), the partial correlations between debugging and programming outcomes controlling for ability and number of errors made were still statistically significant and similar in magnitude to the partial correlations presented in Table 8.3. So, even controlling for the number of errors, discussion about debugging was positively related to achievement. The implication, then, is not that students should be encouraged to make errors, but rather that they should be encouraged to discuss those errors (and subsequent corrections) fully.

*Summary.*    In summary, students' discussions to each other about planning (when it was done at a general level in their own words) and debugging were positively related to several achievement outcomes. Verbalizing planning and debugging strategies to the instructor was largely unrelated to achievement, although some correlations were negative. These results suggest that students should be encouraged to verbalize to each other their strategies for planning the program and for correcting their errors. Their discussions about planning seem to be particularly beneficial if they use their own words to plan chunks of the program at a time, rather than coding single statements at a time. Because previous studies have found that students resist planning their programs, preferring instead to start immediately to write lines of code (Dalbey & Linn, 1984; Galanter, 1983; Pea, 1983; see also Pea & Kurland, 1983), special activities may be required to encourage planning activity. Some possibilities are discussed in the final section of the chapter.

It should be noted that the conclusions just drawn about planning and debugging may also apply to individual learning settings. That is, students working alone may also benefit from trying to formulate their plans in their own words and to plan and debug their own programs before consulting the instructor. Future research is needed to determine whether discussing plans with another student has advantages over formulating similar plans by students working by themselves. The work by Bargh and Schul (1980) and Durling and Schick (1976) on the benefits for learning of preparing to teach another student and verbalizing material to another student suggests that it might.

## STUDENT CHARACTERISTICS PREDICTING
## STUDENT BEHAVIOR

In noncomputer research, several student characteristics have been shown to relate to student-interaction variables. A consistent finding is that the most-able students tend to give the most explanations; less frequently, the least-able students tend to be the target of the explanations (see Webb, 1982c). Other studies have found that gender is a predictor of student behavior in small groups: in above-average mathematics classrooms, females were less successful than males in obtaining help (Webb, 1984b; Webb & Kenderski, 1985).

None of these findings appeared in the studies of LOGO and BASIC computer programming (Webb, 1984a; Webb et al., 1986). Very few of the correlations between student characteristics (including age, gender, previous experience with computers, mathematics ability, spatial ability, nonverbal processing, field independence, and holistic processing) and measures of student behavior were statistically significant, and those that were siginificant formed no consistent pattern.

The lack of relationships between student characteristics and behavior may be explained, in part, by the task and setting. In conventional subject matters, such as mathematics, ability is a status characteristic that influences student behavior: high-status individuals play dominant roles in group work (Dembo & McAuliffe, 1987). Because most of the students participating in the LOGO and BASIC studies had little or no previous experience with computers, the relevant student-ability variables may not have been salient to them. What needs to be tested is whether student characteristics predict behavior among students who have more experience with computers.

In any case, the lack of a significant relationship between ability and the social interaction measures in these studies shows that social interaction was not a proxy for ability. This finding, and the significant partial correlations between social interaction and programming achievement, help support the interpretation that social interaction influences achievement, rather than being a function of it.

## IMPLICATIONS FOR TEACHING
## COMPUTER PROGRAMMING

The results of the studies of LOGO and BASIC computer programming described here suggest that learning in social contexts is beneficial for students who
actively participate in group work. The specific behaviors in these studies that
were found to be positively related to some achievement outcomes were giving
explanations, giving input suggestions, receiving responses to questions, receiving input suggestions, verbalizing planning and debugging strategies to peers,
and to some extent, receiving explanations. These behaviors should be encouraged in the classroom. The behavior found to be negatively related to achievement was receiving no help when needed. This behavior should be discouraged.
The research prediction growing out of this correlational research is that increasing students' active participation in group work (in the ways just described) will
lead to increased learning. This prediction needs to be tested empirically.

In the event that encouraging active participation in group work promotes
greater learning, what can the teacher do to encourage the kinds of interaction
that seem to be beneficial for learning and discourage those that seem to be
detrimental for learning? We present some ideas here that are drawn from
literature on cooperative learning and on learning computer programming. These
suggestions are only loosely related to the results described in this chapter and
most have not yet been tested empirically.

First, teachers can set the stage for productive peer interaction by establishing
a climate that encourages cooperative behavior. A variety of team-building
activities have been designed to promote interpersonal cooperation among students. Some examples are "Interview" and "Roundtable Brainstorming" (Kagan,
1985; Johnson & Johnson, 1975). The comprehensive program developed by
Solomon et al. (1985) includes cooperative activities and games, regular
participation in helping and sharing activities, opportunities to experience others
setting positive examples, role playing, and positive discipline. Graves and
Graves (1985) described an ecological approach for developing cooperative
classroom environments that takes classroom participants through a series of
steps from recognizing the interpersonal skills that are important for classroom
functioning to the ability to participate in creative group problem solving.

Second, teachers can encourage active participation and helping behavior by
using a group reward structure. Instead of receiving individual grades on the
basis of their own performance (individualistic reward structure) or in competition with other students (such as grading on the curve, competitive reward
structure), students are rewarded on the basis of the achievement of all members
of the group. Research in cooperative learning has shown consistently that a
cooperative reward structure promotes helping behavior among students (Johnson, Johnson, & Stanne, 1985, 1986; Slavin, 1983; Webb, 1982c; see also
Dickson & Vereen, 1983). Because the achievement of all students in the group

is part of the grade or score for each individual student, students are motivated to make sure that everyone in the group learns the material.

Third, teachers can encourage students to help each other and can use specific techniques to train students to give explanations to each other and to be responsive to others' need for help. Some techniques might include modeling and demonstrating beneficial behaviors for students, giving students direct instruction on how to give explanations and how to ask for help, giving students practice in helping each other and providing feedback about their interaction, and evaluating a group's role play of effective interaction (for more details, see Lee, Cohn, Oakes, Farivar, & Webb, 1985).

Fourth, teachers can encourage groups to discuss how they will plan their programs before they start writing code and encourage them to use their own words to describe the purpose of the program and how they will write it. Specific techniques that might be adapted from previous research are the following. Teachers can require students to describe the function of computer statements in their own words (Mayer, 1979, 1981). Clements (1985) suggested the following sequence of activities to encourage planning: planning the program on paper, writing it in English or using pictures, breaking it down into component parts, naming variables, acting out the program, translating the program into computer language, and then typing it into the computer. Still another suggestion is to require students to make action diagrams of their programs before writing it (Linn & Fisher, 1983; see also Dalbey & Linn, 1984).

Finally, teachers can encourage students to work with each other to write their programs and correct their errors before consulting with the teacher. Verbalizing their problem-solving strategies (at least planning segments of the program in their own language and debugging their errors) seemed to be beneficial for learning, so this behavior should be encouraged.


## NEXT STEPS FOR RESEARCH

A number of issues need to be investigated to determine the most effective ways of setting up the social context of instruction in computer programming. First is the issue of group composition. Previous research in noncomputer settings shows that certain combinations of students constitute effective groups, whereas other combinations do not. For example, heterogeneous groups on ability promote active interaction between the most-able and least-able members, but sometimes restrict participation by the middle-ability members. Groups that are more uniform on ability tend to result in active and effective participation among all members, for example, all medium-ability students, lows and mediums, or mediums and highs (two exceptions are homogeneous groups with all high-ability students and homogeneous groups with all low-ability students; see Webb, 1982c, 1983).

Group gender composition also seems to have an important impact on participation in group work. Groups with equal numbers of girls and boys may promote more equitable participation than groups with more boys than girls or vice versa (Webb, 1982a). Interestingly, in groups with an unequal number of girls and boys, the girls are less successful than boys in obtaining help, regardless of which gender predominates. Whether or not similar results of group composition will appear in classes learning computer programming remains to be investigated.

A second question for further research concerns the most effective instructional strategies to use to promote beneficial behaviors. The previous section of this chapter suggests some strategies that the teacher might use, but few have been tested empirically. Furthermore, no one has investigated whether some kinds of students might benefit more from some strategies than others.

A third issue is the size of the group. Some studies have found greater variation in participation rates in larger groups than in smaller groups, but none of them found any differences in achievement levels across group sizes (Okey & Majer, 1976; Trowbridge & Durnin, 1984a, 1984b). Because these studies did not compare the achievement of active participants with passive group members, however, we cannot conclude that group size is unimportant. Indeed, one important difference between the two studies reported in this chapter probably did result from the difference between group sizes. One of the most potent findings from previous studies is that, in groups with more than two students, some students do not receive the help they need; their failure to receive help is negatively related to achievement (see Webb, 1982c). In contrast, in the current study of BASIC, with two students per group, students nearly always received answers to their questions. Thus, it seems clear that groups of two and larger than two have different dynamics.

A fourth question is which kinds of computer programming activities should be carried out in a social context and which ones should not. Perhaps the most effective instructional sequence involves individual work for some phases of learning computer programming and group work for other phases. Whether an initial phase of work in which individuals try to plan or write a program before working together to complete it (as in Cheney, 1977) is more or less effective than group work for an entire task has never been investigated.

The fifth issue concerns the length of instruction. The studies reported here were based on relatively short periods of instruction (1 day and 1 week). Investigation of longer-term instruction is needed to determine whether the same pattern of results will generalize over different lengths of training. The few studies of the stability of the relationship between peer interaction and achievement over time give mixed results (Webb, 1984c; Webb & Cullian, 1983), so no predictions can be made here.

Another issue is the importance of nonverbal behavior in programming activities. The studies reported here used audiotapes, not videotapes. Yet, important information may be communicated nonverbally, such as pointing to the screen or keyboard and, of course, typing on the keyboard. Some pioneering methods of capturing nonverbal communication have been developed and carried out by Trowbridge, Bork, and colleagues (Potter, 1982; Trowbridge & Bork, 1981; Trowbridge & Durnin, 1984a, 1984b). By recording students' behavior while working together (video plus audio) and all key pushes of the computer keyboard simultaneously, they can produce simultaneous images of students working together (with audio) and what appeared on the computer screen. Such methods have great promise for the study of peer interaction and learning of computer programming.

The present research also did not clarify the optimal role of the instructor. The best way to clarify this question is to conduct a randomized experiment that compares different styles of instructor interaction with students.

Finally, the present research did not investigate the mechanisms by which peer interaction influences learning. The introduction of this chapter suggests that peer interaction might produce cognitive restructuring in a variety of ways, for example, through conflict resolution, modeling, internalizing the group's strategies and solutions, and reorganizing and clarifying material during explanations. As Forman and Cazden (1985) pointed out, however, the studies proposing these mechanisms typically did not systematically observe peer interaction. Future research needs to systematically analyze peer interaction for evidence of conflict resolution, clarification and restructuring of material, and internalization of group work (e.g., students who initially have difficulty solving problems adopt strategies proposed by the group and apply them successfully to later problems). Forman and Cazden (1985) have done pioneering work in this direction by tracing how problem-solving strategies that first appear during social interaction later become internalized. In pioneering work testing the model of sociocognitive conflict, Bearison et al. (1986) systematically examined the frequency of different kinds of disagreement between students (e.g., verbal, gestural, whether accompanied by justifications or explanations) as predictors of cognitive change. These kinds of systematic analyses of interaction between students are essential to help clarify how peer interaction influences learning.

In conclusion, current research shows how a social context for learning computer programming may be beneficial for achievement. The next steps are to better understand how learning takes place in these settings and, consequently, to refine the social context of instruction to maximize the learning of all participants.

## REFERENCES

Artzt, A. (1979). Student teams in mathematics class. *Mathematics Teacher, 72,* 505–508.
Atwood, M. E., Jeffries, R., & Polson, P. G. (1980). *Studies in plan construction. I: Analysis of an extended protocol* (Tech. Rep. No. SAI-80-028-DEN). Englewood, CO: Science Applications.
Bandura, A. (1969). *Principles of behavior modification.* New York: Holt, Rinehart & Winston.

Bargh, J. A., & Schul, Y. (1980). On the cognitive benefits of teaching. *Journal of Educational Psychology, 72,* 593–604.

Bearison, D. J., Magzamen, S., & Filardo, E. K. (1986). Socio-conflict and cognitive growth in young children. *Merrill-Palmer Quarterly, 32,* 51–72.

Becker, H. J. (1984). *School uses of microcomputers: Reports from a national survey* (Issue No. 6, pp. 1–11). Center for Social Organization of Schools, The Johns Hopkins University.

Berlyne, D. E. (1965a). *Structure and direction in thinking.* New York: Wiley.

Berlyne, D. E. (1965b). Curiosity and education. In J. D. Krumboltz (Ed.), *Learning and the educational process* (pp. 67–89). Chicago: Rand McNally.

Bower, G. H. (1973). Mental imagery and associative learning. In L. Gregg (Ed.), *Cognition in learning and memory* (pp. – ). New York: Wiley.

Bradley, C. (1985). The relationships between students' information-processing styles and LOGO programming. *Journal of Educational Computing Research, 1,* 427–434.

Bronfenbrenner, U. (1970). *The two worlds of childhood: U.S. and the U.S.S.R.* New York: Russell Sage Foundation.

Buckholdt, D. R., & Wodarski, J. S. (1978). The effects of different reinforcement systems on cooperative behaviors exhibited by children in classroom contexts. *Journal of Research and Development in Education 12*(1), 50–68.

Campbell, P. B. (1986, April). *Computers, children, and data.* Paper presented at the annual meeting of the American Educational Research Association, San Francisco, CA.

Cheney, P. H. (1977). Teaching computer programming in an environment where collaboration is required. *Journal of the Association for Educational Data Systems, 11,* 1–5.

Clements, D. H. (1985). Research on LOGO in education: is the turtle slow but steady, or not even in the race? *Computers in the schools, 2,* 55–71.

Cohen, J. (1986). Theoretical considerations of peer tutoring. *Psychology in the Schools 23*(2), 175–186.

Dalbey, J., & Linn, M. (1984). *Making programming instruction cognitively demanding.* Paper presented at the annual meeting of the American Educational Research Association, New Orleans, LA.

Damon, W. (1984). Peer education: The untapped potential. *Journal of Applied Developmental Psychology 5*(4), 331–343.

Dembo, M. H., & McAuliffe, T. J. (1987). Effects of perceived ability and grade status on social interaction and influence in cooperative groups. *Journal of Educational Psychology, 79,* 415–423.

Dickinson, D. K. (1985). *Young children's collaborative writing at the computer.* Paper presented at the annual meeting of the American Educational Research Association, Chicago, IL.

Dickson, W. P., & Vereen, M. A. (1983). Two students at one microcomputer. *Theory into Practice, 22,* 296–300.

Diem, R. A. (1986a). Computers in a school environment: Preliminary report of the social consequences. *Theory and Research in Social Education, 14,* 163–170.

Diem, R. A. (1986b). *The impact of microcomputer technology on selected educational environments: Three case studies.* Paper presented at the annual meeting of the American Educational Research Association, San Francisco, CA.

Doise, W., Mugny, G., & Perret-Clermont, A-N. (1975). Social interaction and the development of cognitive operations. *European Journal of Social Psychology, 5,* 367–383.

Durling, R., & Schick, C. (1976). Concept attainment by pairs and individuals as a function of vocalization. *Journal of Educational Psychology, 68,* 83–91.

Ellis, S., & Rogoff, B. (1982). The strategies and efficacy of child vs. adult teachers. *Child Development, 53,* 730–735.

Forman, E., & Cazden, C. (1985). Exploring Vygotskian perspectives in education: The cognitive value of peer interaction. In J. Wertsch (Ed.), *Culture, communication, and cognition: Vygotskian perspectives* (pp. 323–347). New York: Cambridge University Press.

French, J. W., Ekstrom, R., & Price, L. (1963). *Kits of reference tests for cognitive factors.* Princeton, NJ: Educational Testing Service.

Gagne, R. M., & Smith, E. C., Jr. (1962). A study of the effects of verbalization on problem solving. *Journal of Experimental Psychology, 63,* 12–18.

Galanter, E. (1983). *Kids and computers: The parents' microcomputer handbook.* New York: Putnam.

Gall, M. D., & Gall, J. P. (1976). The discussion method. In N. L. Gage (Ed.), *The psychology of teaching methods* (pp. 166–216). Chicago: The University of Chicago Press.

Genishi, C., McCollum, P., Strand, E., & Hamilton, S. (1985, April). *An observational study of young children and LOGO.* Paper presented at the annual meeting of the American Educational Research Association, Chicago, IL.

Graves, N. B., & Graves, T. D. (1985). Structuring a cooperative learning environment. In R. Slavin, S. Sharan, S. Kagan, R. Hertz-Lazarowitz, C. Webb, & R. Schmuck (Eds.), *Learning to cooperate, cooperating to learn* (pp. 403–436). New York: Plenum.

Hammond, L. K., & Goldman, M. (1961). Competition and noncompetition and its relationship to individual and group productivity. *Sociometry, 24,* 46–60.

Hatano, G. (1986, April). *Enhancing motivation for comprehension in science and mathematics through peer interaction.* Paper presented at the annual meeting of the American Educational Research Association, San Francisco, CA.

Hayes-Roth, B., & Hayes-Roth, F. (1979). A cognitive model of planning. *Cognitive Science, 3,* 275–310.

Heap, J. L. (1986, April). *Collaborative practices during computer writing in a first grade classroom.* Paper presented at the annual meeting of the American Educational Research Association, San Francisco, CA.

Hythecker, V. I., Rocklin, T. R., Dansereau, D. F., Lambiotte, J. G., Larson, C. O., & O'Donnell, A. M. (1985). A computer-based learning strategy training module: Development and evaluation. *Journal of Educational Computing Research, 1,* 275–283.

Jackson, V. C., & Riessman, F. (1977). A children teaching children program. *Theory into Practice, 16,* 280–284.

Jewson, J., & Pea, R. D. (1982). LOGO research at Bank Street College. *Byte, 7,* 322–323.

Johnson, D. W., & Johnson, R. T. (1975). *Joining together: Group theory and group skills.* Englewood Cliffs, NJ: Prentice-Hall.

Johnson, D. W., & Johnson, R. T. (1979). Conflict in the classroom: Controversy and learning. *Review of Educational Research, 49,* 51–70.

Johnson, R. T., Johnson, D. W., & Stanne, M. B. (1985). Effects of cooperative, competitive, and individualistic goal structures on computer-assisted instruction. *Journal of Educational Psychology 77*(6), 668–678.

Johnson, R. T., Johnson, D. W., & Stanne, M. B. (1986). Comparison of computer-assisted cooperation, competitive, and individualistic learning. *American Educational Research Journal, 23,* 383–392.

Kagan, S. (1985). Dimensions of cooperative classroom structures. In R. Slavin, S. Sharan, S. Kagan, R. Hertz-Lazarowitz, C. Webb, & R. Schmuck (Eds.), *Learning to cooperate, cooperating to learn* (pp. 67–96). New York: Plenum Press.

Kuhn, D. (1972). Mechanisms of change in the development of cognitive structures. *Child Development, 43,* 833–844.

Kull, J. A. (1986). Learning and LOGO. In P. Campbell & Fein (Eds.), *Young children and microcomputers.* Englewood Cliffs, NJ: Prentice-Hall.

Langer, E. J., & Imber, L. E. (1979). When practice makes imperfect: Debilitating effects of overlearning. *Journal of Personality and Social Psychology, 37,* 2014–2024.

Lee, K., Cohn, J., Oakes, J., Farivar, S., & Webb, N. M. (1985). *The helping behaviors handbook.* Los Angeles, CA: The Graduate School of Education, UCLA.

Linn, M. C., & Fisher, C. W. (1983). *The gap between promise and reality in computer education: Planning a response*. Paper presented at Making Our Schools More Effective: A Conference for California Educators, San Francisco, CA.

Littlejohn, T. D., Ross, R. P., & Gump, R. V. (1984, April). *Using microcomputers in elementary schools: Implementation issues*. Paper presented at the annual meeting of the American Educational Research Association, New Orleans, LA.

Mayer, R. E. (1979). A psychology of learning BASIC. *Communications of the ACM, 22*, 589–593.

Mayer, R. E. (1981). The psychology of how novices learn computer programming. *Computing Surveys, 13*, 121–141.

Mugny, G., & Doise, W. (1978) Socio-cognitive conflict and structure of individual and collective performances. *European Journal of Social Psychology, 8*, 181–192.

Murray, F. B. (1972). Acquisition of conservation through social interaction. *Developmental Psychology, 6*, 1–6.

Murray, J. P. (1974). Social learning and cognitive development: Modelling effects on children's understanding of conservation. *British Journal of Psychology, 65*, 151–160.

Muller, A. A., & Perlmutter, M. (1985). Preschool children's problem-solving interactions at computers and jigsaw puzzles. *Journal of Applied Developmental Psychology, 6*, 173–186.

Nagy, G., & Pennebaker, M. A. (1971). *A step toward automatic analysis of logically undetectable programming errors* (Research Rep. No. RC-3407). International Business Machines.

Noddings, N. (1985). Small groups as a setting for research on mathematical problem solving. In E. A. Silver (Ed.), *Teaching and learning mathematical problem solving* (pp. 345–359) Hillsdale, NJ: Lawrence Erlbaum Associates.

Okey, J. R., & Majer, K. (1976). Individual and small-group learning with computer-assisted instruction. *Audio-Visual Communication Review, 24*, 79–86.

O'Neill, H. F. (1978). *Learning strategies*. New York: Academic Press.

Paivio, A. (1969). Mental imagery in associative learning and memory. *Psychology Review, 76*, 241–263.

Palincsar, A. S. (1986). The role of dialogue in providing scaffolded instruction. *Educational Psychologist, 21*, 73–98.

Palincsar, A. S., & Brown, A. L. (1984). Reciprocal teaching of comprehension-fostering and comprehension-monitoring activities. *Cognition and Instruction, 1*, 117–175.

Papert, S., Watt, D., diSessa, A., & Weir, S. (1979). *Final report of the Brookline LOGO Project Part II: Project summary and data analysis* (LOGO Memo No. 53). Cambridge, MA: Artificial Intelligence Laboratory, Massachusetts Institute of Technology.

Papert, S. (1980a). *Mindstorms: Children, computers and powerful ideas*. New York: Basic Books.

Papert, S. (1980b). Teaching children thinking. In R. Taylor (Ed.), *The computer in the school* (pp. 161–176). New York: Teachers College Press.

Papert, S. (1980c). Teaching children to be mathematicians vs. teaching about mathematics. In R. Taylor (Ed.), *The computer in the school* (pp. 177–196). New York: Teachers College Press.

Pea, R. D. (1983, April). *LOGO programming and problem solving*. Paper presented at the annual meeting of the American Educational Research Association, Montreal, Canada.

Pea, R. D., & Kurland, D. M. (1983). *On the cognitive prerequisites of learning computer programming* (Rep. No. 18). New York: Bank Street College of Education, Center for children and technology.

Perlmutter, M, Behrend, S., Kuo, F., & Muller, A. (1986). *Social influence on preschool children's problem solving at a computer*. Unpublished paper, University of Michigan.

Perret-Clermont, A.-N. (1980). *Social interaction and cognitive development in children*. (*European Monographs in Social Psychology*, No. 19) New York: Academic Press.

Peterson, P. L., Janicki, T. C., & Swing, S. R. (1981). Ability × treatment interaction effects on children's learning in large-group and small-group approaches. *American Educational Research Journal, 18*, 453–473.

Peterson, P. L. & Janicki, T. C. (1979). Individual characteristics and children's learning in large-group and small-group approaches. *Journal of Educational Psychology, 71,* 677–687.

Peterson, P. L., & Swing, S. R. (1984, April). *Student's cognitions as mediators of the effectiveness of small-group learning.* Paper presented at the annual meeting of the American Educational Research Association, New Orleans, LA.

Peterson, P. L., Wilkinson, L. C., Spinelli, F., & Swing, S. R. (1984). Merging the process-product and the sociolinguistic paradigms: research on small-group processes. In P. L. Peterson, L. C. Wilkinson, & M. Hallinan (Eds.), *The social context of instruction* (pp. 126–152). Orlando, FL: Academic Press.

Piaget, J. (1970). Piaget's theory. In P. H. Mussen (Ed.), *Carmichael's manual of child psychology* (3rd ed., Vol. 1, pp. 703–732). New York: Wiley.

Potter, M. (1982). *Audio tape interface unit: Technical documentation.* Unpublished document, Educational Technology Center, University of California, Irvine.

Raven, J. C. (1958). *Standard progressive matrices.* London, England: H. K. Lewis.

Riel, M. (1983). Education and ecstasy: Computer chronicles of students writing together. *The Quarterly Newsletter of the Laboratory of Comparative Human Cognition, 5,* 59–67.

Rubin, A. (1983). The computer confronts language arts: Cans and shoulds for education. In A. C. Wilkinson (Ed.), *Classroom computers and cognitive science* (pp. 201–217). New York: Academic Press.

Salomon, G. (1983). The differential investment of mental effort in learning from different sources. *Educational Psychologist, 18,* 42–50.

Salomon, G. (1985). Information technologies: What you see is not (always) what you get. *Educational Psychologist, 20,* 207–216.

Schneiderman, B., Mayer, R., McKay, D., & Heller, R. (1977). Experimental investigations of the utility of detailed flowcharts in programming. *Communications of the Association for Computer Machinery (ACM), 20,* 373–381.

Schunk, D. H. (1987). Peer models and children's behavioral change. *Review of Educational Research, 57,* 149–174.

Shade, D. D., Nida, R. E., Lipinski, J. M., & Watson, J. A. (1986). Microcomputers and preschoolers: Working together in a classroom setting. *Computers in the Schools, 3,* 53–61.

Shrock, S., Matthias, M., Vensel, C., & Anastasoff, J., (1985, April). *Microcomputers and peer interaction: A naturalistic study of an elementary classroom.* Paper presented at the annual meeting of the American Educational Research Association, Chicago, IL.

Slavin, R. E. (1977). Classroom reward structure: An analytical and practical review. *Review of Educational Research, 47,* 633–650.

Slavin, R. E. (1983). *Cooperative learning.* New York: Longman.

Solomon, D, Watson, M., Battistich, V., Schaps, E., Tuck, P., Solomon, J., Cooper, C., & Ritchey, W. (1985). A program to promote interpersonal consideration and cooperation in children. In R. Slavin, S. Sharan, S. Kagan, R. Hertz-Lazarowitz, C. Webb, & R. Schmuck (Eds.), *Learning to cooperate, cooperating to learn* (pp. 371–402). New York: Plenum.

Swigger, K. M., & Swigger, B. K. (1984, Spring). Social patterns and computer use among preschool children. *Association for Educational Data Systems Journal,* 35–41.

Swing, S. R., & Peterson, P. L. (1982). The relationship of student ability and small-group interaction to student achievement. *American Educational Research Journal, 19,* 259–274.

Trowbridge, D., & Durnin, R. (1984a). *A study of student-computer interactivity.* Unpublished paper, University of California, Irvine.

Trowbridge, D., & Durnin, R. (1984b). *Research from an investigation of groups working together at the computer.* Unpublished paper, University of California, Irvine.

Trowbridge, D., & Bork, A. (1981, July). *Computer based learning modules for early adolescence.* Paper presented at the 3rd World Conference on Computers in Education, Lausanne, Switzerland.

Vedder, P. (1985). *Cooperative learning: a study on processes and effects of cooperation between primary school children.* Westerhaven Groningen, Netherlands: Rijkuniversiteit Groningen.

Vygotsky, L. S. (1978). *Mind in society: The development of higher psychological processes,* (M. Cole, V. John-Steiner, S. Scribner, & E. Souberman, Eds. and trans.). Cambridge, MA: Harvard University Press.

Vygotsky, L. S. (1981). The genesis of higher mental functioning. In J. V. Mertsch (Ed.), *The concept 'of activity in Soviet psychology.* Armonk, NY: Sharpe.

Webb, N. M. (1980a). An analysis of group interaction and mathematical errors in heterogeneous ability groups. *British Journal of Educational Psychology, 50,* 266–276.

Webb, N. M. (1980b). A process-outcome analysis of learning in group and individual settings. *Educational Pscyhologist, 15,* 69–83.

Webb, N. M. (1982a). Group composition, group interaction and achievement in cooperative small groups. *Journal of Educational Psychology, 74,* 475–484.

Webb, N. M. (1982b). Peer interaction and learning in cooperative small groups. *Journal of Educational Psychology, 74,* 642–655.

Webb, N. M. (1982c). Student interaction and learning in small groups. *Review of Educational Research, 52,* 421–445.

Webb, N. M. (1983). Predicting learning from student interaction: Defining the interaction variables. *Educational Psychologist, 18,* 33–41.

Webb, N. M. (1984a). Microcomputer learning in small groups: Cognitive requirements and group processes. *Journal of Educational Psychology, 76,* 1076–1088.

Webb, N. M. (1984b). Sex differences in interaction and achievement in cooperative small groups. *Journal of Educational Psychology, 76,* 33–34.

Webb, N. M. (1984c). Stability of small group interaction and achievement over time. *Journal of Educational Psychology, 76,* 211–224.

Webb, N. M. (1985). Cognitive requirements of learning computer programming in group and individual settings. *Association for Educational Data Systems Journal, 18,* 183–194.

Webb, N. M., & Cullian, L. K. (1983). Group interaction as a mediator between student and group characteristics and achievement: Stability over time. *American Educational Research Journal, 20,* 411–424.

Webb, N. M. & Kenderski, C. M. (1984). Student interaction and learning in small group and whole class settings. In P. L. Peterson, L. C. Wilkinson, & M. Hallinan (Eds.), *The social context of instruction: Group organization and group processes* (pp. 153–170). New York: Academic Press.

Webb, N. M., & Kenderski, C. M. (1985). Gender differences in small-group interaction and achievement in high- and low-achieving classes. In L. C. Wilkinson & C. B. Marrett (Eds.), *Gender differences in classroom interaction* (pp. 209–236). New York: Academic Press.

Webb, N. M., Ender, P., & Lewis, S. (1986). Problem-solving strategies and group processes in small groups learning computer programming. *American Educational Research Journal, 23,* 243–261.

Weinstein, B. D., & Bearison, D. J. (1985). Social interaction, social observation, and cognitive development in young children. *European Journal of Social Psychology, 15,* 333–343.

Wertsch, J. V. (1979). From social interaction to higher psychological processes. *Human Development 22,* 1–22.

Wilkinson, L. C., & Calculator, S. (1982a). Effective speakers: Students' use of language to request and obtain information and action in the classroom. In L. C. Wilkinson (Ed.), *Communicating in the classroom.* New York: Academic Press.

Wilkinson, L. C., & Calculator, S. (1982b). Requests and responses in peer-directed reading groups. *American Educational Research Journal, 19,* 107–120.

Wood, D., Bruner, J. S., & Ross, G. (1976). The role of tutoring in problem solving. *Journal of Child Psychology Psychiatry, 17,* 89–100.

Wood, D., & Middleton, D. (1975). A study of assisted problem-solving. *British Journal of Psychology, 66,* 181–191.

# 9

# Instructional Conditions in Pascal Programming Classes

Kathryn D. Sloane
Marcia C. Linn
*University of California, Berkeley*

## ABSTRACT

Systematic study of the relationship between instructional practice and learning outcomes can help to build powerful instructional theories. This study examines relationships between students' programming proficiency and instructional conditions in 14 high-school Pascal programming classes. To establish programming proficiency, we assessed students' ability to write programs and students' ability to understand, modify, and analyze programs written by experts. Both students' and teachers' perceptions of instructional conditions were used to characterize the learning environment. We found that instructional conditions predicted student performance on each measure of programming proficiency. Effective instructional conditions included: (a) extensive on-line access; (b) explicit instruction; and (c) frequent feedback. Further, we found that the pattern of programming proficiency varied with classroom conditions. The results help clarify the nature of exemplary instructional environments and suggest principles for instructional theory.

## INTRODUCTION

Although it is universally agreed that the nature of classroom instruction influences student learning, the factors governing such influence are just becoming understood. Efforts to understand classroom learning have featured largely descriptive studies that relate classroom characteristics, such as instructional time and time-on-task, to student learning. We applied this methodology to programming instruction by describing the classroom conditions in high-school Pascal programming classes and examining the extent to which these practices promote proficiency in programming.

Although programming represents a relatively mature use of technology, clear guidelines are not available to teachers on the most effective methods of teaching programming. Historically, programming classes built on experiences of expert programmers who taught themselves. Students were provided with assignments and access to computers and were expected to learn through trial and error and unguided discovery. Feedback consisted of what happened when students ran their programs.

Recent examination of programming classes (Linn, 1985a; Linn & Dalbey, 1985) reveals that some teachers continue to emphasize discovery, some emphasize problem-solving procedures, and some provide extensive feedback. Instruction ranges from situations where all students execute the same comments at the same time (e.g., "everyone type PRINT") to classes where instructors model expert solutions to problems, insist that students simulate the computer before asking for help with a bug, or encourage group problem solving. Feedback ranges from detailed comments on completed assignments to whatever messages the software provides.

Ultimately, we desire an instructional theory that specifies how instruction influences learning (Linn, 1987). To explore the relationship between instructional practice and programming proficiency, we conducted a descriptive study of naturally occurring instruction. Instruction practices vary widely, so we attempted to relate broad differences in practice to broad differences in outcomes.

This study is part of a series of investigations in the Autonomous Classroom Computer Environments for Learning (ACCEL) project. The ACCEL project aims to identify promising instructional practices, refine curriculum materials to reflect research findings, evaluate the materials, and ultimately improve programming instruction by offering more effective curricula.

In this chapter, we examine the relationship between instructional practice and programming proficiency. We focus on elements of the classroom environment that are controlled by the teacher, that reflect decisions made by the teacher regarding the type and quality of opportunities for learning. We identified these elements by examining previous research on effective instruction and by determining desired components of programming instruction.

## IDEAL PROGRAMMING KNOWLEDGE

In the ACCEL project, the outcomes of ideal programming knowledge are characterized as a chain of cognitive accomplishments (Linn, 1985a; Linn & Dalbey, 1986; Linn, Sloane, & Clancy, 1987). The chain culminates in the knowledge held by expert programmers and includes links that build on each other to form a strong integrated understanding of programming. The links selected for the chain reflect observations of expert teachers, discussions with computer center consultants, and opinions from expert programmers (Jeffries, Turner, Polson, & Atwood, 1981; Soloway & Ehrlich, 1984).

The chain begins with the acquisition of features or primitives in a programming language. The next link consists of higher-order language units referred to as templates. Templates are prototypic sequences of code and programmer actions required for a specific function (Linn & Dalbey, 1985). The third link in the chain is that of programming design skills or strategies. Design strategies include decomposing the problem into manageable pieces, implementing the decomposition step-by-step, testing the code that has been implemented, debugging code that does not perform to specifications, and monitoring one's own progress. The final link in the chain consists of generalizable problem-solving skills. Students who have successfully constructed the previous links in the chain can acquire the capability of autonomously generalizing the problem-solving skills learned from programming to other situations.

The ACCEL model and conceptual framework for studying influences on students' progression on this chain of ideal programming knowledge consists of five components and their interrelationships. Cognitive outcomes (ideal programming knowledge) are hypothesized to vary as a function of autonomous study activities (information processing and self-management), which themselves vary with instructional provisions, teacher characteristics, and student characteristics. Our investigations are designed to test the relationships among these factors and to assess their impact on programming proficiency. Ultimately, the project will develop instructional materials that promote autonomous learning activities and emphasize higher links on the chain of ideal programming knowledge.

## RESEARCH ON INSTRUCTIONAL PRACTICE
## AND LEARNING

### Learning Time

The large body of literature on effective teaching and learning has consistently identified key components of quality instruction across a variety of subject areas. Perhaps one of the most salient variables is time-on-task, or *active learning time*. Effective teachers maximize the proportion of time their students are engaged in academic tasks, thus maximizing the students' opportunities to learn and practice the content (e.g., Brophy, 1983; Fisher et al, 1980; Good, 1979; Rosenshine & Berliner, 1978). This generalization is most often applied to students' mastery of basic facts and concepts, but some research suggests that it also applies to more complex cognitive skills. Students who have more practice in applying concepts and problem-solving strategies, in providing explanations for answers, or in synthesizing and evaluating information perform better in these types of cognitive activities than do students whose practice is limited to recalling factual information (e.g., Bloom, 1976; Evertson, Anderson, Anderson, & Brophy).

In programming classes, active learning time has two components: (a) class time devoted to learning and practicing problem-solving strategies, and (b) time spent working on-line. Precollege programming classes often do not provide sufficient time—in amount of instruction or of practice on the computer—for students to develop problem-solving skills. For example, Linn (1985a) described the chain of cognitive accomplishments necessary for learning to program and concluded that precollege courses often address only the language-features link on the chain. Precollege courses fail to address the problem-solving link because they last 12 weeks or less, allow less than 10 hours of on-line access, and lack technical resources (e.g., Clements & Gullo, 1984; Dalbey & Linn, 1985; Pea & Kurland, 1983).

Other researchers have found dramatic differences in the time students spend working on the computer. In precollege programming classes, teachers must determine how much of the class period is to be spent on-line, or how many class periods per week the students work on the computer. Teachers make these decisions based on available resources (e.g., computer/student ratio) and on their judgments regarding the best use of instructional time. These choices are also influenced by the amount of time the computer is available outside of class to work on assignments. Even when the curriculum specifies clear guidelines, the actual allocation of on-line time varies considerably by teacher (Amarel, 1983). It is important to note, however, that students do not always use on-line access productively (Clancy, 1983; Linn & Dalbey, 1985) so access gives only a general indication of potential student benefits. Lack of access clearly limits learning but access alone is not enough to help students learn.

## Explicit Instruction

Effective teachers devote time to explicit instruction in the skills they want their students to learn well. *Explicit instruction in applying concepts and problem-solving strategies* has emerged as a second aspect of the classroom environment that relates to student learning in these areas.

Recent research has indicated the importance of explicit instruction in various subject domains, such as physics (Reif, 1987) and geometry (Greeno, 1978). Explicit instruction has also been identified as an important factor in students' independent learning skills, such as skill in studying scientific texts (Larkin & Reif, 1976) and in preparing for standardized tests in mathematics (Leinhardt & Greeno, 1986).

The literature on programming instruction suggests that explicit instruction in problem solving is extremely important. Explicit instruction in problem solving includes teaching students how to design problem solutions, helping students develop template repertoires, modeling debugging strategies, and explaining how to select exhaustive test cases. In contrast to unguided discovery classes, those providing explicit instruction have far greater success with medium- to low-ability students, presumably because these students lack skill in inferring problem-solving strategies on their own (Doyle, 1983; Eylon & Helfman, 1985; Linn & Dalbey, 1985).

Studies examining potential transfer of problem-solving skills from programming instruction to other domains also indicate the need for explicit instruction. For example, Soloway (in press) described skills students need to solve programming problems. He emphasized the need to explicitly teach step-wise refinement, a component of top-down design. He discussed how students need to learn to combine plans to create a program design, in addition to learning programming discourse rules that result in clear, unambiguous code. These explicit problem-solving strategies, Soloway argued, make teaching programming worthwhile and may apply to problems in other domains.

Explicit instruction includes, but is not limited to, teacher-directed instruction (e.g., lectures). Effective teachers regularly model problem-solving strategies, ask process-oriented questions, and provide opportunities for practice in these types of activities (e.g., Brophy, 1983). They provide a *balance and variety of instructional strategies* including direct instruction, independent learning, and guided practice (e.g., Brophy, 1983; Rosenshine, 1983).

An overemphasis on teacher-directed instruction limits opportunities students have to apply, practice, and learn through doing. Overemphasis on unguided discovery, however, may not be desirable either. A balance of instructional strategies includes (a) opportunities for students to explore and experiment (b) guidance by teachers on what to look for, and (c) interpretation by teachers on what results of these explorations mean in terms of theory, concepts, or facts discussed in textbooks. Class discussions should encourage students to relate topics and concepts, and to hypothesize outcomes.

Explicit instruction must be balanced with opportunities for students to practice and further develop these skills on their own. As Derry and Murphy (1986) reported in their review of the literature on learning ability, the skill of combining information to solve new problems probably requires experience solving problems for which no explicit solution exists. Students need practice combining available information to solve new problems. When instruction overemphasizes direct instruction, students may not get opportunities to practice devising, testing, and revising their own approaches.

## Feedback

The third instructional variable related to student achievement is *feedback*. Students benefit from immediate, specific feedback on their performance in learning activities. To be effective, feedback should help students correct their errors or misunderstandings (e.g., Rosenshine, 1983). Prompt, relevant feedback, coupled with additional practice to strengthen areas of weakness, is particularly important in hierarchical subject domains. When mastery of later skills depends on understanding of previous concepts and skills, effective teachers check students' understanding on a regular basis and spend additional time reviewing or reteaching difficult content.

Thus, the type of feedback is as important as the presence of feedback. Feedback should be responsive to the student and should encourage the students to revise their templates and strategies. Simply responding that an answer is right or wrong does not necessarily lead to this revision. Similarly, providing the student with the correct answer before the student has the opportunity to think about the problem may discourage students from diagnosing their difficulties.

Many studies of programming assess different forms of feedback in the programming environment and examine the effect of feedback on students' learning. Early programming environments provided poor feedback about how programs performed, often indicating only that the program had failed. Recently, programming software developers have added many on-line features such as error diagnoses, simultaneous stepping through the code while executing the program, and intelligent tutoring.

Another approach to providing feedback is through systems that respond to student errors. To build PROUST, for example, Johnson and Soloway (1983) catalogued all the errors students made on one introductory Pascal assignment. The system takes students' programs for this assignment as input, and outputs comments on the assignments. Anderson, Boyle, and Reiser (1985) developed a tutor for LISP programming that analyzes each line of code as it appears and corrects or comments as appropriate. The LISP tutor provides extensive feedback and memory support. However, because the feedback is so extensive (it often supplies the correct code) and occurs immediately, students have little opportunity for reflection.

The research suggests that prompt, detailed feedback is preferred over delayed, incomplete feedback. User-controlled feedback has advantages over feedback that occurs at the same rate and level of detail for all students. As stated previously, effective feedback is responsive to the particular student and encourages the students to think about what they have done and how it can be improved.

## METHODS

### Research Questions and Design

Explicit instruction in problem solving, allocation of time and resources for practice, and the presence and type of feedback provided have consistently emerged as instructional variables that are highly related to student achievement. How do high-school programming teachers apply these strategies in their instruction? Are these variables equally important in programming, or do students do just as well if given the time and resources to work alone? What characteristics of existing Pascal classes promote ideal programming knowledge, that is, problem-solving skills beyond mastery of language features? To address these and other questions, we have conducted a series of investigations to discover current instructional conditions and to explore the effects of interventions designed to improve students' programming knowledge (e.g., see Linn et al., 1987).

The current study contributes to the descriptive phase of the project. Subsequent studies include interventions using project-designed curriculum materials.

### Classes

The classes included in this study are similar in length, purpose, and population of students. All are year-long, Advanced Placement (AP) Pascal programming courses. Many students take the AP course to prepare for the Advanced Place-

CHAPTER 9

TABLE 9.1
ACCEL Sample

| Type of Class | Number of Teachers | Number of Classes | Number of Students | % Male | % Female |
|---|---|---|---|---|---|
| Advanced Placement | 12 | 14 | 242 | 85% | 15% |
| Introductory | | 5 | 123 | 70% | 30% |
| Total | | 19 | 365 | 80% | 20% |

ment test that will give them college credit in programming. Most of the students in these classes are college bound and are interested in taking college-level programming classes. Most teachers consider the AP Test in planning their curriculum. The classes are, therefore, similar in the population of students taking the course and the purpose and focus of the course.

We identified 13 teachers in the San Francisco Bay Area, each at a different school, who were teaching Advanced Placement courses in Pascal. Five of these teachers taught more than one section of Pascal. The additional sections were usually "introductory level" courses. We collected baseline data in all classes, for an initial sample of 19 classes and 365 students. Class sizes ranged from 15 to 31 in the introductory classes and from 10 to 28 in the AP classes (Table 9.1).

As shown in Table 9.1, fewer females than males participate in introductory courses and the discrepancy is much more pronounced in AP courses. The issue of participation of females in programming classes is an issue that deserves further study. Because these classes give students an advantage in college courses, females who want to continue in college should be encouraged to participate (Kersteen, Linn, Clancy, & Hardyck, 1986). Research clearly shows that females who do participate perform as well or better than their male counterparts (Linn, 1985b; Lockheed, 1986; Mandinach & Linn, 1987). Many reasons for lack of participation have been proposed (Linn, 1985b, 1986; Lockheed, 1986), and these need to be addressed in our efforts to increase female participation in programming courses.

## Instruments

### Student Ability and Background

To assess general ability of students, we administered a version of the Raven's Progressive Matrices (16 items).

To assess students' backgrounds and previous experience in programming, we designed the Computer Experience Questionnaire. If students are at different points on the chain of cognitive accomplishments, we would expect them to have different reactions to instructional practices. Prior experience or achievement can also influence current proficiency. We asked students about their prior knowledge of Pascal to determine how far along the chain they had progressed before the current course.

### Students' Programming Proficiency

Students' knowledge in programming was measured by two criteria developed for this study: (a) the Spacetext programming assignment; (b) the Madlibs case study test. Requirements for administering the programming assignment and the case study were that the class must have completed the study of arrays and have completed at least one class assignment using arrays. The programming assignment and case study were administered when the class met the preceding criteria; therefore, classes completed these tasks at different times. When receiving the criteria tasks, classes were roughly equivalent in the experience of the students (given that they all completed the task when they had reached a certain point in the course).

Differences in the pacing of the classes became particularly obvious when scheduling the programming assignment and the case study. The introductory classes did not progress far enough along in the course to complete the programming assignment. Among the AP classes, some had completed arrays before December; others did not complete arrays until late spring. The programming assignment was eventually administered in 14 classes, taught by 12 teachers, with a combined total of 242 students. Of these 14 classes, three completed the programming assignment so late in the year that they did not have time to complete the case study. The case study, therefore, was administered in 11 classes (9 teachers).

*Programming Assignment.* We used Spacetext, a week-long programming assignment, as one assessment of programming proficiency (see Linn et al., 1987). The assignment requires completion of textbook chapters on loops and arrays and at least one assignment using arrays. Each class completed the assignment when they met the criteria, so different classes received it at different times.

Students performed the assignment with minimal teacher help. Teachers clarified the assignment if necessary, but offered no guidance to students. Regular classroom procedures concerning whether students worked individually or in teams were followed. As a result, we can analyze class performance but not individual performance.

*Scoring.* First, we generated an ideal solution to Spacetext (Clancy & Linn, 1986). Then, we scored programs on four dimensions: (a) template sophistication and correctness; (b) accuracy of design; (c) seriousness of bugs; (d) exhaustiveness of tests. A composite score based on these dimensions was used for the analyses.

*Case Study.* Case studies are narrative accounts of an experts' step-by-step solution to a programming problem. The narrative discusses the process of designing, implementing, testing, and debugging a program. These solutions to programming problems illustrate expert problem-solving skills. They make explicit the normally tacit problem-solving information possessed by experts. Decomposition diagrams illustrate how experts made the design manageable. Students see the design choices and examine the reasons experts use to make design decisions.

Case study materials include: (a) a statement of the programming problem and a narrative description of an expert's solution; (b) a listing of the expert's code; (c) study questions to provide practice analyzing the program; and (d) test questions to assess students' understanding of the program solution. Test questions focus on design, testing, debugging, and reformulation of the program, as well as on students' understanding of the use of templates. (See Clancy, 1986; Linn, 1986, for a detailed discussion of the rationale and methods of constructing case studies.)

The Madlibs case study is a solution to a programming problem based on the following story game: A story is generated, with blanks inserted for all of the adjectives; a list of adjectives is generated independently; the objective is to insert the adjectives from the separate list into the story, resulting in an (usually) entertaining combination of adjectives and nouns.

Students received case study materials after completing the Spacetext assignment. They were given three days to study the case study materials and answer the study questions. The program was available on-line, and students were free to run the program and experiment with modifications to the program. On days 4 and 5, students answered test questions similar to the practice study questions.

The two-part test contained a total of five "items" representing different dimensions of programming skills: Debugging, Design (2 items), Testing, and Understanding Templates. As an example, one of the design items posed the possibility of expanding the program to read and insert nouns and verbs, as well as adjectives. Students were asked to explain how they would modify the main program, and/or the relevant subroutines, to produce this desired expansion.

Students worked on the case study with minimal teacher help. Students could work together while studying the case study narrative, running the program, or answering the study questions. The two-part test was administered under standard testing conditions: Students had to answer the test questions alone and could only work on the test during the class period.

The case study represented a totally new way of thinking about programs for most of these students—and for the teachers. Neither students nor teachers were accustomed to reading about programs. Students were accustomed to spending class periods working on-line or listening to lectures. Reading a narrative of how a program was designed, implemented, and tested was a totally new approach. The program was also fairly complex; we found that even some of the teachers were challenged while analyzing the program.

*Scoring.* Tests were scored using protocol designed to assess how accurately and thoroughly the students answered each of the test questions. The Design scale captures the complex problem solving most emphasized in precollege programming courses. Thus, we expected this scale to yield the most information on the relationship between instructional strategies and student performance. This scale is used in the following analyses of the relationship between classroom variables and case study performance.

## Classroom Characteristics and Conditions

In this study, we assessed classroom conditions through multiple measures: (a) student surveys; (b) teacher reports; (c) classroom observations. We analyzed the agreement between teachers' and students' responses, and we compared these results to our own classroom observations.

### Student Survey:
### Classroom Characteristics Questionnaire

This survey assessed three dimensions of the classroom environment: (a) access to computers; (b) explicitness of instruction in problem solving; and (c) presence and type of feedback. (Sample items appear in Table 9.2).

*Computer Access.* Items on this dimension assessed the availability and use of the computer in these Pascal programming classes. Items included the amount of class time devoted to on-line work; the proportion of programming assignments that required on-line access; the total number of hours (in and out of class) that computers were available for student use.

*Explicit Instruction.* This dimension included a variety of items to assess the extent to which instruction in the course was explicitly directed toward problem solving, that is, advanced links on the chain of cognitive outcomes (design, implementation, etc.). Scales on this dimension included: (a) the mode of instruction (emphasis on formal, whole-group lectures versus individualized work with students at the computer); (b) requirements for on-line access (degree to which the teacher explicitly required the students to plan their work and design their program before entering code, etc.); and (c) the "quality" of the formal instruction. This "Quality of Instruction" scale assessed teachers' strategies for presenting, organizing, and explaining programming concepts and principles. Items included the frequency of lectures or class discussions on planning and

TABLE 9.2
Sample Items from Classroom Characteristics Survey

| Question | Response scale (5 points unless noted) |
|---|---|
| **Access to computers** | |
| • How many of the assignments in this class are programming assignments to be done on-line? | "Almost all" to "Almost None" |
| • Students work on-line for most or all of the period. | 0 to 4–5 days per week |
| • Hours/week computers are available for on-line work. | "0–5 hrs" to "16+ hrs" |
| **Explicitness** | |
| • Teacher lectures for most or all of the period. | 0 to 4–5 days per week |
| • Teacher works with individuals or small groups. | 0 to 4–5 days per week |
| • What must you do before you can use the computer (e.g., show a program plan and code to teacher)? | Yes/No |
| **Feedback** | |
| • How often does the teacher grade the assignment? | "Always" to "Never" |
| • When students turn in assignments, how often does the teacher: | |
| • write specific comments on your assignment? | "Always to "Never" |
| • discuss common problems or mistakes with the class? | "Always" to "Never" |
| • describe different ways the assignment could be solved? | "Always" to "Never" |

implementing program solutions, integrating concepts, and considering alternative solutions to a programming problem.

*Feedback.* The survey included four scales on this dimension to determine the explicitness of the feedback procedures and the degree to which feedback procedures emphasized—or reinforced—students' problem-solving strategies. The Presence of Feedback scale assessed the frequency with which the teacher provided feedback to individual students on their programming assignments (e.g., teacher collects, grades, and returns the programming assignments). The Type of Feedback scale considered the extent and focus of individual and group-based feedback on assignments (e.g., teacher writes comments on individuals' assignments; teacher discusses common problems and mistakes with the class; teacher presents solution to programming assignment). The Testing scale assessed the breadth of teacher testing procedures (e.g., whether tests covered more advanced skills such as designing solutions or applying algorithms, in addition to language features). Items on the Grading scale focused on the criteria teachers used to grade programming assignments, specifically if programs were graded on design, implementation, and efficiency, or if grades were based solely on whether or not the program ran correctly.

The original survey contained 62 items, 44 of which are included in these analyses. A few items were deleted because they were redundant or unclear. Most deletions were items related to individual behaviors in the classroom and are not included in this analysis of general class conditions.

The survey was completed by the students in late fall, 1985. By this time—10 to 11 weeks into the academic year—it was assumed that classroom practices were fairly well established.

## Teacher Reports

The teachers completed the same Classroom Characteristics Questionnaire administered to the students. Teachers also completed a survey that provided more information on how and why they choose particular instructional strategies, as well as data on their own background, experience, and training in Pascal programming. Frequent, informal discussions with individual teachers throughout the year enabled us to maintain an ongoing record of the teachers' activities and perceptions of their courses.

## Classroom Observations

All classes were visited by two or more project staff, on separate occasions. The project coordinator also visited the classes on a regular, informal basis. These class visits allowed us to compare the written assessments of classroom activities (from students and teachers) with observations of activities and behaviors.

## Agreement Among Students and Teachers

As a check on the reliability of the student consensus measures used to assess classroom conditions, student and teacher scores on the same survey were compared. Generally, the level of agreement between students and teachers was high. The highest levels of agreement were on variables that assessed resources and routines that are the same for all students in the class: computer access scales; mode of instruction (i.e., frequency of lectures); requirements for working on-line; the presence and type of feedback; and testing procedures.

Students' and teachers' scores were moderately consistent on the Quality of Instruction scale, with teachers displaying a slight tendency for higher scores. That is, these teachers tended to report more emphasis on explicit instruction related to problem solving that did the students. This trend may be due to a bias in the teachers' reports. Teachers may have overestimated their emphasis on discussing the assignment, explaining methods of solving the programming problem, and so on, because they perceived these as appropriate, desirable instructional strategies. An alternative explanation may be that the teachers believed they were providing this type of instruction regularly, but the students in their classes were not fully grasping the intent of the instruction. Because the classes with the lowest levels of agreement on this scale are the classes that performed the lowest on one or both of the proficiency measures, it may be that these teachers' scores are not accurate assessments of the quality of the explicit instruction that their students actually received.

The same trend occurred on the scale assessing how programming assignments were graded. Teachers were more likely to believe that higher grades reflected good program design. This trend may reflect biases in the teachers' reports. An alternative explanation may be that students did not interpret the survey questions correctly.

The scale with the lowest student/teacher agreement is one that is perhaps most sensitive to student perception: the amount of time teachers allocate to working with individuals or small groups. Nearly two thirds of the classes exhibited low levels of agreement on this scale. Students are likely to be basing their responses on how often the teacher worked with them personally. We would expect students in the same class to respond differently, based on their personal experience, and might expect greater differences between students' mean scores and teachers' scores on this item. The direction of the disagreement showed no clear trend, however. Students and teachers were equally likely to assign higher scores on this item.

Given the consistencies between students' and teachers' responses, we chose to use the students' scores (class means) in the analyses. The ranking of classes on each classroom dimension, based on the pooled students' responses, conformed to our observation data. And, assessing classroom conditions through a consensus of students' perceptions is a valid, reliable method of measuring class-level variables (e.g., Fraser, 1986), particularly compared to relying solely on direct observations. Consensus measures involve the pooled judgments of all students in the class. Students' responses are based on their experiences over many lessons, rather than the few class sessions an observer attends. And, students' perceptions of classroom environments often account for more variation in learning outcomes than do variables derived from observations by others (e.g., Fraser & Walberg, 1981).

## ANALYSES

Analyses were performed using class level data (i.e., class means) to relate classroom variables to class performance on proficiency measures. We first analyzed the relationships between classroom variables and class performance on the criteria; then, we grouped classes based on performance and analyzed similarities and differences in *patterns* of classroom variables across different levels of class performance.

The results of these analyses are presented in three sections: (a) analysis of variation across classrooms in classroom variables and in student performance on each of the criteria; (b) analysis of the relationships between classroom practices and students' programming knowledge; and (c) comparisons of patterns of relationships between classroom variables and each of the two measures of students' programming knowledge. In this final analysis, we examined classes performing well on both programming proficiency criteria, poorly on both, and with mixed results, to examine corresponding patterns of class variables. These results suggest conditions and instructional strategies in exemplary classrooms, that is, classes in which students advance furthest along the chain of cognitive accomplishments.

## RESULTS AND DISCUSSION

### Variation Across Classes

There was significant variation among the classes on all measures of *classroom conditions and instructional practices*. The ranges of class scores on these variables, and the results of the analysis of variance among the classes, are reported in Table 9.3.

There was also significant variation among classes in students' *programming knowledge*, as measured by the two criteria.

Class scores on the Madlibs Case Study Test are presented in Table 9.3. Classes are listed in rank order of performance on the Design scale. The Design items required an understanding of the design of the case-study program and of the functions of different components of the program. Students were asked to identify and modify sections of the program to produce desired changes. This scale was perhaps most indicative of students' understanding of the case study program and of their abilities to apply high-level problem-solving skills in programming.

Class scores on the *Spacetext* programming assignment are also presented in Table 9.4. Classes are identified by the code letters from the ranking on case study scores. There was some shifting in class rank on the Spacetext assignment, compared to performance on the case study. This suggests some differences between students' skills in writing a program and their abilities to analyze and think critically about an expert's solution to a programming problem.

### Variables Related to Student Performance

The correlations between measures of student performance and relevant student and classroom variables are presented in Table 9.5.

#### Student Ability and Previous Experience

Student ability, as measured by the Raven Progressive Matrices Test, was not related to performance on either the Spacetext assignment or the case study test.

TABLE 9.3
Classroom Characteristics Questionnaire: Variation Across Classes

| Class Variable | Range of scores (F value) | Interpretation |
|---|---|---|
| Computer Access | | |
| #Days on line | 2.30 to 5.00 ( 8.56*) | 1–2 days to 4–5 days |
| Hours computer available | 1.74 to 3.71 (13.21*) | 0–5 hrs/wk to 16+ hrs. |
| Proportion of on-line assignments | 3.14 to 5.00 (10.35*) | About ½ to Almost all |
| Explicitness | | |
| #Days teacher lectures | 1.67 to 4.00 (20.17*) | 0–1 days to 3–4 days |
| #Days teacher works w/ individuals | 1.50 to 3.86 ( 6.45*) | 0–1 days to 3–4 days |
| Require. for computer access | 0.00 to 3.00 (10.64*) | None to "Show plan and code" |
| Quality of explicit instruction (how often teacher uses strategies) | 2.84 to 3.87 ( 9.76*) | Rarely to Often |
| Feedback | | |
| Presence of feedback | 3.33 to 4.70 (12.58*) | Sometimes to Always |
| Type of feedback | 2.57 to 4.00 ( 6.96*) | Rarely to Often |
| Tests on language features | 2.35 to 3.91 ( 6.40*) | Rarely to Often |
| Tests on Pascal procedures | 1.80 to 2.69 ( 3.69*) | Rarely to Sometimes |
| Grading criteria | 2.00 to 4.00 ( 4.63*) | Correctness only to correct + design, style |

*$F(18, 340)$, $p < .001$

Some of the lowest Raven scores were for classes that performed the highest on the proficiency measures. Classes did not differ significantly on this variable, however. Students who enrolled in these AP programming classes were fairly similar in measures of general ability.

There was variation across classrooms in students' previous programming experience. And, as might be expected, previous experience is correlated with all measures of programming proficiency. Classes ranged from those in which nearly all of the students reported enough prior experience to write a 300-line program in Pascal, to very low percentages of students having this level of prior experience.

To determine the effect of prior experience on the relationship between classroom characteristics and programming proficiency, we calculated partial correlations to control for this student variable. Controlling for students' previous experience did *not* significantly affect the relationships between classroom characteristics and scores on the programming assignment or the case-study scales. Thus, we can conclude that prior experience, although predictive of success on programming problems, did not interact with instructional practice.

TABLE 9.4
Class Means, Standard Errors on Programming Criteria

| Madlibs Case Study Test | | Spacetext Programming Assignment | |
|---|---|---|---|
| Class | Design (max = 40) | Class | Correctness (max = 25) |
| A | 34.00 (0.68) | F | 23.33 (0.24) |
| B | 32.78 (0.62) | B | 23.30 (0.34) |
| C | 32.07 (0.96) | H | 23.20 (0.35) |
| D | 31.98 (0.53) | A | 23.00 (0.59) |
| E | 31.52 (0.54) | E | 23.00 (0.59) |
| F | 31.36 (0.93) | J* | 22.43 (0.69) |
| G | 31.33 (0.75) | C | 22.57 (0.75) |
| H | 30.43 (0.53) | G | 21.71 (1.21) |
| I | 29.30 (0.76) | D | 19.86 (0.97) |
| | | I | 19.75 (1.09) |
| | | K* | 18.75 (1.07) |
| | | L* | 17.27 (0.96) |
| Total mean | 31.63 | | 21.51 |
| (Stand. error) | (0.21) | | (0.46) |
| F Value | 2.58 | | 5.39 |
| (df = 8,161) | p < .01 | (df = 13.191) | p < .001 |

*did not complete case study

## Class Variables and Student Performance

Scanning Table 9.5, there are different patterns of relationship between classroom variables and student scores on the two criteria. These patterns suggest that different dimensions of the classroom environment are supportive of different types of programming knowledge. As discussed previously, the two performance criteria measure different aspects of programming knowledge and skills. The case-study test required an understanding of the design of the case-study

TABLE 9.5
Class Level Correlations:
Student Variables, Classroom Characterictics, and Programming Proficiency

|  | Case Study Questions (N = 11 classes) Designing | Spacetext Assignment (N = 14 classes) Correctness |
|---|---|---|
| Student variables |  |  |
| General ability (Raven) | −.05 | −.03 |
| Previous experience | .48# | .52* |
| Class variables |  |  |
| Computer access |  |  |
| Number of days on-line | .16 | .40# |
| Hours computer available | .54* | .80*** |
| Prop. on-line assignments | .06 | .04 |
| Explicitness |  |  |
| Number of days teacher lectures | .01 | −.58** |
| Number of days teacher works w/ individuals | .42# | .61** |
| Require. computer access | −.19 | .47* |
| Quality of explicit instruction | .83*** | .17 |
| Feedback |  |  |
| Presence of feedback | .60* | .64** |
| Type of feedback | −.14 | .59** |
| Tests: language features | .61* | −.04 |
| Tests: Pascal procedures | .79** | .29 |
| Grading criteria | .26 | .34 |
| Spacetext assignment | .38 | — |

$\#p < .10,$ $^*p < .05,$ $^{**}p < .01,$ $^{***}p < .001$

program and of the functions of different components of the program. The programming assignment assessed students' skills in writing a program—writing and entering code, testing and debugging their own program. The differences in class performance on these two criteria (see Table 9.4) suggests some differences between students' skills in writing a program and their abilities to analyze and think critically about an expert's solution to a programming problem.

In the following, we first discuss relationships between class variables and student performance for *each* of the two criteria, then discuss the implications of these different patterns of instructional support.

### Classroom Variables Related to Performance on Madlibs Case Study

Student performance on the Madlibs case study was significantly related to class variables on each of the three dimensions of the classroom environment.

*Computer Access.* As might be expected, access to computers was positively related to student performance on the case study. Classes demonstrated considerable variation in the number of hours the computer was available for student use. In some classes, access was limited to 8 or 9 hours per week, including class time. In other classes, the computer was available 16 or more hours per week, translating into 10 to 12 hours of computer availability outside of regular class time.

The relationship between computer availability and performance reinforces the importance of having access to resource. Some teachers made the special efforts needed to provide this resource by extending their own time in the computer lab so that students could have access to the computers.

*Explicitness.* Two variables in this dimension emerged as significant predictors of student performance: the proportion of time teachers worked with individuals or small groups and the quality of the explicit instruction.

The variable that emerged as most significant in predicting performance on the case study was the quality of explicit instruction. This variable assessed the extent to which teachers provided explicit instruction in strategies for solving problems, explained difficult concepts, led student discussion about the assignments, and encouraged students to discuss how topics related or how previously learned procedures could be applied to new problems. An emphasis on thinking about the concepts and principles of programming and on analyzing different approaches to solving programming problems emerged as extremely predictive of students' abilities to think critically about the structure and design of a program.

Teachers had to make decisions regarding the balance of group versus more individualized instructional strategies. Some teachers tended to focus more on lectures and whole group instruction, whereas others tended to emphasize on-line work and working with individuals at the computer. This individualized attention appears to be important in helping students learn to reflect on their programming skills and to think carefully about the design and structure of a program. For performance on the case study, distinctions between applying these strategies in group versus individual instruction may not be of critical importance. Rather, what seems to be important is that these types of strategies are utilized, whether in group or individual settings.

*Feedback.* Teachers' efforts to provide feedback to individual students, and to reinforce the mastery of concepts and principles through testing practices, were highly related to students' skills in analyzing the design and structure of programs. Of the five scales on this dimension, three yielded significant positive correlations with student performance: presence of feedback and the two scales assessing the breadth of materials covered on tests. These three assessments of feedback are most relevant to reinforcing the concepts and principles of programming. The two scales related specifically to feedback on programming assignments (type of feedback and grading criteria) were not significantly correlated with case study performance.

To summarize the pattern of relationships between class variables and students' performance on the case study, it appears that explicit instruction in problem solving and in applying concepts and principles of programming is most predictive of students' abilities to analyze the design and structure of a program. It is also important for students to have access to computers outside of class time and access to individualized attention from the teacher. The extent to which the teacher provides individualized feedback, in the form of collecting, grading and returning assignments (presence of feedback) is also predictive of students' performance on the case study. Finally, testing the students on the material covered in class appears to reinforce their understanding of the programming principles and concepts.

### Class Variables Related to Performance on Programming Assignment

The Spacetext programming assignment required students to design a program, write, test, and debug the code, and produce the desired output. This assignment assessed students' on-line skills and was similar to (though perhaps more difficult than) most of their regular class assignments. Classroom practices emerged as strong predictors of student performance on this programming task (see Linn et al., 1987, for a more detailed discussion of students' performance on the programming assignment and for a preliminary analysis of the influence of instructional conditions).

Over half (7 out of 12) of the classroom variables were correlated with class performance on the programming assignment. These variables were equally distributed across the three classroom dimensions: computer access, explicitness, and feedback.

*Computer Access.* Computer access, both in number of class days spent on-line, and in the availability of the computer for student use, was strongly predictive of students' competence in writing programs. Computer availability was the most predictive of scores on the programming assignment of all of the classroom variables. The high relationship between these two variables reinforces the importance of on-line time in learning to program.

We suspect that factors other than sheer availability are contributing to the power of this variable. When students do work on-line (in or out of class), the teacher can devote more time and attention to the individual student, using tutoring strategies rather than group instruction.

A nonlinear relationship emerged between the proportion of on-line programming assignments in the course and students' programming skills. Teachers in high-scoring classes and in low-scoring classes tended to assign a large proportion of programs (compared to reading or written exercises), whereas classes in the middle tended to have fewer programming assignments. Given the vast difference in computer access between the high- and low-scoring groups, we can conclude that students in the exemplary group had more time and more supervision for working on these assignments. Simply assigning large programs is not enough; in order for assignments to be effective, they must be supported by adequate access to computers and to the teacher.

*Explicitness.* The most significant classroom variable in this dimension was the proportion of time teachers worked with individuals or small groups. An emphasis on small group and individual instruction is highly predictive of students' performance on the programming assignment, whereas an emphasis on group lecture is negatively related. In small group or tutoring situations, teachers can tailor their instruction to meet the needs of the individuals. Given the diversity of student backgrounds and the idiosyncratic nature of student errors on programs, more individualized attention and instruction is understandably related to programming proficiency.

*Feedback.* More proficient classes received more feedback on their performance on class assignments from their teachers. There was a strong linear relationship between proficiency in writing programs and the frequency with which teachers collected, graded, and promptly returned students' class programming assignments (presence of feedback). The type of feedback teachers provide is equally important. Students whose teachers wrote comments on their programs, explicitly presented solutions to the programming assignments, or discussed different ways the problem could be solved, performed better on the Spacetext assignment than did students whose teachers did not provide this type of feedback on a regular basis.

Similarly, the extent to which grades on class programming assignments were based on more than simply whether or not the program ran (e.g., the design, use of test cases, etc., also counted toward the students' grades on the assignment) was also related to performance, although not as strongly as these other feedback variables.

In the classes with low scores on the feedback variables, perhaps some of the teachers believed they were providing adequate feedback by observing the students as they worked on programming assignments or by answering questions as they were asked. As several teachers pointed out, grading programs is a difficult and time consuming task. Also, some teachers noted that students receive feedback when they run their programs. These results suggest, however, that the students benefited from explicit efforts to provide individualized feedback on their performance and from discussion of common problems with the class.

The degree to which tests covered mastery of language features was not related to proficiency on the programming assignment. The extent to which tests covered applications of algorithms and Pascal procedures was positively related, although the correlation was not significant with the small number of classes. An emphasis on testing language features probably did not encourage students to use higher-level skills or provide practice in applying algorithms or developing templates.

### Comparing Patterns of Class Variables

There are similarities in class variables predictive of performance on the case study and the programming assignment. For each, the number of hours the computer was available to students (computer access) was related to performance, although it appeared to be much less important for the case-study tasks. The same was true for the proportion of time teachers spent working with individuals or small groups (explicitness) and for the presence of feedback (collecting, grading, and returning class assignments).

Some of the differences in patterns of relationships are probably due to the focus of the classroom scales. For example, the type of feedback scale assessed the extent to which teachers commented on programs, discussed the solution to the programming problems, and so forth. Because this scale focused specifically on feedback on programming assignments, it is understandable that it is more highly related to performance on a similar task (i.e., the Spacetext assignment).

Other patterns of relationships between class variables and student performance show some interesting differences for the case study. These differences are perhaps more informative about the influence of teachers' instructional strategies on students' cognitive achievements in programming courses.

Table 9.6 displays the two-way classification of the classrooms, based on rank performances on the programming assignment and on the case study. The classes are ranked as scoring high, medium, or low on each of the criteria. High scoring classes are those with mean scores of at least 2 standard errors above the total group mean; low-scoring classes scored at least 2 standard errors below the group mean. From this classification table, we can identify classes that performed well on both criteria, those that performed poorly on both, and those that demonstrated mixed patterns of competence.

Two classes, A and B, are the top-ranked classes on both criteria, Class I is the lowest ranked class on both; Class G maintained its middle position on both. The other five classes show some shifting, usually from one level to the next. The exception is teacher H (actually the average of the two classes taught by teacher H). These classes did extremely well on the programming assignment, but scored the lowest on the case study. Classroom observations during the case study revealed considerable problems with the administration of the case study materials. Neither the teacher nor the students displayed much interest in taking

TABLE 9.6
Class Performance: Spacetext Scores by Case Study Scores

Spacetext Programming Assignment

| | High (>2 s.e above mean) | Middle | Low (>2 s.e. below mean) |
|---|---|---|---|
| Column variables | Class / Hrs computer available / #days lecture / Teacher works with individuals / Quality of instruction (V V V V V) | Class / Hrs computer available / #days lecture / Teacher works with individuals / Quality of instruction (V V V V V) | Class / Hrs computer available / #days lecture / Teacher works with individuals / Quality of instruction (V V V V V) |
| Case Study (Design) High | A: X _ X X / X<br>B: X _ X X / X | C: _ X _ X / X _ X | |
| Case Study (Design) Middle | E: X _ X / X X<br>F: X _ X / X X | G: _ X _ / X _ X X | D: _ X X / X _ X |
| Case Study (Design) Low | H: X _ X / X _ X | | I: _ / X X X X |

the assignment seriously and not much time was spent studying the materials or preparing for the test.

From the preceding description of class variables related to the two criteria, four classroom variables were selected to examine patterns of classroom conditions and instructional strategies: (a) hours the computer is available; (b) proportion of lectures, versus (c) works with individuals; and (d) quality of instruction.

Table 9.6 also shows the relative rank of the classes on these four class variables. An X above the line is used to represent a class variable score above the median of the total group (original sample of 14 classes); an *X* below the line indicates a class variable score below the median of the total group.

Patterns of effective classroom instruction demonstrate the differences in instructional support for the two criteria. All of the classes that scored in the highest category on the programming assignment were also highest in computer access; none of the other classes had the same degree of computer availability. Teachers whose students did well on the programming assignment also tended to work with individuals more than they lectured. (The one exception is Class E, the average of the two classes taught by Teacher E.) All of the high-scoring classes on the case study were highest on quality of instruction. The class scoring in the lowest category on both criteria also scored in the lower category on all of the class variables.

Scanning the patterns of rank position on class variables reveals consistencies among the classes at different levels. We begin to see how a strength in one variable, or a lower rank on another, may be influencing student performance on the two criteria.

The two classes that performed in the top ranks on both criteria can be used to compare the patterns of class variables in the other classes. Classes A and B have the same patterns of class variables. Each have high scores on computer access, on working with individuals, and on quality of instruction. These are the only two classes in the total group that seemed to combine attention to individuals with effective presentation and explanation of material. All other classes scored above the median on one of these variables, but not both.

The patterns of class variables are further illustrated in the graphs in Figs. 9.1 and 9.2. Four of the classes were selected: Class B (performed high on both criteria); Class F (performed higher on programming assignment than on case

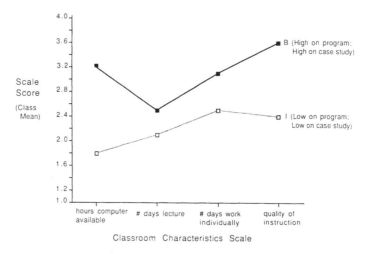

FIG. 9.1.   Patterns of class variables for high and low scoring classes.

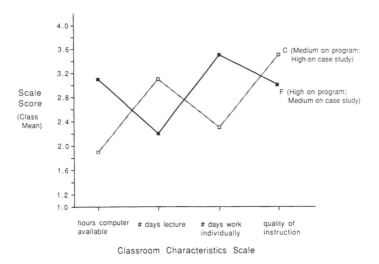

FIG. 9.2.    Patterns of class variables for classes with mixed performance.

study); Class C (performed higher on case study); and Class I (performed poorly on both criteria).

In Fig. 9.1, the class means on the four class variables are compared for Classes B (high on both criteria) and I (low on both criteria). We see the dramatic difference in the degree of computer access and quality of instruction. Each teacher lectured less than he or she worked with individuals, but Teacher I used each method less than Teacher B.

The different patterns of class variables are well illustrated in Fig. 9.2, comparing F and C. These two classes have opposite patterns of performance. Class F was among the highest scoring classes on the programming assignment, but dropped in rank on the case study; class C did just the opposite. Their patterns of class variables are exactly opposite as well, with F higher on computer access and working with individuals, and C higher on lecturing and quality of instruction.

## CONCLUSIONS AND SEARCH
## FOR AN "IDEAL BALANCE"

Results suggest that classroom conditions and the instructional strategies that teachers use do have an impact on students' learning in programming. Consistent with other research, we find that time devoted to work on the computer, providing explicit instruction in problem solving, guiding students' practice by working with them individually, and providing prompt, relevant feedback all have an influence on student achievement.

Further, a balance among these different strategies seems to be important; more is not always better. For example, an overemphasis on lecturing means that there is less time for students to work on the computer, and less time for the teacher to tailor instruction and assist individual students. Conversely, an over-emphasis on independent work at the computer means spending less time presenting, explaining, and discussing the material or strategies all of the students are expected to learn. Students who work at the computer nearly all of the time may not benefit from questions other students ask, or the insights the teacher or other students might share in group discussions.

Many of the teachers we worked with in this project were unsure of the most effective ways to structure the class and organize their instruction. Some believed students would learn best by spending as much time as possible at the computer, learning by "discovery." Others taught programming as they would teach their other subjects (usually mathematics): by breaking the subjects into segments, providing direct instruction on each segment, then giving students exercises to practice new concepts and procedures. Still others are continuing to experiment with different approaches and to work on their own competence (several have very little formal education in programming, but "picked it up on their own.").

Two classes emerged as "exemplary," both in terms of student performance and on what seem to be effective instructional practices. These teachers have found methods of balancing their instructional strategies, of providing direct instruction, individualized attention, and time for students to work and experiment on the computer. They have also developed methods of encouraging students to relate and to integrate the various concepts and procedures covered in the course. Such successes suggest that there may be "ideal," or at least "highly effective," classroom conditions.

## IMPLICATIONS

These results suggest that helping teachers learn to use effective instructional techniques would enhance outcomes from programming courses. Furthermore, such instruction would help teachers identify productive ways to use increased on-line time and provide additional evidence for the need to increase on-line access in precollege programming courses.

Curricular materials could also provide explicit instruction in problem solving. Well-developed instructional materials may assist teachers in presenting and explaining material, and in leading discussions to help students integrate and apply their knowledge. We are currently responding to this need by devising expert solutions of programming problems to describe the strategies used by expert programmers (e.g., Clancy & Linn, 1986). These "case studies" include the problem, a worked out solution, and a commentary describing how an expert achieved the solution. We are currently testing these materials in classrooms, to assess whether these materials help students learn explicit programming strategies.

This study describes the relationship between observable classroom characteristics and student learning. It suggests some factors that appear to influence the effectiveness of programming instruction. Many recent studies of how experts solve problems suggest strategies that students need to learn. Examination of effective programming teachers suggests that those teachers who can explicitly model the strategies used by experts are more effective than others. An interesting question is whether modeling is the most effective mechanism for communicating this information or whether the information could be communicated more abstractly through lectures or principles. We suspect that modeling is particularly important in this instance because the skills students need to acquire are extremely complex and often difficult to communicate verbally.

The recent literature on time on-task or learning time is compatible with our finding that students need time to work at computers in order to succeed in programming. In the case of programming, time on the computer is almost identical to time on-task, because students tend to be extremely diligent when using a computer. An interesting question for further research is why this diligence results. Presumably, a factor in such attentiveness is the feedback available in the situation.

These investigations took place in classrooms where the fundamental goal was to prepare students for success on the Advanced Placement Test. As a result, these can be seen as particularly realistic settings. It is interesting that neither time on-task nor explicit instruction prevailed in the most successful classes, but rather that these two factors were most effective when balanced.

Perhaps an implication of these investigations is the need to integrate varying perspectives on classroom learning in order to fully understand the complexity of this dynamic system. More detailed investigations and analyses are necessary in order to fully understand this process. We hope to provide such results in the future.

## ACKNOWLEDGMENTS

This material is based on research supported by the National Science Foundation under grant DPE-84-70364. Any opinions, findings, and conclusions or recommendations expressed are those of the authors and do not necessarily reflect the views of the National Science Foundation.

## REFERENCES

Amarel, M. (1983). The classroom: An instructional setting for teachers, students, and the computer. In A. C. Wilkinson (Ed.), *Classroom computers and cognitive science* (pp. 15–29). New York: Academic Press.

Anderson, J. R., Boyle, C. F., & Reiser, B. J. (1985). Intelligent tutoring systems. *Science, 228,* 456–467.

Bloom, B. S. (1976). *Human characteristics and school learning.* New York: McGraw-Hill.

Brophy, J. E. (1983). Classroom organization and management. *Elementary School Journal, 83*(4), 265–285.

Clancy, M. (1983). *Experience with the lab model for introductory programming instruction.* Paper presented at Computer Science Colloquium, University of California, Irvine, CA.

Clancy, M. (1986, April). *Designing an ideal Advanced Placement course.* Paper presented at the annual meeting of the American Educational Research Association, San Francisco, CA.

Clancy, M., & Linn, M. C. (1986). *Spacetext expert solution.* Unpublished manuscript, University of California, Lawrence Hall of Science, ACCEL Project, Berkeley.

Clements, D. H., & Gullo, D. F. (1984). Effects of computer programming on young children's cognition. *Journal of Educational Psychology, 76,* 1051–1058.

Dalbey, J., & Linn, M. C. (1985). The demands and requirements of computer programming: A literature review. *Journal of Educational Computing Research, 1*(3), 253–274.

Derry, S., & Murphy, D. (1986). Designing systems that train learning ability: From theory to practice. *Review of Educational Research, 56,* 1–39.

Doyle, W. (1983). Academic work. *Review of Educational Research, 53*(2), 159–199.

Evertson, C., Anderson, C., Anderson, L., & Brophy, J. (1980). Relationship between classroom behaviors and student outcomes in junior high mathematics and English classes. *American Educational Research Journal, 17,* 43–60.

Eylon, B., & Helfman, J. (1985). *The role of examples, generalized procedures, and ability in solving physics problems.* (Tech. Rep. No. P85/5.) Rehovot, Israel: Weizmann Institute of Science.

Fisher, C., Berliner, D., Filby, N., Marliave, R., Cahen, L., & Dishaw, M. (1980). Teaching behaviors, academic learning time, and student achievement: An overview. In C. Denham & A. Lieberman (Eds.), *Time to learn* (pp. 7–32). Washington, DC: Department of Education.

Fraser, B. J. (Ed.). (1986). *The study of learning environments.* Unpublished manuscript, Assessment Research, Northwest Evaluation Association, Science Curriculum and Assessment Project, Salem, OR.

Fraser, B. J., & Walberg, H. J. (1981). Psychosocial learning environment in science classrooms: A review of research. *Studies in Science Education, 8,* 67–92.

Good, T. (1979). Teacher effectiveness: What we know about it now. *Journal of Teacher Education, 30,* 52–61.

Greeno, J. G. (1978). A study of problem solving. In R. Glaser (Ed.), *Advances in instructional psychology.* Hillsdale, NJ: Lawrence Erlbaum Associates.

Jeffries, R., Turner, A., Polson, P., & Atwood, M. (1981). The processes involved in designing software. In J. R. Anderson (Ed.), *Cognitive skills and their acquisition* (pp. 255–283). Hillsdale, NJ: Lawrence Erlbaum Associates.

Johnson, W. L., & Soloway, E. (1985, April). An automatic debugger for Pascal programs. *Byte,* 179–190.

Kersteen, Z., Linn, M. C., Clancy, M., & Hardyck, C. (1986, April). *Previous experience in the learning of computer programming: The computer helps those who help themselves.* Paper presented at the annual meeting of the American Educational Research Association, San Francisco, CA.

Larkin, J., & Reif, F. (1976). Analysis and teaching of a general skill for studying scientific text. *Journal of Educational Psychology, 68,* 431–440.

Leinhardt, G., & Greeno, J. G. (1986). The cognitive skill of teaching. *Journal of Educational Psychology, 78*(2), 75–95.

Linn, M. C. (1985a). The cognitive consequences of programming instruction in classrooms. *Educational Researcher, 14,* 14–16, 25–29.

Linn, M. C. (1985b). Fostering equitable consequences from computer learning environments. *Sex Roles, 13,* 229–240.

Linn, M. C. (1986). *Rationale and classroom uses for step-by-step solutions.* Unpublished manuscript, University of California, ACCEL Project, Berkeley.

Linn, M. C. (1987). Establishing a research base for science education: Challenges, trends, and recommendations. *Journal of Research in Science Teaching, 24*(3), 191–216.

Linn, M. C., & Dalbey, J. (1985). Cognitive consequences of programming instruction: Instruction, access, and ability. *Educational Psychologist, 20,* 191–206.

Linn, M. C., Sloane, K., & Clancy, M. (1987). Ideal and actual outcomes from precollege Pascal instruction. *Journal of Research in Science Teaching, 24*(5), 467–490.

Lockheed, M. (1986, April). *Who uses computers in schools? Findings from a national study.* Paper presented at the annual meeting of the American Educational Research Association, San Francisco, CA.

Mandinach, E. B., & Linn, M. C. (1987). Cognitive consequences of programming: Achievements of experienced and talented programmers. *Journal of Educational Computing Research, 3*(1) 53–72.

Pea, R. D., & Kurland, C. M. (1983). *On the cognitive prerequisites of learning computer programming.* (Tech. Rep. No. 16). New York: Center for Children and Technology, Bank Street College of Education.

Reif, F. (1987). Instructional design, cognition, and technology: Applications to the teaching of scientific concepts. *Journal of Research in Science Teaching, 24*(4), 309–324.

Rosenshine, B. (1983). Teaching functions in instructional programs. *Elementary School Journal, 83*(4), 336–351.

Rosenshine, B., & Berliner, D. (1978). Academic engaged time. *British Journal of Teacher Education, 4,* 3–16.

Soloway, E. (in press). Why kids should learn to program. *Harvard Education Review.*

Soloway, E., & Ehrlich, K. (1984). Empirical studies of programming knowledge. *IEEE Transactions on Software Engineering, SE-10*(5), 595–607.

# 10

# An Introductory Pascal Class: A Case Study of Students' Errors

D. Sleeman
Ralph T. Putnam
Juliet Baxter
Laiani Kuspa
*Stanford University*

## ABSTRACT

This study investigated the sorts of errors made by able high school students at the end of a semester-long Pascal class. Several classes were given a screening test, and each student that displayed a reasonable number of errors was given an individual "clinical" interview. This chapter reports the sorts of errors noted and their frequencies. Further, a crude classification into "surface" and "deep" errors is proposed; finally, we speculate about how easy it would be to remediate the different types of errors.

## INTRODUCTION

The growing availability and use of computers in the past few years has resulted in the introduction of programming courses in many schools. High schools offer instruction in programming on the grounds that it provides students with needed job skills, that it is an important component of computer literacy, or that it is a powerful way to develop problem-solving and analytical-thinking skills. Because programming, particularly in the high school curriculum, is a relatively new phenomenon, we have had a limited understanding of how these students learn to program, the difficulties they have, and the misconceptions they develop. This is a study to access the difficulties that students have when learning to program. Further, as difficulties encountered by students may be age related, this study provides another useful data point to earlier studies with college students. Understanding these errors should serve an important role in improving instruction in this area as well as providing insight into the more general area of the learning of complex skills. It is widely accepted that to program effectively one must:

- have a good knowledge of the syntax and semantics of the target programming language (i.e., have an understanding of the conceptual machine supported by the programming language);
- be able to debug programs; and
- be able to analyze (complex) tasks and design algorithms aimed at solving these tasks.

The ability to understand (or "read") programs is a byproduct of the first two stages. Further, it is generally agreed that the topics in the preceding list are in their order of complexity. A more radical goal, supported by research from several areas of cognitive science (Gentner & Stevens, 1983), would advocate that knowledge should be organized around larger chunks, for example, a loop to add $N$ numbers (Schneiderman, 1976; Sheil, 1981). How this may be achieved—other than by extensive practice—is an important instructional issue. Although intuitively we accept this basic point, in this study we were not able to initiate a new approach to the teaching of Pascal. Moreover, we felt that further information about the difficulties students experience when taught programming using traditional methods would provide additional empirical evidence. When we began our study of programming classes in high schools, we expected to study the three aforementioned stages. However, it soon became clear that a sizable number of students in the classes we studied had significant difficulties with the first stage, and were thus hampered in their attempts to implement and extend programs. Thus, the first stage—students' knowledge of syntax and semantics— became the focus of the study (as opposed to the Soloway group which has studied essentially the *plans* underlying college students' Pascal programs).

As noted earlier, one major component of learning to program is gaining an understanding of the "virtual machine" (Wegner, 1968), or the "conceptual machine" (Norman, 1983), underlying a particular language or a working model of how various constructs in a language function (duBoulay & O'Shea, 1981). A programmer must know, for example, what happens when IF or READLN statements are used. Similarly, cognitive scientists working in other subject domains have postulated mental models of various physical and symbolic systems that people hold (Davis, Jockusch, & McKnight, 1978; Gentner & Stevens, 1983; Larkin, McDermott, Simon, & Simon, 1980). Such studies have relied heavily on interview techniques to reveal the nature of people's errors and misunderstandings. In the current study we have applied this methodology to some of the misunderstandings of the conceptual machine that students hold in the early stages of learning to program in Pascal. We have concentrated primarily on their understanding of fundamental constructs such as variables, assignments, and several control constructs. We have examined to a lesser extent their ability to trace and debug programs.

Research on learning to program and on programming errors has been summarized by duBoulay and O'Shea (1981). The majority of the studies reviewed report the frequency of errors made when using particular constructs in various programming languages (BASIC, FORTRAN, LOGO, and Pascal). A major omission in these studies is that they did not determine the *nature* of the errors associated with various constructs. They presented only the frequencies with which various constructs were used incorrectly in programs written by novice or expert programmers. Programmers who made errors were not questioned to determine the nature of their errors or their misunderstandings.

Ripley and Druseikis (1978) have carried out two classic studies of Pascal. More recently, Soloway and his coworkers analyzed the errors that university students make with Pascal assignments and loop constructs. The majority of their analyses have been carried out on programs collected automatically by the operating system (Soloway, Ehrlich, Bonar, & Greenspan, 1982; Spohrer et al., 1985). They have also used interview techniques to probe students' understanding of the assignment construct, finding that students treated $I := I + 1$ and

SUM:= SUM + N as different entities instead of instances of the same general construct. The *pragmatics* of the situation dominated these students' interpretation (Bonar & Soloway, 1982). Another survey found that 34% of the students believed that the WHILE statement functioned as a daemon. That is, given a WHILE statement of the form

```
WHILE cond DO
    BEGIN S1;
         . . .
             Sn
END
```

after executing a statement Si, of the WHILE body they would check to see whether the cond is still true, if not, they would skip the remaining statements.

The following sections of this chapter discuss the organization of the study, provide an overview of the errors encountered, with some indication of the frequency of their occurrence, and give several summaries of the data—including a discussion of typical students with minor and major difficulties and a classification of the errors noted. The article concludes with suggestions for future studies and an overview.

## LEARNING PASCAL IN HIGH SCHOOL

### Subjects

Students from three high-school classes participated in the study. A pilot study was done with one class of 27 students; two additional classes of 19 and 22 students, respectively, were involved. All three classes were introductory courses in Pascal. Most students had some prior exposure to BASIC; the effect of a previous programming language on a second language is an issue to be considered in future research. Our studies took place toward the end of each course. The majority of the students were from Grades 11 and 12 and had strong math backgrounds (as there were math prerequisities).

### Screening Test

Prior to conducting the Pascal study, we carried out an analogous study of the difficulties students encounter when learning BASIC (Putnam, Sleeman, Baxter, & Kuspa, 1986). For the BASIC study, we had developed an effective screening test and a set of more detailed question sheets focusing on particular topics. The task at the beginning of the Pascal study was to refine these tools. The test used is available from the authors; the following section is extensively illustrated with examples from the test. The purpose of the test is to detect possible difficulties in basic constructs, such as reading and printing data, assignments, and the several control structures provided by Pascal. Nine items require specifying the output produced by short (6- to 14-line) programs, each designed to highlight specific concepts. One task requires the student to debug a program for which a written description of the intent is provided. Two items address a similar task, but each program uses a different control structure. The test took between 15 and 35 minutes for the students to complete. Because we asked questions about programs we had prepared, only the students' reading knowledge of Pascal was tested. It would appear that creating a program would be more complex than understanding a given (short) program, and so we suggest that this test represents a test of minimum competence.

## Procedure

The screening test was pretested with a class of 27 students. Minor changes were made in the test before it was used with the other classes. In general, the test and the questions used in the interviews were fine-tuned for each class to reflect the teaching materials used and the order in which concepts had been introduced.

A screening test was given to each student in the three classes. Each student's performance was evaluated by one of the researchers; in this study, we chose to interview only those students who appeared to be having significant difficulties. (Subsequently, it would be interesting to interview students who appear to be doing well, to probe their understanding of this subject domain and make a comparison with this group.) Interviews were conducted with 9, 15, and 11 students, respectively, from the three classes (in the case of the first class it was not logistically possible to interview all the students for whom an interview was suggested). The interviews were clinical in nature, with interviewers using questions and short programs prepared in advance, but also following up with various probes and programs composed on the spot. The goal was to clarify, as far as possible, the nature and extent of the students' misconceptions about programming concepts.

Students were asked to say what output would be produced by various programs, to trace programs and explain how they worked, and to debug short programs. In several cases, students were asked to trace identical programs with different sets of input data. The discussion of a particular topic generally continued until the researcher was able to decide: (a) the "precise" nature of the student's error, (b) that the student had a variety of possible ways of interpreting a construct, or (c) that the student had little knowledge of a particular concept. The interviewer also made a subjective assessment about his or her confidence in this prediction and also noted how consistently the student had manifested the error(s). Some supplementary items created for individuals are included in the text.

Tape recordings, written notes, and responses generated during the interviews were perused for patterns of errors and misconceptions. Because the study was exploratory and qualitative in nature, no quantitative analysis techniques were used. Findings are discussed in the following sections.

## SUMMARY OF ERRORS ENCOUNTERED

As previously noted, the screening tests were given to 68 students of which 35 were subsequently interviewed. We shall refer to an error as being *frequent* with this population if it occurs with 25% or more of the *interview* population (i.e., 8 or more students), *fairly frequent* if it occurs with 4 to 7 students, and *occasional* if it occurs less frequently (i.e., with 1 to 3 students). Note these figures do not capture the frequency or the consistency with which each error was encountered with individual students; specific comments about these aspects are interspersed throughout this section.

The Appendix at the end of this chapter gives a brief summary of the principal constructs of the Pascal language discussed. Those familiar with Pascal should skip the Appendix; those with less familiarity should read it through carefully at this point, *and* refer to it when each new construct is introduced.

### Difficulties with READLN Statements

Several students had difficulty understanding how a READLN statement assigned values to a variable. Four categories of errors appeared: semantically constrained reads, data read in alphabetic order of the variable names, order of declaration determined the order of reading from the file, and multiple-value reads. (It is difficult to categorize unambiguously many of the errors noted. For example: Is the last error mentioned a "READ" or a "variable" error? In this article we make an arbitrary assignment to a class that seems reasonable; in some cases we discuss possible alternative categories.)

*Semantically Constrained READS* Eleven students believed that a READLN statement used with a meaningful variable name caused the program to select a value based on the name's meaning. (Thus, given the frequency classification discussed earlier this is a *frequent* error.) For example, given the following program:[1]

---

[1]The convention used in this and subsequent programs is that data are provided in brackets immediately following the program; multiple brackets indicate sets of data.

```
PROGRAM B1;
VAR First,Smallest,Largest: INTEGER;
BEGIN
    WRITELN('Enter three numbers');
    READLN(Largest,Smallest,First)
END.
[5 10 1]
```

The students with this error said that 1 would be read into "Smallest," 10 into "Largest," and 5 into "First." The majority of these students exhibited this error consistently on this program and in two other programs where it could occur. The second program used to probe for this error was:

```
PROGRAM B2;
VAR Even,Odd: INTEGER;
BEGIN
    WRITELN('Enter two numbers');
    READLN(Odd,Even);
END.
[2 3]
```

Ten students read 3 into "odd" and 2 into "even."

*Declaration Order Determines the Order of Reading* Students with this problem assumed that if the sequence of variables in the declaration statement differed from the sequence of variables in the READ statement, then the variable list of the declaration statement determined the order in which variables were read. This was a fairly frequent error and it showed up in the following program:

```
PROGRAM B4;
VAR A,B,C: INTEGER;
BEGIN
    WRITELN('Enter three numbers');
    READLN(C,B,A)
END.
[15 25 20]
```

These students argued that A was assigned the first number, B the second number, and C the third number "*because* of the order the variables were declared." Typically, the interviewer then modified the order of the variable declarations and asked the student to rework the task. In all cases the response was consistent with this error.

*Multiple Values Read into a Variable*   This error is a variation of the Semantically Constrained READ error; the name of the variable determines the values that are read, but in the Multiple-Values READ more than one value is assigned to a variable at one time. This frequently occurring error was noted in the following program:

```
PROGRAM B3;
VAR Even,Odd: INTEGER;
BEGIN
   WRITELN('Enter data:');
   READLN(Even,Odd)
END.
[3  2  10  5]
```

These students consistently and confidently said that "Even" was assigned the values 2 and 10 and "Odd," 3 and 5. Frequently, the data set was then changed and the students continued to manifest this error. Further, when multiple-valued variables occurred in a conditional statement these students either said that the *first* value is used for comparison or that the comparison cannot be made or the program loops until the values in the variables have been "used."

### Difficulties with Print Statements

The following three errors occurred occasionally with WRITELN statements:

1. WRITELN('Enter a number: '); caused a number to be read; similarly WRITELN('Enter 4 numbers: '); caused 4 numbers to be read;
2. WRITELN('Enter a number: '); caused the variable name *and* its value to be printed; and
3. After this statement has been executed, the program can *choose* a number from the data statement.
   After we had encountered these students, the following diagnostic sequence was devised:

```
X:= 3;
WRITELN('The value of X is 1');
WRITELN(X);
```

Subsequent students were able to cope with this construction correctly, but we are confident that the students with this error would have given the answer "1", that is, the value "given" to X in the string. This item has been added to our repertoire and will be used subsequently.

## Assignment Statements

The first item of the screening test was designed to detect difficulties with assignment statements; supplementary examples produced for the interviews probed this construct further. Although the several errors only occurred occasionally, a total of nine students had difficulties with assignment statements. The difficulties noted include:

1. A:=B was interpreted as switching the values in the variables, that is, A:=B and B:=A (three students showed this error);
2. The assignment statement causes the instantiated statement to be printed. Given the sequence A:=2; B:=3; A:=B; one student said the computer would print 2 = 3;
3. The assignment statement had no effect (noted with three students); and
4. A:=B was interpreted as A=B by two students. (That is, these students said this construct was the boolean comparison operation.)

## Variables

The most significant "variable" error was the previously mentioned multiple value error. The following errors have also been noted occasionally:

1. Confusion of variables. In the sequence:

READLN(P); Q:= Q+1;

the latter statement is executed as if it were:

Q:= P+1;

2. Values of variables are printed when the variable is encountered on the LHS (left-hand side) of an expression.
3. The value of the LHS variable is printed whenever its value changes.

## Difficulties with Loop Constructions

There were three types of errors common to FOR and WHILE constructs. Additional errors were found only in FOR loops.

*WRITELN Adjacent to Loop is Included in the Loop* Some students interpreted WRITELN statements immediately following loops as though the WRITELNs were actually included in the loops. This error occurred frequently and was noted with nearly half the students interviewed. The programs that highlight this error are:

```
PROGRAM G3;
VAR P,Q: INTEGER;
BEGIN
  Q:= 0;
  WRITE('Enter a number: ');
  READLN(P);
  WHILE P < > 0 DO
    BEGIN
      IF P > 0 THEN
        Q:=Q + 1;
      WRITE('Enter a number:');
      READLN(P)
    END;
  WRITELN(Q)
END.
[1 –1 –3 2 4 0]
```

and

```
PROGRAM A5;
VAR I,X: INTEGER;
BEGIN
  FOR I:= 1 TO 3 DO
  BEGIN
    WRITELN('Enter a number.');
    READLN(X)
  END;
  WRITELN(X)
END.
[6 3 4 2 4 1 8]
```

The students who manifested these errors executed program G3 as if the WRITELN(Q) was part of the WHILE loop, predicting that the program would print each number read rather than only the final value of Q. Similarly, they executed program A5 as if WRITELN(X) was part of the FOR loop giving "6 3 4" as output rather than "4." Curiously enough, those students who consistently made this error with the WHILE loop did not necessarily make it with the FOR loop, and vice versa.

*Data-Driven Looping*    Several students indicated that the number of values in the data determined the times a loop was executed. This error occurred in the following program:

```
PROGRAM A2;
VAR I,X: INTEGER;
BEGIN
  FOR I:= 1 TO 3 DO
    BEGIN
      WRITELN('Enter a number.');
      READLN(X);
      WRITELN(X)
    END
END.
[6 3 4 2 4 1 8]
```

We have observed the following output:

```
6 3 4 2 4 1 8
6 3 4 2 4 1 8
6 3 4 2 4 1 8
```

The students explained that the number of values in the data set determined the number of columns, and the value of the FOR-loop limit (in this case, three) determined how many times the process was repeated. Given 6 2 as input data for this program, this student produced the following output:

```
6 2
6 2
6 2
```

*Scope Problems* Several errors involved incorrectly determining where loops begin and end and which statements are repeated in loops.

1. Only the last instruction of a loop is executed multiple times. The other instructions are executed only once but the last instruction is executed the correct number of times. This error was noticed fairly frequently, but it only occurred in a loop where a WRITELN statement was the last one in the loop (thus it may be this error was caused by the write statement and not the loop construct). For example in a revised form of program A5 where the WRITE(X) is the last statement of the FOR statement, students with this error said that the statement that prints the caption and the statement that reads the X would be executed once, whereas the WRITELN(X) would be executed three times.

2. BEGIN/END defines a loop. Given program A3 following, two students thought that all the numbers in the data set would be printed despite the absence of a FOR or WHILE statement.

```
PROGRAM A3;
VAR X: INTEGER;
BEGIN
   WRITELN('Enter a number.');
   READLN(X);
   WRITELN(X)
END.
[6  3  4  2  4  1  8]
```

In a variant of this error, scope of the loop was determined by indentation. In the case of program D1, several students said that the WRITELN "went together with the FOR loop because they were lined up." (In this case, the students' prediction of how the program behaved was correct; they merely gave an incorrect explanation.)

```
PROGRAM D1;
VAR R,C: INTEGER;
BEGIN
   FOR R:= 1 TO 4 DO
      BEGIN
         FOR C:= 1 TO 3 DO
            WRITE ('#');
         WRITELN
      END
END.
```

3. After a loop is executed, control goes to the first statement of the program. This error was seen occasionally and only in short programs where it *could* be interpreted as reinitializing variables each loop-cycle.

Although each of the scope errors in loops only arose occasionally, the total number of students who had difficulties with the scope concept was approximately one third of those interviewed.

*Errors Specific to FOR Loops*   Two errors were specific to FOR loops:

1. The control variable does not have a value inside the loop (this occurred fairly frequently); and
2. The loop statement acted as a *constraint* on the embedded READLN statement. One student said that only the numbers 3, 2, and 1 could be read with:

```
PROGRAM A5;
VAR I,X: INTEGER;
BEGIN
   FOR I:= 1 TO 3 DO
```

```
BEGIN
    WRITELN ('Enter a number.');
    READLN(X)
END;
    WRITELN(X)
END.
[6  3  4  2  4  1  8]
```

Such students believe that the range of the control variable *determines* the values of the variables that can be read by the READLN statement. Although with these Pascal students this error only occurred once, we have previously noted it occurred frequently with students learning introductory BASIC (Putnam et al., 1986).

## Errors Noted with IF Statements

Four types of errors were noted occasionally with IF statements. However, eight students (or 25%) made at least one of the errors:

1. Program execution is halted if the condition is false and there is no ELSE branch;
2. Both the THEN and the ELSE branches are executed;
3. The THEN statement is executed whether or not the condition is true; and
4. IF <a> THEN <b>; <c>; is interpreted as
   IF <a> THEN <b> ELSE <c>.

## Errors with Procedures

These errors fell into two categories:

1. All statements including those in procedure bodies were executed in the order they appeared (a frequent error); and
2. Procedures are executed when they are encountered in a top-to-bottom scan of the program text (as in #1, preceding) and *again* when they are called (a fairly frequent error).

## Tracing and Debugging

As noted earlier, tracing and debugging were not emphasized in this study, but we did include a program in the screening test and a program in the subsidiary material that highlighted these issues. Further, interviewers frequently asked students to trace other programs if they thought this would help determine the nature of the students' difficulties. From this activity, the several interviewers concluded that at least half of the students could *not* trace through programs systematically. Further, we concluded that these students often decided what the program would do on the basis of a few key statements, and would then "project this insight" onto the program as a whole. For example, some students' interpretation of the following program is dominated by the variable Smallest—"obviously this program is to find the smallest of a set of numbers."

```
PROGRAM I1;
VAR Smallest, Number: INTEGER;
BEGIN
   WRITELN('Enter a number:');
   READLN(Number);
   Smallest: = Number;
   WHILE Smallest < > 0 DO
     BEGIN
       IF Smallest > Number THEN
       Smallest: = Number;
       WRITELN('Enter a number:');
       READLN(Number)
     END;
   WRITELN(Smallest)
END.
[9  5  6  2  0]
```

These students assumed that the first READLN(Number) statement reads the lowest value from the data line because the smallest number is needed in the next statement, Smallest: = Number. This error was noted occasionally and appears to be a variant of the semantic read misconception noted earlier.

Other students interpreted programs based on what would be *reasonable output*. The following program illustrates this:

```
PROGRAM F2;
VAR Number: INTEGER;
BEGIN
   WRITE('Enter a Number:');
   READLN(Number);
   IF Number = 7 THEN
     WRITELN('Unlucky Number');
   IF Number = 10 THEN
     WRITELN('Lucky Number');
   WRITELN(' The Number was', Number)
END.
[4]   [10]   [7]
```

For instance when the number 10 was read, students said something like "Well, it will print LUCKY NUMBER and that's all, so there's no point doing the next line as we know the value must be 10 as it's a lucky number," an analogous explanation was given for the UNLUCKY number. These explanations were encountered frequently.


## SUMMARY OF THE DATA

As the data are both rich and complex we shall attempt several overviews, each of which highlights some aspect.


### Summary of All the Students Interviewed

The interviewers classified each student's performance as having essentially no difficulties, minor, or major difficulties (see Table 10.1).

TABLE 10.1
Summaries of All Students Interviewed

| Assessment | N | Percent |
|---|---|---|
| No difficulties | 3 | 8.6 |
| Minor difficulties | 14 | 40.0 |
| Major difficulties | 18 | 51.4 |

From this we note that three of the students did *not* have any problem in the interview, although the screening test indicates some difficulties. In most cases this discrepancy has been attributed to the students rushing through the test or not taking it seriously. (Note: all three were males.) Of the 68 students who took the screening test, at least 32 students had minor problems, and 18 of them (or 26%) had major difficulties. Anecdotally, teachers report that students debug programs by a trial-and-error method. This study lends support to this view as, in the case of many students, several Pascal constructs are only partially understood (or subject to multiple interpretations), thus a trial-and-error approach is the only realistic alternative!

We found that, even after a full semester of Pascal, students' knowledge of the conceptual machine underlying Pascal can be very fuzzy. The problem is more widespread than we had expected and not totally appreciated by the teachers, who frequently set a performance-based completion criteria for the class. Not unreasonably, programming tasks are completed jointly by several students, often masking the several misunderstandings of the individual students.

## Profiles of Typical Students

So far in this chapter we have given an account of the errors noted in the population with some indication of the number of students who manifested each error. By way of contrast, in this section we describe all the difficulties noted for two students; one was described as having minor difficulties and the other as having major difficulties. These are typical of students we classified as having *minor* and *major* difficulties. This classification is not only based on the number of difficulties noted but on our *subjective* assessment of how easy or hard the errors would be to remove/remediate.

## Example of a Student
## with Minor Difficulties

This student appeared to have two errors:

1. Assignment being interpreted as a switch of variables A:= B is interpreted as A:= B *and* B:= A (the student did not manifest this behavior consistently); and
2. Statements in procedures are executed as they are encountered (the student appeared to be consistent with this error).

   Note too that when we interviewed this class, procedures had only recently been introduced. We believe that these errors could be cleared up with just a little additional instruction.

## Example of a Student
## with Major Difficulties

The errors reported with this student were:

1. Semantically constrained reads (a consistent error);
2. The alphabetic ordering of the variables determined the order in which the data was read (not applied consistently);
3. Read a value when a variable was encountered in a statement (not used consistently);
4. WRITELN('Enter a Number'); caused a value to be read (not used consistently);
5. WRITELN adjacent to a loop construct was considered a part of the loop (a consistent error);
6. The number of data elements determined the number of times a loop was executed (a consistent error);

7. The control variable did not have a value in the loop body;
8. The order of execution of two statements was inverted consistently in the following program:

```
PROGRAM G1;
VAR Number: INTEGER;
BEGIN
   Number:= 0;
   WHILE Number < 5 DO
   BEGIN
      WRITELN(Number);
      Number:= Number + 1
   END
END.
```

This program was executed as if the loop body was:

```
Number:= Number + 1; WRITELN(Number);
```

This behavior, however, was *not* noted with other programs; and

9. Infers a complete program's function based on a small number of commands.

A section of the interview with this student that describes this error is quoted in the section on tracing and debugging. Essentially we believe this student's interpretation of the program was dominated by several key statements in the code and the notion that the machine would act "reasonably." Why, he argued, "would the machine execute the last WRITELN, which gives you the value of the number, when it has already told you that the number was lucky and so you would know it had the value of 10?"

We have classified this student as having major difficulties not only because of the sizable number of difficulties, but because we believe some of the errors/misconceptions would be hard to remediate. For example, we believe that the last two errors, 8 and 9, would be difficult to remediate because the student is calling upon common-sense knowledge. This issue is discussed again in the next section.

## Error Classification

Incorrect variants of virtually every construct in the Pascal language were found with these students. We believe that some misconceptions will be much easier to remediate than others. In the algebra domain, for instance, Sleeman suggested that some errors occur because the user omits one of the substeps of a rule that he essentially knows (Sleeman, 1984); we have called these *manipulative* errors. Other errors indicate that the student has little understanding of basic constructs in the algebra domain. For example, we have seen the following expression:

$$3X + 4X = 19 \text{ changed to } X + X = 19 - 3 - 4$$

We have referred to errors of this sort as being *parsing* errors. To generalize this classification to programming, and possibly to other domains, we propose referring to these classes of errors as *surface* and *deep* errors.[2] An example of a surface error in the programming domain is interpreting the statement A:=B as switching the value of the two variables. Semantic READ errors imply a lack of understanding of variables (also encountered in algebra, Kuechemann, 1981) and should be classed as deep errors. Moreover, we believe that inferring the function of a program from a few key instructions is a deep error and one that arises from the user bringing common-sense reasoning to bear on a formally defined domain. Semantically constrained reads and the inference of function from a few statements can be explained by the user attributing to the machine the reasoning power of an average human. We refer to this subclass of errors as the "reasonably human" error class. Pea made similar observations and conclusions (Pea, 1986).

## SUMMARY

The tentative conclusion of this study is that in programming as in other domains (e.g., mathematics) there are basically two types of errors: (a) those due to lack of attention or knowledge and (b) those caused by the interaction of the student's knowledge of the formally defined domain with his common-sense knowledge.

## ACKNOWLEDGMENTS

This chapter draws heavily on Sleeman D., Putnam R. T., Baxter J., & Kuspa L. (1986). Pascal and High School Students: a study of errors. *Journal of Educational Computing Research, 2, 5–23*. Reprinted with permission from Baywood Publishing Company, Inc.

We wish to thank the teachers and students who participated in this study. Haym Hirsh and Alan Char helped with the interviewing. Marcia Linn provided access to an earlier test of BASIC programming. We also thank the Study of Stanford and the Schools for providing funding.

---

[2]Following the recent distinctions introduced to designate the level of an expert system's knowledge of its domain.

## APPENDIX: EXAMPLES OF THE PRINCIPAL
## PASCAL STATEMENTS DISCUSSED

### READ Statement

Pascal actually reads values from the data-stream in order, so if the program and data are:

```
PROGRAM B1;
VAR First,Smallest,Largest: INTEGER;
BEGIN
   WRITELN('Enter three numbers');
   READLN(Largest,Smallest,First)
END.
[5 10 1]
```

Largest would be assigned the value 5, Smallest 10, and First 1. Note that a variable can contain only a single value at any point. (This note is relevant to all the difficulties that arise with READLN statements.)

### Print Statement

The WRITELN command merely causes whatever is in the string to be printed on an output device, say a terminal. It has no *effect* on any of the user defined variables. So

```
WRITELN('Set variable X to 999')
```

has *no* effect whatsoever on the value of the variable $X$.

### Assignment Statement

```
A:= 2   (sets the value of variable A to 2)
B:= 3   (sets the value of variable B to 3)
A:= B   (sets the value of A to B, i.e. to 3, and 2 is "overwritten")
```

A standard variable can contain only a single value at any point in the program's execution.

### Variables

Variables are entities that are used to retain intermediary values of computations. Suppose we need to calculate the annual rainfall of Glencoe—a nontrivial computation. If this value were to be processed in several ways, it would be economical to store the value in a variable and not to have to recalculate it for each subcalculation.

## Loop Constructs

There are three main types of loop constructs in Pascal, namely FOR, WHILE, and REPEAT. The first two have been discussed in this chapter. There is also a further conditional statement in Pascal, the CASE statement, which has not been discussed in this paper.

```
FOR I:= 1 TO N DO
    BEGIN
        S1;
        . . . . . . . . . . . .
        Sn
    END
```

executes the statements in the loop in the order in which they occur for each value of $I$, that when I= 1, = 2,. . . . = N.

```
WHILE P = 0 DO
    BEGIN
    S1
    . . . . . . . . .
    Sn
    END
```

checks if $P = 0$, and if it is, it then *executes* the body of the loop, thereby executing statements S1 . . . Sn (whatever they are). Then the controlling condition is tested *again,* and if the test is true, the loop body is executed again. This continues until the condition is not true, that is, until $P \neq 0$, when control passes to the next statement in the program, that is, the one after the WHILE statement.

## Conditional Statements

There are two forms of IF statement in Pascal:

```
IF cond THEN S1;
    and
IF cond THEN S1 ELSE S2;
```

In the first type, if the condition, for example, $P = 0$, is true, then the statement S1 will be executed. If the condition is false, then the Pascal statement *after* the IF statement would be executed.

In the second type of IF statement, if the Condition is true, the statement S1 is executed, if it is not true, then statement S2 is executed. In both cases the next statement to be executed would be the one *after* the IF statement.

## Procedures

Although there are several types of procedures in Pascal, for the purposes of this study they may be thought of as *subroutines*. If in a sequence of statements a subroutine is encountered, control passes to the subroutine, and at the end of executing the subroutine, control in returned to the statement after the subroutine call.

## REFERENCES

Bonar, J., & Soloway, E. (1982). *Uncovering principles and novice programming* (Res. Rep. No. 240). New Haven, CT: Department of Computer Science, Yale University.

Davis, R. B., Jockusch, E., & McKnight, C. (1978). Cognitive processes in learning algebra. *Journal of Children's Mathematical Behaviour, 3,* 1–320.

duBoulay, B., & O'Shea, T. (1981). Teaching novices programming. In M. Coombs & J. Alty (Eds.), *Computing skills and the user interface* (pp. 147–200). London: Academic Press.

Gentner, D., & Stevens, A. L. (Eds.). (1983). *Mental models.* Hillsdale, NJ: Lawrence Erlbaum Associates.

Kuechemann, D. (1981). Algebra. In K. M. Hart (Ed.), *Children's understanding of mathematics: 11–16* (pp. 102–119). London: Murray.

Larkin, J. H., McDermott, J., Simon, D. P., & Simon, H. A. (1980). Models of competence in solving physics problems. *Cognitive Science, 4,* 317–345.

Norman, D. A. (1983). Some observations on mental models. In D. Gentner & A. Stevens (Eds.), *Mental models* (pp. 7–14). Hillsdale, NJ: Lawrence Erlbaum Associates.

Pea, R. D. (1986). Language-independent conceptual "bugs" in novice programming. *Journal of Educational Computing Research, 2,* 25–36.

Putnam, R. T., Sleeman, D., Baxter, J. A., & Kuspa, L. (1986). A summary of misconceptions of high school BASIC programmers. *Journal of Educational Computing Research, 2,* 459–472.

Ripley G. D., & Druseikis, F. C. (1978). A statistical analysis of syntax errors. *Computer Languages, 3,* 227–240.

Sheil, B. (1981). The psychological study of programming. *Computing Surveys, 3,* 101–120.

Shneiderman, B. (1976). Exploratory experiments in programmer behaviour. *International Journal of Computer Information Science, 5,* 123–143.

Sleeman, D. (1984). An attempt to understand student understanding of basic algebra. *Cognitive Science, 8,* 387–412.

Soloway, E., Ehrlich, K., Bonar, J., & Greenspan, J. (1982). What do novices know about programming? In A. Badre & B. Shneiderman (Eds.), *Directions in human/computer interaction* (pp. 27–54). Norwood, NJ: Ablex.

Spohrer, J. C., Pope, E., Lipman, M., Sack, W., Freeman, S., Littman, D., Johnson, L., & Soloway, E. (1985). *Bug catalogue: II, III, IV* (Tech. Rep. No. 386). New Haven, CT: Department of Computer Science, Yale University.

Wegner, P. (1968). *Programming languages: Information structures and machine organization.* New York, NY: McGraw-Hill.

# 11

# Learning and Transfer of Debugging Skills: Applying Task Analysis to Curriculum Design and Assessment

Sharon McCoy Carver
*Carnegie Mellon University*

## ABSTRACT

By taking an information-processing approach to the teaching and learning of
LOGO programming, we have been able to foster students' high-level debugging
skills such that they can be transfered to debugging tasks in nonprogramming
contexts. In this chapter, we describe the highlights of our research program and
attempt to integrate our findings with those of researchers with other perspectives.
First, we specify a task analysis to make explicit the cognitive processes and
knowledge necessary for debugging. We then report the results of two pilot studies
showing that students in two different LOGO courses were not able to acquire
effective debugging skills by discovery. Next, we present the debugging curriculum we designed, based on our task analysis, in an attempt to foster students'
learning. Finally, we describe the results of two studies assessing students' acquisition and transfer of debugging skills after explicit instruction about the skill
components. We contend that the specificity of our task analysis enabled us to
design an effective curriculum for helping students to acquire debugging skills to
such a degree that they were able to use them effectively even outside the
programming domain.

## RESEARCH PERSPECTIVE

One of the primary justifications for including computer programming in the
precollege curriculum is that students can acquire generalizable high-level skills,
such as planning, problem decomposition, and debugging, from this unique
problem-solving domain (Clements & Gullo, 1984; Linn & Fisher, 1983; Papert,
1972, Soloway, this volume; Winston, 1977). Although previous attempts to
demonstrate students' acquisition and transfer of low-level skills, such as knowledge of particular commands, have been relatively successful (Dalbey & Linn,
1984; Garlick, 1984; Gorman & Bourne, 1983; Littlefield et al., this volume),
demonstrating mastery and transfer of high-level skills has been extremely
difficult (Clements & Gullo, 1984; Garlick, 1984; McGilly, Poulin-Dubois, &
Shultz, 1984; Pea, 1983). We contend that students are not learning high-level
skills simply because these skills are not explicitly taught. No one would expect
students to master English composition with explicit instruction only in gram-

matical sentence construction. Students also need to be taught techniques for combining sentences into paragraphs and larger units for various types of communication, such as arguments, critiques, narratives, and so forth. In a similar way, we must teach students both the low-level and the high-level skills for mastering programming languages.

In order to focus instruction on high-level skills, we must go beyond the readily identifiable behavioral objectives typically stressed in programming courses (e.g., write a program to draw a house using procedures for a square and a triangle) to the underlying cognitive objectives (e.g., develop skills for decomposing program specifications into programmable units). As Lehrer et al. (this volume) indicate, we must use the programming medium as a scaffold for instruction rather than a substitute for it. Unfortunately, such scaffolding is difficult to build, and cognitive objectives are difficult to reach because the component skills are typically left unspecified. Our perspective is that a detailed task analysis of high-level thinking skills is essential for designing explicit instruction to teach cognitive-skill components.

In addition to developing specific cognitive objectives for programming instruction, we must develop appropriate evaluation techniques. Researchers' learning and transfer assessments must focus precisely on the skill components that have been targeted in the instruction. Only when we both provide explicit instruction focused on high-level skills and demonstrate that students have acquired them in the programming domain can we expect to find those skills used beyond programming as broadly applicable cognitive skills. In Greeno's (1976) words,

> the explicit statement of instructional objectives based on psychological theory should have beneficial effects both in design of instruction and assessment of student achievement. The reason is simple: we can generally do a better job of accomplishing something and determining how well we have accomplished it when we have a better understanding of what it is we are trying to accomplish. (p. 123)

In this chapter, we discuss our threefold approach to fostering high-level, transferable, debugging skills. First, we *analyzed the debugging task* to specify the necessary skill components. We describe our model of debugging skill and report two pilot studies demonstrating which components of effective debugging skill elementary school children did and did not discover on their own. Second, we *designed a curriculum* to make the difficult skill components explicit to students. We focus here on our translation of the debugging model into a curriculum to foster children's debugging skill. Third, we *designed tests* to evaluate students' learning and transfer of specific skill components. We report two studies demonstrating that elementary school children did learn effective debugging skills after explicit instruction and were able to transfer these skills to debugging tasks in nonprogramming domains. Our central claim is that the effectiveness of our instruction for promoting students' acquisition of generaliz-able debugging skills in a LOGO context relied heavily on our specification of the components of debugging skill.

## MODELING THE DESIRED SKILL

Imagine the following debugging situation. A child is asked to write a program to draw the sailboat pictured in Fig. 11.1a. Figure 11.1b shows buggy output that the child would see if the SAILBOAT program, in Fig. 11.1c, was run.

Children typically respond ineffectively to debugging situations such as this. Many of them panic and call the teacher insistently, making no attempts to correct the situation until help arrives. Others quickly erase their code and begin again without ever understanding their error. The few who do attempt to debug their code do so by checking each command in the program, usually in order of

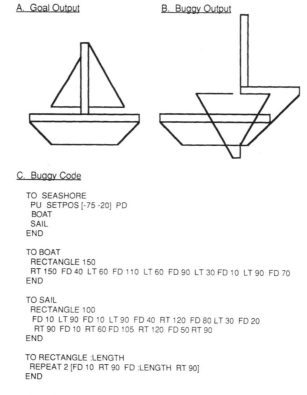

A. Goal Output     B. Buggy Output

C. Buggy Code

```
TO SEASHORE
  PU SETPOS [-75 -20] PD
  BOAT
  SAIL
END

TO BOAT
  RECTANGLE 150
  RT 150 FD 40 LT 60 FD 110 LT 60 FD 90 LT 30 FD 10 LT 90 FD 70
END

TO SAIL
  RECTANGLE 100
  FD 10 LT 90 FD 10 LT 90 FD 40 RT 120 FD 80 LT 30 FD 20
  RT 90 FD 10 RT 60 FD 105 RT 120 FD 50 RT 90
END

TO RECTANGLE :LENGTH
  REPEAT 2 [FD 10 RT 90 FD :LENGTH RT 90]
END
```

FIG. 11.1.    A graphics debugging situation. The student's goal is to write a program to draw the sailboat A; she can gather clues about the identity and location of the bugs from the faulty output B to narrow her search in the program code C.

execution, until the bug is found. In any case, ineffective debugging skills act as a bottleneck to developing other programming skills; students who spend large amounts of their computer time waiting for the teacher, rewriting code, or laboriously checking every command are unlikely to enjoy programming enough to persist through the hundreds or thousands of hours necessary to develop programming proficiency.

The first step in alleviating this bottleneck and providing students with a high-level skill that might be useful in other domains beyond programming is to specify a precise task analysis of debugging skill. Our task analysis was specified in the form of a computer-based tutorlike production system that was intended to capture, in concrete form, the decision processes, knowledge, and subskills necessary for efficient debugging. The model can debug LOGO graphics and LOGO list-processing programs with one or more syntactic (grammar) and/or semantic (usage) bugs.

In general, a production-system model is designed to simulate human thinking and behavior. It consists of a set of rules, called "productions," that specify the action to be taken if certain conditions exist. The conditions include the goal that the model is trying to achieve and the information currently available in working memory (the set of known facts). A production is selected and executed only when the appropriate conditions exist; thus, the current state of the environment determines which actions will be performed. The actions include updating or adding to working memory and/or goal memory.

The productions in our model represent our task analysis of debugging skills in the LOGO context.[1] The model's goals correspond to the steps in the debugging process and its productions represent general and specific heuristics used for efficient debugging. The low-level subskills assumed by the model include running programs, editing code, and so on; these skills are currently taught in most LOGO courses and are, therefore, not the focus of our curriculum or of the discussion in this chapter. Rather, the model is designed to capture the high-level skills of effective debuggers. It follows a standard debugging procedure and, like a tutor, requests information about the particular situation as it proceeds. When we run the model, we can simulate students with different debugging ability by providing more or less accurate information. The computer model can locate bugs quickly and efficiently if it is given appropriate information; otherwise it resorts to serial search, much like the novices described earlier. We use these simulations of debuggers at various skill levels both to determine what procedures and heuristics to teach our students and to evaluate the skill levels students have reached at different test times.[2]

---

[1]The model is implemented in GRAPES, a goal-restricted production system (Sauers & Farrell, 1982).

[2]Additional details about the system are available elsewhere (Carver, 1986; Carver & Klahr, 1986).

Our model describes effective debugging as a five phase process. Figure 11.2 shows a flow diagram representation of the five phases and an English version of the system's production rule for creating that hierarchy of goals. Both representations convey the same idea. If there is a bug, then the debugger should attempt to identify the likely bug type and the likely bug location. For example, in the situation pictured in Fig. 11.1, the only type of commands that could cause the boat side to be too long are move commands, and the only commands that could cause the sail to be upside down are turn commands. One could also predict that the boat-side bug would be located in the BOAT procedure and that the sail-orientation bug would be located in the SAIL procedure. In fact, even without knowing the order in which segments were drawn, one could further specify the location of the sail orientation bug; it must be early in the procedure, because the shape of the sail itself is correct. Effective debugging depends heavily on clues about the probable identity and location of the bug to focus the debugger's search. With that type of information in mind, the debugger should be able to limit search to only particular locations for particular types of commands. Without such clues, the debugger must resort to serial search through the code.

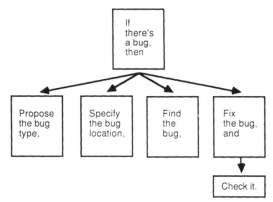

A. Flow Diagram Representation

B. Production Rule Representation

```
IF  the goal is to evaluate a program
    and
    the desired output and the actual output
    are not the same,
THEN set a subgoal to identify the bug type
    and
    set a subgoal to identify the bug location
    and
    set a subgoal to find the bug
    and
    set a subgoal to fix the bug.
```

FIG. 11.2. A general view of the debugging process. The five basic phases involved in effective debugging can be represented either as a flow diagram A or as a condition-action rule from our production system model B.

In either case, once the bug is found, the debugger must make the correction and retest the program to verify the correction.

Because the model's goals and heuristics are central to the debugging curriculum that we present later, we describe them in more detail in the following sections. In addition, we provide examples of the model debugging a list-processing program to contrast the focused and serial search strategies more fully.

## Goals Direct the Solution

The debugging model's goal structure corresponds to the five phases described earlier. A tree representing the model's goal structure is shown in Fig. 11.3. The system has a set of productions corresponding to each goal to represent the different responses a debugger would have to the same goal in different situations. The "situations" are represented by the contents of the system's working memory. Productions with *test* and *evaluate* goals start the system and evaluate the success of each debugging attempt (i.e., whether the program plan and its output match). The *describe* and *propose* productions describe the discrepancy between the program plan and the program's buggy output and propose possible bugs and ways to discriminate among them. Productions with *represent* and *specify* goals look for structural clues to the bug's location. If the model has successfully gathered clues about the bug's identity and location, then the *find* productions can isolate the bug without having to *interpret* each command and *check* its correctness. The *change* and *replace* productions then identify the appropriate correction and change the program listing accordingly. Finally, the *test* goal is reset so that the correction can be verified.

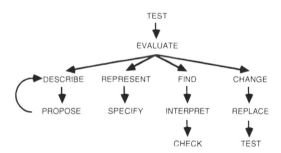

FIG. 11.3. The goal structure of the debugging model. According to our model, effective debuggers first test a program to evaluate its outcome. If a bug exists, they describe the problem and attempt to propose a likely cause. Based on their representation of the program structure, they try to identify the likely location of the bug. This clue gathering should allow them to find the bug without interpreting and checking the outcome of many commands. They then generate the change, replace the bug with the correct commands, and retest the program, beginning a new cycle. (From Carver & Risinger, 1987.)

## Heuristics Narrow the Search

The system has two sets of debugging heuristics, one set for identifying the type of bug (*describe* and *propose* productions) and one set for representing the location of the bug in the program (*represent* and *specify* productions). Appropriately using both sets of heuristics focuses the search for the bug. Heuristics for identifying the bug consist of mappings between observed discrepancies and potential bugs. For example, an orientation discrepancy (such as with the boat's sail in Fig. 11.1) can be caused only by a turn command, a RighT turn, a LefT turn, or a SETHeading command. These may not be one-to-one mappings, however; heuristics may suggest several types of bugs. In that case, the system may either request further information from the user to distinguish among alternatives or may simply suggest scanning for either possibility. For example, when a variable name gets printed instead of its value, the model would suggest looking for a variable name that has a quote instead of a colon or a variable name that has been enclosed in brackets.

Heuristics for locating the bug involve knowledge of program structure types. For example, if the program is identified as having subprocedure structure, the model would ask for information about which subprocedure was likely to contain the error, and it would confine its search to that subprocedure unless no bug could be located there. If no subprocedure clue is available, the model will seek other structural clues, such as location within a REPEAT or an IF statement or location after a particular command. For example, if the debugger can identify a correct command that was executed before the bug occurred, the model will use that command as a marker and begin its search after that command.

## Modeling Different Levels of Skill

Contrasting two simulated attempts to debug the example program shown in Table 11.1 will clarify the importance of the goal structure and heuristics just described. These simulations differ only in the amount of accurate information given to the model about the bug's identity and location.

First, we simulate a situation in which the debugger is very knowledgeable (Table 11.2). The model is provided with information about both the discrepancy and the program structure; this information is listed on the right-hand side of the trace. Here the simulated debugger classifies the problem as list processing without an error message and then identifies the discrepancy type as *printvariable*, because the variable name JOB was printed instead of its value TV REPAIR. The model responds that the bug causing that discrepancy is likely to be incorrect punctuation. It also asks the debugger to input the name of the variable. The debugger is then asked a series of questions about the likely location of the bug. This simulated debugger knows that the program *LIVING* has subprocedures and that the bug is likely to be in the procedure *JOB*. Because

TABLE 11.1
A typical list-processing bug. This debugging situation in LOGO list processing is the basis for
the example simulations we discuss in this chapter. We assume that the debugger has access to
the buggy code A and the buggy output B on-line. The last line of the output should read, "TV
REPAIR IS AN INTERESTING JOB." (From Carver & Risinger, 1987.)

A. Buggy Code

```
TO LIVING
   PRINT [DO YOU LIKE LIVING IN PENNSYLVANIA?]
   MAKE "LIVING READWORD
   IF EQUALP :LIVING "YES [WHERE] [WORKING]
END
TO WHERE
   PRINT [WHERE DO YOU LIVE?]
   MAKE "WHERE READLIST
   (PRINT :WHERE [IS A NICE PLACE TO LIVE.])
END
TO WORKING
   PRINT [TOO BAD, DO YOU LIKE WORKING HERE?]
   MAKE "WORKING READWORD
   IF EQUALP :WORKING "YES [JOB] [PRINT [I DON'T EITHER.]]
END
TO JOB
   PRINT [WHAT IS YOUR JOB?]
   MAKE "JOB READLIST
   (PRINT "JOB [IS AN INTERESTING JOB.])
END
```

B. Buggy Output

```
?living
DO YOU LIKE LIVING IN PENNSYLVANIA?
no
TOO BAD, DO YOU LIKE WORKING HERE?
yes
WHAT IS YOUR JOB?
tv  repair
JOB IS AN INTERESTING JOB.
?
```

the model has been given knowledge about both the likely identity and the likely
location of the bug, it locates the bug immediately (i.e., without having to
interpret and check the outcomes of any commands). The model prompts the
debugger to input the necessary fix, makes the specified change, and directs the
debugger to retest the subprocedure *JOB* and then the main procedure *LIVING*.
Because the fix is correct and no other bugs exist, the debugging episode is
complete.

Figure 11.4a shows the goal tree generated during this high-information
simulation. Each number refers to one subgoal; the information content of the
trace is included next to the corresponding subgoal number. Figure 11.4b shows
the goal tree generated during a low-information simulation. The simulated
debugger responds to the model's prompts by giving it no information, so the
model has no clues to either the bug's identity or location. In this case, the model
starts searching for the bug in the main procedure and continues checking each

TABLE 11.2
A high knowledge debugging simulation. The production system requests information about
the current debugging situation. To simulate a high-knowledge debugger, we provided complete information in response to the prompts so the system located and corrected the bug after
minimal search. (From Carver & Risinger, 1987.)

| | |
|---|---|
| Run the program LIVING. | -->ok |
| Did the outcome match the plan [yes or no]? | -->no |
| | |
| What type of discrepancy is there [graphics or lists]? | -->lists |
| Did you get an error message [yes or no]? | -->no |
| What is the discrepancy between the plan and outcome? | |
| [printvariable, wrongvalue, notmatching, extent, | |
| extrapart, wrongpart, missingpart, or ?] | -->printvariable |
| | |
| The variable has probably been quoted or put in brackets. | |
| Use a colon when printing variables. | |
| What is the name of the variable? | -->JOB |
| Look for PRINT "JOB or PRINT [ ... :JOB ...]. | |
| | |
| Does the LIVING program have subprograms [yes or no]? | -->yes |
| Is the bug in a subprogram [yes or no]? | -->yes |
| Which subpart is wrong? | -->JOB |
| | |
| The bug is "JOB in JOB. | |
| | |
| How should the fix be made? | |
| [change, delete, or insert] | -->change |
| What should "JOB have been? | -->:JOB |
| | |
| Run the program JOB. | -->ok |
| Did the correction fix the problem? | -->yes |
| Run the program LIVING. | -->ok |
| Did the outcome match the plan [yes or no]? | -->yes |

command in order of execution until the bug is found. Each time a subprocedure
call is encountered, the debugger is given another chance to provide information
about the likely location of the bug. Once again, none is entered so the model
continues its serial search until the debugger identifies "JOB as the bug.

The contrasts between the model's behavior in the high- and low-information
simulations are striking: The former required only 16 subgoals, whereas the latter
requied 68. The high-information simulation represents the ideal case in which
the bug is completely specified and its location is known. The system's goals and
heuristics were used efficiently to narrow the search for the bug. In the low-
information situation, little use is made of the *describe*, *propose*, *represent*, and
*specify* goals so none of the heuristics for narrowing the debugger's search are
used, and debugging proceeds by brute force, one command at a time. Most of
the extra subgoals are the result of this serial search. For the purpose of this
simulation, we assumed that the interpretation of commands in the low-

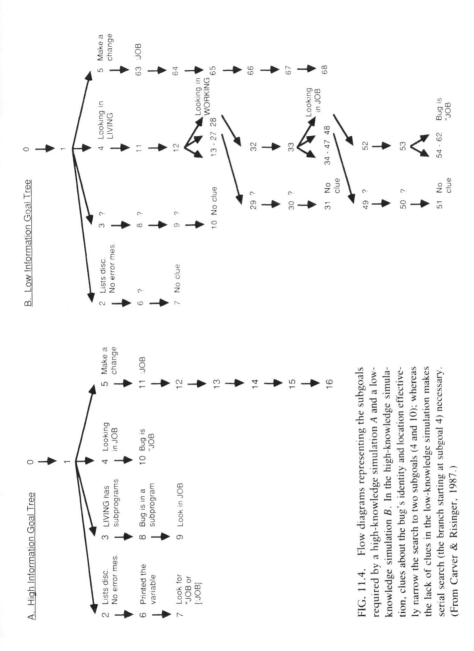

FIG. 11.4. Flow diagrams representing the subgoals required by a high-knowledge simulation *A* and a low-knowledge simulation *B*. In the high-knowledge simulation, clues about the bug's identity and location effectively narrow the search to two subgoals (4 and 10); whereas the lack of clues in the low-knowledge simulation makes serial search (the branch starting at subgoal 4) necessary. (From Carver & Risinger, 1987.)

269

information simulation correctly identified the bug. If this had not been the case, the difference between the two traces would have been even more striking because repeated debugging cycles would have been necessary.

## EVALUATING DISCOVERY LEARNING

We used our various skill-level simulations as standards for measuring the debugging skills students acquired, by discovery, from LOGO experience. In this section, we briefly present evidence from two pilot studies that children do not acquire effective debugging skills on their own. To motivate the debugging curriculum that we present in the next section, we focus here on the debugging skill components responsible for the students' poor performance. The first pilot study took place in the context of a typical, short-term, structured LOGO graphics course. In contrast, the second pilot study took place in the context of a unique, long-term, unstructured LOGO course. At the end of both LOGO courses, the students were still ineffective debuggers, because they used primarily serial search debugging techniques.

### A Short-Term, Structured Environment

In order to assess students' developing debugging skills in a structured environment but without any special focus on debugging skills, we taught a 24 hour LOGO graphics course to nine second- and third-grade students, ranging in age from 7;1 to 8;9, in 12 two-hour sessions over a 3-week period (Carver & Klahr, 1986). New material was introduced by the teacher, and the students did activities presented on handouts. They were then encouraged to explore variations on the current theme in order to understand a concept's flexibility (e.g., in a lesson on using REPEAT to generate curves, students would be encouraged to try changing each of the inputs to discover its effect).

In this context, we assessed the acquisition of debugging skills, particularly those corresponding to the model's goals and heuristics. In addition, we assessed several of the subskills in isolation. Debugging skills were monitored three times throughout the LOGO course by asking students to debug six short programs, each containing one bug. For each program, students were given a color drawing of the intended output and were directed to run the buggy program. They were then asked to describe the problem with the output and to fix the bug. The experimenter recorded any clues the students mentioned, the search strategy they used, and each change they made in the code. Students' developing abilities to generate move and turn commands (to hit a target on the screen), to interpret the outcome of commands (to predict what a procedure would produce on the screen), and to maneuver within the LOGO environment (to edit procedures) were also monitored three times during the course.

On all three debugging tests, children's primary difficulty was in finding the bug, not fixing it. They had difficulty interpreting and checking commands in the program as they searched for the bug; they frequently counted incorrect commands as correct and identified correct commands as the bug. On tests designed purely to assess children's ability to predict the outcome of LOGO graphics procedures, children also performed very poorly and did not show improvement during the course. Children made correct drawings for only 19% of the 162 problems. They made errors in measurement of angles and distances as well as in placekeeping (i.e., they skipped commands, read commands twice, or iterated the wrong number of times in a REPEAT statement). Errors such as these severely handicapped the students on the debugging tests because they did not develop effective search strategies.

Students were able to *test* and *evaluate* the program to see whether or not the actual output matched the desired output, often before the program had finished running. They made little use, however, of the *describe, propose, represent*, and *specify* goals. The few clues they did gather about the bug's identity were vague and rarely discriminated between potential bugs. In addition, the clues that had been gathered were seldom used to narrow the search for the bug, so the students had to *find* and *change* the bug using step-by-step examination of the program code. Students used serial-search strategies so extensively that they did not even skip commands that could not have been the bug; they consistently checked color commands even though the color was never discrepant.

Though students did not improve in terms of their search strategies, they did improve in the accuracy of their corrections. For the 54 problems given at each test time, the students made a total of 99, 81, and 70 changes to correct the programs (i.e., closer to one change per bug fixed). This improvement is the result of two developing subskills. On the pure editing tests (given marked hard copy), children became more efficient during the course. On the first test, children made a average of 75% more keystrokes than necessary to complete the editing tasks. By the second test, they made only 57% more keystrokes than necessary, and by the third test, only 45%. Children also improved on pure command-generation tests. Their ability to choose left and right turns from varying turtle orientations improved markedly during the course. They made almost perfect judgments from a 0° orientation even on the first test, but their judgments from 180° improved from 33% correct on the first test to 85% on the third test. Judgments from four other intermediate orientations improved to even higher levels. The children's estimation of angles and distances was consistently good throughout the course. In other words, children did have the editing and command-generating skills necessary for making corrections in the code, but they had difficulty finding the bugs in the first place.

In summary, the students in this typical short-term, structured graphics programming course did not develop the effective search-narrowing heuristics used by our debugging model. Instead they continued to use serial search and made frequent errors when locating the bug because they misinterpreted commands. They did, however, develop the ability to correct bugs once they had been located.

## A Long-Term, Unstructured Environment

Though the children in the first pilot study did not develop effective debugging skills after 24 hours of LOGO experience, they may have done so if they had been given substantially more experience. In collaboration with Papert's research group at MIT, we tested this possibility. We assessed the debugging skills of fifth-grade students given extensive unstructured LOGO experience (approximately 200 hours). At the end of this time, we gave a graphics debugging test (containing six bugs) to 15 of the best programmers from advanced work classes.

In spite of having 200 hours of programming experience, only one of the subjects was able to find and fix all of the bugs quickly. He gathered effective clues about the identity and location of the bug and, therefore, was able to use focused search. Nine of the subjects were ineffective debuggers because, like the subjects in the first pilot study, they had considerable difficulty interpreting and checking commands. They relied heavily on serial search and required considerable help from the experimenters in order to locate the bugs. Five of these students also made multiple changes between program tests so they had difficulty determining which of their changes had fixed the bug. The five remaining students chose to rewrite the buggy procedures rather than to debug them. They required less help from the experimenters but spent more time debugging, because they had to write their own procedures and then debug them. One student even rewrote his own procedures when they did not work the first time.

## Poor Learning from Discovery

Results from both pilot studies show that students rarely developed effective debugging skills on their own, even after extensive experience with LOGO. Most of them did not learn to gather clues about the bug's identity or location, which could have narrowed their search. Instead they relied primarily on serial search, which was ineffective because of difficulty interpreting the effects of commands.

The remainder of this chapter discusses how these difficulties might be alleviated for children in a LOGO programming environment. Our general claim is that students can learn effective high-level skills, such as debugging, when the components of those skills are specified and taught directly. We demonstrate how we designed an explicit debugging curriculum from the goal structure and the heuristics that are central to effective debugging in our simulation model. Then we present results from two studies designed to test the effectiveness of our curriculum.

We implemented two LOGO courses which, aside from the explicit debugging instruction, were typical. Twenty-two third- to sixth-graders in a local Montessori school participated in the first LOGO course, which consisted of 50 hours of LOGO graphics and list processing over a 6-month period. Thirty-four sixth graders in a local private girls' school participated in the second LOGO course which consisted of 25 hours of LOGO list processing. All lessons were taught in a guided discovery manner and included time for self-initiated projects. The intervention of the teacher in the students' work was kept to a minimum (see Webb & Lewis, this volume), but new program commands and ideas were introduced in a structured way and beginning activities for using the new concepts were initiated by the teacher. Because the memory load of early programming is high, reminders of all commands and concepts were provided for students.

Our first goal was to discover whether students could learn the debugging skills used by the model when those skills are taught directly. In both studies, we monitored students' debugging skills at several times during their LOGO course to identify which of the component skills they developed. The second goal was to demonstrate whether debugging skills, once learned, are transferable to tasks requiring similar skills. We designed a variety of nonprogramming tasks that required debugging of written directions to achieve a well-specified goal. Students' performance on these tasks was assessed both before and after students were exposed to our curriculum and had experience debugging in a LOGO environment. The following sections describe the debugging curriculum and then the learning and transfer assessments in each of these courses.


## DESIGNING EXPLICIT INSTRUCTION

In addition to using the debugging model to characterize student skill levels, we used the it as the basis for designing curriculum to teach components of debugging skill explicitly (Carver, 1986). The cognitive objective of the debugging curriculum was for students to acquire the same goal structure as the model, especially the initial phases where clues to the bug's identity and the program structure are gathered to narrow the search for the bug. With only slight rewording of the goal structure shown in Fig. 11.3, particularly the interactive prompts the model gives the user, we produced a step-by-step debugging procedure to teach the students. To highlight the similarity between the model and the instruction, Fig. 11.5 shows the debugging procedure students were taught in terms of the flow diagram of the simulation model. The curriculum also included some of the specific heuristics the model uses to map discrepancies onto likely bugs and to focus search on particular parts of the program. All of the possible problem–cause mappings could not be taught, so students were directed to keep records of problems and causes they encountered. They used record sheets with two columns headed: "If this goes wrong," and "Then check for this bug."

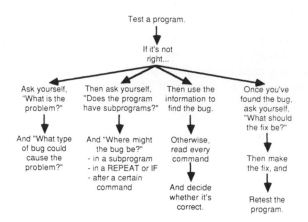

FIG. 11.5. Our debugging curriculum. The debugging procedure taught to students is a step-by-step translation of our model's goal structure. The procedure is represented here in terms of the goal structure flow diagram in Fig. 11.3 to highlight their similarity. (From Carver & Risinger, 1987.)

This simple curriculum was designed for students who already have 6 to 8 hours of programming experience, including one lesson on using subprocedures to compartmentalize parts of the program, especially parts that could be reused. By this time, students have learned the basic commands and have done enough programming to have experienced the difficulty of debugging. Because of their own frustration, they perceive the usefulness of the debugging skills being taught.

During the debugging lesson, the teacher introduced the step-by-step debugging procedure, and the students used the debugging steps to correct the bugs in purposely buggy programs (written by the experimenter) as well as in their own and other students' programs. Only one half-hour lesson was devoted explicitly to debugging; throughout the rest of the course, however, students were frequently encouraged to use the debugging procedures and challenged to find and record new clues. Our thesis is that after explicit debugging instruction, students will develop effective debugging strategies in the LOGO context and transfer them to nonprogramming contexts.

## ASSESSING LEARNING AFTER INSTRUCTION

Because transfer is not possible without learning, we must demonstrate that students have actually acquired debugging skills before assessing transfer. In order to specify precisely which debugging skills students could acquire from our curriculum and have available for transfer to the nonprogramming tasks, we monitored students' debugging skill development during two LOGO courses.

We first selected tasks on which students' debugging skill components would be apparent, evaluated performance measures such as speed and efficiency of debugging, and analyzed students' debugging behavior in terms of their strategies (goals and heuristics).

## Debugging Computer Programs

Students were asked to debug programs written and bugged by the experimenter. We used programs that the students had not written themselves so that the bugs would be the same for all students. In order to ensure that students understood what the buggy program was supposed to do, we gave them an opportunity the previous week to write their own version of the program. During the debugging test, then, students were given the experimenter's buggy programs on-line and asked to fix all the bugs. The students were allowed to work until the program ran correctly or until one class period had elapsed, whichever came first.

The programs used for the debugging test were well-structured; in other words, they made appropriate use of subprocedures and other LOGO substructures such as iteration, conditional statements, and recursion. Bugs were added to each program by the experimenter. The bugs were chosen so that the discrepancies they caused in the output would be fairly independent either in space (usually for graphics) or time (usually for list processing) so that the problem caused by one bug would not obscure the problem caused by any other bug. The only other criterion for bug selection was that there be a variety of discrepancy types in each program.

## Using Protocol Data

Our primary source of data was subjects' verbal and behavioral protocols. We used such data because we consider it an accurate reflection of the complex cognitive processes we are attempting to assess. The students' behavior on all of the tests was videotaped to get a detailed record of the intermediate steps in their solution processes. The videotape contained a visual record of all debugging activity, an auditory record of all verbalizations by the subject and the experimenter, and a record of an elapsed-time indicator (accurate to the nearest second). In addition, students were encouraged to think aloud so that the goals, strategies, and knowledge influencing their solutions could be recorded (Ericsson & Simon, 1984). In order to give students an opportunity to attempt as much of each test as possible during the allotted time and, thereby, maximize the amount of data collected, the experimenter intervened to provide help when impasses were reached.

The protocols were transcribed directly in terms of the model's goal structure by categorizing each statement and action according to goal type. Transcripts were divided into episodes based on the test goal. A new cycle began each time the subject ran a program or ran a series of programs without doing anything else in between. Figure 11.6 shows what a transcript for the high-information trace discussed in the previous section would look like. The transcript begins with a test of the program *LIVING*. A negative evaluation is indicated by the comment, "Oh no!" The discrepancy was described as, "it printed JOB instead of TV repair." and the bug proposed as, "The variable doesn't have a colon." The students know that the program representation includes subprocedures, and one student asks, "Which subprogram should we try?" The other specifies the buggy subprocedure as "Job." They edit the subprocedure *JOB* and scan for a variable called JOB. "JOB is isolated and understood to be the bug. "It should be a colon." says one student. The students then replace the quote with a colon and exit the editor to retest the program. After transcribing the videotapes in this manner, the protocols were used as the basis for performance measures, such as speed, efficiency, and accuracy, as well as for characterizations of subjects' debugging strategies.

## Using the Model to Predict Learning

Our predictions about subjects' debugging performance and strategies were based on our debugging model. Evidence of effective debugging skills was derived from students' verbalizations during debugging and from their actual debugging behavior (the time they took, the code they searched, and the changes they made, etc.). As our example simulations demonstrated, greater knowledge input results in narrower search for the bug (fewer goals); developing debugging

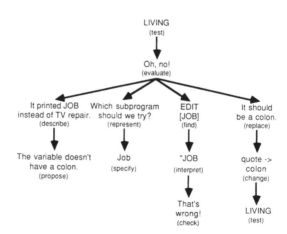

FIG. 11.6.   A debugging protocol transcript. Protocols were transcribed directly onto flow diagram forms like the one shown here. Capital letters indicate what the student typed; lower case letters indicate verbalizations. The corresponding goal names are included in parentheses beneath each entry.

skill should, therefore, result in decreased debugging time (though the model makes no absolute predictions about debugging time). If all the knowledge input to the model is accurate, the bug can be located and corrected all in one cycle through the model (from the initial goal to test the program to the final retest goal). Developing accuracy in debugging should therefore result in fewer debugging cycles needed to locate and correct bugs (i.e., greater efficiency). In addition to these performance measures, we expected that students using focused search would mention more clues about bug location and bug identity before they began their search than students using serial search. They should also search only parts of code related to the bug and edit only commands similar to the bug. In the next two sections, we discuss two separate studies using these assessments to monitor students' development of effective debugging skills after exposure to our debugging curriculum.

## Third- to Sixth-Graders Working in Pairs

Our first assessments of learning and transfer after explicit debugging instruction took place in the context of a 50-hour LOGO course at a local Montessori school. All 22 of the third- to sixth-grade students received the same LOGO instruction, including explicit instruction in debugging. We used a between-subjects design in which half of the students began with graphics and then moved into list processing, whereas the other half took the two minicourses in the reverse order. (See Fig. 11.7) There were no significant differences between the students taking graphics first and those taking list processing first in terms of age, standardized achievement scores, or access to computers at home.

Debugging performance was measured three times during each minicourse (1, 2, and 3 for graphics and 4, 5, and 6 for list processing in Fig. 11.7), so students took a total of 6 debugging tests. The first debugging test was taken after special attention to subprocedures but before debugging instruction. Tests were not counterbalanced with test time; they corresponded, instead, to the concepts being learned at that period in the course. Each debugging test contained six bugs. For the graphics tests, five of the bugs were semantic bugs, whereas only one was a syntactic bug. Syntactic errors include misspellings, inappropriate punctuation or spacing, and other errors that interrupt the running of the program. Semantic errors do not stop the program from running but do cause faulty output. Because syntax tends to be more of a problem for list processing, those tests contained three syntactic and three semantic bugs.

From our past experience, we expected that the children would have difficulty giving think-aloud protocols in the cognitively demanding debugging situation. For this reason, children worked in pairs throughout the course and for the debugging tests. We felt that the joint effort would require verbal communication of strategies for and knowledge about the task. Such communication between the partners was recorded on videotape, as previously described.

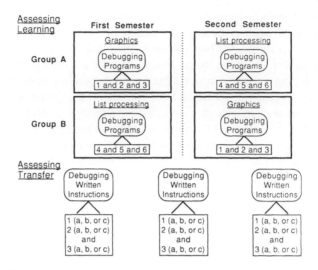

FIG. 11.7. The design of Study 1. The learning design shows LOGO experience, with debugging tests given a total of six times for each group. The transfer design indicates that transfer tests were given before the first minicourse, between minicourses, and after the second minicourse. At each transfer test time, each student took one version (a, b, or c) of each of three test types (1, 2, and 3).

### Between-Subject Comparisons

Because the two groups of subjects took the two minicourses in different orders, we could compare the debugging strategies and performance on the same tests of students who had no prior debugging instruction or experience with students who had debugging instruction and experience in another LOGO domain. For example, all of the students had the same amount of LOGO graphics experience when they took Test 1 (see Fig. 11.7), but Group B had previous debugging instruction and experience in LOGO list processing. If the students in Group B learned the general goal structure of debugging in list processing, they should be able to apply it in graphics, because our model shows that the goal structure is identical for debugging LOGO graphics and list-processing programs. Similarly, if the same students have learned effective bug identity and location heuristics in list processing, at least some of them should be applicable in graphics because our model has several discrepancy-bug mappings (primarily those dealing with syntactic errors) and program structure clues that apply to both domains. In addition, the subskills required by the debugging process, such as editing, running programs, and so forth, are similar in graphics and list processing.

The goal of the debugging analysis was to document which of the debugging skills the students were able to acquire from the direct instruction provided in both LOGO minicourses. For the purpose of this general description, the within minicourse tests are considered essentially as three trials, and the scores have been averaged to get a score for each minicourse as a whole. More detailed descriptions of the results and statistical analyses can be found in Carver (1986). There was no comparison group (a group that got no explicit instruction in debugging); however, these results can be compared to the results from the pilot studies. We present evidence that when given debugging instruction based on the performance model, students were able to acquire effective debugging skills. Without such instruction, students in the pilot studies debugged poorly.

## Speed and Efficiency

We expected that students would require less time to correct each bug in the second minicourse than in the first if their strategies shifted from brute force to more focused search, which requires fewer subgoals. In fact, the average time students spent per bug decreased significantly from 9 minutes 6 seconds in the first minicourse to only 5 minutes 25 seconds in the second. As debugging skill improves, students should also take fewer cycles (each isolated test goal initiates a cycle) to fix each bug. Students' debugging efficiency improved significantly by about 1 cycle per bug from the first to the second minicourse (from a mean of 2.9 to a mean of 2.05 cycles per bug). In the second minicourse, several pairs of students averaged close to a perfect score of 1 cycle per bug and a few actually took fewer than one cycle per bug because they fixed several bugs in one procedure without exiting to retest the program in between.

## Clue Gathering

The goal structure of efficient debugging, presented to the students in our curriculum, stresses the value of seeking clues to narrow the search. As students' understanding of that goal structure and their knowledge of discrepancy-bug mappings and of location clues increases, they should begin to make more comments about the bug's likely identity and/or location before suggesting a command as the bug. Students made very few comments overall, perhaps because the task was so cognitively demanding. They described the discrepancy aloud for about half of the cycles, but they proposed bugs for only about $\frac{1}{4}$ or $\frac{1}{3}$ of the cycles. Location descriptions were more frequent than bug proposals but were still offered for less than half of the cycles. The accuracy of students discrepancy descriptions was nearly 100% in both minicourses; whereas the accuracy of the bug proposals and bug location comments remained constant at about 75%. The important change was that students were more likely to make these statements *before* beginning to search for the bug in the second minicourse. The proportion of discrepancy comments made prior to search increased from less than 65% on tests in the first minicourse to over 80% on tests in the second. Similarly, the proportion of early bug proposals increased from only 25% to over 50% and the proportion of early bug location comments increased from 75% to

85%. Particularly for bug proposals, the students began to gather clues early in order to focus their search.

## Search Behavior

Increasingly focused search should also cause a decrease in erroneous search, that is, the number of correct subprocedures the students erroneously edit and the number of false alarms they make (correct commands they identify as the bug). The number of times the students looked into a subprocedure that did not contain the bug (or information relevant to the bug such as variable values) should decrease as the students learn to use clues for locating the bug. The subprocedure structure of the buggy programs was easy for the students to recognize because the subprocedures that had been loaded were displayed on the computer screen at the beginning of the test. Students rarely misjudged which subprocedure did which part of the program because the subprocedure names were related to their function. The mean number of times subjects looked into a program that did not contain the bug ranged from 2 to 3 per test (i.e., per 6 bugs) in both minicourses. Most of these errors resulted from forgetting the names of the programs or forgetting what subprocedures existed. The amount of brute force search (reading and checking each command in a program) did decrease from the first minicourse to the second. The number of instances of brute force search decreased from a mean of 20 to a mean of 7 out of a possible 66. The number of correct commands that were misidentified as the bug (false alarms) dropped from 293 in the first minicourse to 177 in the second.

## Summary

In summary, after having only one lesson that focused on debugging, students' debugging speed and efficiency improved. They began to use the new strategies we had taught, especially by asking themselves which subprocedure was likely to contain a particular bug. They could, however, have made more use of the list of discrepancy-bug mappings. They memorized some of the more common mappings early, but many students used their problem–cause mapping chart only as a last resort. Nonetheless, they used brute force strategies less often and made fewer false alarms. In fact, most of them did better than the LOGO teachers tested by Jenkins (1986) on the same programs.

One difficulty with this study was that all of the comparisons were made between pairs of subjects. It is, therefore, impossible to go beyond these aggregate results to trace individual patterns of learning and the relationship between those patterns and the successfulness of skill transfer. We designed the second study to alleviate these problems by doing the testing individually rather than in pairs and by using within-subject comparisons.

## Sixth-Graders Working Individually

In order to monitor individual students' improvement more precisely, we implemented a second LOGO course, including only list processing. All 34 of the sixth-graders at a private girls' school participated in this study. We used isomorphic tests and counterbalanced them with test time so that we could do within-subject comparisons of debugging performance and strategies. In addition, half of the students in our sample took the LOGO course during the first semester, whereas the rest, the control group, were in study hall. Those in study hall took list processing during the second semester.

The design of this study is depicted in Fig. 11.8. All students were scheduled for two 40-minute computer periods per week. We then randomly assigned half of each class to the computer condition and half to the control condition. The girls in the computer condition attended a LOGO list-processing class two periods per week for the first semester, whereas the girls in the control condition were in study hall. Half way through the year, the girls in the control condition switched to taking the list-processing class and the others began attending study hall.

During the list-processing course, the girls took two programming and two debugging tests to monitor their developing debugging skills—one shortly after the debugging instruction and one near the end of the course. Two isomorphic

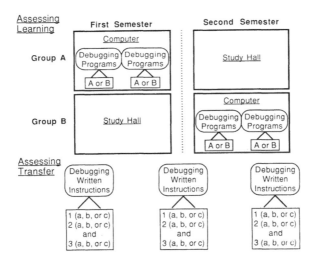

FIG. 11.8.   The design of Study 2. The learning design shows LOGO experience, with debugging tests given twice for each group. The transfer design indicates that transfer tests were given before the first semester, between semesters, and after the second semester. At each transfer test time, each student took one version (a, b, or c) of each of three test types (1, 2, and 3). (From Carver & Risinger, 1987.)

program descriptions were used so that they could be counterbalanced with test time. In addition, two sets of eight bugs (five semantic and three syntactic) were added to the two isomorphic programs. The sets of bugs were isomorphic in the sense that they caused similar discrepancies at the same point in the program output. Further details are included in Carver and Risinger (1987).

At each test time, each student was given one class period to write a program according to one of the program descriptions. During a subsequent class period, the student was asked to fix a program written (according to the same description) and bugged (with one of the sets of bugs) by the experimenters. At the second test time, each student used the other program description and was asked to fix a program bugged with the other set of bugs.

### Within-Subject Comparisons

Once again, the goal of the debugging analysis was to document which of the model's skills the students were able to acquire from the direct instruction. Because we used isomorphic tests counterbalanced with test time, we can compare subjects' performance on the first test to their performance on the second test. From the program debugging transcripts, we measured improvements in speed and efficiency and coded students' clue-gathering and search strategies. There were no differences between program type or bug set so all results are collapsed across these variables. Because most of the analyses were identical to those used for the previous study, we describe only the differences as we present these new results. In addition, these data were collected during the first semester of the study; the second semester data have not yet been analyzed.

### Speed and Efficiency

As in the first study, students' performance on quantitative measures of debugging skill improved during the course. The students' mean debugging speed decreased from 9 minutes 36 seconds per bug on the first debugging test to 4 minutes 43 seconds on the second. Students also took fewer cycles to fix each bug on their second test. The mean number of cycles students took to fix each bug decreased significantly from 3.02 on the first test to 1.60 on the second, which is approaching perfect efficiency.

### Clue Gathering

From the protocol data, we did not see improvement in students' use of bug identity clues. On both debugging tests, students averaged slightly more than one discrepancy description per debugging cycle and were accurate 90% of the time. This high accuracy rate, similar to that found previously, is not surprising because describing the discrepancy between the goal output and the actual output requires no knowledge of programming or debugging. In contrast, students did not propose a bug on every debugging cycle. The percentage of cycles on which they proposed bugs decreased slightly from 63% on the first test to 50% on the second, and the accuracy of their comments increased slightly from 30% to 40%. This result indicates that students were still having some difficulty finding clues to the likely bug before looking at the program code. One reason for this difficulty was that students made ineffective use of their lists of discrepancy-bug mappings. They rarely recorded new mappings after the debugging lesson and consulted their listing only after prompting.

In contrast, students' use of location clues did improve. The proportion of cycles on which students commented about the structure of the program increased significantly from only 19% on the first test to 34% on the second test. The accuracy of these comments increased slightly from 74% to 95%. In conjunction with the increase in comments students made about the structure of the program, the frequency with which they specified the bug location increased slightly from 67% to 82%, and their accuracy rate remained constant at about 60%. In general, students' comments reveal a slight increase in the clues they gathered about the bug's likely location, but their actual search behavior demonstrates increasingly narrow search more dramatically.

## Search Behavior

The number of times the students looked into a subprocedure that did not contain the bug (or information relevant to the bug) should decrease as the students learn to use location clues. The number of subprocedures students entered (per bug fixed) decreased significantly from 4.42 on the first test to 2.26 on the second test. Part of this decrease can be attributed to a significant decrease in the number of correct subprocedures students erroneously edited (1.13 per bug fixed on the first test and .46 per bug fixed on the second). Increased attention to the structure of the program may also contribute to the decrease because students may need to look into correct subprocedures to find information about flow of control less often. Students should also make fewer false alarms as they learn to use clues to the bug's identity. The number of correct commands that were misidentified as the bug and subsequently changed (false alarms) decreased significantly from the mean of 7.29 on the first test to a mean of 2.41 on the second.

## Summary

In summary, after the one lesson focusing on debugging, students began to develop effective debugging strategies. Students took less time and fewer cycles to fix each bug on the second debugging test than on the first. Our results demonstrate improvement in students' debugging skills by showing that their search is restricted to a small portion of the program and to a more specific type of bug. Students were slightly more likely to mention accurate clues about the bug's likely identity and location on the second test, whereas they were less likely to change inappropriate types of bugs and search inappropriate locations. According to our qualitative and quantitative measures, students in both of our courses had begun to use focused search as an effective debugging strategy in the LOGO context. On a more anecdotal note, the character of students' responses to bugs during regular classroom programming, that is, apart from the testing situation, also changed considerably. Students learned to deal with bugs quickly and efficiently with a minimum of insistent requests for help and a very limited amount of code rewriting. By the end of both courses, students sought help from the instructor only for the most insidious bugs.

The research we have described so far has demonstrated that students can learn high-level debugging skills when the component skills are appropriately specified and taught explicitly. We must now address the issue of whether the skills students have acquired are general enough to transfer beyond the programming domain to tasks requiring similar skills. In both studies, we compared students' performance on noncomputer debugging tasks before and after their debugging instruction in the LOGO context. Regarding the pre–post transfer assessments, however, only the second study included a control group receiving no LOGO experience (and no debugging instruction). Therefore, we focus our discussion on contrasting the results for the experimental and control groups in the second study and include results from the first study only to show that we obtained similar results in two different contexts.

## ASSESSING TRANSFER

The goal of the transfer assessments was to discover which of the knowledge and skills available for transfer from the program-debugging context are actually applied in new instances. By making the goal structure and knowledge required by effective debugging concrete, our debugging model provides a way to advance the specificity of predicted transfer effects, the choice of tasks where debugging skills would be useful, and the type of measures used to assess both strategy acquisition and corresponding improvements in performance.

### Debugging Written Directions

Our noncomputer transfer tests all involved detection and correction of errors in a written set of instructions about how to achieve a well-specified goal. These tasks are similar to LOGO debugging in three ways.

First, the instructions given at the beginning of each transfer session and the cover story for each item were designed to highlight the debugging nature of the tasks. Program debugging is viewed as a situation where a programmer has given the computer commands; the computer follows the commands perfectly, but something goes wrong because one of the commands is wrong. The debugger's job is to find the bug in the commands and fix it so that next time it will run correctly. The instructions for debugging written directions mimic the program debugging situation:

> Today I would like you to read three stories. In each story, someone gives someone else directions. The person follows the directions perfectly, but something goes wrong because one of the directions is wrong. Your job is to find the problem with the directions and fix it so that next time it will be done correctly.

The second similarity is that information about the desired and actual output was provided before the written directions could be viewed, just as discrepancy information is available from test runs in debugging situations. In two of the three test types, this information was pictorial; however, in the third, it was tabular. From the pictures and tables, subjects could gather clues about the identity of the bug and its probable location, just as they could in the program-debugging situation.

Third, the lists of directions were structured in ways similar to LOGO, primarily like subprocedures. This structuring was accomplished by the addition of headings between sections of directions to label their purpose. Subjects could use the headings to determine which sections of the directions were likely to contain the bug, just as they could use the subprocedure names to guide their search for program bugs.

Three types of tests were chosen, on the basis of informal pretests, to span a range of difficulty. The easiest problems involved directions for arranging something (setting a table, building with blocks, or arranging furniture). The next easiest problems involved directions for distributing something (paying wages, delivering trees, or ordering food). The most difficult problems involved directions for traveling somewhere (playing golf, visiting airports, or running errands). The tasks were always presented in order of increasing difficulty so that students would not do poorly on an easier test purely as a result of being frustrated by a harder one. Students worked on the tests individually and were asked to "read and think aloud" while they worked. All work was done in a test packet that contained the three stories, pictures or tables comparing the desired outcome with the actual outcome, and the lists of directions.

## Variety of Solution Strategies

The following example will show how the model's brute-force strategy (low-information search) and selective-search strategy (high-information search) would solve one of the transfer items. Table 11.3 shows the plan and outcome for the wage-distribution problem. Table 11.4 lists the accompanying directions. Before viewing the table, students read the following cover story.

TABLE 11.3

Discrepancy information. Comparing the two columns in this table could yield clues about the identity and location of the bug in the accompanying written directions. In LOGO programming, comparing the desired and the actual output can provide similar information. In this case, the hourly rate for the busboys is too low.

| | | Amount Earned | Amount Paid |
|---|---|---|---|
| Cooks | | | |
| | Mary | $50 | $50 |
| | Bert | $75 | $75 |
| | Gary | $75 | $75 |
| | Jason | $65 | $65 |
| Waiters and Waitresses | | | |
| | Claire | $40 | $40 |
| | Bill | $40 | $40 |
| | Sally | $45 | $45 |
| | Tom | $20 | $20 |
| | Mary | $30 | $30 |
| Busboys | | | |
| | Gary | $15 | $12 |
| | Wayne | $25 | $20 |
| | Tom | $50 | $40 |

Mr. Handy owns a family restaurant that has 11 employees. He was out of town on payday so he asked his wife to pay the workers. He gave his wife a list of directions.

The table on the next page shows how much each employee earned. Mrs. Handy followed her husband's directions *perfectly*, but there was *one* problem with the directions so some of the workers did not get the proper amount of money. The table on the next page also shows how much each worker actually got paid.

*Change* or *add* one thing to fix Mr. Handy's directions so everyone will get the right amount of money.

Comparison of the two columns in Table 11.3 reveals that Gary, Wayne, and Tom were underpaid. Closer inspection may reveal that they were all busboys and that they each received $\frac{4}{5}$ of what they earned. A solver who knows to look for Gary, Wayne, and Tom might scan the directions until reaching one of those names. This strategy would lead to false alarms on the lines describing the cook named Gary or the waiter named Tom. A solver who knows to look in the directions for the busboys will ignore the other directions and focus only on the busboy ones. In contrast, solving this problem would be quite tedious for someone using a brute-force strategy, as many children did on the pretest. The solver would read each line, calculate the expected salary, and check the table to make sure it was correct until the incorrect direction was located.

TABLE 11.4

Buggy written directions. The directions are structured with sections, similar to subprocedures in programming, so the use of location clues is possible. A student using focused search would only consider directions for paying the busboys or those directions referring to employees named Gary, Wayne, and Tom.

---

Here are the directions Mr. Handy gave to his wife.

To pay the cooks,
    Pay Mary $50.
    Pay Bert $25 more than Mary.
    Pay Gary the same amount as Bert.
    Pay Jason $10 less than Gary.
To pay the waiters and waitresses,
    Pay the waiters and waitresses $5 for every hour they worked.
    Pay Claire and Bill for 8 hours each.
    Pay Sally for one more hour than Claire.
    Pay Tom for half as many hours as Bill.
    Pay Mary for 2 more hours than Tom.
To pay the busboys,
    Pay the busboys $4 for every hour they worked.
    Pay Gary for 3 hours.
    Pay Wayne for 2 more hours than Gary.
    Pay Tom for twice as many hours as Wayne.

Change or add one thing to fix these directions.

---

Solvers with all of these strategies could locate the bug and change the hourly rate from $4 to $5 for the busboys. The search process, not the success rate, is what distinguishes the different strategies. However, solvers who search more of the directions might be more likely to false alarm and, therefore, be less successful.

## Using the Model to Predict Transfer

The goal of the transfer analysis was to determine whether the focused search strategies learned from the explicit debugging instruction in the LOGO environment would transfer to similar debugging situations not involving programming. As with the learning assessments, verbal and behavioral protocols, transcribed from videotapes of the test sessions, were our primary source of data. Students who learn the importance of seeking clues to narrow their search in the LOGO context may transfer this practice to the new task.

Because we expect the difference between subjects who have acquired effective debugging skills and those who have not to be in the search process not the outcome of that process, the central measure in our transfer analysis is a qualitative assessment of the subjects' search strategies. Subjects' choice of debugging strategies was expected to shift toward more efficient strategies if they were able to transfer the focused search strategies they demonstrated in the

LOGO context. Students were reading and thinking aloud so their search process was easily traceable. From the transcripts, we first classified each student's strategy for *reading* each set of buggy instructions. Three qualitatively different strategies were possible:

1. *Focused search (F)*. The student selectively focuses only on the appropriate subsection of the instructions and/or on the part near the bug or referring to the bug.
2. *Self-terminating brute-force search (S)*. The student reads every instruction until the bug is located and then disregards the rest.
3. *Brute-force search (B)*. The student reads every instruction.

We also classified each subject's strategy for *simulating* the buggy directions, that is, actually interpreting the effect of a direction by referring back to the discrepancy information. For simulating, the subject may use any of the three strategies in the preceding list or may simulate no instructions at all (*N* for no strategy). We expected that more subjects would use focused search strategies for reading and simulating directions after having acquired debugging skills in the LOGO context than before. Subjects in the control (study hall) condition were, therefore, not expected to improve.

We also predicted that the accuracy of fixes would improve as a result of more focused search. Students should process fewer lines so the number of false alarms should decrease, causing their overall accuracy to increase. Once again, the control group was not expected to improve. On the other hand, we did not predict differential improvement on measures of skills that we did not model, teach, or test. These nondebugging skills include reading skills (such as comprehension or speed), math skills (useful for correcting buggy distribution directions), or map skills (useful for correcting buggy travel directions).

## Within-Subject Comparisons in the Second Study

We assessed the debugging skills of all 34 students from the second study in a noncomputer context at the beginning of the year, in the middle of the year (after half of the girls had been given explicit debugging instruction in the LOGO context), and at the end of the year. At each of the three test times, each student took three types of transfer tests (1, 2, and 3 in Fig. 11.8), all of which involved debugging a written set of instructions about how to achieve a well-specified goal, as previously described. One-third of the students took each version at each time (a, b, or c in Fig. 11.8). Our transcriptions of the videotaped tests focused on the components of the model's debugging skill. The results described here include only the pre- and midtest analysis.

## Clue Gathering

On both the pre- and midtests, students in both groups (computer and study hall) spent about 30 seconds looking at the discrepancy information before turning to the directions. Their comments at both test times were restricted to orientation to the type of discrepancy information ("This is what they earned and this is what they got.") and descriptions of the discrepancy ("These should be paid more."). As with the LOGO debugging, most of the discrepancy descriptions were correct. Students made few comments, however, about the likely identity of the buggy directions, presumably because they had inadequate knowledge about the discrepancy-bug mappings in the transfer domains. Students made comments about the likely location of the bug only on the distribution tests where the discrepancy information was presented in a table with section headings. Here, the location clue was salient, and the accuracy of students' comments was high for both groups on both tests. The difference between the computer and control groups emerges only when the actual search process is considered.

## Search Behavior

As we predicted, differential improvement did occur between the computer and control groups in terms of their actual search process. Two experimenters categorized each subject's strategies on each test, with an interrater reliability of 86%. Figures 11.9a and b show the percentage of strategy usage for the two groups on the pre- and midtests. Each subject debugged three sets of buggy directions at each test time so the total number of strategy scores equals three times the number of subjects.

The upper left cell in Fig. 11.9a shows that the brute-force reading/no simulating strategy (column B, row N) was used 44% of the time. This cell represents the worst strategy combination (read exhaustively and never seek discrepancy information), whereas the bottom right cell (focused reading/ focused simulating) represents the best strategy combination. Therefore, the expected shift for the computer group was from the top left cells to the bottom right cells. Analysis of the column and row marginals in Fig. 11.9a reveals that students in the computer group shifted significantly toward more focused strategies for both reading and simulating. Comparable analysis for the control group data shown in Fig. 11.9b shows no such shift.

## Accuracy

Because the computer group did demonstrate better search strategies, we also expect them to make more accurate corrections. The changes subjects made were scored as either correct or incorrect. In order to be scored as correct, subjects had to debug the directions rather than merely add to them. In the preceding example,

### A. Computer Group

**Pretest (N=54)**

Reading Strategy

| Simulating Strategy | B | S | F | |
|---|---|---|---|---|
| N | 44 | 4 | 6 | 54 |
| B | 15 | - | - | 15 |
| S | 0 | 18 | - | 18 |
| F | 4 | 2 | 7 | 13 |
| | 63 | 24 | 13 | |

**Midtest (N=51)**

Reading Strategy

| Simulating Strategy | B | S | F | |
|---|---|---|---|---|
| N | 14 | 6 | 4 | 24 |
| B | 20 | - | - | 20 |
| S | 0 | 15 | - | 15 |
| F | 2 | 8 | 31 | 41 |
| | 36 | 29 | 35 | |

### B. Control (Study Hall) Group

**Pretest (N=51)**

Reading Strategy

| Simulating Strategy | B | S | F | |
|---|---|---|---|---|
| N | 31 | 2 | 0 | 33 |
| B | 35 | - | - | 35 |
| S | 0 | 16 | - | 16 |
| F | 2 | 0 | 14 | 16 |
| | 68 | 18 | 14 | |

**Midtest (N=51)**

Reading Strategy

| Simulating Strategy | B | S | F | |
|---|---|---|---|---|
| N | 14 | 8 | 4 | 26 |
| B | 25 | - | - | 25 |
| S | 0 | 21 | - | 21 |
| F | 6 | 8 | 14 | 28 |
| | 45 | 37 | 18 | |

FIG. 11.9. Change in search strategies after debugging instruction in Study 2. Numbers indicate the percentage of subjects using each strategy combination in A the experimental group and B the control group. N means no search, B means brute force search (every direction), S means self-terminating search (every direction up to the bug), and F means focused search (only directions near the bug or similar to the bug). There was a significant shift toward focused reading and simulating strategies for students after debugging instruction in the LOGO context but not for students in study hall. (From Carver & Risinger, 1987.)

a student would not be scored as correct if she added a direction at the bottom of the page saying something like, "Pay Tom $10 more." The proportion of computer students who accurately debugged the directions increased from 33% on the pretest to 55% on the midtest. In contrast, the accuracy rate of the study-hall group remained constant (41% and 39%).

### Checking Fixes

In addition, as a result of computer debugging experience, students in the computer group more frequently checked the directions *after* making a change. The transfer tasks provided no opportunity to rerun the directions after making a change as is possible in computer programming; however, some students attempted to mentally resimulate the effect of the change to test its correctness. On the pretest, students in the computer group read a total of 109 lines and simulated 94 lines after making fixes. The number of lines they checked by reading and simulating increased on the midtest to 157 and 160. The number of lines checked after a fix changed little for the control group (136 to 143 for reading and 119 to 133 for simulating). This checking strategy contributes to the increase in accuracy of corrections, because checking the fix after it has been made can lead to discovering an incorrect fix. One thing that computer students have clearly learned from debugging experience is that the fix may be wrong or may make things worse. Our debugging model always instructs the user to recheck the program once a fix has been made. Even though retesting is not easy for debugging noncomputer directions, students demonstrated that they knew a very important goal: to check the fixes. They were able to transfer that part of their strategy despite having to tailor it to a new situation.

To summarize, the focused search strategies students acquired in the LOGO context were transfered to nonprogramming contexts involving debugging written directions. Students' increasingly focused search and increased checking after making a fix resulted in a greater accuracy of fixes. After explicit debugging instruction, based on a detailed task analysis, students both acquired and transfered focused search strategies for debugging. The following sections provide further support for this claim by presenting similar results from the first study and by demonstrating the relationship between individual student's acquisition and transfer scores in the second study.

## Similar Results in the First Study

The first study included a within-subjects pretest/posttest comparison of performance on the noncomputer debugging tasks identical to the second study. (See Fig. 11.7.) A midtest was also included to monitor transfer after the first minicourse only.

As in the second study, students made few presearch comments. However, the number of comments students made about the possible location of the bug in the directions increased from 9 on the pretests to 16 on the midtests to 22 on the posttests (out of a possible 66). Also, the students needed less help describing the discrepancy between the desired and actual outcomes; instances of help decreased from 19 to 9 to 4 for the three test times (also out of 66). Apparently, the students were paying more attention to the outcome information prior to beginning their search.

Figure 11.10 shows the reading/simulating strategy combinations for each test time. There were no differences between Groups A and B so the data have been collapsed across group. The total number of combinations per test time should have been 66 (22 subjects × 3 tests at each time); the actual totals are slightly lower due to several videotape failures.

Computer Group (graphics and list-processing combined)

Pretest (N=61)

Reading Strategy

|  | B | S | F |  |
|---|---|---|---|---|
| N | 45 | 17 | 3 | 65 |
| B | 8 | - | - | 8 |
| S | 3 | 17 | - | 20 |
| F | 2 | 0 | 5 | 7 |
|  | 58 | 34 | 8 |  |

(Rows labeled Simulating Strategy)

Midtest (N=65)

Reading Strategy

|  | B | S | F |  |
|---|---|---|---|---|
| N | 20 | 18 | 8 | 46 |
| B | 0 | - | - | 0 |
| S | 2 | 21 | - | 23 |
| F | 3 | 3 | 25 | 31 |
|  | 25 | 42 | 33 |  |

(Rows labeled Simulating Strategy)

Posttest (N=51)

Reading Strategy

|  | B | S | F |  |
|---|---|---|---|---|
| N | 12 | 15 | 0 | 27 |
| B | 5 | - | - | 5 |
| S | 3 | 19 | - | 22 |
| F | 8 | 15 | 23 | 46 |
|  | 28 | 49 | 23 |  |

(Rows labeled Simulating Strategy)

FIG. 11.10. Change in search strategies after debugging instruction in Study 1. Numbers indicate the percentage of subjects using each strategy combination. N means no search, B means brute force search (every direction), S means self-terminating search (every direction up to the bug), and F means focused search (only directions near the bug or similar to the bug). There was a significant shift toward focused reading and simulating strategies for students after debugging instruction in the LOGO context.

The students' behavior on the pretests was very much like the brute-force strategy of the debugging model. The top left cell shows that the predominant strategy (45%) was to read all the commands and simulate none. A change in focus on the later tests is apparent from the decrease in the percentage of combinations in the upper cells and left columns and the corresponding increase in the lower right cells. By the midtest, most students had shifted to a more focused strategy for reading directions. Two thirds of the students simulated none of the lines on their first reading of the directions on the pretest. Some students had shifted to a more focused simulation strategy by the midtest, but half of the students were still not simulating any commands. By the posttest, half of the students were using focused strategies.

In addition to improved strategies, the students made more correct fixes on later tests regardless of the order in which they took the minicourses. The percentage of subjects who made the correct change increased from an average of

33% on the pretests to 56% on the midtests to 64% on the posttests. The students' mean search time decreased significantly from the pretest to the posttest as a result of the shift to the selective search strategy (from 4 minutes 50 seconds on the pretest to 3 minutes 41 seconds on the midtest to 3 minutes 4 seconds on the posttest). The improvements on these tasks were primarily a result of increasing use of location clues. Also, the number of students who read and simulated lines after the initial bug was identified increased significantly from the pretest to the posttest (from an average of 2 students—out of 22)—on the pretests to an average of 8 students on the midtests to an average of 11 students on the posttests).

To summarize, the focused search strategies these students acquired in the LOGO context were transfered to the nonprogramming context as in the second study. Students' increasingly focused search and increased checking after making a fix resulted in decreased search time and greater accuracy of fixes. Both studies showed that in programming and nonprogramming contexts, the debugging search strategies shifted toward more focused search. However, in addition to demonstrating that transfer occurs on the group level, it is also important to determine the relationship between the amount individual students improve in the LOGO context and the strength of their transfer.

## Tracing Individual Learning and Transfer Patterns

Because all of the testing in the second study was done individually, it is possible for us to go beyond the aggregate results to test whether the subjects whose debugging skills improve most in the debugging course are also the ones whose strategies improve most on the transfer test. In order to facilitate such correlational analysis, we had to convert our strategy classifications for the transfer test into a numerical score. We did this by simply giving 0 points for No Strategy, 1 point for Brute Force, 2 points for Self-terminating Search, and 3 points for Focused Search. Because each subject gets two strategy scores (reading and simulating) for each of three tests at each test time, possible scores range from 0 to 18. We are not arguing that these strategies are, in fact, equidistant on a strategy continuum but rather that this simple scoring will reflect the strategy differences. The computer group's mean score increased significantly from a mean of 7.00 to a mean of 11.06 from the pretest to the midtest. The means for the study-hall group did not increase significantly (7.76 on the pretest and 9.35 on the midtest).

For the experimental group, there was a significant correlation of .52 between students' changes in strategy scores from the pretest to the midtest and their changes in debugging efficiency from Test 1 to Test 2 during the LOGO course. All students either improved on both measures or failed to improve on both; there were no students who improved in LOGO debugging but got worse on the transfer task and no students who got worse in debugging but improved on the transfer task. Similarly, there was a significant correlation of .58 between students' change in strategy scores relative to their decrease in debugging time per bug fixed. For the control group, with the exception of two students, the change in strategy scores from the pretest to the midtest clustered around zero; in other words, with no LOGO experience there was no change in LOGO debugging efficiency and no change in transfer test search strategy.

We found a similar lack of transfer due to a lack of learning in the second pilot study (long-term, unstructured environment without debugging instruction). We gave one set of transfer tests (essentially a posttest) to the 15 students who had had 200 hours of LOGO experience and to 15 of their schoolmates who were not in the LOGO project. Both groups performed at the level of pretest performance by the students in both of our debugging instruction studies. Without debugging instruction, students did not demonstrate effective debugging skills in programming or nonprogramming contexts. Fay and Mayer (this volume) presented evidence of a similar learning–transfer relationship. In their study, children who continued to demonstrate egocentric misconceptions even after LOGO training did not improve on spatial cognition tests; whereas those who had no egocentric misconceptions at the end of the training did demonstrate improvement.

These results demonstrate the possibility of tracing individual patterns of learning and transfer from programming experience. Evidently, there are positive cognitive consequences for those students who do learn effective skills from LOGO programming. We are in the process of conducting more detailed analyses of this type in an attempt to specify more precisely the consistency of students' strategy use across tasks within and between domains as well as the factors that determine the extent to which individual students will learn and transfer our instructional material.

## SUMMARY AND CONCLUSIONS

The underlying assumption of all the research perspectives represented in this volume is that teaching and learning computer programming is valuable to some degree, despite past difficulty demonstrating just that. Soloway (this volume) says quite explicitly that programming is a good domain for teaching high-level skills, such as boundary conditions, simulation, and problem simplification. The key point in his claim, though, is the teaching, not the domain itself. In fact, Sloane and Linn (this volume) have already provided correlational evidence that student learning is enhanced in situations where teachers emphasize explicit strategies.

The goal of our research program has been to provide evidence that particular instruction, rather than LOGO itself, is what has potential for yielding significant cognitive consequences for students. Our specific goals were to determine whether children can learn debugging skills from computer programming if the component skills are precisely specified and taught directly and, then, whether the skills are generally transferable once they have been learned.

We specified a model of effective debugging skill that emphasized the importance of gathering clues about a bug's identity and location for focusing one's search for bugs in program code. From two pilot studies, we have found that without explicit instruction in debugging, students do not learn debugging skills from either a structured or an unstructured course, even with 200 hours of LOGO experience. Difficulties with debugging have also been demonstrated among LOGO teachers (Jenkins, 1986) and in the adult novice debugging literature (Gould, 1975; Gugerty & Olson, 1986; Jeffries, 1982; Katz & Anderson, 1986; Kessler & Anderson, 1986). In our two extensive studies, we included one debugging lesson, derived directly from our debugging model, in two otherwise conventional LOGO courses and assessed students' learning and transfer of debugging skills. In these two contexts, we found that students did learn to debug effectively and that they could transfer their debugging skills to similar nonprogramming contexts. Students demonstrated better debugging strategies, took less time, and were more accurate on transfer tests of debugging in nonprogramming contexts after debugging instruction than before. Students who did not receive debugging instruction in the LOGO context did not improve on the transfer tests. In addition, among the computer students in the second study, there was a positive correlation between the amount of improvement in LOGO debugging and the amount of strategy shift on the transfer tests.

There is a striking contrast between these positive results and the largely negative results from previous studies of the transferability of high-level problem-solving skills from computer programming experience (Garlick, 1984; McGilly et al., 1984; Mohamed, 1985; Pea, 1983). The key to our students' acquisition and transfer of debugging skills was our careful task analysis of the components of debugging skill and our explicit debugging instruction. Lehrer et al. (this volume) also provide suggestive evidence that the particular skills students learn and transfer from programming courses depends heavily on the focus of instruction in those courses. Furthermore, preliminary reports from Clements and Merriman, Littlefield et al., and Perkins (all in this volume) emphasize the importance of precise instruction regarding strategies, particularly at the metalevel. We suggest that the use of precise cognitive models of skill components, similar to the one we described for debugging, could be used as the basis for more effectively designing instruction to foster other high-level problem-solving skills in programming and nonprogramming domains.

## ACKNOWLEDGMENTS

This research was supported in part by a National Science Foundation Graduate Fellowship. The research was further supported by a grant jointly funded by the Program for Research in Teaching and Learning and the Program for Applications of Advanced Technology at the National Science Foundation (MDR-8554464). Many thanks to my collaborators, David Klahr and Sally Clarke Risinger, who made significant contributions to this work and to my colleagues, Kevin Dunbar and Carolanne Fisher, who made helpful comments on an earlier draft of this chapter.

## REFERENCES

Carver, S. M. (1986). *LOGO debugging skills: Analysis, instruction, and assessment.* Doctoral dissertation, Department of Psychology, Carnegie-Mellon University, Pittsburgh, PA.

Carver, S. M., & Klahr, D. (1986). Assessing children's LOGO debugging skills with a formal model. *Journal of Educational Computing Research, 2*(4), 487–525.

Carver, S. M., & Risinger, S. C. (1987). Improving children's debugging skills. In G. Olson, S. Sheppard, & E. Soloway (Eds.), *Empirical studies of programmers: Second workshop* (pp. 147–171). Norwood, NJ: Ablex.

Clements, D. H., & Gullo, D. F. (1984). Effects of computer programming on young children's cognition. *Journal of Educational Psychology, 76*(6), 1051–1058.

Dalbey, J., & Linn, M. (1984, April). Spider world: A robot language for learning to program. In *Proceedings of the American Educational Research Association Conference.* New Orleans, LA: AERA.

Ericsson, K. A., & Simon, H. A. (1984). *Protocol analysis: Verbal reports as data.* Cambridge, MA: MIT Press.

Garlick, S. (1984). *Computer programming and cognitive outcomes: A classroom evaluation of LOGO.* Unpublished Honors Thesis, The Flinders University of South Australia.

Gorman, H. Jr., & Bourne, L. E., Jr. (1983). Learning to think by learning LOGO: Rule learning in third grade computer programmers. *Bulletin of the Psychonomic Society, 21*(3), 165–167.

Gould, J. D. (1975). Some psychological evidence on how people debug computer programs. *International Journal of Man–Machine Studies, 7,* 151–182.

Greeno, J. G. (1976). Cognitive objectives of instruction: Theory of knowledge for solving problems and answering questions. In D. Klahr (Ed.), *Cognition and instruction* (pp. 123–159). Hillsdale, NJ: Lawrence Erlbaum Associates.

Gugerty, L., & Olson, G. M. (1986). Comprehension differences in debugging by skilled and novice programmers. In E. Soloway & S. Iyengar (Ed.), *Empirical studies of programmers* (pp. 13–27). Norwood, NJ: Ablex.

Jeffries, R. (1982, March). A comparison of the debugging behavior of expert and novice programmers. In *Proceedings of the American Educational Research Association.* New York, NY: AERA.

Jenkins, E. A., Jr. (1986). *An analysis of expert debugging of LOGO programs.* Unpublished manuscript.

Katz, I. R., & Anderson, J. R. (1986). *An exploratory study of novice programmers' bugs and debugging behavior.* Poster session presented at the Empirical Studies of Programmers Conference, Washington, DC.

Kessler, C. M. & Anderson, J. R. (1986). A model of novice debugging in LISP. In E. Soloway & S. Iyengar (Ed.), *Empirical studies of programmers* (pp. 198–212). Norwood, NJ: Ablex.

Linn, M. C., & Fisher, C. W. (1983, December 17). The gap between promise and reality in computer education: Planning a response. In *Making our schools more effective: A conference for California educators.* San Francisco, CA: ACCCEL.

McGilly, C. A., Poulin-Dubois, D., & Shultz, T. R. (1984). *The effect of learning LOGO on children's problem-solving skills.* Unpublished manuscript.

Mohamed, M. A. (1985). *The effects of learning LOGO computer language upon the higher cognitive processes and the analytic/global cognitive styles of elementary school students.* Unpublished doctoral dissertation, School of Education, University of Pittsburgh, Pittsburgh, PA.

Papert, S. (1972). Teaching children thinking. *Programmed Learning and Educational Technology, 9,* 245–255.

Papert, S. (1980). *Mindstorms: Children, computers and powerful ideas.* New York: Basic Books.

Pea, R. D. (1983, April). LOGO programming and problem solving. In *Proceedings of the American Educational Research Association Conference.* Montreal, Canada: AERA.

Sauers, R., & Farrell, R. (1982). *GRAPES user's manual.* Pittsburgh, PA: Department of Psychology, Carnegie-Mellon University

Winston, P. H. (1977). *Artifical intelligence.* Reading, MA: Addison-Wesley.

# 12

# New Directions
# in Educational Computing
# Research

Robert H. Seidman
*New Hampshire College Graduate School*

## ABSTRACT

This chapter provides comments on two aspects of the research presented in the preceding chapters. First, this chapter focuses on research comparing explicit instruction and discovery methods of instruction for teaching computer programming. Second, this chapter focuses on the conditions required for transfer of cognitive skills learned in computer programming environments.

## INTRODUCTION

The chapters in this book represent some of the most promising research and clear thinking on two important and related questions: (a) What are the most efficacious *environments* for promoting the learning of computer programming in and of itself, while at the same time (b) directing this learning toward the *transfer* of cognitive skills to extraprogramming environments?

In this chapter, I focus on research results having to do with *explicit instruction* in computer programming and cognitive skills versus *unguided* or discovery learning of programming and indirect instruction in cognitive skills. In addition, I focus on the *structure* of the learning environment surrounding the particular

299

programming language and its relationship to programming mastery. I also examine research pertaining to the cognitive preconditions and extant conditions for the *transfer* of cognitive skills, including the question of whether or not programming mastery is a prerequisite condition.

In my attempt to discern the basic outlines of an emerging research direction concerned with environmental (curricular and pedagogical) aspects of programming instruction and with transfer effects under such environments, I necessarily leave it to the reader to judge individual chapters on methodological grounds and relevance criteria. The research in this volume speaks to us in different ways, and I make no attempt to cover all of the multitudinous ideas and results that appear between these covers. This is a narrowly focused project, but one which, hopefully, will be helpful to those who are interested in the perspective that I pursue.

This chapter presents an integrative overview of the research reported in this book with respect to the aforementioned topics. Outlined is a new direction in educational computing research—a direction that shifts the focus from the programming language, per se, to the surrounding educational environment.

## THE EFFICACY OF COMPUTER
## PROGRAMMING ENVIRONMENTS

Clearly, a major justification for teaching a computer programming language to children is that it fosters cognitive skills and facilitates the transfer of these skills to nonprogramming situations. But as Salomon and Perkins (1987), Johanson (1988) and others have pointed out, research has not for the most part supported this general claim. One of the hypotheses offered by Johanson to explain this failure is lack of "curricular sophistication." Very simply, *the instruction does not embody the objectives.* Learning a particular programming language does not in and of itself necessarily promote higher-level learning and transfer of cognitive skills. Apparently, the instructional environment surrounding the language *must* be conducive for transfer. That is, higher-level cognitive skills must be explicitly taught within a curricula paradigm that uses the computer programming language as a *vehicle* for instruction. Salomon and Perkins (1987) suggested that the conditions for even "low road" transfer of cognitive skills are, for the most part, unreachable given current levels of programming instruction.

Soloway et al. (this volume) present a cogent argument for teaching *process* principles, rather than product principles for effective programming mastery and for potential transfer of cognitvie skills. Soloway et al. introduce the notion of teaching "variability exploration skills" using Pascal as a programming language vehicle while at the same time offering very explicit analysis and design criteria (variability heuristics) that apparently need to be learned for possible transfer to other domains. Here, Pascal is the vehicle, and a carefully thought out *process model* is the shadow curriculum for teaching higher order strategies geared toward extraprogramming transfer.

Although the Soloway et al. research sets the tone for the movement toward explicitly teaching cognitive skills within a programming environment, Clements and Merriman (this volume) set the *framework* within which to discuss many of the other chapters. Their research is divided into three parts. They first make the case for the *reflection* of Sternburg's information-processing componential model of cognitive processes in the LOGO language environment. Then they present a series of experiments designed to tailor the instructional environment to aspects of the theoretical model, which may promote transfer of componential and metacomponential skills. Finally, they present related research and speculate on how to structure an idealized LOGO environment in order to more readily facilitate cognitive-skill transfer.

This is an important piece of research for several reasons. It attempts to embed LOGO and its environment within a theoretical framework, which provides a standard against which to measure efficacy. It also develops new instruments to measure transfer of specific cognitive skills. Soloway et al.'s chapter (like other chapters in this volume) provides many concrete suggestions for practitioners who want to create pedagogically efficacious environments for maximum transfer effectiveness. In addition, Clements and Merriman advance the seemingly outlandish proposition that mastery of LOGO programming may not be a factor in the transfer of some cognitive skills. This is not unlike the proposition put forth, within a theoretical framework, by Salomon and Perkins (1987) who argued that "far" transfer will depend primarily upon the "high road" and that high-road transfer does *not* necessarily require programming mastery.

Although it is heartening to see experiment and practice so closely identified with and informed by theory, it is not surprising that the LOGO language and its associated environments are in some ways isomorphic to the particular cognitive theory that Clements and Merriman advance. After all, the theoretical model they use is itself derived from computer information-processing theory and software implementation practice and thus draws heavily upon computational metaphors. Almost any procedural computer language (and its accompanying environment) would reflect the theory in a more than superficial way. LOGO's physical, screen "turtle" makes it attractive to some Piagetian developmentalists, as well, who see in it a potential "matching environment" between the concrete and formal operational stages of development.

Clements and Meriman's research results, in a sense, take the pressure off of the LOGO language (and by association, other procedural computer programming languages) by introducing, what Perkins et al. (this volume) call a "meta-course," which includes explicit instruction geared toward helping students exercise their metacomponential and knowledge-acquisition skills. Clements and Merriman report mixed success from their experiments. As is the case with most pioneering research, they raise more questions than they answer. For example, what can they tell us about the validity and reliability of their new assessment instruments? How can they control for, and take into consideration, the individual cognitive predispositions of novice programmers such as those described by Fay and Mayer (this volume)? It would be interesting to consider how exposure to LOGO and its accompanying environment affects skill transfer as framed by other cognitive theories. The reader might wish to consider, for comparison purposes, the work of Lehrer et al. (this volume) which utilizes aspects of control theory and artificial intelligence principles in the development of their theoretical framework.

It is most interesting to note that Clements and Merriman did not care to even measure mastery of LOGO programming (and then correlate it with cognitive skill transfer) as some of the other studies reported in this volume did. In their literature review, Clements and Merriman find that mastery of programming was *not* consistently a significant factor in the transfer of cognitive skills. What then is a significant factor? Clement and Merriman seem to think that it is the overall environment within which LOGO is embedded, at least with respect to the particular environment that they set up in their experiments.

The notion, if substantiated, that cognitive skill transfer can apparently take place without LOGO programming mastery could serve as an argument *against* teaching the LOGO language, per se, but *for* keeping aspects of its environment (the metacourse). However, it might turn out that the vehicle, LOGO, is indispensible for making the environment work, whereas mastery is less important than immersion in the environment and explicit instruction in desired cognitive skills. This stands in direct contrast to the results of the Fay and Mayer research reported in this volume.

Although Clements and Merriman suggest that environment, rather than programming mastery, might be more decisive in aiding cognitive skill transfer, Perkins et al. (this volume) argue that pedagogical environment is *crucial* in making it easier to learn computer programming. Unlike Clements and Merriman, their environment was not specifically designed to promote transfer. Both research groups, it seems, believe that merely teaching a computer programming language is not enough to ensure programming mastery and cognitive skill transfer. A *special* environment needs to be created. This, of course, was Papert's original point (Papert, 1980, 1987), although he has been widely interpreted as claiming that the LOGO language alone could provide such an environment.

Perkins et al. quite rightly point out that procedural programming is problem-solving and precision intensive and is, therefore, quite difficult to learn. This provides yet another argument for abandoning procedural in favor of logic programming. From the results of careful clinical intervews of naive BASIC programmers, the research team discovered: the need for an efficacious model of the computational machine (process); the lack of good problem-solving strategies; and problems in personal confidence and control. All influence BASIC mastery.

A solution is to construct a "metacourse," which is comprised of a series of lessons put together to address these problems. The course, an experiment in instructional design, purports to teach metacognitive skills to enhance programming mastery. The results of their experiment are promising and the notion of a metacourse is a refreshing one—it raises the teaching of computer programming from the merely technical to something that potentially encompasses the education of higher-level skills.

Perkins et al. wisely point out that the metacourse may be able to be oriented toward one or the other, but not both: (a) good programming and (b) transfer of general cognitive skills. They suggest that a "bridge course" might be necessary to accomplish both goals. In fact, they argue for programming instruction (within differently constructed environments) toward three distinct ends: good programming (technical), cognitive skills (higher level competencies) and cultural (social demands/understanding). Educational computing researchers might do well to consider whether and how the construction of such environments might address these distinct goals.

Littlefield et al. (this volume) lend support to the shift away from pure discovery learning of programming toward more carefully structured instructional environments. The research distinguished between structured, unstructured, and mediational (where the teacher explicitly focuses on and teaches for transfer of skills) methods. The research results indicate that such a mediational method facilitate transfer, as measured by tests that closely resemble the LOGO environment.

The Littlefield et al. research supports the Perkins et al. contention that curricula cannot necessarily be all things for all purposes. The results show that a structured method is more effective in fostering programming mastery than an unstructured method, whereas the mediational method seems to aid more in transfer. One of the Littlefield et al. conclusions seems to be at odds with Clements and Merriman in suggesting that programming mastery is necessary in order for transfer to occur.

## CONSTRUCTING APPROPRIATE
## EDUCATIONAL ENVIRONMENTS

Like Clements and Merriman, Lehrer et al. (this volume) base their environment upon a theoretical framework. Control theory leads them to identify cognitive, metacognitive, and epistemic consequences of learning to program and a hierarchy of control. From this, the researchers derive pedagogical implications, which guide them in setting appropriate experimental environments (e.g., reminding conditions).

The three experiments that they report are all good examples of well conceived studies grounded in theory and, taken together, tend to show that transfer needs a "well-organized body of LOGO-related knowledge" in certain circumstances. In addition, LOGO mastery enhanced the experimental group's ability to understand certain extraLOGO concepts. The environments were decidedly *not* unguided. They were "carefully crafted instructional contexts" in which problem constraints were emphasized.

The research results provide evidence that the environment was in part responsible for metacognitive transfer (e.g., with regard to reminding). To the researchers credit, they examined the much neglected notion of self-structure and noted its importance in computer-based learning. In addition, some of their conclusions supported the need for wide access to computers, a result also found in Sloan and Linn's research (this volume).

The shift toward computational environmental concerns, require great attention to the construction of pedagogically efficacious instructional paradigms. Carver's research (this volume) is an excellent model of the process of arriving at such a paradigm. Her thesis is that high-level skill transfer cannot occur unless skills are specified and explicitly taught. Through a task analysis, she identified cognitive processes and knowledge necessary for successful program debugging. Next, she designed a curriculum to foster debugging skills and designed measures to evaluate skill learning and transfer. Carver's research is an excellent model of how educational computing research can inform and influence practice.

Carver's five-phase production system model of debugging behavior and her description of student interaction with it (within a programming environment) approaches what Salomon (1988) calls, "AI in reverse." Here, students model and "internalize" the behavior of "intelligent" computer systems. In Carver's words: "The cognitive objective of the debugging curriculum was for students to acquire the same goal structure as the model. . . ." As it was with Littlefield et al., Carver's transfer tests were very close to the structure of LOGO programs. One is led to wonder whether or not comparable results would be obtain if the overt disparity between test and learning environment were greater?

Nevertheless, Carver offers a methodological paradigm for analyzing learning situations and then constructing specific curricula for explicit instruction geared toward cognitive skill transfer. Although production system models are not the only type of idealized process approaches available, it seems to me that these particular types of expert systems may prove to serve many pedagogical and descriptive needs quite well.

The Sleeman et al. (this volume) research analysis goes to great lengths in order to identify certain student errors in Pascal programming. This kind of analysis is necessary as a first step in understanding errors and their sources and in devising remediation strategies. However, we need to ask whether teaching method is the culprit (with regard to errors) or whether we are confronted with fundamental cognitive misconceptions like the kind reported by Fay and Mayer (this volume)? The next move, in applying Carver's curriculum-construction paradigm to the Sleeman et al. research results, would be to construct a theory of the errors and then an expert system model. When explicitly utilized, this model might help students learn higher-level skills that would not only help them remediate specific programming bugs, but might also foster transfer to extraprogramming environments.

Sloan and Linn (this volume) identify four instructional variables, based in part upon what they call a "chain of cognitive accomplishments" that influence computer-programming proficiency. Explicit instruction is one of these variables. The researchers proceeded along the same lines as Carver, but on a more macroscale and without constructing an instructional model from or for their research. Essentially, they gathered data that enabled them to identify existing instructional strategies and to determine existing relationships with programming achievement, among other things. Sloan and Linn promise future research to develop and utilize explicit instructional strategies and materials.

The results of their data gathering indicated that exlicitness of instruction in problem-solving strategies is predictive of programming success and that adequate access to computers was crucial for this success. This latter result confirms the Lehrer et al. findings. The former results add support to other research studies, which seem to suggest that too much independent work (pure discovery approach) is not efficacious in teaching programming. No effort was made by Sloan and Linn to assess cognitive transfer effects.

An important part of any computer environment is its social structure: for example, should programming instruction occur individually or in small groups and what should be the level of peer interaction? Webb and Lewis (this volume) provide a very useful literature review that is used as the framework for their investigations of specific kinds of behavior in small groups with regard to achievement in computer programming. Their research is an important contribution to knowledge of how best to structure the use of computers in order to facilitate learning computer programming. Their results indicated that actively participating in group discussions as well as giving and receiving explanations and input suggestions were beneficial for fostering programming proficiency.

Webb and Lewis found that student discussions with one another about planning and debugging strategies were positively related to achievement. A surprising result was that student verbalization of planning and debugging to an instructor was negatively or not at all related to programming achievement. This suggests a much needed reevaluation of the role of the instructor in the teaching/ learning process. Webb and Lewis were able to conclude that group initiating behavior was probably not based upon the need for help and that the instructor's behavior was mostly reactive and indirect. Thus, it appeared to be group working style that, more than anything else, accounted for the high frequency of asking the instructor questions. The help that the instructor did provide may have been an impediment to students developing their own problem-solving strategies. Although the researchers were justifiably cautious about drawing implications from these particular results due to the limitations of their experiment, their results do raise a question about the *appropriate* role of the instructor in the learning environment. Interestingly, Webb and Lewis were able to determine from their data that social interaction was not a proxy for ability and that social interaction influenced achievment, rather than the other way around.

The Webb and Lewis results suggest the need for an explicitly designed social environment that would surround the programming curriculum. The environment would consist of a set of activities (e.g., teachers encourage a climate of cooperative behavior and active participation) explictly designed to foster computer-programming learning. The researchers raise a number of important, and as yet, unanswered questions such as: What is the optimum group size and length of instruction? This question is of particular interest given the relatively short duration of programming instruction in the Webb and Lewis studies. Like most basic research, Webb and Lewis raise many more research questions than they answer.

The Fay and Mayer (this volume) chapter is important for a number of reasons. It is a reminder that we must be alert to the cognitive preconceptions that students bring into their learning environments. Some of these preconceptions turn out to be *misconceptions* and are a hinderance to learning. In addition, we need to be sensitive to student developmental and cognitive stages in order to determine limitations to learning.

Fay and Mayer adopt a cognitive chain paradigm and posit stages in the learning of programming skills: syntactic knowledge, semantics of LOGO, and the semantics of the domain of interest (e.g., spatial). Syntactic problems may be related to "fragile knowledge" as defined by Perkins et al. (this volume), but problems of acquiring semantic knowledge seem to have more to do with preconceptions that the learner brings to the programming experience. For example, egocentric-type errors apparently decrease with age, lending some support to the impact of developmental stage—a reality that curriculum designers must face.

Even if the target skill is explicitly taught in the programming domain, Fay and Mayer point out that developmental misconceptions may mitigate against semantic understanding and thus foil transfer. Clearly, readiness to learn a concept (or the need to unlearn one) is important for learner success. But just what is the nature of the match between programming instruction, learning and appropriate cognitive developmental level? On what particular dimensions can this match take place? These questions present significant challenges to researchers and curriculum designers alike. There has been precious little work in this area and Fay and Mayer's contribution is a welcome one.

With regard to the transfer of knowledge from one domain to another, Fay and Mayer again propose a stage approach: syntactic and then semantic knowledge must be acquired in the programming domain before the latter knowledge can be recognized as relevant for the new domain and achieve transfer. The results of their study showed that this is the case for LOGO as applied to spatial navigation. The close match between the programming and nonprogramming domain tasks related to cognitive transfer indicates that learning programming alone is probably not enough even for effective "near transfer." Like the Carver study, there are indications that *explicit attention* to matching specific transferable skills within the learning domain to the nonprogramming domain is necessary for transfer to occur. This is consistent with the environmental theme that emerges from many of the studies reported in this volume.

## CONCLUDING THOUGHTS

To Fay and Mayer's claim that programming mastery is affected by the learner's cognitive misconceptions, Clements and Merriman might reply that although this may be true, it is *not* crucial to the transfer of cognitive skills. What's a practitioner to think about this, much less do about it? Perhaps mastery of a programming language is a prerequisite for the transfer of only certain cognitive skills and not for others. For some skills we might not want to intervene to correct programming misconceptions if programming mastery is not required for cognitive transfer. This seemingly paradoxical situation is made even more complex when one thinks about the Perkins et al. proposed "bridge course," which is itself directed toward cognitive-skill transfer using programming mastery as a vehicle. What would it be like for learners to be frustrated at failing to master the computer language but satisfied at mastering higher level cognitive skills?

It appears that the emerging target of research in this area is the investigation of environments that foster higher-order thinking through computer programming. Although for many researchers the condition for cognitive-skill transfer is programming proficiency, for some, mere exposure to the programming experience is sufficient. However, as the diversity of the research reported in this volume attests to, there is no clear-cut agreement as to just what constitutes higher-order thinking much less on what constitutes an efficacious transfer environment. What counts for or against including one or another cognitive skill in the higher-order thinking transferable catagory? What are effective instruments to measure cognitive transfer? Clarity here might help researchers focus their energies in potentially fruitful areas.

Finally, much of the research reported in this volume appears to lend credence to the Salomon and Perkins (1987) explication of the conditions for transfer associated with the low and high road. The results of many of the studies seem to support taking the high road in order to effect transfer. As Salomon and Perkins (1987) put it: "In the long run, carefully designed curricula, improved programs of teacher training, and similar means may make possible the routine implementation of programming instruction that has an impact on cognitive skills" (p. 164). Perhaps the research emphasis needs to be less on fostering programming proficiency and more on constructing educational environments to effect high-road transfer. To this end, research might attempt to determine whether or not procedural computer programming is the best way, amongst multiple methods, to achieve cognitive skill transfer. Perhaps we will see future studies where cognitive-skill transfer results due to procedural computer programming environments are compared with the results of other approaches (including nonprocedural computer programming) to the same problem.

The studies and thinking presented in this volume point to major new directions in educational computing research. They serve to advance our knowledge about the conditions under which successful teaching of programming and transfer of cognitive skills occur. These research pieces will undoubtedly help, in important ways, to set the educational computing research agenda.

## REFERENCES

Johanson, R. P. (1988). Computers, cognition, and curriculum: Retrospect and prospect. *Journal of Educational Computing Research, 4,* 1–30.

Papert, S. (1980). *Mindstorms: Children, computers and powerful ideas.* New York: Basic Books.

Papert, S. (1987). Computer criticism vs. technocentric thinking. *Educational Researcher, 16,* 22–30.

Salomon, G. (1988). AI in reverse: Computer tools that turn cognitive. *Journal of Educational Computing Research, 4,* 123–139.

Salomon, G., & Perkins, D. N. (1987). Transfer of cognitive skills from programming: When and how? *Journal of Educational Computing Research, 3,* 149–170.

# Author Index

Numbers in *italics* indicate pages with complete bibliographic information.

# Subject Index

Boldface numbers indicate entire chapters.